'Schumpeter's great book has been a classic since its publication in 1942. But the Great Crash of 2008 has made it even more relevant than before. Capitalism has been called into question and Socialism has gained popularity as a claimed alternative; worrying global developments are now threatening Democracy. This present volume is timely and forward-looking.'

Geoffrey Hodgson, *Professor in Management, Loughborough University London*

'The perspective of the informed lay public on how modern capitalist economies work long has been Schumpeterian. However, today's academic economic discipline recognizes Schumpeter hardly at all. This book makes the case for bringing the Schumpeterian perspective to the center of our discipline's thinking and writing. I could not agree more. And readers who have any doubts about this are highly likely to be persuaded by the books well developed argument.'

Richard Nelson, *Professor of Economics, Emeritus, Columbia University*

'Joseph Schumpeter might have been the most complete economist of the 20th century: linking technology, finance, development, and crises across the history of economic thought. Yet, his popularity peaked in the early 1990s when his metaphor of "creative destruction" explained fast economic growth without inflation. Now Burlamaqui and Kattel have done us all a big favour by bringing together an outstanding group of researchers who have brought Schumpeter's thoughts back into the core of today's problems. Their volume is a most useful antidote against neo-classical economic orthodoxy at a time when this is sorely needed!'

Erik S. Reinert, *Professor of Technology Governance and Development Strategies, Tallinn University of Technology, Estonia and Chairman of The Other Canon Foundation, Norway*

Schumpeter's *Capitalism, Socialism and Democracy*

2017 marked the seventy-fifth anniversary of Schumpeter's *Capitalism, Socialism and Democracy*, a work acknowledged as one of the most insightful books written in the twentieth century. It retains a contemporary quality, and still invites criticisms, new interpretations, and extensions and across disciplines.

This book, in addition to re-examining Schumpeter's seminal work and undertaking a twenty-first-century update of its main themes, brings together leading social scientists to provide contemporary amendments, extensions – or eventually refutations – of key elements of Schumpeter's vision and thesis. Issues covered include a new take on creative destruction, the contours of a theory of innovative enterprise, finance and financialisation, a critique of the secular stagnation thesis, Schumpeter's contributions to a theory of the entrepreneurial state, his conception of socialism and its current relevance for understanding the 'China model' as well as a rekindling of his democracy thesis for our times.

Bringing together leading international contributors, this book provides fresh perspectives on ideas that continue to be hugely relevant to contemporary social sciences and a guide for understanding the current tensions among capitalism, the state and democracy. These chapters will be of interest to economists, social scientists and anyone with an interest in modern capitalism.

Leonardo Burlamaqui is Professor of Economics at the Department of Economic Evolution, State University of Rio de Janeiro, Research Scholar at the Levy Institute – Bard College (New York), and Adjunct Professor at Graduate Program in Public Policies and Development Strategies at the Federal University at Rio de Janeiro. He is also a member of the International Joseph Schumpeter Society.

Rainer Kattel is Professor of Innovation and Public Governance at UCL Institute for Innovation and Public Purpose, UK, and Research Professor at Ragnar Nurkse School of Innovation and Governance, Tallinn University of Technology, Estonia.

Routledge Studies in the History of Economics

For more information about this series, please visit www.routledge.com/series/SE0341

Schumpeter's *Capitalism, Socialism and Democracy*

A Twenty-First-Century Agenda

Edited by Leonardo Burlamaqui and Rainer Kattel

LONDON AND NEW YORK

First published 2019 by Routledge

2 Park Square, Milton Park, Abingdon, Oxfordshire OX14 4RN
52 Vanderbilt Avenue, New York, NY 10017

Routledge is an imprint of the Taylor & Francis Group, an informa business

First issued in paperback 2020

British Library Cataloguing-in-Publication Data
A catalogue record for this book is available from the British Library

Library of Congress Cataloging-in-Publication Data
Names: Burlamaqui, Leonardo, author. | Kattel, Rainer, 1974 – author.
Title: Schumpeter's capitalism, socialism and democracy: a twenty first century agenda/Leonardo Burlamaqui, Rainer Kattel.
Description: 1 Edition. | New York: Routledge, [2019] | Series: Routledge studies in the history of economics
Identifiers: LCCN 2018043351| ISBN 9781315618043 (ebook) | ISBN 9781138669697 (hardback)
Subjects: LCSH: Schumpeter, Joseph A., 1883–1950. Capitalism, socialism, and democracy. | Socialism. | Capitalism. | Democracy.
Classification: LCC HX86.S337 B87 2019 | DDC 335–dc23
LC record available at https://lccn.loc.gov/2018043351

ISBN: 978-1-138-66969-7 (hbk)
ISBN: 978-0-367-66298-1 (pbk)

Typeset in Bembo
by Wearset Ltd, Boldon, Tyne and Wear

To my beloved and engaging discussant daughter, Valentina Burlamaqui

Leonardo Burlamaqui

To my parents

Rainer Kattel

Contents

Figures

Tables

Contributors

Fred Block – Professor of Sociology (Emeritus), University of California, Davis.

Leonardo Burlamaqui – Professor of Economics, Department of Economic Evolution, State University of Rio de Janeiro and Research Fellow at the Levy Economics Institute, NY.

Beniamino Callegari – Lecturer, Department of Law and Governance, Norwegian Business School.

Rainer Kattel – Professor of Innovation and Public Governance at UCL Institute for Innovation and Public Purpose, UK, and Research Professor of Ragnar Nurkse School of Innovation and Governance, Tallinn University of Technology, Estonia.

William Lazonick – Professor of Economics, Co-Director of the Center for Industrial Competitiveness College of Fine Arts, Humanities and Social Science UMASS, Lowell, NY.

Francisco Louçã – Professor of Economics, Lisbon School of Economics and Management, Lisbon University.

John Mathews – Professor Emeritus, Macquarie Graduate School of Management, Macquarie University, Sydney, Australia.

Mariana Mazzucato – Chair in the Economics of Innovation and Public Value, University College London (UCL), Founder and Director of the UCL Institute for Innovation and Public Purpose.

John Medearis – Professor and Chair, Department of Political Science, University of California, Riverside.

L. Randall Wray – Professor of Economics at the Levy Economics Institute, Bard College, NY.

1 Introduction – *Capitalism, Socialism and Democracy* at 75

New interpretations and new dimensions

Leonardo Burlamaqui and Rainer Kattel

The year 2017 marked the seventy-fifth anniversary of Schumpeter's *Capitalism, Socialism and Democracy* (*CSD*), a work acknowledged as one of the most insightful books in the social sciences written in the twentieth century. It has been widely discussed since its publication and deserved a special celebration volume when it reached 40 (Heertje 1981). From our perspective, far from being a 'collection of essays' in economics, sociology and politics, *CSD* is in fact an attempt to capture the essential dimensions of capitalism's dynamics, and its potential future, from a multidisciplinary perspective; an analytical framework that remains essential for understanding capitalist economic and social dynamics, democratic politics and development trajectories today. The contemporary relevance of *CSD*, its freshness and scope allow, and ask for, new interpretations, extensions and criticisms, which is what makes it worthwhile, almost mandatory in fact, to dedicate a volume to its diamond anniversary.

However, in contrast with most previous *CSD*-related discussions, including most in Heertje's edited collection, our aim in this volume is less about revisiting and scrutinising the book per se and more concerned with accessing Schumpeter's core theory and theses, and providing contemporary extensions, reinterpretations or eventually refutations of his arguments. In short: this is not a book about another book, but is rather a set of reflections on the contemporary relevance and, largely, forgotten broadness and scope of Schumpeter's *agenda*. The boldness of *CSD*, announced by its title, consists in linking politics and social structures to the economy, instead of simply discussing economic evolution per se. The task Schumpeter embraces is rather to connect economic transformation with institutional, political and cultural changes, as well. In this lies, perhaps, the most fundamental relevance of *CSD* for today. In times when many governments and international organisations are seeking ways how to make innovation and institutional reform serve wider societal challenges – the challenges coming from the impact of industry 4.0, AI or climate change – *CSD* offers, we suggest, the most provoking framework for a comprehensive understanding not only of the 'economics of innovation', but also of its 'politics', of its impacts on the social strata, interest groups and corporations that gain, but also the ones that suffer, from fast-paced structural transformation and how they react to it (Taylor 2016 and Juma 2016 explore this avenue in more detail).

Indeed, in *CSD* Schumpeter presents an analytical framework for thinking about how capitalism evolves – as a system of creative destruction but also as an institutional web and a cultural phenomenon – and suggests tools for how both corporations and the state *could* manage it.[1] Furthermore, while most economists, both orthodox and heterodox, see market failures as the vantage point to analyze policy tools for speeding innovations and managing welfare measures in general (see key statements in Arrow 1962 and Nelson 1959), in *CSD* Schumpeter presents the foundations of a creative-destruction paradigm for understanding how the system evolves and a market-shaping institutional framework for business organisations and the state to manage its evolution (Burlamaqui 2006; Mazzucato 2017).

Let us pause here and give the reader a more concrete taste of what she will find in the contributions to the volume. The book is divided into two parts: new interpretations and new dimensions. The first is basically concerned with 'updating' Schumpeter's analysis, mostly by criticising and rekindling it, while the second is more focused on recovering and expanding his agenda. Obviously, this is not an 'iron-caged' division. There are overlaps, but we think that it provides some clarity to the reader in following the chapters' sequence.

In the first part, the common point to underline is the, somewhat overlooked, theme of the feasibility of merging evolution with equilibrium, or 'Schumpeter's basic ambition' in Andersen's terms (2009, Chapter 1). This is the subject of Louçã's contribution to the volume, but it is also prominent in both Burlamaqui and Callegari's discussions: the question of why Schumpeter did not reject the Walrasian paradigm he could not properly use or link rigorously with either development or cycles. Callegari stresses this eloquently by pointing out that '[t]he adoption of the Walrasian equilibrium as a theoretical closure allows Schumpeter to build a model, but the resulting conflicts in underlying assumptions lead to severe inconsistency (Chapter 4 in this volume).

In Chapter 2, Burlamaqui scrutinises these theoretical inconsistencies of Schumpeter's two major works on development, the *Theory of Economic Development* (*TED*) and *Business Cycles* (*BC*), highlights their conceptual innovations and indicates how the inconsistencies are finally resolved in *CSD* by dropping equilibrium and espousing creative destruction. He claims that *CSD* marks a radical rupture in Schumpeter's theorising about capitalist dynamics. Until then, economic *cycles* were for Schumpeter the key organising framework within which economic evolution was conceived. Schumpeter's theory of cycles, both the *Theory of Economic Development* (*TED*) and *Business Cycles* (*BC*), begins and ends in equilibrium. In fact, Andersen (2009, 2–3) argues that 'Schumpeter's basic ambition was to complement equilibrium economics with an evolutionary economics that analyses capitalist economic evolution.'

Burlamaqui takes issue with that interpretation stressing rupture, not continuity, between *CSD* and Schumpeter's two previous works on development. He shows that in *CSD*, especially from Chapter 7 on, a new paradigm takes shape. Competition by means of innovation – Schumpeterian competition as we know it today – *replaces* cycles as the core for understanding capitalism's evolution. Furthermore, both equilibrium and perfect competition are completely dismissed and considered incompatible with change. Creative destruction is born.[2] In the following three chapters, Schumpeter advances the sketch of a theory of corporate capitalism operating under oligopolistic, but dynamic, competition, which is conducive to increased innovations and fast-paced technological progress. In that sense, *CSD* provides us with an entirely new paradigm to analyse and to theorise about capitalism. The 'creative-destruction paradigm', as Burlamaqui terms it, is the outcome – a new but at the same time also somewhat surprisingly underdeveloped paradigm. The radical nature of this new departure was scarcely noticed (Nathan Rosenberg, 1994, being a laudable exception to the rule).

Burlamaqui closes the chapter indicating that, to date, there is no comprehensive account of Schumpeter's creative-destruction paradigm understood as a theory of capitalist dynamics as a whole. The need for a fresh look is crystal clear here and this is a theme in need of further research and elaboration. His contribution is an attempt to lead the way as to how this should be done.

In the following chapter, Louçã addresses the same issue, the paradoxical nature of Schumpeter's work, but does it on a much bigger scale than Burlamaqui. For Louçã the equilibrium versus evolution 'anomaly' was the most serious, since it concerned the backbone of Schumpeter's approach and analysis of capitalism. But it was hardly the only one permeating his thinking. To substantiate his claim, Louçã offers the reader a tour de force in reviewing a large chunk of Schumpeter's writings, where he highlights a whole set of ambiguities in the author's intellectual and political trajectory.

First, there is Schumpeter's approach to liberal democracy, which he did not particularly like, but was not ready to openly dismiss. Democracy, for Schumpeter, Louçã explains, is a powerful method of social organisation and decision, and a legitimate one, but it is companionable with the imposition of terror on some minorities (or majorities, as it comes), since it is a method, and a vulnerable one, not an end in itself. In Schumpeter's approach, the jury is still out on the efficacy of the method (see also Medearis' contribution in this volume).

Second, the conflict between his political and economic evaluations of authoritarian regimes, which emerged in the 1930s, especially the Nazi regime, is also noticeable. While condemning the Nazi political extremism and social perversity, Schumpeter praised its industrial rationalisation policies and its role as an entrepreneur.[3]

Third, there are Schumpeter's attitudes towards anti-Semitism, which again he condemned but also displayed mixed feelings about on a case-by-case basis. His pronouncements on the Marschak and Samuelson episodes alluded to by Louçã testify to that.

Fourth, his recognition that the big bureaucratised corporations with retained earnings and R&D departments were much better at endogenising innovation, even 'automatising' them, collides with his regret that this same trace would render the 'heroic entrepreneur' obsolete.

Fifth, there is Schumpeter's odd relationship to what should be the 'gold standard' for economics; he retains physics, but, at the same time, flirts with zoology, organic analogies and – at the very end of his career – economic and business history (his 'final thesis'). Louçã aptly summarises the point by indicating that 'in the general epistemological stance, Schumpeter certainly praised the authority and clarity of physics; but when concrete economic concepts were at stake, he denied any significant influence from physics.' Furthermore, Louçã does not see *CSD* as a coherent work, and much less as offering a new paradigm for economic analysis. In this he diverges from Burlamaqui's interpretation in the previous chapter.

Louçã closes his chapter in a truly 'Schumpeterian fashion', offering the reader two different – and almost opposing – paths to follow. On one hand, he states that 'it is possible to conclude that Schumpeter defined the social process as an intrinsic dynamic disturbance of equilibrium through the creation of novelty – the innovative mutation – and this was precisely what defined his evolutionary framework.' This is clearly a statement underlying the confusing nature of Schumpeter's legacy and of the potential risks of its adoption as a source of inspiration or as a theoretical guideline. On the other hand, Louçã's closing paragraph openly praises the author:

> Schumpeter is one of the most modern of all economists because he felt, studied and discussed contradictions and tensions in the evolution of the developed economies. In that sense, Allen is right again: he had a paradoxical life and career, produced paradoxical ideas and books, had a career of failure which was, as a whole, a great success.

What seems to be uncontroversial is the need for additional thinking and research on those issues, given the fact that, as Burlamaqui suggests in his first contribution,

> [e]quilibrium-based thinking remains, despite its distance from any kind of empirical grounding, a powerful iron cage that traps whoever gets into it. Easy to get in, extremely difficult to get out. In that sense, economic theory constitutes a very strange case of applied social science, where the mostly revered analytical tool [equilibrium, or in modern parlance, DSGE models] is in fact a rather poor lens for understanding the way the real economy works and evolves.
>
> (Chapter 2 in this volume, note 2)

In this regard, one should not expect much help from the vast majority of contemporary 'neo-Schumpeterians'. Their research agenda ended up shrinking

Schumpeter's analysis to the sector level in order to discuss the relationship between market structures, technical change, firm organisation and innovation.[4] They provided us with fine case studies of industries, sectors and technological trajectories, but ended up trapped in a model-building competition with the mainstream that largely ignored the broadness of Schumpeter's original approach as well as his agenda. The result was, in Callegari's felicitous phrase, 'a Schumpeterian-neoclassical synthesis'.

Additionally, there is the need to explore more thoroughly the intertwining dimensions of economic evolution and social/institutional change. Callegari takes up this task in his chapter in the book. His main assertion is that *CSD* makes essentially two major contributions: the first to the analytical structure, by modifying a crucial element of the methodological approach, and the second in terms of theoretical propositions, by extending the contents of the theory itself to the conditions of trustified capitalism.

The first consists in the expansion of the concept of regime, an exogenous set of institutional rules, in the more general idea of order, including the socio-political conditions required for its preservation.

The second points to the broader implications of expanding the concept of entrepreneurship. In *CSD*, Callegari submits, Schumpeter suggests that the entrepreneurial function should be expanded to include the mechanism of conversion of profits into rents, thus giving rise, through a retained stream of income collected via innovation diffusion, trade secrets and intellectual property protection, to the oligopolistic firm. This brings in a complex mix of economic, social and political results that deserves attention: 'when the entrepreneur is characterised as a dynamic rent-seeker, each business cycle will lead to a progressive concentration of the productive sector' (Callegari, Chapter 4 in this volume). Furthermore, when entrepreneurs and rent-seekers inhabit the same individual, organisation or social strata, both economics and politics tend to become much harder to decipher. Top technological performers can also be tax-avoiding experts and lobbyists advocating for strong rent-seeking based intellectual property regimes.[5] The cases of Apple, Google and the 'new digital monopolies' in particular, and the financialisation of formerly 'industrial conglomerates' in general, are cases in point. This is a discussion that is catching fire in the specialised media and already has the European Commission trying to counteract it through its competition policy decisions – including huge fines – on Google, Microsoft and others. Updating Schumpeter's analysis can certainly help in this matter.

Not surprisingly, updated analyses lead us straight to an expanded Schumpeterian agenda – or perhaps, more fairly, to recovering and expanding Schumpeter's agenda. That constitutes the second part of the book. Here some of the leads, and missing pieces, of Schumpeter's original thinking are pursued. One of the most prominent, and also intriguing, refers to the role of credit and finance and financial systems' dynamics more generally in Schumpeter's creative-destruction paradigm.

In Chapter 2, Burlamaqui indicates that although credit is a definitional trace of capitalism in Schumpeter's theory, it is almost absent from *CSD*. Furthermore, given its 'definitional trace' status, there is relatively little discussion of the inner workings of the financial system in his books altogether. Even though *TED* (Chapters 3 and 5) and *BC* (Chapters 3 [section D] and 4 [section C][6] and a multitude of sharp observations in the books' historical chapters) provide extremely valuable material that influenced, for instance, Hyman Minsky and many others, no deep analysis of financial entrepreneurship – especially financial innovation –, liquidity and leverage concerns, financial fragilisation or the need for financial regulation are to be found in his analytical framework. Nor is the possibility of 'financialisation' of non-financial firms culminating in unproductive or even destructive entrepreneurship, to use Baumol's terms, given much thought.

Mazzucato's and Wray's contribution is an effort to address those lacunae, so is Lazonick's. Mazzucato's and Wray's analysis is based on a synthesis of the main contributions of Schumpeter, Keynes and Minsky. From Schumpeter they borrow two insights: the first is that it is critical to understand the innovation process in order to begin to analyze the dynamics of the capitalist economy, and, second, part of this understanding concerns the fact that innovation needs appropriate types of finance. From Keynes they borrow two central elements: the theory of effective demand and his argument that when the 'capital development of a country becomes the by-product of the activities of a casino, the job is likely to be ill done' (*General Theory*, Chapter 12). From Minsky they borrow the recognition that the dynamics of the capitalist system are not necessarily stabilising, and that when finance is brought into the analysis, the picture tends to get worse. Like Minsky, they turn orthodoxy's 'invisible hand' metaphor on its head: market forces are destabilising, and the instability can be contained only by reverting to convention and institution building, including establishing confidence in future outcomes, financial supervision and regulation.

After linking these three sets of ideas, their main conclusions are that although finance is crucial for development and structural change, as Schumpeter pioneered in stressing, the financialisation of the economy does not promote development. On the contrary, it impairs it. And this is largely because, as Minsky stressed, the 'banker' is not only the ephor of capitalism, but also its key source of instability. Following this thread of analysis, they point to the fact that when finance runs 'free' it tends to become self-destabilising and prone to destructive entrepreneurship.[7] The financial system, instead of financing development starts to finance itself and to 'go Ponzi'. Overleveraging, pure speculation, value-destructing financial innovation and even fraud replaces long-term funding. They test their analytical framework by applying it to the US and the UK.

Mazzucato and Wray close the chapter by highlighting the crucial importance of public sources of funding for innovation and development, a theme that both authors have developed at length in previous works; and by suggesting a set of financial reforms that would induce the private financial system to resume its role of ephor of development instead of remaining casino managers – populated by billionaire managers to be sure – working to enrich themselves and their rentier clientele.

Bill Lazonick's chapter addresses some of these same points discussed by Mazzucato and Wray but from a different angle: he proposes a 'theory of innovative enterprise'. As Burlamaqui notes in passing in Chapter 2, Schumpeter had a theory of development by means of innovation but not a theory of the firm, which constituted an important gap in his theoretical scaffolding. However, this lacuna started to be filled by Edith Penrose with her highly original 1959 book *The Theory of the Growth of the Firm*.[8] Her work never penetrated the mainstream economics profession – no surprise here – but became a huge hit in the business strategy departments of prestigious universities,[9] where it turned into the bedrock of the 'resource-based approach to the firm', which later gave rise to the 'dynamic capabilities perspective on the firm'. Both are still highly praised in the business literature, but they both gave very little room for a crucial 'Schumpeterian' trace: the central role of finance.

Here is where Lazonick's contribution takes up the task of expanding the agenda. Lazonick first contributed to the theme we are exploring by rekindling Chandler's Schumpeter-inspired business history and turning it into a 'theory of business organisation' (Lazonick 1991). Although the 1991 book did not focus on finance, Lazonick's subsequent work was quick to recognise the importance of the 'finance link' to the theory of the firm.[10] His most recent research output is the 'theory of innovative enterprise' that he displays in his contribution to this volume. In that framework, the way finance and financial metrics interact with corporate governance and how this organisational packet works inside the corporation is central to understanding corporate performance.

Lazonick opens his chapter stating that 'the theory of innovative enterprise is a conceptual framework for analyzing how an economy can achieve sustainable prosperity.' Key in his account is the type of corporate governance and strategies forged for the 'growth of their firms'. The Schumpeter-Penrose-based strategy and governance approach are well known and result in a virtuous cycle. It is the retain-and-reinvest regime, where companies retain corporate revenues and use them along with external funding to invest in productive capabilities, including those of the labour force, that can generate innovative processes, products and markets. Corporate growth and diversification results, along with structural transformation of the economy.

However, there is another governance regime, which Lazonick labels the 'maximise shareholder value' approach, which delivers completely different results. This 'maximise shareholder value' approach adopts a 'downsize-and-distribute' corporate strategy. Under a downsize-and-distribute regime, senior corporate executives – incentivised by stock-based pay and pressured by short-term financial interests – focus on cost-cutting, downsizing the labour force and distributing corporate revenues to shareholders in the forms of cash dividends and stock repurchases.

This governance approach induces the 'financialisation of the corporation' and is the flip-side of the 'financialisation of the economy' discussed by Mazzucato and Wray. Consequently, it also contributes to the reversal of Schumpeter's 'ephor model' as well as its outcomes. When short-term financial interests dictate the rules, non-financial corporations start to behave like pure financial agents with no other commitments than short-term gains instead of long-term growth, which results in unproductive – or destructive – entrepreneurship (Baumol), resulting in a zero-sum game instead of the positive sum attached to the Schumpeterian governance regime.

Lazonick explains and documents how this reversal in corporate governance approaches contributed to the current deterioration of the US economy and its social tissue, an economy (and society) that displayed a tendency toward stable and equitable growth in the immediate post-World War II decades, but entered from the last half of the 1970s into an era of unstable employment, inequitable income distribution, crumbling infrastructure and sagging productivity.

Similarly to Mazzucato and Wray, Lazonick closes his chapter with suggestions on how to restore the conditions for sustainable growth. He concentrates on the need to revive and refine the Schumpeter-Penrose approach[11] to corporate expansion, to which he contributes by providing the 'theory of the innovative enterprise', and to eradicate the 'maximising shareholder value' approach to corporate governance, characterised as an ideology of value extraction without a theory or practice of value creation (see also Mazzucato 2018). Financial re-regulation and corporate governance reform are at the core of his prescriptions.

Fred Block opens his chapter with the following sentences: 'Returning to Schumpeter's *Capitalism, Socialism and Democracy* after seventy-five years is not at all an antiquarian exercise. On the contrary, it is vitally important for anyone trying to understand our current political economic situation.' As already underlined above, that is precisely the aim of this book. In Block's contribution, the issue addressed is a key debate academics, policy makers and dedicated media are facing: the spectrum of 'secular stagnation'. Raised by Larry Summers from a more theoretical and policy perspective in 2014 and 2016, the theme gained new ammunition with the publication of Robert Gordon's 2016 book *The Rise and Fall of American Growth*.

Gordon's main thesis is that the extraordinary century of US economic growth from 1870 to 1970 has ended, and the US entered a new period in which major headwinds make it highly likely that economic growth will continue to occur at a much slower pace than before 1970. As Block notes, this is a recurring theme in economics and economic history. The term 'secular stagnation' last flourished in the 1930s and early 1940s; it was raised more prominently by Alvin Hansen at Harvard and originated a discussion in which Schumpeter got directly involved. His arguments then are still valid today, and Block makes good use of them.

Block's critique of Gordon unfolds along three areas: measurement problems, deficient knowledge or understanding of current technological disruptions and lack of a proper theoretical framework for his narrative. In the measurement area, Block indicates that Gordon completely ignores one of the most important changes in recent decades: the extraordinary proliferation in the variety of consumer goods available in any given category, and goes further, stating that this is only the tip of the iceberg; in that sense he, in fact, ignores some of the key qualitative changes in economic output.

This echoes very closely Schumpeter's own complaints in *CSD* regarding the lack of understanding of how development should be accessed:

> New commodities escape or are inadequately represented by an index which must rest largely on basic commodities and intermediate products. For the same reason improvements in quality almost completely fail to assert themselves although they constitute, in many lines, the core of the progress achieved — there is no way of expressing adequately the difference between a motorcar of 1940 and a motorcar of 1900 or the extent to which the price of motorcars per unit of utility has fallen.
>
> (Schumpeter 1942, 66)

The core of Block's measurement critique resides in Gordon's acceptance of total factor productivity (TFP) as an adequate yardstick. As he indicates, the single biggest problem with Gordon's study is his reliance on trends in TFP in the period from 1970 to the present. In fact, reliance on TFP assumes that GDP is an accurate measure of the growth in economic output. Yet, given the complete rejuvenation of the economic space brought through by innovations and general-purpose technologies, with productivity rising in an increasingly intangible cluster of services while their prices fall (although we know we got more productive with the flood of 'Apps' in our possession, how do we measure the productivity of the 'App economy'?), GDP growth means less and less for evaluating economic performance.[12]

Here we get to the core of Schumpeter's apt differentiation between *growth* and *structural transformation*, which is what Block finds lacking in Gordon. From a Schumpeterian perspective, an economy can be substantively transformed and made more efficient without growing much.[13] Producing and investing more efficiently can very well involve less growth, but it will involve substantial structural change. In fact, that is exactly what structural transformation is about: getting more with less.

Additionally, Block points out that, in fact, it is possible to assemble data showing that Gordon's pessimism about current technologies is off the mark. Examples include a study by Graetz and Michaels (2016), which found that quality adjusted prices of industrial robots declined by 80% between 1990 and 2005 or an annual rate of 5% per year, and a report by Nykvist and Nilsson (2015) showing that the cost of lithium-ion battery packs for electric cars fell at an annual rate of 14% between 2007 and 2014 with indications that the declines have accelerated more recently.

The most important dimension of Block's argument, however, is that Gordon lacks a proper theoretical framework to apply to his narrative. Quite surprisingly, Block adds, Gordon only mentions Schumpeter once in the book, and totally misses the two most important Schumpeterian points on technological forecasting: first, that if the recent economic history of technology teaches us anything, it is that the past is a poor guide to the future. One can never extrapolate future outcomes from past or current trends (be it the 1890s or 1970s). Technological uncertainty is a fact. Second, as Schumpeter argues in *CSD*,

> [t]echnological possibilities are an uncharted sea ... (and) from the fact that some of them have been exploited before others, it cannot be inferred that the former were more productive than the latter. And those that are still in the lap of the gods may be more or less productive than any that have thus far come within our range of observation.
>
> (Schumpeter 1942, 155)

Had Gordon taken these premises seriously, his prediction would have been much more cautious.[14] Block closes his chapter by pointing to the importance of institutional and policy arrangements – with a prominent role for the state[15] – and institutional change to understand technological dynamics and progress and, conversely, of institutional inertia and misguided policies to account for stagnation and poor economic performance.[16] Here, in countering the most recent incarnation of technological pessimism, Block shows how Schumpeter's insights and analytical framework remain extremely handy as well.

Having said that, let us add that the attentive reader could be wondering about the mention of slow growth and sagging productivity in the US when we summarised both Mazzucato and Wray and Lazonick's arguments, linking them to Gordon's main thesis of 'technological diminishing returns'. That would be misplacing them. The point here is that both Mazzucato and Wray and Lazonick's dismal diagnoses of the US and UK economic performances are finance-based, and not due to some scarcity of available knowledge and technology or innovation opportunities. They originate in badly regulated finance, the financialisation of the economy and their implications, and reflect a diversion from the Schumpeterian development regime, not its theoretical inadequacy.

In John Mathews' chapter, the insights generated by Schumpeter in *CSD* are applied to the rise of new green industries in China, with a focus on their evolutionary dynamics and potential to disrupt established fossil-fuel industries in the West. Mathews argues that the Schumpeterian account that builds on insights spelt out in *CSD* provides the best explanation for this current global green shift and its Chinese driver. He starts by confronting the fact that as China, India and other industrialising giants grow, they are faced with an inconvenient truth: they cannot rely on the Western industrial development model. Therefore, largely by necessity, a new approach to development is needed and is already emerging in the East, with China leading the way in building green industry at scale.

The core elements of this emergent industrial model are: (1) the enhancement of energy security by basing energy systems on manufactured energy devices; (2) the enhancement of resource security by restructuring the economy along circular lines (closing industrial loops) rather than the traditional linear economy; and (3) greening of finance to drive the transition. Mathews' key claim is that this emergent model of green industry constitutes a major process of creative destruction, which fits Schumpeter's framework perfectly. He uses the concept of a Kondratiev-like technological wave to characterise its main traces.

They include drastically declining costs (where the argument is that their costs are declining for fundamental reasons related to the fact that they are products of 'technology-fed manufacturing'); unlimited supply of renewable energy sources (and recirculation of material inputs, potentially endlessly); and demonstrated potential for incorporation in power systems, food production, water regeneration and in manufacturing and transport generally, i.e. right across the economy. At that point, Mathews introduces China's emerging leadership in that 'greening wave' and links it to the two Schumpeterian core levers: finance and entrepreneurship. In China's case, they both happen to be public. He indicates that the key element is the role played by finance, particularly state entrepreneurial finance – and here we see China playing a leading role in greening its financial system and giving full rein to development banks, especially the China Development Bank.

Examples in this endeavour include the China Development Bank's lines of credit to Chinese solar photovoltaic (PV) companies like LDK and Yingli Solar, and to wind power companies like Goldwind, thus propelling them to leadership in the China market and subsequently to global dominance. Mathews underlines the importance of the presence of a national strategy to manage the transition process as well as the bold actions of a mission-oriented entrepreneurial state. Both issues can be traced back directly to Schumpeter, as Burlamaqui shows in the concluding chapter of the book, where Schumpeter reveals himself – quite surprisingly indeed – as a fierce advocate of an entrepreneurial state and backing up a 'creative-destruction management' strategy as one of its building blocks.

Mathews concludes the chapter sustaining that, essentially, greening is a massive process of creative destruction – a destruction of the entire fossil-fuel industrial order and its supersession by an alternative energy and resources order based on renewable inputs. In his own words, '[t]his is a powerful application of Schumpeter's conceptual apparatus in a new, twenty-first-century setting.'

We can add here that the mission-oriented Chinese entrepreneurial state provides a stark contrast with the neo-liberal-oriented Western model of industrialisation of finance and financialisation of industry,[17] which invites the question of which of them is more capable of delivering the type of structural transformation Schumpeter theorised about. In that regard, perhaps a more useful way to characterise the Chinese regime is 'Socialism with Schumpeterian characteristics', rather than 'Socialism with Chinese characteristics', an official expression of the Chinese Communist Party that does not have any meaningful content. This is a theme that will reemerge in the closing chapter of the book.

John Medearis' chapter, 'Domination, weak judgement and the dilemmas of contemporary Schumpeterian democrats', is devoted to discussing contemporary implications of Schumpeter's mature theory of democracy as it is exposed in *CSD*. According to Medearis, Schumpeter's theory of democracy 'combined qualified advocacy of minimal democratic electoral institutions with a behavioural account of voters as irrational and incapable of living up to the standards of "classical" democratic theory'. However, he affirms, in contemporary democratic theory these elements of Schumpeter's political thought have split off from each other, with scholars he terms 'institutional Schumpeterians' and 'behavioural Schumpeterians', each adopting only part of what for Schumpeter was an integral approach. Representative scholars of the institutional realm include Adam Przeworski and Ian Shapiro, while Christopher Achen and Larry Bartels are key figures of the behavioural camp.

Medearis' line of reasoning proceeds in three interconnected routes. The first involves establishing that there are, in fact, two different and distinct schools influenced by Schumpeter, characterised by selective borrowings from his democratic theory. The second consists in critically analysing these approaches and demonstrating the weaknesses inherent in institutional and behavioural Schumpeterianism, which grow in each case out of the new purposes to which they try to put Schumpeter's ideas, as well as from attempting to secure one major element of his political thought without drawing or relying on others. The third, and most relevant, dimension of his argument shows that these distinctive weaknesses of institutional and behavioural Schumpeterians, significant in their own right, also lead to a common inadequacy, a difficulty identifying and analysing an increasingly manifest challenge to Western democracies in the twenty-first century: the rise of populist and white nationalist movements and parties.

Medearis' argument is a new take on 'Schumpeterian politics', and it is nuanced and complex. In a nutshell, his objections to each camp can be summarised as follows: institutional Schumpeterians cannot show that devices for limiting access to state power are sufficient for a robust democratic programme to resist the many contemporary forms of social and political domination at work today. Behavioural Schumpeterians' efforts to show that most voters are non-ideological, as they understand the term, are inherently dubious – and they leave their proponents unable, by definition, to identify specifically ideological challenges to democratic life.

Despite many differences in tone, language and tactics, Medearis argues, these challenges have common ground. They aim to protect or extend the social position of racial or ethnic groups that have been traditionally dominant. Therefore, their threat to democratic life arises from the fact that they often seek to relegate members of other racial or ethnic groups to less-valuable forms of citizenship, as well as their frequent embrace of authoritarian policies and political tactics.

After a lengthy analysis of both camps' main theses and shortcomings, Medearis returns to Schumpeter's own blend of institutional and behavioural elements, indicating how we can still learn from it and use it today: to fully appreciate Schumpeter's elite conception of democracy and its behavioural and institutional theses, Medearis asserts, it is necessary to view them in the context of what he would have termed his 'vision' of social structure and historical change. This vision had at its core the ideas that all societies were led by classes whose special aptitudes made them indispensable in their time, and that capitalism was in decline in the twentieth century – slowly approaching replacement by democratic socialism.

This transformation did not happen, in fact almost the reverse seems to be true. However, the challenges brought by the spread of democratic ideologies directly influencing policy changes, something Schumpeter deemed politically destabilising, might help to explain the reasons for this reversal of fortunes. Medearis' approach provides a bridge for that hypothesis:

> In both contemporary Europe and the US, there is growing evidence of the resurgence of movements of traditionally dominant ethnic and racial groups that believe their position is threatened by out-groups such as immigrants, and so embrace programmes to degrade the value of others' democratic citizenship, often by extraordinary political means that undermine democratic commitments to democratic rights and procedures.

To which he adds: 'Similar evidence shows that Donald Trump was propelled into office significantly by the same social forces and beliefs.'

Summing up, in the context of increased radicalisation of political ideologies and political parties and increasing influence of new information-diffusion technologies by social media – both real and fake – on voter behaviour and with the availability of big-data-based tools to gauge and 'direct' voter conduct, as evidenced by the recent Cambridge Analytica scandal, Schumpeter's theory of democracy can still shed light on the contemporary malaise of Western democratic politics – with provisos derived from the analysis provided in his chapter. Medearis finishes his contribution along these lines by stating that

> [a] democratic theory that incorporated critical analysis of anti-democratic and undemocratic ideologies could build on Schumpeter's own understanding of ideology critique: a study of how groups understand the social

world and explain to themselves their place in it, and the implications this has for politics.

Finally, the issues of state, socialism and socialisation of investment. These themes clearly point to an obvious and badly needed extension of Schumpeter's theoretical approach: the incorporation of the state. These issues are tackled by Burlamaqui in the closing chapter of the book, which opens with the assertion that, historically, successful paths to capitalism included the state, more often than not, as a central actor.[18] The chapter recovers Schumpeter's important, but unsystematic, comments on State action and leadership in several of his works and suggests they present the seeds for a proper conceptualisation of an entrepreneurial state.

Following Schumpeter's observations on 'state action', Burlamaqui submits that what results is an institution that, through history, exercised the functions of market-maker, macro-strategist, venture capitalist in chief (forging and funding industries, and crafting innovation and technology policies) and creative-destruction manager (stimulating the creative part of the process in order to speed productivity enhancement and innovation diffusion and acting as a buffer to its destructive dimension). These traces, he adds, are the building blocks of a proper theory of the state as an 'entrepreneur',[19] and, Burlamaqui affirms, they are all in Schumpeter. Quite explicitly in his discussion of socialism – not of capitalism – in *CSD*, but also hidden in his historical chapters in *BC*, in side observations in *TED* as well as in several papers and even footnotes.

After documenting their presence and discussing them, Burlamaqui submits that Schumpeter's Entrepreneurial State offers a solid, and original, analytical framework, which, once made explicit, enriches his own theoretical edifice. Furthermore, the Schumpeterian input on state action complements previous studies on the Asian developmental state providing them an 'economics' they, in general, lack.

Last, the chapter also attempts to revive and rekindle Schumpeter's conception of socialism, which has an entrepreneurial state and the socialisation of investment as its core, and apply it to contemporary China. The key point here is the claim that China provides a case where the core Schumpeterian propositions about Socialism are alive, well and at work: China demonstrates that, as Schumpeter suggested, properly organised, 'socialism' can beat 'capitalism' in the terrains of speedy and leapfrogging growth, technological catching-up, economic efficiency, and poverty alleviation, largely by exercising public (entrepreneurial) leadership, funding and socialising strategic investment initiatives, and managing creative destruction.

The final takeaway is both theoretical – the incorporation of the state as a key factor (in fact a protagonist) in enabling capitalism to evolve by providing infrastructure, sponsoring technological breakthroughs, steering innovation diffusion, shaping markets and forging development strategies – and analytical: a re-interpretation of the nature of 'socialism with Chinese characteristics' – a meaningless expression as already mentioned – as 'socialism with Schumpeterian characteristics'.

Now we invite the reader to advance to the chapters and get a proper understanding and evaluation of the material we just summarised. Paraphrasing Schumpeter, we are sure she will find plenty to learn from, but also material to 'shoot at'.

Acknowledgements

The editors would like to thank our fellow collaborators for accepting to contribute to an unconventional proposal by not-well-known researchers and especially for their patience in waiting, far more than what would be acceptable – even in the intricate craft of book editing – for the conclusion of the project. We also thank Routledge, especially Lisa Lavelle and Ingebert Edenhofer, for the same reasons.

Notes

1 The state constitutes a vastly overlooked dimension of Schumpeter's analysis, which is indicated by both Callegari and Burlamaqui in their contributions and discussed in more detail by Burlamaqui in the last chapter of the book.

2 The reader should note the full convergence between these statements and Douglass North's 'final thesis' in his 2005 book *Understanding the Process of Economic Change*, where he explicitly states that '[w]we live in an uncertain and ever changing world that is continually evolving in new and novel ways. Standard theories are of little help in this context' (vii). From a Schumpeterian perspective it's quite a victory: The dean of the New Institutional Economics, and a Nobel prise winner, deferring to the evolutionary perspective in economics.

3 See Burlamaqui's chapter (Chapter 10) in this volume for a further discussion of this last point.

4 By neo-Schumpeterians we mean roughly the generation *after* Stopler, Rosenberg, Nelson, Winter, Freeman, Lundvall and other founding fathers of the 'Schumpeterian renaissance' in the 1970s and 1980s. These towering figures were truly 'Schumpeterians' with broad agendas and employing a wide range of enquiry methods and research techniques. We are inspired by them. In contradistinction, the neo-Schumpeterians we have in mind, and criticise, are those who reduced Schumpeter's work to a caricature of what it is. A representative group of them are the 'model-builders' united around the *Journal of Evolutionary Economics*, which also constitutes a large chunk of the papers at the bi-annual Schumpeter Society Conferences. Both in the journal and more and more in the conferences, one can find hundreds of hyper-abstract equilibrium models aiming to somehow advance Schumpeter's legacy and insights. They may have captured and developed a dimension of Schumpeter's work: the one that revolves around linking evolution with equilibrium. This approach is amply criticised in this book for its internal inconsistency; it was explicitly rejected by Schumpeter in *CSD* and, we sustain, does little to contribute to a proper understanding of how capitalism actually works and evolves. Summing up, this group was successful in developing what Callegari labels as a 'Schumpeterian-neoclassical synthesis' but can hardly claim to be in track with Schumpeter's broad agenda and his recommended methods of inquiry summarised in his 'final thesis'. If alive, Schumpeter would probably shy

away from these heirs. Perhaps what we have here is a case of 'bastard Schumpeterianism'? (See Burlamaqui, Chapter 2, and Louçã, Chapter 3, for discussions on Schumpeter's final thesis).

5 Big Pharma is the sector that excels in lobbying for these rent-seeking IP-based regimes. See Bessen and Meurer 2008 for an apt discussion of this subject.

6 There is a wealth of observations on financial issues in *BC*'s historical chapters, but they are pulverised and unsystematic, not leading therefore to a coherent approach to the matter.

7 Schumpeter had already pointed to that possibility when describing the 'secondary wave' in *Business Cycle*. See Burlamaqui, Chapter 2, section on '*Business Cycles*: theoretical failure, first-class business history and Minskyan seeds' in this volume for the relevant passages on that matter.

8 In the book, Schumpeter is quoted only three times and in footnotes, but Penrose's whole framework is not only compatible with Schumpeter's but actually a complement to his theory. For the relevant references, see Burlamaqui, Chapter 2, section on '*Capitalism, Socialism and Democracy*: creative destruction as new departure point for economic analysis' in this volume.

9 Harvard, Wharton and Berkeley are cases in point.

10 In fact, financial issues received detailed treatment in 'Controlling the Market for Corporate Control' ICC, 1992, which initiated his critique of agency theory, see www.newsweek.com/2017/04/14/harvard-business-school-financial-crisis-economics-578378.html. During the 1990s, he wrote a number of papers with Mary O'Sullivan on the finance of industry comparing the US, UK, Germany and Japan, and in 2000 they published a study criticising the 'Maximizing shareholder value' corporate strategy, which became his most cited paper. Since 2007 Lazonick has developed a systematic study of buybacks and the looting of the US business corporation under the lens of his evolving 'theory of innovative enterprise'.

11 Which is alive and doing extremely well in China, as Burlamaqui shows in the concluding chapter of the book.

12 Mokyr complements the argument denouncing that '[e]conomists have different measures of innovation, and all of them are flawed', adding: 'TFP can grow (or not) regardless of technological progress, and considerable technological progress can take place that does not get recorded as TFP growth' (2017, 20).

13 Should the reader pay a visit to Tokyo, the capital of the 'two lost decades' country, she will understand perfectly what is at stake: shining new infrastructure, completely rejuvenated neighbourhoods (Roppongi for instance) and a vastly expanded transportation network.

14 Here we ask the reader to pause for a minute and look at the ongoing and upcoming transformations brought by automation/robotisation, artificial intelligence and DNA manipulation. Does it look like any major productivity blow is implausible?

15 A theme to which he, Mathew Keller and collaborators produced a pioneering contribution, see Block and Keller 2011.

16 For an acute analysis of how special interests – losers of innovation – can politically organise in order to undermine entrepreneurship and innovation, an argument espoused by Schumpeter, see Bessen 2015.

17 The apt phrase belongs to Michael Hudson.

18 The fact that mainstream economic theory has very little to say about the role of the state in economic transformation should appal us all. Despite a whole tradition of institutional reformers and policy-makers going back (at least) to Antonio Serra, Oliver Cromwell, J.B Colbert, A. Hamilton, F. List, O. Bismarck, the Meiji reformers, and, more recently, to F.D. Roosevelt, G. Vargas, G. Marshall, J. Monet, K. Adenauer, Lee Kuan Yew, Park C. Hee, Chiang Kai-shek and Deng Xiaoping. In point of fact, economic theory in general was and is mute in regard to the state as a key agent of economic modernisation, industrialisation and

economic and social stabilisation. It had to wait for Keynes (and Weber, to a lesser extent) to open up the *potential* to properly access its role. Nevertheless, if we look back at the last 40 years, Schumpeter's dictum would fit like a glove: 'They [the profession] learned a lot ... and unlearned even more' in that timeframe. See Reinert 2007 for a wonderful exposition of that forgotten – or never documented before – 'history of economic policy and economic transformation.'
19 See Ruttan 2006, Block and Keller 2011, Mazzucato 2013 and Weiss 2014 for complementary analyses of the US case, the whole literature on the developmental state (for instance Johnson 1982, Wade 1990, Woo 1991, Woo-Cummings 1999, Vogel 2011, Kim and Vogel 2011) for Asia and Musacchio and Lazzarini 2014 for Brazil.

References

Andersen, E.S. (2009). *Schumpeter's Evolutionary Economics: A Theoretical, Historical and Statistical Analysis of the Engine of Capitalism.* London: Anthem Press.

Arrow, K.J. (1962). Economic welfare and the allocation of resources for innovation. In: R. Nelson (Ed.), *The Rate and Direction of Technical Change* (pp. 609–626). New York: National Bureau of Economic Research.

Bessen, J. and M.J. Meurer (2008). *Patent Failure: How Judges, Bureaucrats, and Lawyers Put Innovators at Risk.* Princeton, NJ: Princeton University Press.

Block, F. and Keller, M.R. (Eds.) (2011). *State of Innovation: The U.S. Government's Role in Technology Development.* Boulder, CO: Paradigm.

Bessen, J. (2015). *Learning by Doing: The Real Connection between Innovation, Wages, and Wealth.* New Heaven, CT: Yale University Press.

Burlamaqui, L. (2006). How should competition policies and intellectual property issues interact in a globalised world? A Schumpeterian perspective. Working Papers in Technology Governance and Economic Dynamics no. 6. Available at http://technologygovernance.eu/files/main//2006042407123939.pdf.

Graetz, G. and Michaels, G. (2016). Robots at work. London School of Economics, Centre for Economic Performance, *Working Paper No. 1335.*

Heertje, A. (Ed.) (1981). *Schumpeter's Vision – Capitalism Socialism and Democracy After 40 years.* New York: Praeger.

Johnson, C. (1982). *MITI and the Japanese Miracle: The Growth of Industrial Policy: 1925–1975.* Stanford, CA: Stanford University Press.

Juma, C. (2016). *Innovation and its Enemies: Why People Resist New Technologies.* New York: Oxford University Press.

Kim, B.K. and Vogel, E.F. (Eds.) (2011). *The Park Chung Hee Era.* Cambridge. Harvard University Press.

Lazonick, W. (1991). *Business Organisation and the Myth of the Market Economy.* Cambridge: Cambridge University Press.

Lazonick, W. and O'Sullivan, M. (2000). Maximizing shareholder value: A new ideology for corporate governance. *Economy and Society,* 29(1), 13–35.

Mazzucato, M. (2013). *The Entrepreneurial State.* London: Anthem Press.

Mazzucato, M. (2017). Mission-oriented innovation policy: Challenges and opportunities. UCL Institute for Innovation and Public Purpose Working Paper, IPP WP 2017–01. Available at www.ucl.ac.uk/bartlett/public-purpose/publications/2018/jan/mission-oriented-innovation-policy-challenges-and-opportunities.

Mazzucato, M. (2018). *The Value of Everything: Making and Taking in the Global Economy.* London: Penguin.

Mokyr, J. (2017). The past and the future of innovation: some lessons from economic history. Research paper, Departments of Economics and History Northwestern University.

Musacchio, A. and Lazzarini, S.G. (2014). *Reinventing State Capitalism*. Cambridge. Harvard University Press.

Nelson, R.R. (1959). The simple economics of basic scientific research. *Journal of Political Economy*, 67(3), 297–306.

Nykvist, B. and Nilsson, M. (2015). Rapidly falling costs of battery packs for electric vehicles. *Nature Climate Change*, 5, 329–332.

Penrose, E.T. (1959). *The Theory of the Growth of the Firm*. New York: Sharpe.

Reinert, E. (2007). *How Rich Countries Got Rich and Why Poor Countries Stay Poor*. London: Constable & Robinson.

Rosenberg, N. (1994). Schumpeter: Radical economist. In: Y. Shionoya and M. Perlman (Eds.), *Schumpeter in the History of Ideas*. Ann Arbor, MI: The University of Michigan Press.

Ruttan, V. (2006). *Is War Necessary for Economic Growth?* Oxford, Oxford University Press.

Schumpeter, J.A. (1942). *Capitalism, Socialism and Democracy*. New York, Routledge.

Taylor, M.Z. (2016). *The Politics of Innovation: Why Some Countries are Better than Others at Science and Technology*. Oxford. Oxford University Press.

Vogel, E.F. (2011). *Deng Xiaoping and the Transformation of China*. Cambridge, MA: Harvard University Press.

Wade, R. (1990). *Governing the Market: Economic Theory and the Role of Government in East Asian Industrialisation*. Princeton, NJ: Princeton University Press.

Weiss, L. (2014). *America Inc.: Innovation and Enterprise in the National Security State*. Ithaca, NY: Cornell University Press.

Woo, J.E. (1991). *Race to Swift: State and Finance in Korean Industrialisation*. New York: Columbia University Press.

Woo-Cummings, M. (Ed.) (1999). *The Developmental State*. Ithaca, NY: Cornell University Press.

Part I

New interpretations

2 Creative destruction as a radical departure

A new paradigm for analysing capitalism

Leonardo Burlamaqui

> The long wrangle about 'measuring capital' has been a great deal of fuss over a secondary question. The real source of trouble is the confusion between comparisons of equilibrium positions and the history of a process of accumulation.
>
> (Robinson 1978, 135)

Introduction

In the Schumpeter Society's Kyoto 1992 conference Nathan Rosenberg delivered a brilliant paper later published with the provocative title 'Schumpeter: Radical Economist' (Rosenberg: 1994). In the paper, Rosenberg begins by stating that according to him, *Capitalism, Socialism and Democracy* was the 'mature statement of the most radical scholar in the discipline of economics in the twentieth century' (1994, 41). He went further:

> Rather, it is my intention to show the quintessential later Schumpeter … held views that were not only radical, but are deserving of far more serious attention than they receive today, even, or perhaps especially from scholars who think of themselves as working within the Schumpeterian tradition.
>
> (Ibid.)

Rosenberg's statements are sharp, on the mark, but were almost completely overlooked. This chapter will pick up where he left off and argue that after 75 years of its publication, *Capitalism, Socialism and Democracy* (*CSD*) still is a vastly unexplored work in the sense that if offers a whole new paradigm to analyse the way capitalism works. It does that by not only criticising the core assumptions of the prevailing neoclassical theory. That is well known and has merited plenty discussion. What was largely overlooked is that *CSD* also provides a new framework where Schumpeter's previous theoretical innovations concerning the specific contours of an evolutionary system fall in place. The chapter will argue that from a theoretical perspective, *CSD* marks a radical departure from Schumpeter's previous analytical framework, the one he used in both his *Theory of Economic Development* (*TED*) and in *Business Cycles* (*BC*), published only three years before.

Until *CSD*, Schumpeter's theory of development was, in fact, a theory of cycles rooted in equilibrium, and one which gets more complicated and out of touch with actual capitalism dynamics as he moves from the basic Juglar cycle, which supports the basic model of *TED*, towards the contortions he throws himself into, in *BC*, where he tries to 'merge' three different cycles (Juglar, Kondratiev and Kithins), all rooted in equilibrium as well, and apply the resulting scaffolding to an historical interpretation of capitalist evolution since the industrial revolution. Schumpeter's analyses both in *TED* and *BC* are, despite many challenging propositions to both neoclassical and Marxist orthodoxies, rooted in equilibrium, as we will see, which turns his theory as a whole into a rather incoherent body of work since it tries to merge equilibrium analysis (which translates as absence of change) with evolution (which equals change) in the same theoretical body. That doesn't work well, as the author would make explicit only in *CSD*.[1,2]

My contention in this chapter is that only in *CSD* does a fully radical, 'Schumpeterian', Schumpeter emerge.[3] In the book, competition *replaces* cycles and takes centre stage as the key process guiding economic evolution. Creative destruction, the kernel of competition, is presented as an openended process filled with turbulence, instability and uncertainty. Equilibrium is finally removed from the framework and perfect competition is totally thrown away, and labelled as basically inefficient (if it ever came to exist). Bigness, when subjected to competition by means of innovation, is efficient. Coupled with growth, it provides a win–win solution for capitalists, workers, shareholders, consumers and fiscal revenues. 'Monopolistic practices' (dominating firms, oligopolistic market structures, price fixing, mark-up manipulation, market niches' creation, as well as planned idle capacity) are understood as competitive business strategies rather than oligopolistic inefficiencies. Super-profits are the seeds of super-investments and job creation. Unemployment and idle capacity are the norms (again: equilibrium is gone). Capitalism is neither 'harmonious', it's filled with conflicts, nor bound to economic collapse. It's a victim of its own success due to institutional entropy.[4]

Now, if we couple those propositions with the brilliant, but underdeveloped, innovations from *TED*, and the largely ignored 'macrofinancial' elements of Schumpeter's secondary wave, provided in *BC*, a new paradigm – out of equilibrium and centred in creative destruction – emerges. That new paradigm still has to be properly worked out since, to my knowledge, the analyses and discussions of Schumpeter's works largely bypassed that 'reconstruction strategy' and the vast majority of neo-Schumpeterians who attempted to follow up on Schumpeter's agenda are still working inside the 'iron cage' of equilibrium.[5]

The chapter will proceed as follows: I will present a compressed view of Schumpeter's own evolution highlighting the evolutionary elements on the first two books of his 'evolutionary trilogy', *TED* and *BC*[6] (Andersen 2009), severing them from 'equilibrium theorising' to which they are attached in both works, and integrating those same elements into the 'creative-destruction' framework forged in *CSD*. My contention is that the result is an updated Schumpeterian departure point for economic analysis.

Schumpeter's theory of economic development: brilliant theoretical innovations on shaky equilibrium foundations

Andersen (2009) performed a magnificent task by scrutinising Schumpeter's trilogy (*TED*, *BC* and *CSD*), pointing to its strengths and its weakness. His work will be very difficult to match on that front and I will certainly not pursue that goal. Rather, I will take advantage of his effort but with a very different goal. Andersen's ultimate objective was to show the complementarity among the trilogy and the imperative of analysing the three books together (2009, 137–139). He also submits as his book's core propositions '(1) that Schumpeter's basic ambition was to complement equilibrium economics with an evolutionary economics that analyses capitalist economic evolution; and (2) that his major contributions to economics relate to his attempts to fulfil that ambition' (2009, 2–3).

I am in full agreement with his first proposition, but will proffer that Schumpeter largely failed to accomplish this self-imposed task. As for the second proposition, I'll part ways with Andersen and side with Rosenberg (1994), extending and deepening his framing of *CSD* as a radical departure from Schumpeter's earlier attempts to complement equilibrium economics with evolutionary economics.

TED's major weakness was, as mentioned, that the explanation of development and structural change are wrapped in equilibrium. The development process starts from equilibrium, the circular flow described in Chapter 1, and ends in equilibrium. The end of each cycle is a (new) equilibrium position from which a new cluster of innovations can emerge. The closing chapter in the book (Chapter 6: 'The business cycle') provides ample evidence of that:

> In this sense, therefore, we come to the conclusion that according to our theory there must always be a process of absorption between two booms, ending in a position approaching equilibrium, the bringing about of which is its function.
>
> (1997, 244)

> Recession has a function: to disseminate the innovation cluster and to restore equilibrium …' (ibid.). 'With this qualification, then, we return to our conclusion that the economic nature of depression lies in the diffusion of the achievements of the boom over the whole economic system through the mechanism of the struggle for equilibrium.
>
> (1997, 250)

The quotations speak for themselves. *TED* presents a framework where development, is constructed as a theory of business cycles in the Austrian tradition in which equilibrium is key.[7] It is assumed as an anchor or attractor towards which the system inexorably gravitates. Schumpeter *assumes* that as a *fact* without ever explaining *why* development should unfold like this and, specially, precisely *how* once deviated from an initial (assumed) equilibrium position, it would converge to another one. The 'convergence problem' that resulted in so much debate in the field without solid results (Ingrao and Israel 1990; Hahn 1992, Chapter 1; Hahn and Petri: 2003) is simply assumed away.

The process of economic development is a well-behaved theory of cycles where the invisible hand is at work through crises/recessions. They 'clean' the system, restoring the equilibrium, though as a condition for the next 'wave of prosperity'. A strong flavour of Marx's 'laws of motion' is tentatively blended with Walrasian absence of motion. The concoction is not particularly successful from a theoretical point of view.

That major weakness in Schumpeter's scaffolding was spotted and elegantly showed by Nelson (2012, 903):

> At the time, he was writing TED Schumpeter seemed to believe that his theory of economic dynamics and neoclassical equilibrium theory of prices, while oriented to different phenomena, could co-exist comfortably. My argument is that they couldn't. Schumpeter's theory of innovation driven economic development not only put forth a different view of what was most important about capitalist economies. It diverged from theory that stressed equilibrium conditions regarding the assumed general context for economic action taking. It was virtually impossible to buy conceptually into both at the same time.

TED was, after all, an incoherent theoretical construction. Nevertheless, it was also brilliant, filled with striking ideas and conceptual innovations. Let me point first that Chapter 2, where the main new ideas about development are presented, is *not* built as a theory of cycles. Rather, the phenomenon under scrutiny is *endogenous economic change*.

> By development, therefore, we shall understand only such changes in economic life as are not forced upon it from without but arise by its own initiative, from within.
>
> (1997, Kindle Locations 2055–2056)

What's important to keep in mind here is that, in my reading, Chapter 2 provides a more flexible and open-ended platform for understanding the broad contours of development than the closing one (Chapter 6). Second, innovations are the endogenous dynamic forces in the system and the root cause of change, and their definition is broad: not only new technologies, but also products, forms of organisations, markets' source of supply. Therefore, development analysed from that perspective should be a complex, multifaceted, institutionally grounded process, not easily, or desirably, caged into a mathematical model. Third, finance is at the core of the process.

> The capitalistic credit system has grown out of and thrived on the financing of new combinations in all countries, even though in a different way in each (Locations 2166–2167). To provide … credit is clearly the function of that category of individuals which we call capitalists.
>
> > (1997, Kindle Locations 2150–2151)

> In this sense, therefore, we define the kernel of the credit phenomenon in the following manner: credit is essentially the creation of purchasing power for the purpose of transferring it to the entrepreneur, but not simply the transfer of existing purchasing power (Locations 2840–2842). To bridge it is the function of the lender, and he fulfils it by placing purchasing power created ad hoc at the disposal of the entrepreneur.
>
> > (1997, Kindle Locations 2850–2851)

Much before Keynes's concept of monetary-production economy or Minsky's Wall-Street paradigm, Schumpeter characterises capitalism as a financial system where investment bankers are the shapers of structural transformation via their funding choices. They are the true capitalists, the ephors of the system:

> The money market is always, as it were, the headquarters of the capitalist system, from which orders go out to its individual divisions, and that which is debated and decided there is always in essence the settlement of plans for further development. All kinds of credit requirements come to this market; all kinds of economic projects are first brought into relation with one another, and contend for their realisation in it.
>
> > (1997, Kindle Locations 3142–3144)

Fourth, credit, not savings, is the key element for investment to take place. Money and credit are endogenous. Loans create deposits and bankers are the 'financial entrepreneurs' who preform that crucial role.[8]

> It is always a question, not of transforming purchasing power which already exists in someone's possession, *but of the creation of new purchasing power out of nothing* – out of nothing even if the credit contract by which the new purchasing power is created is supported by securities which are not themselves circulating media – which is added to the existing circulation. And this is the source from which new combinations are often financed…. *The banker, therefore, is not so much primarily a middleman in the commodity 'purchasing power' as a producer of this commodity.*
>
> > (1997, Kindle Locations 2218–2219, my emphasis)

Fifth, bankers[9] are the fundamental possessors of animal spirits. It's their money that's at stake, not the entrepreneurs'.[10]

> The entrepreneur is never the risk bearer.... In our example, this is quite clear. The one who gives credit comes to grief if the undertaking fails.... Risk-taking is in no case an element of the entrepreneurial function.
>
> (1997, Kindle Locations 3377–3380)

Sixth, entrepreneurs, despite not bearing financial risks, are the linchpin of innovation. Schumpeter oscillates, between personalising them as 'new men founding new enterprises'[11] and treating entrepreneurship as a function that is always crucial for development but necessary coming from individuals – it could be carried by corporations or even the state. However, he would clarify that distinction only in *CSD*. In *TED*, the two uses frequently overlap.

> The carrying out of new combinations we call 'enterprise'; the individuals whose function it is to carry them out we call 'entrepreneurs'.
>
> (1997, Kindle Locations 2226–2227)

What matters the most for analytical purposes is that entrepreneurs – or the entrepreneurial function – are a condition for development by means of innovation. Entrepreneurs are the ones, equipped with a vision and a strategy, who break two barriers to innovation: uncertainty and the resistances of the status quo. The first comes from the future, from not knowing it, and the second from the past, both the path-dependence of tradition and from those whose economic, social or political positioning in the system will be threatened by successful innovations.

> Carrying out a new plan and acting according to a customary one are things as different as making a road and walking along it.
>
> (1997, Kindle Locations 2353–2354)

> Of course, he must still foresee and estimate on the basis of his experience. But many things must remain uncertain.... The third point consists in the reaction of the social environment against one who wishes to do something new. This reaction may manifest itself first of all in the existence of legal or political impediments.
>
> (1997, Kindle Locations 2377–2378)[12]

Leadership, vision and strategy are the distinguishing features of the entrepreneur. These are necessary skills for creating new structures, new markets, new methods of production, organisation and consumption. This is an absolutely apt description of core capabilities for innovation in contemporary capitalism.[13] One can only bow to Schumpeter's ingenious way of presenting them in 1912. Furthermore, in the Schumpeterian saga the entrepreneur is both the hero and the 'victim' of change. He is the change-maker but also the one whose gains will vanish when innovations diffuse and imitation takes charge.

> ... The entrepreneurial function is attached 'to the creation of new things, to the realisation of the future value system. It is at the same time the child and the victim of development'.
>
> (1997, Kindle Locations 3630–3632)

It's worth noticing here that there is a curious[14] reversal of roles with reference to Marx, for whom the worker is the hero and the victim, the one who creates the surplus-value but also the victim of the way the surplus is appropriated. For Marx, the core conflict in the system is between capital and labour. For Schumpeter it is between innovation and tradition, new and old.

Seventh, entrepreneurial profits are the outcome of temporary monopolisation of market opportunities and creatures of development. They can show up as the result of decreasing costs, increasing margins, or both. They originate from surplus creation or surplus transfers, but cannot be understood à la Marx, as value extracted from labour power.

> Entrepreneurial profit is a surplus over costs. From the standpoint of the entrepreneur, it is the difference between receipts and outlay in a business.
>
> (1997, Locations 3241–3242)

> The creation of a new good which more adequately satisfies existing and previously satisfied needs is a somewhat different case. In this case the possibility of profit rests upon the fact that the higher price received for the better commodity surpasses its costs, which are likewise higher in most cases.
>
> (1997, Locations 3340–3341)

> Since the entrepreneur has no competitors when the new products first appear, the determination of their price proceeds wholly, or within certain limits, according to the principles of monopoly price. Thus, there is a monopoly element in profit in a capitalist economy.
>
> (1997, Locations 3606–3607)

Schumpeter does not provide any deep discussion of the 'origins of profit' or a new approach to a 'theory of value', but he gives us a hint. Profits result from temporary monopolisation of business opportunities created by credit and entrepreneurship. Therefore, investment bankers and entrepreneurs are the main originators of the surplus resulting from increased productivity created by 'new combinations' or innovations. What is worth noticing is that his formulation produces a 'positive sum' approach to surplus distribution: profits rise, prices fall, real-wages rise, consumption increases, interest and dividends are positive and fiscal revenues tend to rise as well. Later, in *CSD*, Schumpeter would help clarify that by stating that entrepreneurs 'generally create what they exploit' (1942, 101). Here we can speculate if there is room for a 'productivity theory of value'. The core argument is that structural transformation is a process where, over time, everybody benefits.

Eighth, within this cumulative change environment, propelled by different clusters of innovations, and filled with uncertainty, there is no tendency for profits – or the rate of profit – to equalise, nor any proportionality 'law' between investments and returns (the more one invests the bigger the returns).[15]

> Entrepreneurial profit is not a rent like the return to differential advant- ages in the permanent elements of a business; nor is it a return to capital, however one may define capital....

> So that *there is no reason for speaking about a tendency towards equalisation of profits which does not exist at all in reality*: for only the jumbling together of interest and profit explains why many authors contend for such a tend- ency, although we can observe such extraordinarily different profits in one and the same place, at the same time and in the same industry.
>
> (1997, Kindle Locations 3620–3621)

> And the total amount of profit actually obtained in a given time, as well as the profit realised by an individual entrepreneur, may be much greater than that necessary to call forth the entrepreneurial services which were actually operative.
>
> (1997, Locations 3646–3647)

These, equalisation and proportionality 'laws', are common assumptions in every economic theory dealing with profits and competition – including Marx where competition tends to redistribute surplus-value and equalise profits and the proportionality law also holds, the difference residing in that it is a negative correlation (the falling rate of profit sketched in Volume 3). Nevertheless, both propositions are, as Schumpeter suggests, wrong: anchored on perfect competition hypothesis, they are not validated by empirical data at any time in capitalism's history.

In contrast, Schumpeter's heretic propositions, both when they were made and now, hold true in capitalist reality. A look at Fortune 500 or any other index or company data over time shows how right he was. Profits do not tend to equalise, and an initial investment of US$400,000 in a company called WhatsApp in 2009 – later upped to eight million by Sequoia Capital – resulted in a 19 billion acquisition by Facebook in 2014. In Schumpeter's parlance, individual effort is often disproportionately rewarded in capitalism.

Ninth, capital is – as in Marx – a social relation of production: but it's not the Marxian capital–labour nexus, but credit. It links bankers to entrepreneurs. Therefore, capital is – as in Marx – control over the productive process.

However – as in Keynes and Minsky – the financial system is the collective ephor who exercises that control.

> We shall define capital, then, as that sum of means of payment which is available at any moment for transference to entrepreneurs.… The kernel of the matter lies in the credit requirements of new enterprises.
>
> (1997, Locations 3079–3123)

> With this proviso, only one fundamental thing happens on the money market, to which everything else is accessory: on the demand side appear entrepreneurs and on the supply side producers of and dealers in purchasing power, bankers' (1997, Locations 3126–3128) … 'Thus, the main function of the money or capital market is trading in credit for the purpose of financing development.
>
> (1997, Location 3147)

Evidently Schumpeter's focus in *TED* is a development-oriented financial system, or, one could venture, he is isolating that function of financial system for analytical purposes. The fact that most financial systems are, today, far away from his picturing doesn't make it less valuable – which doesn't mean it is comprehensive (see my critique below). On the contrary, the paucity of Schumpeterian bankers and productive entrepreneurship helps to explain the low growth-path of most OECD economies, or secular stagnation, to pick a trendy term, and one that Schumpeter refused to endorse many times in his works (see Block's chapter in this book). However, if we turn to the few financial systems that still have development as a priority – China is the obvious candidate – most of *TDE*'s analysis still applies, with the proviso that China's development banks are also public banks. The fact that Schumpeter never gave a proper attention in his theory to the role of the state in creating and financing innovations and, therefore, forging development[16] is a striking puzzle, and another gap that needs updating.[17]

Tenth, interest is characterised as a monetary-financial phenomenon. In a lengthy discussion with Bohm-Bawerk's time-related theory of interest, Schumpeter refutes his former professor and proposes a conceptual framework that would later be picked up by Keynes. A caveat is needed here. Once more, Schumpeter isolates one type of interest for analytical purposes: 'productive interest' which is interest attached to development-innovation projects. While not denying the existence of other types of interests (consumption-related, for instance) he doesn't think they are key for development. Therefore, productive interest is his focus in the book.

> … Obviously they [interest rates] could also exist in the circular flow where there is no development.… But they do not constitute the great social phenomenon that needs explaining. This consists of interest on productive loans.
>
> (1997, Locations 3758–3759)

From the lender perspective, bankers, issuing credit for funding innovation is a risky operation, filled with uncertainty and which requires exercising their 'animal spirits'. Their liquidity decreases and their 'exposure' goes up.[18] For them, interest is a source of income (their earnings), but lending means reducing the bank's liquidity, with the interest rate as the expression of that. Although the discussion is not phrased in Keynes's parlance the meaning is clearly convergent. Schumpeter extends his discussion adding the entrepreneur's perspective. For him, interest constitutes the price of purchasing power, and a tax on future profits. From that angle, Schumpeter concludes that although a means to development, interest (as opposed to credit) is, in fact, a brake on development.

> Interest is not, like profit for example, a direct fruit of development in the sense of a prize for its achievements. It is on the contrary rather a brake on development, a kind of 'tax on entrepreneurial profit'.
>
> (1997, Kindle Locations 4581–4582)

It's worth noticing two points here. First, there is another 'Schumpeterian' structural conflict playing out besides 'old and new'. The one between entrepreneurs and bankers or, more generally, between debtors and creditors.[19] This adds an institutional dimension, a 'sociology of conflict', to the core of the theory of economic development and this reinforces its incompatibility with equilibrium theorising. Second, the observation that interest rates are a brake on development is an important policy statement, and another one which would be explored by Keynes as well.[20] The discussion concludes with a tentative conciliation:

> Certainly, this is not sufficient to condemn it, even if one includes condemnation or approbation of things in the tasks of our science. Against the condemnatory verdict we can assert the importance of the function of this 'ephor of the economic system,' and we may conclude that interest only takes away something from the entrepreneur which would otherwise accrue to him, and not from other classes.
>
> (1997, Locations 4582–4584)

However, when we get to Chapter 6, the theory of economic development becomes a theory of cycles. And of equilibrium as well. Here the foundations turn 'shaky'. Schumpeter struggles with an impossible task: to merge equilibrium and structural change under the same framework: a 'two strokes' cyclical movement: prosperity or boom and depression[21] (Andersen 2009, Chapter 9). That was an odd choice. Understandable from the recognition that there was a respectable tradition of cycle theories by the time Schumpeter was working on the book (from Juglar to the Austrian variety, from Wicksell to Aftalion and Spiethoff; and from Marx to Tugan-Baranovsky), but rather perplexing if we examine *TED*'s seventh chapter, which was not published in English until

2002.[22] The chapter was, however, partially discussed by Shionoya in his seminal 1995 book. There Shionoya reproduces a lengthy quote from Schumpeter that should make us pause.

> It follows from our entire thought that a dynamic equilibrium does not exist.… Development in its ultimate nature *disturbs an existing static equilibrium and does not have a tendency to return to a previous equilibrium.* Development alters the data of a static economy.… *Development and equilibrium are opposite phenomena excluding each other.*
>
> (Schumpeter 1912, 489, quoted by Shionoya 1985, 39, my emphasis)

This is a brilliant statement … that poses a major puzzle. How does one reconcile what is spelled out so clearly in this paragraph with the previous six chapters of the book? Why in a substantial rewriting of the book for the English translation published in 1934 was it not incorporated or even mentioned? Even more sobering, why in *Business Cycles* (1939), which Schumpeter saw as his magnum opus, is equilibrium kept as the starting and central point of his construction at the cost of clarity, coherence and adherence to his own historical narrative, as so many of his heavy-weight reviewers noted?[23]

We will never have definitive answers to those questions, but they belong mostly to intellectual history, and only indirectly to economic theory. Instead of searching in the dark, let me point to three ways where equilibrium acts as a 'spoiler' in Schumpeter's model, adding confusion and incoherence instead of clarity and adherence to actual historical processes.

First, since equilibrium is assumed as the starting point of each cycle, full employment and full capacity utilisation have to be in place. This imposes the surprising result that prosperity is accompanied from its beginning by scarcity of consumer goods and inflation, since entrepreneurs have to deviate productive resources from current uses towards innovations. That scarcity will only be eliminated when a new crop of products reaches the market.

> First, the new entrepreneur's demand for means of production, which is based upon new purchasing power — the well-known "race for means of production" (Lederer) in a period of prosperity — *drives up the prices of these'.…* Secondly, the new products come on the market after a few years or sooner and compete with the old.… This appearance of the new products *causes the fall in prices, which on its part terminates the boom,* may lead to a crisis, must lead to a depression, and starts all the rest.
>
> (1997, Kindle Locations 4983–4998)

Oscar Lange pointed to the paradox of Schumpeter's logic – and model – in his review of *Business Cycles* (1941, 192–193):

> In the pure model [which is the one utilised in *TED*] we encounter only an output cycle and a price cycle. The price cycle follows the usual

pattern. ... but the output cycle follows the opposite of the usual pattern. Total output remains unchanged during prosperity and increases (as result of innovations) during recessions.[24] The output of consumers' goods even decreases during prosperity (because innovations bid away the factors). Thus, we obtain a fall of real income consumed during prosperity and an increase during recession.... A queer picture indeed.

Indeed ... and those logic contortions are, I submit, a direct imposition of having equilibrium as the starting point. Otherwise, neither should prices increase at the bottom of prosperity, only in its 'bubble phase', since the system would be below full employment, nor should total output remain the same − not to mention decreasing output of consumer goods. Idle capacity utilisation would assure that result. In addition, the 'profit cycle' is equally curious. During prosperity, producers of means of production (some at least) accrue a profit, since their resources are bid at higher prices by entrepreneurs. Consumption goods producers also make a windfall due to supply contraction pairing with rising nominal wages. Entrepreneurs themselves don't get anything except debt (they are quasi-Ponzis!). By definition, they are labouring to put together the new combinations and will only become eligible for a windfall *after* the innovations materialise. But then depression starts. So, old business profits during prosperity and innovators during depression. Somehow both group's gains will have to disappear as mandated by equilibrium before another prosperity has chance to unfold. To paraphrase Lange, another 'queer picture'.

Finally, we reach what I think is the core weakness of *TED*: the completely *unnecessary* forcing of equilibrium into the model, its introduction as a *deus ex machina* and − worst − its teleological role, the 'deity' from which all else flows.

> The second reason explains why a new boom does not simply follow on: because the action of the group of entrepreneurs has in the meanwhile altered the data of the system, upset its equilibrium, and thus started an apparently irregular movement in the economic system, which we conceive as a struggle towards a new equilibrium position.
>
> (1997, Kindle Locations 5033–5035)

The boom 'upsets' the systems equilibrium, which has to be restored so that entrepreneurial activity and innovations can resume. Why? What exactly does the expression 'upsets its equilibrium' mean?

> Just as the struggle towards a new equilibrium position, which will embody the innovations and give expression to their effects upon the old firms, is the real meaning of a period of depression as we know it from experience, so it may likewise be shown that this struggle must actually lead to a close approach to an equilibrium position: on the one hand, the

driving impulse of the process of depression cannot theoretically stop until it has done its work, has really brought about the equilibrium position.

(1997, Kindle Locations 5140–5143)

How? What are the *mechanisms* through which the equilibrium position – with zero profits, zero interest rate, no loans, no excess demand in any corner of the system, full employment and no entrepreneurs in action – comes to existence? How long does it last? The reader will not find the answers in the book. Furthermore, how does the banking system – the ephor – survive with no loans and no earnings (zero interest rates)?

> In this sense, therefore, we come to the conclusion that according to our theory there must always be a process of absorption between two booms, ending in a position approaching equilibrium, *the bringing about of which is its function.*
>
> (1997, Kindle Locations 5169–5171, my emphasis)

Paradoxically, despite harshly condemning Marx for his mechanical treatment of capitalism via laws of motion and 'mere mechanics of masses of capital' which 'together with a faulty theoretical technique, accounts for many cases of non-sequitur and for many mistakes' (1942, 32), Schumpeter should be charged along similar lines. *TED*'s Chapter 6 constitutes a case of poor theorising of how equilibrium turns into development and how development softly lands back into equilibrium, along with faulty technique in properly explaining how equilibrium works. These shortcomings account for many mistakes and many cases of non-sequitur.

Nevertheless, the same reasoning Schumpeter used to ultimately praise Marx, after critically scrutinising his theory, should be applied to him:

> The non-sequitur ceases to be a fatal objection if what does not follow from Marx's argument can be made to follow from another one; and even downright mistakes and misinterpretations are often redeemed by the substantial correctness of the general drift of the argument....
>
> (Schumpeter 1942, 32)

I will contend, in the section on '*Capitalism, Socialism and Democracy*: creative destruction as new departure point for economic analysis', that this is precisely what is accomplished through reinterpreting Schumpeter in the light of *CSD*. Once disentangled from equilibrium, all *TED*'s brilliant theoretical innovations stand out and can easily be inserted into the creative-destruction paradigm that emerges in 1942. That conceptual restructuring allows for previous development theorising to achieve coherence. A new departure point for analysing capitalism appears. However, before getting to that discussion, a brief reference to *Business Cycles* is necessary.

Business Cycles: theoretical failure, first-class business history and Minskyan seeds

Schumpeter had great expectations about his 1939 two-volume, 1,050-page book. It was supposed to be his *magnum opus*, his coronation as the best economist in the world (one of his ambitions according to several anecdotal references). From a theoretical standpoint, it was a disaster. As already mentioned, the book was widely reviewed by several top-ranking economists working at the time, a few of which would get Nobel prises later on. Simon Kuznets, Jan Tinbergen, Alvin Hansen, Oscar Lange, Henrik Grossman are worth mentioning but they hardly exhaust the luminaries club. All of them were highly critical of the book, especially its theoretical structure.

The reasons are not difficult to discern. The underlying theory remained wrapped in equilibrium, which per se could be digestible by almost all critics, all – save Grossman – preachers of equilibrium theorising. The problems came from trying, again, to blend equilibrium and evolution without realising this was an impossible task, especially if concerned with Schumpeter's type of evolution: continuous change. '… evolution is a disturbance of existing structures and more like a series of explosions than a gentle, though incessant, transformation' (1939, 1964, Kindle Locations 1644–1645, Kindle Edition).

But *BC* aspired to an even more difficult task: to blend equilibrium with a four-phase cycle[25] and wrap the combo into a three-cycle duration (Kitchin, Juglar and Kondratiev – or four according to Samuelson, see infra). No proper theoretical (causal) links or mechanisms are proposed to articulate and tie together the cycles coherently. They are superimposed on each other. The work proceeds by trying to compress data, statistics and economic history into an equilibrium-cum-multiple-cycles framework in order to explain 'theoretically, statistically and historically' the development of capitalism since the industrial revolution. Not a humble goal.

> Barring very few cases in which difficulties arise, it is possible to count off, historically as well as statistically, six Juglars [eight to ten-year business cycles] to a Kondratieff [50 to 60 years] and three Kitchins [40 months] to a Juglar – not as an average but in every individual case.
>
> (Schumpeter 1939, 169)

Why this was so, Schumpeter, concedes, 'is indeed difficult to see' (ibid., 173). The project failed. In a 1998 lecture to the Federal Reserve Bank of Boston, Paul Samuelson – Schumpeter's most famous student – and the pope of the highly influential 'neoclassical synthesis' – pictured the book asperously:

> My Harvard teacher Joseph Schumpeter's 1939 two-volume treatise is almost a parody of eclecticism: It described short cycles under the Kitchin-Crum terminology; then the good old business cycle of allegedly eight to ten years' periodicity was labeled Juglar cycles; and of course,

there were also the long waves of Kondratieff and the Sunday newspaper supplements. But that was not the whole of it. In between Juglars and Kondratieff's came Kuznets's intermediate cycles in construction and immigration, with an alleged approximate periodicity of 18 to 20 years. The tortured epicycles of pre-Copernicus Ptolemaic astronomy had nothing on Schumpeter.

(Samuelson 1998, 1)

Oscar Lange, although in a more amicable way was equally sceptical:

> Professor Schumpeter's three cycle scheme is open to serious criticisms largely on empirical grounds … the Kitchin cycle is based on meager evidence. The empirical material on which it has been observed refers almost exclusively to the monetary sector of the economy.… The kondratiefs are much better established empirically.… But there is serious doubt whether the kondratiefs can be properly called cycles.
>
> (Lange 1941, 192)

Simon Kuznets' review was particularly mortifying. It extends to 14 pages and shows no mercy in pointing out a host of problems and incoherencies. After providing a succinct but well composed briefing of the book, the author starts to raise questions:

> … further reflection and even partial scrutiny of the evidence presented in the two volumes raise a host of crucial questions and disturbing doubts.
>
> (Kuznets 1940, 262)

Discussing the unidimensional causal mechanism for the three cycles, Kuznets objects:

> Discontinuity of opportunity can be assumed only in reference to the most momentous innovations such as steam power, electricity etc., i.e. innovations that bear upon the Kondratieff cycles. We can hardly expect significant fluctuations in the stock of innovation opportunities of the type that are associated with the Juglar or the Kitchin type.
>
> (Kuznets 1940, 264)

Proceeding to the assemblage of data and theory, he throws another grenade:

> The difficulties encountered in the matter of inflection points and the paucity of formal statistical analysis in the treatise lead to a doubt weather Professor Schumpeter's concept of equilibrium and the four-phase model of business cycles are such to permit of application to statistical analysis.
>
> (Kuznets 1940, 265)

In respect to the existence of Kondratiev cycles (causality, duration, recurrence, proper measurement) Kuznets adds:

> the questions raised bears most upon the establishment of the Kondratief cycles.... Nor has a satisfactory theory been advanced as to why these 50 year swings should recur: the explanation tends to emphasise external factors (inventions, wars, etc.) without demonstrating their cyclical character in their tendency to recur as result of an underlying mechanism.
>
> (Kuznets 1940, 267)

The final blow is overwhelming:

> The critical evaluation above of what appears to be important elements in Professor Schumpeter's conclusions viewed as a systematic and tested exposition of business cycles yields disturbingly destructive results. The association between the distribution of entrepreneurial ability and the cyclical character of economic activity needs further proof. The theoretical model of the four-phase cycle about equilibrium level does not yield a serviceable statistical approach. The three-cycle schema and the rather rigid relationship claimed to have been established among the three of cycles cannot be considered, on the basis of the evidence submitted, even tolerably valid.; nor could such validity be established without a serviceable statistical procedure. The core of the difficulty seems to lie in the failure to forge the necessary links between the primary factors and concepts (entrepreneur, innovation, equilibrium, etc.) and the observable cyclical fluctuations in economic activity.
>
> (Kuznets 1940, 270)[26]

What peace still holds after this *blitzkrieg*? Not much apparently. Much later, Rosenberg and Frischtak (1984), Chris Freeman (1982) and others would return to those criticisms, but none with the verve and analytical deepness of Kuznets. Given that, one could quip that Keynes' General Theory's publication in 1936 was more a blessing than a curse since it avoided more attention being given to the repercussions of Schumpeter's treatise.

The bottom-line conclusion here is that the book was, *as a whole*, a major theoretical failure. It did not elevate Schumpeter's status as a theorist among his peers. Nevertheless, it achieved two important results that would survive its bad reputation as a work of economic theory. Those results were harvested mostly by business and technology historians. Thomas Mac Craw, the late 'vice-doyen' (after Alfred Chandler Jr) of business history studies at Harvard Business School raised them in a concise way:

> *Business Cycles* was Joseph Schumpeter's least successful book, measured by its professed aims and several other yardsticks. Yet the book has two vital aspects that have largely been over-looked. First, the prodigious

research that went into its writing caused a significant change in Schumpeter's thinking about capitalism. It moved him to a more historical and empirical approach that shaped nearly all his subsequent work. And second, much of the book constitutes a preview of modern, rigorous business history ... *Business Cycles* is a noble failure that paid unexpected dividends both to the author and to scholarship.

(McCraw 2006, 231)

McCraw had a point here. Indeed, *Business Cycles*' 'historical chapters' constitute its best feature. Well-written, although long, they are a gold-mine for economic, business and technology historians. Packed with detailed accounts of companies' histories and technologies' development in tandem with the economic-industrial histories of the United States, England and Germany, those chapters are still an invaluable source of *histoire raisonée*, as Schumpeter wanted them to be.

The work of Chandler, McCraw, Amatori, Hikino, Lazonick and their collaborators are the direct heirs of Schumpeter's detailed incursions into the evolution of business and technology since the industrial revolution. And this was an important dimension of *Business Cycles* (Chandler 1977; Lazonick 1993; Landes 1969; Mokyr 1990). Furthermore, the widespread rejection of the Kondratiev cycle didn't prevent the spreading of 'technological revolutions'', 'waves' or 'paradigms' as key elements in subsequent neo-Schumpeterian investigations and in classics of technological history such as Freeman and Louçã (2001) and Perez (2002).

Last but not least, and very importantly on the theoretical front, *BC* included a hidden gem, a sophisticated extension of *TED* that provides a brilliant explanation of how the credit creation–innovation nexus leads to a much bigger outcome: the secondary wave. Not discussed in *TED*, the secondary wave is a macro-financial outcome that contains the most detailed analysis by Schumpeter of *how* the initial cluster of localised entrepreneurial activity and credit creation spreads through the system via an interaction of multiplier effects, monetary expansion and non-innovation-related credit creation leading to increasingly reckless business and banking practices. Prosperity once analysed as a macro-financial process turns ultimately destabilising. It ends in over-indebtedness coupled with deteriorating expectations and shrinking profits and cash-flows, which ultimately reverses expansion, dragging the system into a recession and a period of 'abnormal liquidation', which, most likely, will force the system into a depression (Schumpeter 1939, Chapter 4, Section C). Yes, that's Minskyian theorising before Minsky:

If innovations are being embodied in new plant and equipment, *additional consumers' spending will result practically as quickly as additional producers' spending*. Both together will spread from the points in the system on which they first impinge, and create that complexion of business situations which we call prosperity. Two things are then practically sure to happen. First, old firms will react to this situation and, second, *many of them will 'speculate' on this situation.*

(Schumpeter 1939, 1964, Kindle Locations 2483–2486, my emphasis)

The resulting situation is perfectly described by Keynes's multiplier paired with additional credit creation and casino-type financial speculation. The expansion triggered by entrepreneurial activity and credit creation takes off, evolves via cumulative causation mechanisms and positive-feedback loops and exhibits distinctive traces of Minskyan financial fragilisation:

> But in doing this many people will act on the assumption that the rates of change they observe will continue indefinitely, and enter into trans-actions which will result in losses as soon as facts fail to verify that assumption. New borrowing will then no longer be confined to entre-preneurs, and 'deposits' will be created to finance general expansion, each loan tending to induce another loan, each rise in prices another rise.
>
> (Kindle Locations 2491–2492)

Dialoguing with Fischer, Schumpeter goes further in specifying the sources and processes of over-indebtedness and financial fragilisation:

> Once a prosperity has got under sail, households will borrow for pur-poses of consumption, *in the expectation that actual incomes will permanently be what they are or that they will still increase; business will borrow merely to expand on old lines, on the expectation that this demand will persist or still increase; farms will be bought at prices at which they could pay only if the prices of agricultural products kept their level or increased.*
>
> (Kindle Locations 2523–2526, my emphasis)

In those passages we can see, very clearly, the roots of Minsky's financial fra-gility hypothesis: over-indebtedness resulting from validation of over-optimistic expectations and riskier – or reckless – business and banking practices along with shrinking cash-flows and collapsing collateral values. Schumpeter's 'macro-finance' is on solid ground here, and offers a sneak preview of how hedged agents become speculative and then Ponzis:

> The speculative position is likely to contain many untenable elements which the slightest impairment of the values of collateral will bring down. Part of the debt structure will crumble. Freezing of credits, shrink-age of deposits, and all the rest follow in due course.
>
> (Kindle Location 2558)

What we have here is nothing less than a financial theory of innovation-led investment coupled with a 'destabilising stability' approach to credit cre-ation and expansion. A financial theory of creative destruction, in short.[27]

At that point, one wonders why Minsky never cited these passages as part of his sources of inspiration, always referring to Keynes and Simons instead. This silence only started to change in 1986, as we'll see shortly. Yet even then, Minsky's take on Schumpeter, although sharp, is not free from ambiguities.

Summing up, in *BC*'s 'second approximation', the macro-financial four-phase cycle includes prosperity, recession, depression and recovery. There is a wealth of analysis of the financial dimension encompassing and interacting with the innovation-led 'wave'. This is the closest Schumpeter gets to a 'financial theory of creative destruction', something that would be lost in *CSD* and totally eradicated in the neo-Schumpeterian paradigm that emerged in the eighties and nineties.

In a book celebrating a Marx-Schumpeter-Keynes centennial, Minsky contributed with an essay filled with penetrating – but very critical – thoughts about Schumpeter's legacy and its relationship with Keynes'. In a chapter titled 'Money and crisis in Schumpeter and Keynes', he writes:

> The crisis of capitalism evoked a magnificent theoretical performance from Keynes; Schumpeter's response was banal.
>
> (1986b, 112)

To which he adds:

> Schumpeter's 1939 Business Cycles is a retrogression from his 1911 Theory of Economic Development. The three cycles – Kitchin Juglar and Kondratieff – of Schumpeter's business-cycle theory is mechanical and the vast presentation of data is numbing rather than enlightening.
>
> (1986b, 114)

In comparing the two authors' rival assessments of the Great Depression, Minsky praises Keynes and sharply criticises Schumpeter:

> The difference in the import of Keynes and Schumpeter over 50 years since the culmination of the crisis in the collapse of 1933 is that Keynes interpreted 1933 as a source for repudiating prior theories whereas Schumpeter interpreted the events as reinforcing the basic validity of his earlier views.
>
> (1986b, 114)

Surprisingly though, Minsky ends his essay on a rather positive note towards Schumpeter, and the need to bridge his vision and insights with Keynes':

> The task confronting economics today may be characterised as a need to integrate Schumpeter's vision of a resilient intertemporal capitalist process with Keynes' hard insights into the fragility introduced into the capitalist

accumulation process by some inescapable properties of capitalist financial structures.

(1986b, 121)

This is a statement I fully subscribe to.[28] Unfortunately, not much progress has been made in that direction so far. In addition, I submit that Minsky's 'task' can only be accomplished if we understand (a) the depth of the rupture between Schumpeter pre-*CSD* equilibrium-dependent analysis and his core propositions submitted in that book; (b) how *TED*'s theoretical innovations and *BC*'s macro-financial approach to economic fluctuations ought to be, once severed from equilibrium and the three-cycle framework, fully incorporated into this creative-destruction paradigm, since they all fall into place there; and (c) why *CSD*'s analytical framework, once rekindled, provides the scaffolding of a new paradigm for analysing capitalism, one that takes the institutional dimension seriously and is not at odds with empirical reality.

Furthermore, the resulting synthesis delivers a much more coherent alternative to Schumpeter's previous models of multiple cycles-cum-equilibrium-cum-evolution, and opens the space for a full integration with Keynes' and Minsky's theorising about short- and long-term expectations, asset pricing under uncertainty, financial innovation and its impact on liquidity, leverage and financial fragility; and, last but not least, explains the advantages of a substantial degree of socialisation of investment in order to pair rapid economic transformation with financial stability.[29]

Capitalism, Socialism and Democracy: creative destruction as new departure point for economic analysis

The book starts with a thorough analysis of Marx's work. The review is carefully done. It contains serious objections but also big praise. The reason why Schumpeter opens *CSD* with this lengthy discussion of Marx's legacy is not difficult to figure out. Marx always exercised a deep influence on him, and the whole book is written as a dialogue-reaction with-to Marx (and Marxism). And this matters to my thesis – the radical departure – because in the course of his evaluation of Marx, Schumpeter already introduces several hints of his departure from the previous 'skin', the equilibrium-cum-evolution attempted synthesis.

While discussing Marx's theory of 'compulsive accumulation' by capitalists, he basically praises it and introduces the key role of competition as the engine of change:

As a matter of fact, capitalist economy is not and cannot be stationary. Nor is it merely expanding in a steady manner. It is incessantly being revolutionized from within by new enterprise, i.e., by the intrusion of new commodities or new methods of production or new commercial opportunities into the industrial structure as it exists at any moment ... Economic progress, in capitalist society, means turmoil.

To which he adds:

> And, as we shall see in the next part, in this turmoil competition works in a manner completely different from the way it would work in a stationary process, however perfectly competitive. Possibilities of gains to be reaped by producing new things or by producing old things more cheaply are constantly materializing and calling for new investments ... In order to escape being undersold, every firm is in the end compelled to follow suit, to invest in its turn and, in order to be able to do so, to plow back part of its profits, i.e., to accumulate. Thus, everyone else accumulates.
>
> (Schumpeter 1942, 31–32)

In the opening chapter of the books' second part, where the theoretical rupture is performed, before introducing the concept of 'creative destruction' Schumpeter makes two points whose *evolutionary* implications are worth recalling: first, that 'the capitalist engine is first and last an engine of mass production' where the 'masses' were the biggest beneficiaries of structural transformation. The pertinent quote has become a classic:

> Queen Elizabeth owned silk stockings. The capitalist achievement does not typically consist in providing more silk stockings for queens but in bringing them within the reach of factory girls in return for steadily decreasing amounts of effort.
>
> (Schumpeter 1942, 67)

Second, that due to the proliferation of new products and services, along with quality improvements of existing ones, the overall benefits of progress, as well as the extent of the fall of real prices over time, are highly underestimated by indexes and largely ignored by existing theory:

> There is no doubt some things available to the modern workman that Louis XIV himself would have been delighted to have yet was unable to have—modern dentistry for instance.
>
> (Schumpeter 1942, 67)

> New commodities escape or are inadequately represented by an index which must rest largely on basic commodities and intermediate products. For the same reason improvements in quality almost completely fail to assert themselves although they constitute, in many lines, the core of the progress achieved – there is no way of expressing adequately the difference between a motorcar of 1940 and a motorcar of 1900 or the extent to which the price of motorcars per unit of utility has fallen.
>
> (Schumpeter 1942, 66)

Next to go down in the theoretical metamorphosis is the three-cycle frame-work. Wave is the new concept. No more well-behaved regular cyclical movements poorly linked to each other, but successive technological revolutions:

> The same fact stands out still better if we glance at those long waves in economic activity, analysis of which reveals the nature and mechanism of the capitalist process better than anything else. Each of them consists of an 'industrial revolution' and the absorption of its effects. These revolutions periodically reshape the existing structure of industry by introducing new methods of production ... [in a] process of recurrent rejuvenation of the productive apparatus [that] spell disturbance, losses and unemployment.
>
> (Schumpeter 1942, 68)

By now, Schumpeter is already in full 'evolutionary mode'. No references to equilibrium or perfect competition. Or, more precisely, a big blow to the latter, along with a truly original reconceptualisation of competition dynamics seen as a recurrent attempt to establish and exploit market niches through differentiation strategies or 'de-commodification':

> Neither Marshall and Wicksell nor the classics saw that perfect competition is the exception and that even if it were the rule there would be much less reason for congratulation than one might think.[30] ... And as regards practically all the finished products and services of industry and trade, it is clear that every grocer, every filling station, every manufacturer of gloves or shaving cream or handsaws has a small and precarious market of his own which he tries – must try – to build up and to keep by price strategy, quality strategy – "product differentiation" – and advertising.
>
> (Schumpeter 1942, 78–79)

A prelude to creative-destruction-based competition, which would be recognised later as 'Schumpeterian competition', this prior concept of 'competition by means of product differentiation'[31] merits a brief comment. Along with 'creative destruction' it provides the basis for a general theory of competition – not only 'technological revolutions' produced by the diffusion of general-purpose technologies, but business as usual competition – in which the key goal is the temporary monopolisation of market opportunities regardless of size or market-share. Once this is attained *every* business has the potential to become a temporary price- or cost-maker and consequently a windfall-collector or rent-collector.[32] – collector. Perhaps we should conceive it as monopolistic competition without homogeneous cost curves and with no convergence towards equilibrium. This is a remarkably accurate conception of how competition *really* works, which escapes the drawbacks of both perfect competition and the static oligopoly models of Cournot, Bertrand and contemporary textbooks. Schumpeter is straightforward:

> As soon as the prevalence of monopolistic competition or of oligopoly or of combinations of the two is recognized, many of the propositions which the Marshall–Wicksell generation of economists used to teach with the utmost confidence become either inapplicable or much more difficult to prove. This holds true, in the first place, of the propositions turning on the fundamental concept of equilibrium i.e., a determinate state of the economic organism, toward which any given state of it is always gravitating and which displays certain simple properties.
>
> (Schumpeter 1942, 79)

The old 'skin' is gone. A new Schumpeter emerges: capitalism equals *change* which equals *turmoil* which collides with *equilibrium* and whose main agents are corporations (either big or small) who survive and prosper, competing, relentlessly, through innovations, differentiation strategies and market-niche creation. Debunking the economic profession as a whole (himself included), Schumpeter argues:

> If *we* economists *were given less to wishful thinking and more to the observation of facts*, doubts would immediately arise as to the realistic virtues of a theory that would have led us to expect a very different result.
>
> (Schumpeter 1942, 81–82, my emphasis)

From that new approach, traditional theorising is turned upside-down: bigness is efficient *because* competition is fierce and threatening.

> As soon as we go into details and inquire into the individual items in which progress was most conspicuous, the trail leads not to the doors of those firms that work under conditions of comparatively free competition but precisely to the doors of the large concern ... – and a shocking suspicion dawns upon us that big business may have had more to do with creating that standard of life than with keeping it down.
>
> (Schumpeter 1942, 82)

This provides the opening for the full blown 'creative-destruction' approach to economic analysis:

> The essential point to grasp is that in dealing with capitalism we are dealing with an evolutionary process.... Capitalism, then, is by nature a form or method of economic change and not only never is but never can be stationary.... The fundamental impulse that sets and keeps the capitalist engine in motion comes from the new consumers' goods, the new methods of production or transportation, the new markets, the new

forms of industrial organization that capitalist enterprise creates.... Similarly, the history of the productive apparatus is a history of revolutions.

(Schumpeter 1942, 83)

This is an approach whose crowning statement, so often quoted, was never exploited to its full potential:

This process of Creative Destruction is the essential fact about capitalism. It is what capitalism consists in and what every capitalist concern has got to live in.

(Schumpeter 1942, 83)

In scarcely seven pages, where very paragraph exudes brilliance, a new paradigm for economic and social analysis is born. In his own words: first, since we are dealing with a process whose every element takes considerable time … we must judge its performance over time (83). Second, since we are dealing with an organic process … every piece of business strategy acquires its true significance only against the background of that process and within the situation created by it. It must be seen in its role in the perennial gale of creative destruction (84). Third, from that perspective, business strategies and decisions have to be understood as an attempt to deal with a situation that is sure to change presently – as an attempt by those firms to keep on their feet, on ground that is slipping away from under them (84).

Once these propositions are accepted, a new modus operandi unwraps. The central element to retire is the prevailing conception of competition.

As soon as quality competition and sales effort are admitted into the sacred precincts of theory, the price variable is ousted from its dominant position … *in capitalist reality as distinguished from its textbook picture*, it is not that kind of competition which counts but the competition from the new commodity, the new technology, the new source of supply, the new type of organization (the largest-scale unit of control for instance) – competition which commands a decisive cost or quality advantage and which strikes not at the margins of the profits and the outputs of the existing firms but at their foundations and their very lives. *This kind of competition is as much more effective than the other as a bombardment is in comparison with forcing a door.*

(Schumpeter 1942, 84–85, my emphasis)

Furthermore, competition by means of innovation spreads not only from existing competitors, but from potential ones as well. Potential competition is, paraphrasing Rumsfeld, a 'known unknown': it is hardly necessary to point out that competition of the kind we now have in mind acts not only when in being but also when it is merely an ever-present threat. It disciplines before it attacks. The businessman feels himself to be in a competitive situation even if he is alone in his field (85).[33]

The chapter closes with well-known, and deserved, grandeur:

> Now a theoretical construction which neglects this essential element of the case neglects all that is most typically capitalist about it; even if correct in logic as well as in fact, it is like Hamlet without the Danish prince.
>
> (Schumpeter 1942, 86)

Per contra, a theoretical construction where creative destruction is front and centre allows for all the innovations advanced by Schumpeter in *TED*, but which did not find an appropriate fit there. First, development *is* structural transformation. Its main features are irreversibility, uncertainties, industry shake-ups, social turmoil, big fortunes made and lost, regional dislocations, bankruptcies, winners and losers. There is no place for equilibrium – or equilibrium theorising in conceptualising it.

Second, development unfolds in *waves*, cumulative industrial revolutions that rejuvenate the economic landscape, which implies fluctuations in economic activity but not regular, recurring, or multiple, cycles.

Third, competition is its engine and innovations its fuel. All types of innovations play a part: products, processes, financial, organisational, legal, political, institutional, radical, incremental, productive and destructive. As such, any type of regularity is out of the picture and competition is anything but perfect: rivalries, conflicts, resistances, entry and exit barriers, sunk costs, price fixing, planned idle capacity and all sorts of 'monopolistic practices' are among its nuts and bolts. They are business strategies carved to deal with 'known unknowns' and 'unknown unknowns'.[34]

Fourth, in that environment there is no theoretical reason for profit rates to ever equalise. In the case of old business, not yet disrupted by new ones, what happens is progressive commodification, which leads to compressed margins, but not even then should profits equalise: as Edith Penrose so brilliantly showed, inputs are homogenous but resources tend to be unique to firms (1959, Chapters 2 and 3). One main implication of that approach is that even commodities with identical international price will not necessarily have the same cost structures. Therefore, variations in margins and rates of return will be the norm.

Fifth, by the same token, 'uncertainties', bankruptcies and 'winners and losers' preclude any rule tying amounts invested to returns. The WhatsApp case was referred to, and business reports and newspapers are filled with other examples. Conversely, look at the airline or restaurant business: for the vast majority of firms, the hardest goal to achieve is to turn a consistent profit on a regular basis, despite huge investments.[35]

Sixth, returns do turn up permanently. Either as 'Schumpeterian', innovation-based profits or as 'Ricardian rents', sprung from incomplete diffusion, differentiation strategies, or 'fences on imitation' (trade secrets, location, branding, reputation and intellectual property rules and regulations in general).[36] What logical reasoning and empirical observation shows is that only the 'iron cage' of perfectly competitive equilibrium prevented their recognition as outcomes of successful strategising under fierce competition.[37] As for their origin or source, a forgotten – and never-resolved debate in political economy – Schumpeter doesn't settle the question, but his remark that Schumpeterian entrepreneurs, collectively, 'largely create what they exploit' deserves further inquiry (Schumpeter 1942, 101). As Barak Obama remarked, 'they didn't build it alone', and there are cases of pure exploitation,[38] or rent-keeping.[39] However, from an evolutionary perspective, the links between technological creativity, innovation and surplus seem solid (Landes 1969; Chandler 1977; Mokyr 1990). They should be further scrutinised. Notwithstanding, permanent profits exist 'collectively', as surplus, and are appropriated via different mechanisms,[40] but at the firm level they don't. The rise and fall of business dynasties is one of the main traces of capitalism's evolution (Schumpeter 1942, 18).

Seventh, the creative-destruction approach allows for win–win situations in surplus distribution: if the 'Schumpeterian development package' succeeds, everybody improves: profits, real-wages, productivity, variety, quality, dividends, consumption and fiscal revenue all rise, while prices and effort spent to produce and deliver the goods fall. In that framework, big profits are often the seeds of big investments, job creation and robust growth. On the other hand, unemployment becomes a 'normal' feature of the system, and not one Schumpeter applauded, which points to another convergence with Keynes. In that realm, Schumpeter's version of 'the economic possibilities of our Grandchildren' (1942: Chapter 5) largely mimics Keynes' 1930 essay, and anticipates current debates about 'basic income'. Discussing the implications of both cyclical downturns and technological progress for unemployment, Schumpeter affirms: 'whether lasting or temporary, getting worse or not, unemployment undoubtedly is and always has been a scourge' (1942, 70).

And adds:

> … for obviously the suffering and degradation – the destruction of human values – which we associate with unemployment, though not the waste of productive resources, would be largely eliminated and unemployment would lose practically all its terror *if the private life of the unemployed were not seriously affected by their unemployment.*

> (Ibid., my emphasis)

Eighth, while entrepreneurs still play a key role in carrying out innovations and, therefore, in forging progress, there is an important change of emphasis in *CSD*. In the age of big concerns and 'bureaucratisation of innovation', it's not so much entrepreneurs presented as 'new men', but the 'entrepreneurial function' that matters. Taking on board Weber's analysis of rationalisation as a major feature of modern capitalism (Beetham 1985; Collins 1986), Schumpeter sees the routinisation of innovation as a key transformation in capitalism's economic structure, and a linchpin of his thesis of socialism coming as a result of capitalist success (1942, Chapter 12). However, in opposition to many interpretations of his prognosis, what he envisaged was innovation speeding up, not slowing down.[41] That metamorphosis was strengthening, not weakening, the system although eroding the *order*. It was his ticket to the well-known diatribe on the true pacemakers of socialism. It was '… not the intellectuals or agitators who preached it but the Vanderbilts, Carnegies and Rockefellers' (Schumpeter 1942, 134).

Diatribes apart, the importance of the entrepreneurial function for my argument is that it frees Schumpeter's approach from romanticising entrepreneurship, and lends the concept a more solid basis. In fact, Schumpeter never developed a theory of the firm, but Penrose's resource-based theory and the dynamic-capabilities approach to innovation and strategy pioneered by Winter, Teece, Pisano and others filled that gap (Penrose 1959; Levin *et al.* 1987; Teece and Pisano 1994; Teece 1998; Winter 2003; Lazonick and Teece 2012). They provided a genuine Schumpeterian theory of the firm that flourished in business strategy departments, but never made it to economics. Too bad for economics.

Furthermore, the entrepreneurial function may be performed by individuals, corporate teams – big or small – or cooperatives. As McCraw aptly put it: 'Entrepreneurs whether they operate in big firms or small ones, old companies or start-ups-are the agents of innovation and creative destruction' (2006, 7). More importantly, but never conceptualised by Schumpeter, or his followers, it can also be carried out by the state.[42] Schumpeter recognises that, but makes just brief mentions to it in his works, with no proper links to his theory. (See Burlamaqui 2000 for a first attempt to explore that subject and Chapter 10 in this volume for an extended discussion).

As was argued above, the absence of the state in his theorising about structural change is a theoretical flaw in his work, although less so in terms of historical analysis. Yet, Schumpeter was aware of both the importance of state action for assisting capitalist rationalisation[43] or forging industrial policies, as well as the limitations of his model in producing stability or full employment spontaneously out of depressions, as I showed in point seven, above. This is made even more clear is his deference of state action and 'Keynesian' measures to rescue a depressed economy sunk in liquidity preference and bankruptcies[44]:

> … it has been repeatedly emphasized that depression, unlike recession, is a pathological process to which no organic functions can be attributed. *The case for government action in depression remains, independently of humanitarian considerations, incomparably stronger than it is in recession.*
>
> (1964, Ch. 3, Kindle Locations 2692–2693, my emphasis)

Scrutinising his thinking on that subject is certainly not an easy task. Notwithstanding, there is no structural impediment to remedying these shortcomings on how the state can be incorporated in his analytical framework.

On the contrary, for a twenty-first-century updated agenda it's a require-ment. As just mentioned, I will try to follow that path, ahead in the book.

Ninth, with equilibrium out, *stability* comes in to replace it. However, stability[45] is an institutional construct, not a 'natural feature' of the economic structure. Stability is achieved through institutional coherence and resilience; it is an outcome of structural transformation, agreed conventions, rules and regula-tions, which means that is very difficult to discuss it without introducing state action, public policy and public (and international) organisations. Economic stability is, therefore, a subject that cannot be confined to economic theory, moreover it's an evolving process as well. In fact, one of *CSD*'s greatest achieve-ments is its blending of economic theory and economic sociology. In Schum-peter's analysis, institutional stability contexts usually become unstable over time. In this he clearly precedes Minsky's 'destabilising stability' catch phrase.[46] The whole discussion about the 'civilisation of capitalism' and its erosion is a master-class in institutional analysis, regardless of the accuracy of its forecasts.[47]

The core of his message is that institutions are the main buffers of instab-ility as well as the tools for building stability in a creative-destruction environ-ment. Economic stability depends on organisational coherence and institutional robustness, which are not subject to abstract theorising or model-ling. Furthermore, stability is not an assured feature of the system, but rather the result of a complex set of legal and organisational arrangements. However, the argument deepens in complexity; these institutional constellations often tend to become outdated and dysfunctional: destabilising, rather than stabilis-ing features. In one sentence: institutions are the anchors of stability through the creation of regularities, and institutional change is an essential part of structural transformation, yet it is also a disruptive force, which tends to turn those regularities into destabilising forces in an evolutionary environment.

Finally, there is an, apparently, enigmatic absence in the 'creative-destruction paradigm': finance. As we have seen, in both *TED* and *BC*, banking and credit creation are key, defining, features of capitalism. In both works Schumpeter defines capitalism by the finance–innovation nexus. 'Capitalism is that form of private property economy in which innovations are carried out by means of borrowed money which in general though not by logical necessity implies credit creation' (Schumpeter 1939, 216). As discussed above, credit is not only the lever of innovations but a social relation of pro-duction: capital. Bankers are defined as 'ephors' of the system and 'reckless banking' flagged as a major source of turning recessions into depressions in Schumpeter's four-phase cycle (1939, 264). Entrepreneurs are 'debtors' and finance percolates through both books. In contradistinction, none of those are contemplated in *CSD*. There are scarce mentions of credit and banking, and they are located either in the book's first part, devoted to Marx, or in the third, in which the subject is socialism, not capitalism. This is a puzzle, and one that as far as I'm aware, was never properly discussed or clarified by com-mentators, critics or reviewers (yet see O'Sullivan 2005 for insightful incur-sions on this subject).

One way to make sense of that puzzle is to suggest Schumpeter's 'radical departure' didn't include his take on finance and its role in development and structural transformation. We know he struggled strenuously and was not satisfied with his own 'Treatise on money' which was never finished, but on the relationship between finance, innovations and development, Schumpeter seemed to be at peace with what he had previously written. In particular, *BC*'s penetrating 'macro-financial' analysis of the secondary wave provides a clear anticipation of Minsky's financial fragility hypothesis.

Another way to interpret it is by returning to Schumpeter's 1928 'economic stabilisation thesis', where he argues for a diminished role for credit creation and bank-based finance in explaining big corporations' expansion: 'Although credit creation still plays a role, both the power to accumulate reserves and the direct access to the money market tend to reduce the importance of this element in the life of a trust' (Schumpeter 1928, 70–71). This leads directly to the suggestion that banks became less important in financing creative destruction. This interpretation suggests finance wasn't really missing from *CSD*. It was still there, but had changed its relevance in the period of 'trustified capitalism'.

That appears to be Minsky's interpretation as well. In a 1992 paper titled 'Schumpeter and finance', he writes:

> The role of bankers as the *ephors* of the decentralized market economy was reduced when government took over the responsibility for the adequacy of profits to aggregate demand. The flow of profits that followed from the deficits of government and from debt-financed housing construction meant that the internal cash flows of firms could finance their investments. Managements of established firms which had some market power that protected them from competition could be independent of their investment bankers.
>
> (1992, 110)

Minsky's statement reveals a remarkable convergence, in conclusions, regarding the stabilisation of what he termed 'managerial' and Schumpeter's 1928 analysis of 'trustified' capitalism.[48] However, consistent with both authors' perception of capitalism as an evolving institutional structure (Minsky 1992, 113), it was not likely that this structure would last forever. For Schumpeter, economic and institutional evolution – bureaucratisation and rationalisation on all fronts, endogenisation of the innovative process plus cultural changes – would bring about a major economic and institutional transformation he suggested could be labelled 'socialism'. His *BC*'s 'historical outlines' chapters and *CSD*'s discussion of 'socialism' provide us with a useful framework for interpreting the Asian developmental states, and especially China, as I will show in this volume's closing chapter. For Minsky, 'managerial capitalism' would be transformed into 'money manager' capitalism, which would bring the ephor back in, but a very different kind of ephor: Keynes's financial casino manager instead of Schumpeter's investment banker.

In another Schumpeter-related paper, titled 'Schumpeter: finance and evolution' (1990), Minsky completely reverses his previous scepticism and pays generous tribute to his former professor:

> Schumpeter and Keynes are compatible for they both defined the problem of economics as the analysis of a monetary production economy. Financial entrepreneurship and therefore financial evolution are central to Schumpeter's vision of the process of economic development. Innovations in financial relations since World War II validates this interpretation of Schumpeter's vision.
>
> (1990, 51)

To which he adds, a few pages on[49]:

> Schumpeter's banker financed the creative part of creative destruction ... the Schumpeterian [banker] is *not* our own day's master of the corporate raid and the leveraged buyout.
>
> (1990, 11)

However, Minsky's own analysis on the 'return of finance' is made clear in the 'Schumpeter and finance' paper just referred to:

> The emergence of return and capital-gains-oriented blocks of managed money *resulted in financial markets once again being a major influence in determining the performance of the economy*. However, unlike the earlier epoch of finance capitalism, the emphasis was not upon the capital development of the economy but rather upon the quick turn of the speculator, upon trading profits.
>
> (1992, 111–112, my emphasis)

These are sharp observations, and, from my discussion of Schumpeter's theoretical structure, they hit a nerve. In Schumpeter's theory of development, what is central is not really 'finance' understood as the financial system as a whole, but mostly credit, and credit that serves a specific purpose: development. Banks are analysed, fundamentally, as the providers of credit, understood as the vehicle for innovations. That means they are proxies for development banks, and Schumpeter's bankers are, in fact, venture capitalists. Their 'function' is, indeed, to finance the 'creative part of creative destruction'. There is little discussion of the financial system's other features, characteristics or flaws.

Apart from *BC*'s fine discussion of their role in magnifying prosperity and, simultaneously, producing the roots of depression through financial fragilisation, Schumpeter doesn't really get 'inside' the financial structure nor, especially, how it evolves and innovates. Neither financial innovation nor the liabilities side of the banks' balance sheets are incorporated in the analysis. In contrast to Minsky (and Keynes) debt is not a structural problem in his cycle except for turning otherwise 'therapeutic' recessions into 'pathological' depressions or 'abnormal liquidation periods' that will ultimately – mysteriously, one could add – find their way back to equilibrium. Entrepreneurs are the 'typical debtors' in the system, but they seem to end up always paying their debts. Those who fail file for bankruptcy, but the banking system apparently does not face any serious liquidity or solvency problems.[50]

This is clearly another place where the 'creative-destruction paradigm' needs amendments,[51] and where Keynes' and Minsky's theorisings prove superior and are needed. Keynes' financial theory of asset pricing along with his investment theory of business fluctuations, once incorporated, could generalise Schumpeter's innovation-led investment approach, turning it into a finance-based theory of strategic asset creation and liabilities management. Minsky devised the need for that bridge long ago:

> Keynesian theory, centering around the pricing of assets, capital and financial, in an economy where profits exist because development is the normal state, offers just the analytical framework in which the power of Schumpeter's vision becomes evident.
>
> (1990, 67)

Such a theory would enable the full incorporation of leverage, liquidity preference, and solvency constraints into Schumpeterian competition, and deliver a more sophisticated, and empirically grounded, financial dynamics to a Schumpeter-based, and Keynes-Minsky rekindled analysis (along the lines suggested by Keynes 1936, Chapter 17; Minsky 1975, Chapters 4–5, 1986a; Kregel 1997).

Minsky's financial fragility hypothesis coupled with his 'Wall Street paradigm' would also be of service. Their fitness would consist in incorporating financial innovation, debt and the liabilities side of both bankers and entrepreneurs balance sheets into the theory's core. This, in turn, would allow for coupling Schumpeterian development with the *permanent* build-up of financially fragile positions that could impede the adoption of otherwise perfectly sound innovation strategies. Additionally, Minsky's financial analysis would provide an explanation for a type of banking dynamics where financial innovation can become quite destructive and end up financing, most likely through securitisation, the destructive side of creative destruction; and for a type of financial system that fosters *destructive creation* instead of creative destruction, as the 2007 global financial crisis so vividly showed. The outcome will certainly reshape, update and improve the robustness of this new paradigm (cf. Minsky 1986a, 1986b, 1990, 1992; Burlamaqui and Kregel 2005; Kregel 2014, Part III). Both Lazonick and Mazzucato and Wray provide useful inroads in this matter in their contributions to this volume.

This was already clearly perceived by Minsky in his 1990 paper:

> The economic theory that integrates Schumpeter and Keynes, which unifies what is usually called the real and the financial, improves our understanding of capitalist economies.
>
> (1990, 51)

Unfortunately, this economic theory is not at our disposal yet. Best-case scenario, it's a work in progress.[52]

Conclusion

Schumpeter started his academic life trying to blend equilibrium and evolution, Marx and Walras. This permeated his whole career and was never fully discarded, as can be seen in many passages of his *History of Economic Analysis*, published after his death, or in papers such as 'The historical approach to business cycles' published in 1949, the year before he passed away, where we read right in the opening section[53]:

> I am as much as anyone can be convinced of the necessity of bringing to bear upon the study of business cycles the whole of our theoretical apparatus and not only aggregative dynamic schemata but also our equilibrium analysis.
>
> (1949 [2005], 322)

It is *really* difficult to understand the persistent reference to equilibrium after its crystal-clear rejection in *CSD*.[54] Nevertheless, Schumpeter appears to have changed his mind over the course of his life, and the inflection point seems to reside in *Business Cycles*, as pointed by McCraw. While working on the book, Schumpeter must have become bothered by the incongruity between the massive data and historical material he was processing and his 'model'. The – many – discouraging reviews he got certainly contributed to a reconsideration of analytical assumptions and priorities, and this produced his 'final thesis'. The 'thesis' seems to indicate his progressive detachment from equilibrium and a move towards economic and business history, industry case studies, business reports and corporate balance sheets as *the* fundamental tools for economic analysis (1949, 322–324).

> To let the murder out and to start my final thesis, what is really required is a large collection of industrial and location monographs all drawn up according to the same plan and giving proper attention on one hand to the incessant historical change in production and consumption functions and on the other hand to the quality and behavior of the leading personnel.
>
> (1949, 328)

However, it is still rather disturbing that Schumpeter delivers his 'final thesis' in the same paper in which he starts by paying his respects to equilibrium analysis. Nevertheless, the 'final thesis' is reinforced in *History of Economic Analysis*, in a well-documented passage:

> What distinguishes the 'scientific' economist from all the other people who think, talk, and write about economic topics is a command of techniques that we class under three heads: history, statistics, and 'theory.' The three together make up what we shall call Economic Analysis. [Later in this chapter, J.A.S. added to these three a fourth fundamental field, Economic Sociology.] … Of these fundamental fields, economic history – which issues into and includes present-day facts – is by far the most important. I wish to state right now that if, starting my work in economics afresh, I were told that I could study only one of the three but could have my choice, it would be economic history that I should choose.
>
> (1954, 12)

The equilibrium puzzle remains, and we will never know what accounts for its resilience.[55] What really matters here is that if we side with the 'final thesis', almost all the neo-Schumpeterian descendants of Schumpeter chose the other side of the divide. They stuck with equilibrium, espoused neoclassical assumptions[56] and progressively more mathematically oriented research and modelling strategies that largely forgot history. The *Journal of Evolutionary Economics*, the International J.A. Schumpeter Society's major outlet, is a living proof of that. In my, admittedly unconventional interpretation, this was a big mistake: it narrowed down Schumpeter's agenda, dramatically, instead of developing and expanding its boundaries.

To sum up, let me try to sketch 'in desperate brevity', as Schumpeter was fond of saying, what a radical, Schumpeter-based and Keynes-Minsky rekindled approach to economic and institutional analysis, although still in need of proper development, should have as its building blocks:

1   Capitalism is a historical process in which change (not equilibrium) is the most relevant feature. Change, therefore, should be *the* object of investigation in an evolutionary research programme.
2   Economic agents are creative and firms – the main economic units – are agents of transformation. Knowledge skills and organisational – dynamic – capabilities are cornerstones of competitive advantage for both banks and firms.
3   Competition, understood as creative destruction, and as a selection mechanism is the engine that propels economic change.
4   Innovations – applications of new ideas and/or methods to the economic sphere – are the main fuel of that engine.
5   Credit and innovations function both as 'levers of riches' and as uncertainty creators; their interplay is at the root of the system's twin operating features: progress and conflict.

6 Financial innovations are central to financial evolution, yet also linchpins to unstable, financially fragile, and often financially unsustainable development processes.

7 Financial fragility springs from the relationship between 'technological' and financial innovation, indebtedness and uncertainty.

8 Profit rates tend to differentiate (not to equalise) and no 'proportionality law' between investments and profits applies.

9 Institutions and public policy are the main tools for building stability through the establishment of conventions, rules and regulations that create regularities and convergence of expectations.

10 Regularities are not fixed but rather a result of complex arrangements, which can turn into destabilising forces in a creative-destruction environment.

11 States, more precisely entrepreneurial states, are pillars of successful development processes.

12 The main causal chain in the operation of the system runs from policymakers', bankers' and entrepreneur's decisions as to the determination of investment, the speed of technological change, productivity increases and employment profiles.

In conclusion, I'll subscribe to McCaw's position in his inspired review of *CSD*:

> Does Joseph Schumpeter's *Capitalism, Socialism and Democracy* rank with the most important works of economic history of the twentieth century? Of course, it does. Has there been a more penetrating analyst of capitalism than Joseph Schumpeter? No, I do not think there has.
>
> (McCraw 2000, 1)

However, for the reasons given in this chapter, it needs to be updated.

Acknowledgements

I want to thank Dick Nelson, Fred Block, Randall Wray, Jan Kregel, Adriano Proença, John Mathews and Rainer Kattel for their useful comments, with the usual proviso that the neck I am sticking out here is my own.

Notes

1 Actually, Schumpeter spells out this contradiction quite clearly in his seventh 'lost' chapter from *TED*, which was not published in English until 2002. I will get to that later in the chapter. However, let me submit here that this – the equilibrium or not-equilibrium question – was always a big problem for economists in general which attempted/attempt to deal with capitalism as a system of conntinous change, given the fact that equilibrium theory revolves around finding the conditions in which the system is in *rest mode*, or in which it does not have any endogenous mechanism

pushing for change. For a different interpretation of the 'Walrasian' element in Schumpeter's theory, although recognising its incompatibility with the mechanisms of change, see Callegari's chapter in the book. Furthermore, both Callegari's analysis and conclusions are, besides being independently constructed, strongly convergent with my own in this chapter.

2 From Marx to Marshall, Schumpeter, Keynes; from Robinson to Krugman, Stiglitz, Baumol, Blinder, Rodrik and beyond. Despite their brilliance, originality, wealth of knowledge and unorthodox policy prescriptions, all those 'celebrity economists' never parted ways with equilibrium analysis, which means they never fully embraced an evolutionary, out-of-equilibrium, approach to economic theory. Noticeably, their most original and interesting contributions did not depend on the scaffolding of their training. Equilibrium-based thinking remains, despite its distance from any kind of empirical grounding, a powerful iron cage that traps whoever gets into it. Easy to get in, extremely difficult to get out. In that sense, economic theory constitutes a very strange case of applied social science, where the mostly revered analytical tool is in fact a rather poor lens for understanding the way the real economy works and evolves. The failure to predict, or properly understand, the biggest crises of capitalism (1929 and 2008) provides just one hint of a much bigger failure of understanding. The mantra that 'the government is out of money', repeated left and right, provides another one. The practical consequences are dire. Equilibrium-based theorising leads to policy prescriptions that destroy regions, assets, corporations and lives. In that sense, contemporary Nobel-less radical thinkers such as Scitovsky, Hirschman, Galbraith, Shackle, Minsky, Godley and Kregel deserve to take a bow.

3 And submerges shortly after, going back to the previous attempts to reconcile equilibrium and evolution, or 'Marx and Walras'.

4 Or 'cultural contradictions', as Daniel Bell would propose in his seminal 1976 book, some of which are regaining force, as I write, in our Trump-Brexit-anti-emigration era. Pair that with ISIS, 'war on Islam', white supremacism, and the rise of both left and right anti-establishment movements and we have Huntingtonian injections of clashes of civilisations taking form. Given this cluster of instabilities in capitalism's order, there is certainly room for an excursus on the 'new cultural contradictions of capitalism' that would have to take Schumpeter, Bell and Huntington as its primary analytical sources.

5 Obviously that generalisation has to be qualified. A few neo-Schumpeterian economists resisted the 'equilibrium trap', among them Rosenberg, Lazonick, Nelson, the 'young' Dosi, Best, Shionoya, Andersen, Mazzucato and the business scholars behind the 'dynamic capabilities approach' in strategic management. Regretfully, all of them still paid scarce attention to one of the key features of Schumpeter's original approach: the role of finance. As a result, we have neo-Schumpeterian theorising as Hamlet with the Danish prince but without the ephor....

6 Let me apologise to the reader in advance for the abundant number of Schumpeter's quotes. They would not be needed if the thesis advanced here was common sense. I don't think it is. Therefore, it is worth providing proper documentation by quoting from the original sources.

7 I say 'seems' because it really does not. As I will show later (section on '*Capitalism, Socialism and Democracy*: creative destruction as new departure point for economic analysis'), not only can the equilibrium apparatus be removed, granting the analysis more theoretical coherence, but Schumpeter himself spells this out in the seventh 'lost' chapter (not translated into English until 2002) of *TED*.

8 'The businessman as a rule first becomes the bank's debtor in order to become its creditor, that he first "borrows" what he uno actu "deposits"' (1997, Locations 2724–2725).

9   Old-school investment bankers (Hilferding's banks are the proxy here), not the 'modern gamblers'.

10 'Shareholders per se, however, are never entrepreneurs, but merely capitalists, who in consideration of their submitting to certain risks participate in profits (1997, 2573–2574).

11 'It is not the owner of stage-coaches who builds railways' (1997, Kindle Location 2105).

12 See Taylor 2016 for a thorough development of these arguments with several case studies to illustrate them.

13 See, for instance, the essays in Lazonick and Teece 2012.

14 And most likely intended.

15 Obviously profits and the rate of profit would equalise, at zero, after the complete diffusion of a cluster of innovations, as Schumpeter points out more than once in the book. But this would be an equilibrium position where the absence of change would be the case. 'Without development there is no profit, without profit no development' (1997, Kindle Locations 3632–3633). As already noted, this – the equilibrium position – is a shaky foundation for the whole *TED* edifice, but once it is removed, which happens in *CSD*, it all falls into place. The section on '*Capitalism, Socialism and Democracy*: creative destruction as new departure point for economic analysis in this chapter will give a compressed picture of how it does so.

16 There is a whole trail of mentions to the state exercising 'entrepreneurial functions' in capitalism and I will flesh them out in Chapter 10, but although extremely important, and necessary, for an institutional reframing of his analysis where the state becomes a key player. They are peripheral and do not form part of his theoretical model.

17 In *all* economic theories of development. The 'developmental state' approach is brilliant and a major step ahead in filling that hole, but its major architects are political scientists and sociologists. There is no economic theory that takes the state as a major player in the workings of capitalism (please do not confuse this with a plea for an 'economic theory of the state', which, by the way, is also lacking).

18 Recall they create purchasing power out of thin air, not from previously stocked reserves.

19 Max Weber has highlighted this conflict better than Schumpeter. See Collins 1986, Chapter 5.

20 The fact that most of the OECD has extremely low, or zero, interest rates now doesn't contradict the argument. It just proves Keynes right in respect to the way he plugs long-term expectations into his model, stating that they are far more important than the level of interest rates in shaping investment decisions.

21 The use of concepts is confusing. Schumpeter conflates 'prosperity' and 'boom' and uses depression to characterise what in fact should be termed a recession. Only in *BC* would he make these distinctions, under the four-phase model, and achieve more precision in that realm.

22 Thanks to a laudable effort by John Mathews, it appeared in *Industry and Innovation Special Issue*, titled 'Schumpeter's 'lost' seventh chapter' (Vol. 9, Numbers 1/2).

23 The ones by Oscar Lange, Simon Kuznets Jan Tinbergen, Alvin Hansen and Henrik Grossman are particularly devastating. More recent comments by Chris Freeman and Hyman Minsky are equally damaging. I will refer to them below.

24 Depressions, in Schumpeter's *TED* terminology.

25 Instead of the two-phase model used in TED.

26 Henrik Grossman, a well-known Marxist, delivers a similar point in his review. After describing Schumpeter's four-phase cycle and the problems arising from the way the return to equilibrium is framed by the author, Grossman remarks:

Schumpeter solves all these theoretical difficulties with a word 'adaptation'. He never describes the process of adaptation. The desired result of it – equilibrium – is introduced as a *deux ex machina*. If this 'adaptation" takes place, the system functions "satisfactorily" and we are in "equilibrium'.

(1941, 185)

27 However, the cycle analysis, as a whole, still suffers from the weaknesses of a poorly conceived attempt to blend it with equilibrium. Here's a typical passage: 'But when depression has run its course, the system *starts to feel its way back to a new neighborhood of equilibrium*. This constitutes our fourth phase. We will call it Recovery or Revival' (Schumpeter 1964, vol. 1, Kindle Locations 2575–2576, my emphasis).

28 And have tried to contribute to, co-authoring an essay with Jan Kregel, published as a discussion paper in 2000 (Kregel and Burlamaqui 2000) and in an abridged version in 2005.

29 This last topic will be discussed in Chapter 6 below.

30 Including Schumpeter himself until 1939.

31 Note the convergence with Sraffa's' 1926 paper on the 'Laws of return'.

32 If the differentiation process persists.

33 Examples abound. IBM never understood the potential of its PC, until it was too late. Detroit was nearly destroyed by Toyota and is again under threat by Tesla, Google and co. Did the music industry understood the potential of Napster? Blockbuster was destroyed by a new business model: Netflix. How many retailers understood they were under attack by Amazon until they filed for bankruptcy? That's the way capitalism evolves, and that's what Schumpeterian competition is about (cf. Bell 2001; Srinivasan 2017).

34 In the economics literature – heterodox for sure – Rumsfeld has an illustrious predecessor: Shackle and his concept of 'unknowledge' (see Earl and Littleboy 2014).

35 There is only one place where this proportionality rule between 'investment and return' does not seem absurd to me: treasuries.

36 Cf. Burlamaqui, Castro and Kattel 2013.

37 Bill Lazonick aptly names them 'organisational successes' in contrast to the mainstream, never well-explained, rubric of 'market failures' (1991).

38 Semi-slave contracts and slave wages service Apple, Nike, Amazon – shameful 'celebrity firms' whose practices have been disclosed – but this is true of almost all corporations.

39 Strong IP rules and regulations and all sorts of legal monopolies, for instance.

40 Including the way the tax code is shaped, which brings the state and political coalitions straight to the centre of economic analysis, despite the marginal attention they get from economic theory.

41 The way I see it, what tends to confuse interpreters here is Schumpeter's passage stating that:

To sum up this part of our argument: if capitalist evolution – 'progress' – *either ceases or becomes completely automatic*, the economic basis of the industrial bourgeoisie will be reduced eventually to wages such as are paid for current administrative work excepting remnants of quasi-rents and monopoly gains....

(1942, 134, my emphasis)

Schumpeter's thesis was never that it would cease, but rather that it would become routine: 'Thus, economic progress tends to become depersonalised *and automatized*' (133, my emphasis).

42 This is hardly a new discovery in the history of economic thought. It had already been pointed out by, among others, Adam Smith in his chapter on 'The expense of public works and public institutions' in *The Wealth of Nations, Book V*:

The third and last duty of the sovereign or commonwealth, is that of *erecting and maintaining those public institutions and those public works*, which though they may be in the highest degree advantageous to a great society, are, however, of such a nature, that the profit could never repay the expense to any individual, or small number of individuals; and which it, therefore, cannot be expected that any individual, or small number of individuals, should erect or maintain.

(2003 [1776], 508, my emphasis)

In contrast to the 'invisible hand', this statement seems to have got lost. Even the encyclopaedic Schumpeter didn't profit from it. By contrast, if we search the history of economic policy, the state's central role in economic transformation is prominent. From Serra to Cromwell, Hamilton, Carey, List, the German Historical School and the Meiji reformers there is a whole tradition of discussing and performing state action which we now know about (Reinert 2007). More recently, after the flood of books on the Asian developmental state, there is virtually no room for doubt. The state is a key player in development and structural transformation. Economic theory never got that right, Schumpeter included. Hubert Henderson's exchange with Keynes suggesting the state as an 'entrepreneur-in-chief' (1943) could have opened a new window but it wasn't explored. Mazzucato's fine book on the entrepreneurial state was not forged directly as remedy to this theoretical flaw, but helped to raise deserved attention to the matter and provided a new window of opportunity. Let's exploit it from a theoretical perspective.

43 In *BC*, in a brief mention to government direct financing of enterprise, the Brazilian government gets his attention: 'Government fiat might also serve the purpose of financing enterprise. The Brazilian government, for instance, financed coffee plantations by this method in the seventies' (1964, Chapter 3, Kindle Locations 1850–1851).

44 However, there are also several passages where the emphasis is put on polices that act as potential brakes on entrepreneurial dynamism or conduits towards socialisation. As Swedberg remarks, 'Schumpeter detested everything that Roosevelt stood for and was convinced that he would ruin the United States in one way or another' (2003, 34). The essay, 'The march into socialism', written in 1949, shortly before his death, is a good example of this 'anti-Keynesian' approach. (The essay appears as an appendix to later editions of *CSD*.)

45 Or instability, which is the final message of both *CSD* and of its predecessor, the essay on 'The instability of capitalism' (1928, reprinted in Clemence 1951, Chapter 3). However, this is not a particularly well-discussed theme in Schumpeter's works, which deserves further scrutiny. It appears he thought that 'trustified capitalism' would become economically more stable via big corporations, but its institutional structure would progressively turn more unstable. The overall result would be an institutional outcome. Hence the tile 'The instability of capitalism' rather than 'The stability of capitalism'. A noticeable flaw here, that I will refer to below, is that Schumpeter totally missed finance and financial dynamics in his prognosis. Financial evolution is a no-show in *CSD*. It is where Keynes and Minsky should be brought on board, as I will briefly indicate below.

46 Although the way they conceptualise it differs substantially (see Note 48 below).

47 Which, in my view, still largely holds if we see it as a 'long-term' potential scenario, not a 'prediction'. In fact, much of Schumpeter's institutional-sociological-cultural analysis was updated, as mentioned, by Daniel Bell in his classic 1976 book.

48 There is, indeed, a high degree of convergence in conclusions, but not in analysis: in his 1928 essay 'The instability of capitalism' Schumpeter returns to the notion of stages, a recurrent theme of his reflection. Contrasting 'competitive' with 'trustified'

capitalism, Schumpeter submits that in the latter the big concern reigns and credit creation performs a different, less important, role:

> Although credit creation still plays a role, both the power to accumulate reserves and the direct access to the money market tend to reduce the importance of this element in the life of a trust.... It is easy to see that the three causes alluded whilst that accentuated the waves in competitive, must tend to soften them down in trustified.
>
> (1928, 70–71)

The meaning seems clear: it's Schumpeter prognosis, in this paper, of the progressive stabilisation of a formerly unstable economy. A cursory reading of that passage could suggest a precursor of Minsky's 1986 book and 1992 paper. Quite the reverse: what Schumpeter is predicting here is a *structural stabilisation* of the capitalist system (as opposed to its 'politico-legal-institutional' *order*, which tends to destabilise). While Minsky's discussion of stability frames it as a policy-institutional construction where Big Government and Big Bank perform the tasks of stabilising an otherwise structurally unstable financial system, for Schumpeter it seems the financial system's *structure* has become more stable. His analysis is reinforced in *CSD* where a progressively more stable economic structure clashes with a progressively more unstable order. References to credit and banking system are absent. Summing-up, although 'destabilising stability' is a common feature of both Schumpeter and Minsky's analysis, their explanations are quite divergent. Yet, Schumpeter's trajectory on that matter is certainly not easy to decipher. Nonetheless, an analytical perspective that reunites credit and finance with competition by means of innovation opens the door for bridging the 'creative-destruction' and the 'Wall Street' paradigms.

49 Minsky is 'reading' Schumpeter through his own theory here. Innovations in financial relations since World War II validate his theory, for sure, but although financial innovation is *mentioned* by Schumpeter's, it's hardly a central feature of his theory.

50 In his historical narrative, although finance and bankruptcies show up, as already mentioned, theory and history don't really connect to each other well. A typical statement is the following:

> difficulties incident to the adaptation to a new fiscal policy, new labor legislation, and a general change in the attitude of government to private enterprise had made the Depression worse. Most serious of all, particularly in the United States, there had been a wholly unnecessary epidemic of bank failures.
>
> (Schumpeter quoted by McCraw 2006, 350)

51 The other, just to recall, is a proper role for the state in forging, or helping to forge, structural transformation.

52 To my knowledge, the best starting point for that theory is provided by Minsky himself in his 1990 paper referred to above.

53 This is one of Louçã's main points in his contribution to this volume.

54 As I mentioned before, equilibrium is an analytical 'iron cage' that is easy to get into but very difficult to get out of.

55 Lack of self-confidence to disrupt established paradigms? Not likely. Schumpeter, of all economists, was not shy in shaking up the conventional wisdom of the profession or reviewing his own previous ideas. So, clarifying this puzzle is a window of opportunity for intellectual-history-minded Schumpeter scholars.

56 For example: Say's law is ever-present in the hundreds of models published in the *Journal of Evolutionary Economics*.

References

Andersen, E.S. (2009). *Schumpeter's Evolutionary Economics: A Theoretical, Historical and Statistical Analysis of the Engine of Capitalism*. London: Anthem Press.

Bell, D. (2001). *The Future of Technology*. Petaling Jaya, Malaysia: Pelanduk Publications.

Beetham, D. (1985). *Max Weber and the Theory of Modern Politics*. New York: John Wiley & Sons.

Burlamaqui, L. (2000). Evolutionary economics and the role of state. In: L. Burlamaqui, A.C. Castro and H.-J. Chang (Eds.), *Institutions and The Role of the State*. Cheltenham, UK: Edward Elgar.

Burlamaqui, L. and Kregel, J. (2005). Innovation, competition and financial vulnerability in economic development. *Revista de Economia Política, 25*(2): 5–22.

Burlamaqui, L., Castro, A. and Kattel, R. (Eds.) (2013). *Knowledge Governance: Reasserting the Public Interest*. London: Anthem Press.

Chandler, A. (1977). *The Visible Hand: The Managerial Revolution in American Business*. Cambridge, MA: Harvard University Press.

Clemence, R.V. (Ed.) (1951). *Essays of J.A. Schumpeter*. Boston, MA: Addison-Wesley Press.

Collins, R. (1986). *Weberian Sociological Theory*. Cambridge: Cambridge University Press.

Earl, P. and Littleboy, B. (2014). *G.L.S. Shackle*. Basingstoke, UK: Palgrave Macmillan.

Freeman, C. (1982). Innovation and long cycles of economic development. Seminário Internacional, Universidade Estadual de Campinas, Campinas, 25–27 August 1982.

Freeman, C. and Louca, F. (2001). *As Time Goes By: From the Industrial Revolutions to the Information Revolution*. Oxford: Oxford University Press.

Grossman, H. (1941). Business cycles. *Zeitschrift für Sozialforschung* 9.1: 181–189.

Hahn, F. (Ed.) (1992). *The Market: Practice and Policy*. Basingstoke, UK: Palgrave Macmillan.

Hahn, F. and Petri, F. (Eds.) (2003). General Equilibrium: Problems and Prospects. New York: Routledge.

Henderson, H. (1943). Note on the problem of maintaining full employment. In: *The Inter-War Years and Other Essays*. Oxford: Oxford University Press,1955.

Ingrao, B. and Israel, G. (1990). The invisible hand: economic equilibrium in the history of science. Cambridge, MA: MIT Press.

Keynes, J.M. (1936). *The General Theory of Employment, Interest and Money*. New York: Harcourt Brace.

Kregel, J. (1997). The theory of value, expectations and Chapter 17 of *The General Theory*. In G.C. Harcourt and P.A. Riach (Eds.), *A 'Second Edition' of The General Theory* (2 vols). London: Routledge.

Kregel, J.A. and Burlamaqui, L. (2000). Finance, competition, instability and development: The financial scaffolding of the real economy. Paper presented to meetings of the Other Canon Group, Venice, Italy (pp. 1–56).

Kregel, J.A. (2014). *Economic Development and Financial Instability: Selected Essays*. London: Anthem Press.

Kuznets, S. (1940). Schumpeter's business cycles. *The American Economic Review, 30*(2): 257–271.

Landes, D.S. (1969). *The Unbound Prometheus: Technological Change and Development in Western Europe from 1750 to the Present*. Cambridge: Cambridge University Press.

Lange, O. (1941). Review of *Business Cycles*. *Review of Economics and Statistics*, November.

Lazonick, W. (1991). *Business Organisation and the Myth of the Market Economy*. Cambridge: Cambridge University Press.

Lazonick, W. and Teece, D.J. (Eds.) (2012). *Management Innovation: Essays in the Spirit of Alfred D. Chandler, Jr.* Oxford: Oxford University Press.

Levin, R.C., Klevorick, A.K., Nelson, R.R., Winter, S.G., Gilbert, R. and Griliches, Z. (1987). Appropriating the returns from industrial research and development. *Brookings Papers on Economic Activity*, 3: 783–831.

McCraw, T.K. (2000). Review of Joseph A. Schumpeter's *Capitalism, Socialism and Democracy*. Economic History Association (EH.net).

McCraw, T.K. (2006). Schumpeter's business cycles as business history. *Business History Review*, 80(2): 231–261.

Minsky, H. (1975). *John Maynard Keynes*. New York: Columbia University Press.

Minsky, H. (1986a). *Stabilizing an Unstable Economy*. New Haven, CT: Yale University Press.

Minsky, H. (1986b). Money and crises in Schumpeter and Keynes. In: H.-J. Wagener and J.W. Drukker (Eds.), *The Economic Law of Motion of Modern Society*. Cambridge: Cambridge University Press.

Minsky, H. (1990). Schumpeter: Finance and evolution. In: M. Perlman (Ed.), *Evolving Technology and Market Structure: Studies in Schumpeterian Economics* (pp. 51–73). Ann Arbor, MI: Michigan University Press.

Minsky, H. (1992). Schumpeter and finance. Hyman P. Minsky Archive. Paper 280 http://digitalcommons.bard.edu/hm_archive/280.

Mokyr, J. (1990). *The Lever of Riches: Technological Creativity and Technological Progress*. Oxford: Oxford University Press.

Nelson, R.R. (2012). Why Schumpeter has had so little influence on today's main line economics, and why this may be changing. *Journal of Evolutionary Economics*, 22(5), 901–916.

O'Sullivan, M. (2005). Finance and innovation. In: J. Fagerberg, D.C. Mowery and R.R. Nelson (Eds.), *The Oxford Handbook of Innovation*. Oxford: Oxford University Press.

Penrose, E. (1959). *The Theory of the Growth of the Firm*. Oxford: Oxford University Press.

Perez, C. (2002). *Technological Revolutions and Financial Capital*. Cheltenham, UK: Edward Elgar.

Reinert, E. (2007). *How Rich Nations Got Rich … And Why Poor Countries Stay Poor*. London: Constable Press.

Robinson, J. (1972). The second crisis of economic theory. *The American Economic Review*, 62(1/2), 1–10.

Rosenberg, N. (1994). Joseph Schumpeter: radical economist. In: Y. Shionoya and M. Perlman (Eds.), *Schumpeter in the History of Ideas* (pp. 24–58). Ann Arbor: The Univeristy of Michigan Press.

Samuelson, P.A. (1998). Summing up on business cycles: opening address. *Conference Series-Federal Reserve Bank of Boston*. Vol. 42. Federal Reserve Bank of Boston, 1998.

Schumpeter, J.A. (1928). The instability of capitalism. In: R.V. Clemence (Ed.), *Essays of J.A. Schumpeter*. Boston, MA: Addison-Wesley Press, 1951.

Schumpeter, J.A. (1939). *Business Cycles* (2 vols.). New York: Mac-Graw Hill.

Schumpeter, J.A. (1942). *Capitalism, Socialism and Democracy*. New York: Routledge.

Schumpeter, J.A. (1949). The historical approach to *Business Cycles*. In: R.V. Clemence (Ed.), *Essays of J.A. Schumpeter*. Boston, MA: Addison-Wesley Press, 1951.

Schumpeter, J.A. (1954). *History of Economic Analysis* (E.B. Schumpeter Ed.). Oxford: Oxford University Press.

Schumpter, J.A. (1964). *Business Cycles* (2 vols.). McGraw Hill, Kindle Edition.

Schumpeter, J.A. (1997). *The Theory of Economic Development*. Routledge, Kindle Edition.

Shionoya, Y. (1985). *Schumpeter and the Idea of Social Science: A Metatheoretical Study*. Cambridge: Cambridge University Press.

Smith, A. (2003). *The Wealth of Nations*. New York: Random House.

Srinivasan, B. (2017). *Americana: A 400-Year History of American Capitalism*. Penguin. Kindle Edition.

Taylor, T.M. (2016). *The Politics of Innovation: Why Some Countries Are Better Than Others at Science and Technology*. Oxford: Oxford University Press.

Teece, D. and Pisano, G. (1994). The dynamic capabilities of firms: An introduction. *Industrial and corporate change*, 3(3): 537–556.

Teece, D.J. (1998). Capturing value from knowledge assets: The new economy, markets for know-how, and intangible assets. *California Management Review*, 40(3): 55–79.

Winter, S.G. (2003). Understanding dynamic capabilities. *Strategic Management Journal*, 24(10): 991–995.

3 Schumpeter and the dynamics of capitalism

The place of *Capitalism, Socialism and Democracy*

Francisco Louçã

Rosenberg once argued that Schumpeter was the 'most radical scholar in the discipline of economics in the twentieth century' since 'he urged the rejection of the most central and precious tenets of neoclassical theory' (Rosenberg 1994, 41). The author was very emphatic: 'Indeed, I want to insist that very little of the complex edifice of neoclassical economics, as it existed in the late 1930s and 1940s, survived the sweep of Schumpeter's devastating assaults' (ibid.). Based essentially on *Capitalism, Socialism and Democracy* (Schumpeter 1942)[1] and on the preface to the Japanese edition (Schumpeter 1937) of *Theory of Economic Development*, Rosenberg identifies the alleged devastating assaults by Schumpeter against the neoclassical paradigm: since change is the decisive feature of capitalism and it means a permanent tendency towards disruption, and since equilibrium has no welfare advantage since it means no progress, innovation is alien to rational-equilibrating decision-making; in this context, the 'circular flow' described capitalism deprived of the essential movements of change and is therefore merely a simplification; as a consequence, Schumpeter committed himself to the historical analysis of this process of mutation as an alternative to the equilibrium paradigm (ibid., 44–45, 48, 50, 56). But the whole case is based on partial evidence, given the fact that the same Schumpeter denied all these claims in other moments, including in posterior writings.

In any case, one very essential point is clear: Schumpeter was opposed to the neoclassicals in the very definition of the research programme, since his theme was technological and institutional change, and this is typically ignored and annihilated in the orthodox view by the *ceteris paribus* conditions (ibid., 50–51). As a consequence, one of the problems for the interpretation of Schumpeter is why he did not reject the neoclassical paradigm he could not use or follow. Indeed, he held to the framework of the equilibrium paradigm through all his scientific writings, even when he added or counterposed his evolutionary views. This paradox, not recognised by Rosenberg in his radical remarks, is the essential question, or, as Allen puts it, in the most complete and authoritative biography of Schumpeter:

> Paradox, failure, disaster, and disappointment were the keynotes of Schumpeter's life and work. He lived a paradoxical life and had a paradoxical

career. He thought paradoxical ideas and wrote paradoxical books. Time
and time again he failed as a scientist, scholar, politician, businessman, and
even as a human being.... Yet, paradoxically this career of failure was, in
its totality, a success.

(Allen 1991, Vol. 1, 4)

This paradox is never clearer than in regard to the Walrasian grand scheme of
general equilibrium and to his alternative view of cycles and innovation as the
prime movers of modern capitalism. Yet, again, Schumpeter astonished the
profession when, in his *Capitalism, Socialism and Democracy* (hereafter *CSD*) he
anticipated the collapse of capitalism and the eventual triumph of socialism.

Yet this paradox ceased to be read as a crucial part of the book. In fact, for
some years the interpreters and discussants of *CSD* emphasised the importance of the concept of democracy there suggested by Schumpeter; more
recently, his analysis of capitalism has been highlighted by controversies on
the nature of the contemporary economies. These different perceptions of the
book only indicate that, indeed, we really have three different books, scarcely
related: one on capitalism, another on socialism, another on democracy. I will
discuss the three concepts following the reverse order of Schumpeter, beginning with his idea of democracy.

This chapter briefly discusses the paradox as highlighted by the political
context of Schumpeter's career in the first section, or 'Democracy', the argument on socialism and capitalism as presented in *CSD* in the second section,
the notion of evolution in the third section and finally the implications of this
book and other contributions by the author on the debates, past and present,
on stagnation.

Schumpeter inside his political conundrum

Schumpeter's right-wing political views were well known to his friends and
close academic circles. Even when he left Germany in 1932 for his chosen
US exile, Schumpeter was not opposed to Nazism – although, of course,
unaware of what was to happen later on. At the time, Schumpeter showed
great ambivalence in relation to the dramatic events going on: 'I am often in
a state akin to despair', he wrote to Frisch two days before the burning of the
Reichstag.[2] As Hitler tightened his grip on power, he still stated: 'As to
Germany, I find it very difficult to form an opinion. Recent events may
mean a catastrophe but they also may mean salvation',[3] and 'I know something of the government which preceded Hitler's and I can only say that I am
quite prepared to forgive him much by virtue of comparison.'[4]

Schumpeter, who lived in Germany until 1932, even advised some of his
students to join the Nazi party. In his farewell speech to the University of
Bonn he included the following astonishing remarks: 'What enormous subjective individual possibilities there might be for a young man of today if
there were any who, not deprecating economic techniques, felt like a

National Socialist', and defined Nazism as 'a powerful movement which is singular in our history' (quoted in Allen 1991, Vol. 1, 284–285).[5] Later, in his personal diary, Schumpeter asked himself why he had changed his attitude towards Germany from the World War I to World War II: 'I cannot understand at all this *revirement* of my sympathies [for Germany] since 1916' (in Allen 1991, Vol. 2, 139).[6]

Paradoxically again, Schumpeter's earlier life seemed to contradict this evolution. Indeed, he had been part of the Austrian social-democratic government in 1919 as minister for finance, for six short months (but it is conjectured that the prime minister chose him in order to benefit in the political game from his conservative credentials). Yet, the impact of the later evolution, both in Russia and in Central Europe, leading to the rise of the Nazi movement and to the collapse of democracies, may have oriented him to a more reactionary point of view, his '*revirement* of sympathies'.

In Swedberg's introduction to an edition of *CSD* it is revealed that, while writing the book, Schumpeter was under investigation by the FBI for possible espionage, considering his public pro-Nazi or at least not-anti-Nazi positions, and his wife was also under scrutiny for potential pro-Japanese sentiments (Swedberg 1992, x). Although this is anecdotal (and was inconsequential), the suffering evolution of Schumpeter's views is relevant to understand the context of the writing of his more successful book – and the more political one.

These views are not apparent in the book. On the contrary, not only does Schumpeter anticipate the victory of the USSR ('Stalin will emerge as the true victor' of the war, *CSD*, 373) but he also takes distance from the Central European dictatorships, as he discusses democracy as the convenient method of social organisation, although pointing out its vulnerability. Yet, as we shall discuss in the next section, this concept of democracy is not an important part of the core of the book, which is the allegation that capitalism may die and socialism may eventually win. The most unpredictable advocate of socialism, Schumpeter, stunned academia as he announced socialism as the successful force of the middle of the century.

The fact that his own views on the conflict ravaging through Europe and the world were not presented in *CSD* may only be interpreted through different hypotheses: he may have intuited that his position was untenable in the US in 1942; he may have changed his mind or simply hesitated on what to think. Furthermore, contrary to the Nazi actions and while commenting on dangerous European affairs, Schumpeter identifies anti-Semitism in the popular culture and states that, on the 'slaughtering of Jews', 'we should certainly not approve of these practices', pointing this out as the extreme case of popular views that can be imposed on formal democratic grounds but that are inacceptable (*CSD*, 241, 242). The example serves Schumpeter, as he argues about the distinction between the democratic method and the outcomes of decisions. He states:

> Democracy is a political method, that is to say, a certain type of institutional arrangement for arriving at political – legislative and administrative

– decisions and hence incapable of being an end in itself, irrespective of what decisions will produce under given historical conditions.

(Ibid.)

Democracy, for Schumpeter, is a powerful method of social organisation and decision, but it is companionable with the imposition of terror on some minorities (or majorities, as it comes), since it is a method, and a vulnerable one, not an end in itself.

His own personal experience, through the period of great tempests in world politics – he closely followed the Russian Revolution, the rise of Hitler, the preparations for the World War – may have changed or impacted on his concept of democracy. But, unlike many of his readers, I believe that his notion of democracy is instrumental and a limited one, if not dangerous. If democracy is only a technology for decision-making, a method to reach deliberations, then it would really be compatible with different forms of authoritarianism or racism. If democracy has no content, as substantiated in constitutional rights, guaranteed by a culture of equality, then it may become a tool for social destruction, as it has been on so many occasions.

The experience of Schumpeter himself proves that he felt at odds with this very concept of democracy, considering his European life. An example of such limitation of the concept of democracy as a method and not as the rule of law and statute rights is the persecution of the Jews, which was, of course, a very relevant problem in 1942, as it is today, precisely an example that is invoked by Schumpeter. In order to understand Schumpeter's position on the matter – and his paradox on this – the available evidence on his views and actions in relation to the contemporary debates on anti-Semitism is summarised in the following.

In different moments, Schumpeter opposed the nomination of some colleagues of Jewish descent, but this should be attributed mostly to their political activism. It is also to be noted that in other cases he helped the same men against anti-Semitic persecution. One example was Jacob Marschak. In 1932 Schumpeter opposed the election of Marschak as a fellow of the Econometric Society and, indeed, tried to prevent him from getting a prominent position in the newborn movement. For this reason, he quarrelled with Frisch, who criticised his opposition for non-scientific reasons, namely attributing it to his anti-Semitism or anti-socialist motivations, and tried to convince him to correct the course of action.[7]

Frisch noted Schumpeter's opposition as being politically motivated:

I take it that your reference to Marschak being biased in his selection of Fellows means that Marschak is a Socialist and that he therefore is trying to get Socialists into the picture. I knew that Marschak is a Socialist, but I have a very strong impression that in the matters of the Econometric Society he is guided uniquely by scientific motives.[8]

Schumpeter responded very soon afterwards:

> No. You do me an injustice: I am not so narrow as to object to anyone because he is a socialist or anything else in fact. If I did take political opinion into consideration I should be much in favour of including socialists in our list of Fellows. In fact, I should consider it good policy to do so. Nor am I or have I ever been an anti-Semite. The trouble with Marschak is that he is both a Jew and a socialist of a type which is probably unknown to you; his allegiance to people answering these two characteristics is so strong that he will work and vote for a whole tail of them and not feel satisfied until we have a majority of them, in which case he will disregard all other qualifications. This is in the nature of a difficulty. But personally, I like him immensely and I think a lot of him.[9]

This was not satisfactory for Frisch: 'I must admit that I am very surprised about your views on Marschak.'[10]

After the first selection of fellows, Frisch insisted on including Marschak in the next group to be elected, and he won the day. Four years later, Schumpeter used the same argument against the selection of Marschak as the research director for the Cowles Commission: Marschak is a 'highly competent and highly trained economist and statistician.... Of course, he is a Jew and a socialist and it is more than likely that he will try to draw other Jews and socialists after him.'[11] Nevertheless, it remains obvious that the crucial point was his organised political activity rather than any other motive: instead, Schumpeter recommended Oskar Lange, who was also a socialist and whose wife was a Jew (which would mean trouble if returning to Europe, Schumpeter rightly argued).[12]

Although Schumpeter refused to condemn the Hitler government, it is certain that he generously supported colleagues persecuted by the German government. It is also fair to say that, after the confrontation with his friend Frisch over Marschak, Schumpeter tried to set up a commission in the US to help German economists under threat and sent Mitchell a list of Jews in need of assistance, given the danger of Nazi persecution. In this instance, he highly recommended Marschak, 'probably the most gifted scientific economist of the exact quantitative type now in Germany.'[13] He also wrote to the Rockefeller Foundation asking for help for Marschak.[14]

Other examples prove that, in spite of his anti-Semitism, in practical matters Schumpeter often rejected the discrimination against Jews: for instance, he supported the appointment of Samuelson against the opposition of an anti-Semitic head of department, which ignited a major clash in the faculty. Even if his tortured private diary included several anti-Jewish and racist remarks, in his professional life Schumpeter met the requirement of cordiality and human solidarity with those persecuted by racism and xenophobia. Democracy as a method – the method that allowed Hitler's electoral victory and that would eventually establish that, if consulted, a majority of the

German people could have at the time accepted the war and the Holocaust – contrasted with the attitude of Schumpeter himself, who, on several occasions, tried to avoid or to diminish the impact of that method for colleagues and institutions he could influence.

In any case, the successive episodes exhibiting his mistrust of politically engaged Jews, as well as his opposition to Rooseveltian politics and previous sympathies towards the then new German government, naturally accentuated the surprise of Schumpeter's colleagues when he produced *CSD*, with its astonishing claim of the viability of socialism and its impending victory.

The victory of socialism and the collapse of capitalism

CSD is a strange book indeed. It includes a collection of successive chapters not clearly related to each other, beginning with one on Marx, then another following chapter on the question 'Can capitalism survive?', although Schumpeter's answer is unrelated to Marxian theory. His reply to the question is indeed the *motum* of the book: 'Can capitalism survive? No, I do not think it can.' In the following, the author qualifies this statement: capitalism will fall provided its leaders continue to act as in the present, and only in that sense is the outcome 'inevitable' (*CSD*, 61). But what makes the book interesting is not the well-informed, although biased, view of Marx, or any theory of collapse inspired by Marx's views of the contradictions of capitalism, but instead the connection – again, a paradoxical one – between the author's concept of innovation and the discussion on the future of capitalism.

The argument for socialism is weak at best.[15] For Schumpeter, a socialist economy and political regime can work, given that 'it would eliminate the cause of the cyclical ups and downs whereas in the capitalist order it is only possible to mitigate them'; it would generate fewer conflicts and less waste; it would command that 'moral allegiance' lacking under capitalism; and, finally, it could produce more self-discipline, 'hence less need for authoritarian discipline that there is in the society of fettered capitalism' (*CSD*, 95, 198, 211–212). While discussing 'socialism' the author refers exclusively to the Soviet experience, that which was available by that time; he does not use the available information, scarce but still relevant, on the historical facts having led to the Stalinist regime. The civil war just after the revolution, the outcome of the internal struggle in the ruling party and the liquidation of the internal and external oppositions, the social question with the land owners, the kulaks, and then the New Economic Policy, the failure of the German uprising and the impact of the civil war in China: all these topics are mostly ignored by Schumpeter. But, essentially, he could not have missed the evidence of the difficulties of the social regime and its economic programme, to the point of considering that it could mobilise 'less need for authoritarian discipline' than in other societies.

Furthermore, as the debates on 'market socialism' or the 'socialist calcu-lation debate' had emerged since the 1920s and engaged not a few of the people Schumpeter knew, including Friedrich Hayek and Oskar Lange in prominent roles, he could not have ignored these arguments. In other words, 'socialism' was an unclear concept for Schumpeter, in historical analysis, in political definitions and in economic terms, and my inclination is to consider that, as he frequently did, Schumpeter just used the argument in order to '*épater le bourgeois*' and to convene shock and astonishment in order to propose his views.[16] If that was the case, the essential argument of *CSD* boils down to the problem with capitalism and should be read and interpreted in that sense – indeed, not the eventual victory of socialism but the discussion on the con-tradictions of late capitalism is the theme for which the book is remembered and commemorated. It is certainly here that the book reaches its best argu-ment and produces it best lines.

His analysis of the dangers that capitalism is facing is partly based on the fail-ures of economic theory and mostly on the analysis of the structural conditions for development. The immediate theoretical argument is that the dominant liberal views would lead to deepening a recession when it emerged: 'under the conditions created by capitalist evolution, perfect and universal flexibility of prices might in depression further destabilise the system, instead of stabilising it as it no doubt would under the conditions envisaged by general theory' (*CSD*, 95). As this was written a dozen years after the beginning of the Great Depres-sion, the phrase must be attributed to a discussion on theoretical alternatives, not necessarily on practical actions (Schumpeter detested the non-liberal altern-ative of Roosevelt and opposed his politics in any way possible).

The structural conditions for development in mature capitalist economies are indeed what mostly concerned the author. Yet, in his systematic presenta-tion of innovation as creative destruction, Schumpeter takes a contradictory position: on one hand he complains about the gigantism and anonymity of the economic organisation of big firms, since the entrepreneurs are replaced by bureaucrats and the direct responsibility of the owners is substituted by the abstract value of shares, and on the other hand he defends the monopoly as better suited for promoting investment and risking a high level of expenses on research (*CSD*, xvii). Notwithstanding, it is the first argument that emerges in *CSD* as the dominant one.

Schumpeter calls the consequence of the process of industrial and financial concentration the 'obsolescence of the entrepreneurial function' (ibid., 131f.). As his views on entrepreneurship and innovation are well known,[17] and are the topic of other chapters in this book, I will only briefly indicate the per-manence and centrality of the topic in what was the central theme for Schumpeter until *CSD*: the nature and causes of the cycles and crises in capi-talist economies. This he summarised in a paper in the December 1927 issue of *Economica*, discussing, apart from outside disturbances, the importance of seasonal fluctuations, cycles, long waves of a Kondratiev type, and the secular trend, and emphasising that we confess to a feeling that it is the two last named [long waves and trends] which will have before long absorbed the attention of the workers in this field, and that the problems of the cycle cannot be dealt with quite satisfactorily without reference to them.

(Schumpeter 1927, 288)

Innovation is the explanation for these deeply moved fluctuations:

We shall, therefore, have explained the cycle when we have explained those booms which are so clearly before our eyes ever since (at least) the Napoleonic wars.... Those booms consist in the carrying out of innovations in the industrial and commercial organisms. By innovations I understand such changes of the combination of the factors of production as cannot be affected by infinitesimal steps or variations in the margin.... The recurring periods of prosperity of the cyclical movement are the form progress takes in capitalistic society.

(Ibid., 295)

Progress or evolution is moved by the cycles, and the cycles are due to innovation. But – here enters the scepticism of *CSD* – innovation is automatised by a new business environment and organisation, sidelining the deviant spirits and avoiding new ideas, with tremendous social consequences, namely the self-expropriation of the bourgeoisie:

Since capitalist enterprise, by its very achievements, tends to automatize progress, we conclude that it tends to make itself superfluous – to break to pieces under the pressure of its own success. The perfectly bureaucratized giant industrial unit not only ousts the small and medium-sized firm and 'expropriates' its owners, but in the end it also ousts the entrepreneur and expropriates the bourgeoisie as a class which in the process stands to lose not only its income but also what is infinitely more important, its function.

(*CSD*, 134)

The social machinery leading to this social danger is, for Schumpeter, moved by the evolution of the idea of property and the very concentration of capital:

The capitalist process, substituting a mere parcel of shares for the walls and the machines in the factory, takes the life out of the idea of property. It loosens the grip that once was so strong.... Dematerialized, defunctionalized and absentee ownership does not impress and call forth moral allegiance as the vital form of property did. Eventually there will be nobody left who really cares to stand for it – nobody within and nobody without the precincts of the big concerns.

(Ibid., 142)

This sociology is based on feelings and impressions, and it constitutes more of a manifesto than an analysis supported by evidence; the notion that 'there will be nobody left who really cares to stand for it' (given 'absentee ownership') is too naive to merit the confrontation with facts. These are indeed the pages of the strongest claims by the author, and those less related to any sort of economic interpretation of the real-life processes.

It is obvious that by that time the author was unsatisfied with the ability of the profession to understand major economic changes,[18] which might explain his strong statements that allow for no indifference, but his defence of his most powerful argument is deficient at best: innovators and entrepreneurs are compared to the 'armored knights' in the Middle Ages, and current accumulation leading to giant firms based on 'dematerialized, defunctionalized and absentee ownership' is compared to the process of social and technological change that destroyed their function and position (*CSD*, 133). The comparison is certainly not kind to the entrepreneurs, even if it adds some fuel to the argument on the obsolescence of innovation under late capitalism. Furthermore, as with so many historical analogies, this one is predicated upon the certainty of an outcome: the 'armored knights' could not prevent being defeated by modern warfare techniques and by the evolution of social organisation. In any case, this appears to be an ad hoc argument rather than a thorough discussion about the evolution of capitalism.

In the next section I will argue that Schumpeter's own brand of evolutionism is responsible for this vulnerability.

The evolution of Schumpeter's evolutionism

Schumpeter's lifelong project was to create a general theory superseding but including that of Walras, an economist he admired more than all others, but whose theory was considered to be wrong if taken in isolation, since it only accounted for static processes. Therefore, a truly general theory ought to include equilibrium and statics, as well as disequilibrium and dynamics, i.e. economic processes describing the reality of capitalism. This was repeatedly emphasised by Schumpeter in his most important works and represented his crucial contribution to the study of innovation, as he categorically stated in his last major book, *HEA*:

> Social phenomena constitute a unique process in historic time, and incessant and irreversible change is their most obvious characteristic. If by Evolutionism we mean no more than recognition of this fact, then all reasoning about social phenomena must be either evolutionary in itself or else bare upon evolution.
>
> (*HEA*, 435)

This section presents a brief look at how this peculiar concept of evolutionism is formed. What was Schumpeter's evolutionism? Which were his fundamental concepts, and how did they establish his analysis of the contradictions of capitalism, a system that should be walking to its death in the middle of the twentieth century, with a world war going on and of then still uncertain destiny?

In Schumpeter's first book, *Das Wesen und der Hauptinthalt der Theoretischen Nationalökonomik*, published in 1908, when he was 25 years old,[19] a long appreciation of the Methodenstreit was included, the intense debate on method that opposed the Austrian theorist (Menger) and the German Historical School (Schmoller), between the 1890s and the 1910s. Although expressing his concern about the artificial separation between theoretical and historical methods, Schumpeter took the side of Menger, under whose influence he had studied at the University of Vienna. By that time, he was a supporter of the marginalist school and mainly of the Walrasian approach.[20] The book dealt with the general equilibrium and static analysis:

> In the center of the book stands the problem of equilibrium, the importance of which is only slight from the viewpoint of practical applications of theory, but which is nevertheless fundamental for science.... The theory of exchange, price and money, and ... the exact theory of distribution are based on it....
>
> (*DW*, quoted in Allen 1991, Vol. 1., 61–62)

This presentation is very curious, since it indicates in a very early statement the limitation of the equilibrium analysis – its near irrelevance for practical applications – but, in spite of it, its central status in the 'pure' theory, describing the 'changeless order and system in which everything fits together perfectly' (quoted in Allen, ibid., 81). This is a precocious statement of the paradox, as alluded to in the opening of this chapter, and indeed Schumpeter maintained the same attitude through all his life.

Both his general equilibrium framework and his doubts about its applicability were present in his discussion with Walras. In 1909, Schumpeter travelled to Switzerland and visited the ageing Walras, who received and praised the book that he considered a fair presentation of his own theories – although he thought until the very end of the interview that it was Schumpeter's father's (Swedberg 1991, 31; Allen 1991, Vol. 1, 84). Schumpeter described this visit only in 1937, in the Japanese preface to *TED*, according to whom Walras argued

> that of course economic life is essentially passive and merely adapts itself to the natural and social influences which are acting on it, so that the theory of a stationary process constitutes really the whole of theoretical economics and that as economic theorists we cannot say much about the factors that account for historical change, but must simply register them.... I felt very strongly that this was wrong and that there was a source of energy within the economic system which would of itself disrupt any equilibrium that might be attained.
>
> (Schumpeter 1937, 159–160)

There are substantial reasons for accepting this account.[21] First, it corresponds to Walras's approach of economic fluctuations, namely to his metaphor of the economy as the surface of a lake, permanently disturbed but always getting back to equilibrium (Walras 1883, 207–208; Schumpeter, *HEA*, 999). Second, and much more relevant to the present purpose, it indicates the nature of the questions asked by Schumpeter to Walras and his rejection of the general equilibrium solution for those questions. Although this did not affect the reverence of Schumpeter towards Walras, it certainly suggested that he thought that the Walrasian scheme should be completed and that otherwise it would be wrong.

It is also certain that the 1908 book already presented some clues for the future discussion about the entrepreneur. Schumpeter was influenced by an economist of the early nineteenth century, Riedel, who stressed the role of innovations in economic life, by the previous work on the entrepreneur by Thuenen or Bohm Bawerk and particularly by his teacher, Wieser, who was under the ultra-romantic influence so important in Germany at the time. For Wieser, just as for J.B. Clark, a figure of a 'great man' and some 'heroic individualism' was defined in economics, just as Spencer did in sociology and Nietzsche in philosophy (Streissler 1994, 19f., 34). Entrepreneurship had been interpreted since 1908 as the function of carrying the adventuresome innovation (Allen, ibid., 47), and would therefore be the locus for that 'heroic entrepreneur'.

The following book, *Theory of Economic Development*, published two years after the visit to Switzerland, presented his agenda for the study of development and change. As Schumpeter himself stressed in another preface to the English edition of *TED*, the ideas of this book were wholly formed in 1907–1909 (Schumpeter 1935, 5), before the meeting with Walras, and did not change afterwards (Schumpeter 1927, 289). The contrast between their theories is obvious and will be explored in a while. And the continuity in Schumpeter's own thought and writings was successively emphasised by the author, as in 1941, in the Spanish preface to *TED*, when Schumpeter argued that there was no change in his general vision of the capitalist economy from the first edition of that book (Schumpeter 1944, 9).

Yet, this consolidated theory of economic mutation did not challenge the eminent place of Walras in Schumpeter's Olympus. In 1910, Schumpeter published a biographical article on Walras, later reproduced in *TGE* (1997): the general equilibrium theory was praised as being able to 'illuminate' the purely economic relations by 'one single fundamental principle' (*TGE*, 112), and the author was presented as 'an enthusiastic admirer of Walras', 'the greatest of all theoreticians' (ibid., 139, 140), who defined 'the only truly general theory to be formulated in the whole history of economics' (ibid., 442n.). In 1935, Schumpeter stressed again his acceptance of the Walrasian concept of equilibrium (Schumpeter 1935, 4); this was once more repeated in 1939 (*BC*, 45). In 1942, *CSD* presented the Walrasian system – and no longer the Physiocratic, as in *EDM* – as the foundation of economics. In *HEA*, he still stressed the general equilibrium paradigm as the 'Magna Carta of exact economics' (*HEA*, 968), a term he had used in *BC*.

In 1911, in *TED* (1911), Schumpeter presented these conclusions as the distinction between the 'circular flow' and 'development', the main economic processes in action (*TED*, 1961, 145). The circular flow, the 'missing link' in economic causality (*EDM*, 43f.) supposedly discovered by the physiocrats, described

> how each economic period becomes the basis for the subsequent one, not only in a technical sense but also in the sense that it produces exactly such results as induce and enable the members of the economic community to repeat the same process in the same form in the next economic period; how economic production comes about as a social process, how it determines the consumption of every individual and how the latter in its turn determines further production....
>
> (*EDM*, 43)

In other words, this is the stationary process or the condition for equilibrium, which are analytically equivalent (*BC*, 42n., also 68). On the other hand, development was defined as a quantum jump in the social conditions of the system, 'that kind of change arising from within the system which so displaces its equilibrium point that the new one cannot be reached from the old one by infinitesimal steps' (*TED*, 1961, 47n., also 1935, 4). But the 'static conditions' exclude the cycle but not growth: in fact, 'growth', defined as the combination of the evolution of capital accumulation from savings and of the population,[22] was included in the notion of static equilibrium (Schumpeter 1927, 289f.). Equilibrium was thus defined as a 'shifting center of gravitation' in a system that also generates the internal impulse for change, that is, for the rupture of the equilibrium conditions. While development accounted for the nature of the change (*BC*, 560n.), equilibrium described the absorption of change (Schumpeter 1937, 159), that is, was defined as the stability property of the system.

The real economic system cannot be understood without the integration of both processes for Schumpeter: in fact, even if he sometimes indicated that 'perfect' equilibrium was never really present (*BC*, 52) and that it was a 'methodological fiction' (ibid., 964), or if he criticised Walras's and Clark's presentation of real prices oscillating around equilibrium (*HEA*, 999, 1000n.), his general approach was to argue for an integrated account of the development process as including both change and equilibrium. In his 'first approximation' to the theory of the business cycle, equilibrium existed at the end of the depression and before the prosperity. In the 'second approximation', when the 'secondary wave' was considered and the cycle was described in four phases, equilibrium conditions were met at two of the inflexion points,[23] namely when the recession leads to depression and when the revival leads to prosperity and a new cycle is supposed to begin.

As previously noted, Schumpeter distinguished between statics and dynamics, as Mill previously did, as two real processes, although he noted that without disturbances the system would be 'static',[24] but that those disturbances necessarily arise from inside the system itself, or that they exist and change the structure of the economy. In other words, the system could, but would not, be static in that sense. In 1908, Schumpeter argued that the central question for 'pure' economics was statics and equilibrium – which surely deserved the approval of Walras – and considered dynamics a marginal phenomenon (*DW*, quoted in Bottomore 1992, 171), despite some rhetorical declarations about dynamics as 'the land of the future' (*DW*, quoted in Swedberg 1991, 29–30). But he changed his opinion.[25]

This clearly indicates the one-sidedness of the previous argument by Rosenberg. Indeed, Schumpeter formed a very early global sketch of his theory, published and argued for it, acknowledging that the Walrasian system of stationary processes and static analysis was 'wrong', namely incomplete and unable to deal with change and development. But, even so, he still considered Walras the main modern economic theorist, the only one to create a science comparable to the achievements of physics and the exact sciences.

The following pages are concerned with this obvious contradiction between the definition of physics as the authoritative model for sciences and the attempt to deny the incorporation of mechanistic influences into the province of economics.

From evolution to evolutionism

Schumpeter insisted all through his work that the concepts of dynamics and statics he was endorsing were ultimately traceable to zoology and not to mechanics, in spite of the evidence, namely the declarations of their creators. But, at the same time, he presented physics, or mechanics, as the standard for science. For instance, after acknowledging Clément Juglar's role in the definition of a theory of the cycle, he concluded that:

> And so we have reached a stage, perhaps for the first time, where facts and problems are before all of us in a clear and in the same light, and where analysis and description can cooperate in something like the spirit of physical science.
>
> (Schumpeter 1927, 287)

For Schumpeter, Walras was certainly the major protagonist in the development of economics in the direction of the rigour of physics. His theoretical system of general equilibrium, the simultaneous system of equations determining all prices and quantities, was described as the perfect analogue for the exact features of physics:

> Walras is in my opinion the greatest of all economists. His system of economic equilibrium, uniting, as it does, the quality of 'revolutionary' creativeness with the quality of classical synthesis, is the only work by an

> economist that will stand comparison with the achievements of theoretical physics.

> (*HEA*, 827)

And:

> It is the outstanding landmark on the road that economics travels toward the status of a rigorous and exact science.

> (Ibid., 829)

Physics was described as a paradigm for sciences only in *HEA*, the last great text of Schumpeter, on which he worked for the last years of his life. Nowhere in his work was there another indication of a different science having this central epistemological role. And physics was also mentioned when Schumpeter needed to present an argument of authority: since those criticising his views did not accept his notion of clusters of innovation, he argued in 1935 that these were postulated by the theory, just as hypotheses were formulated in physics, 'irrespective of what might be adduced for or against their objective truth' (Schumpeter 1935, 6).

Finally, physics was also mentioned in order to present new methods (for example, the impossibility of isolating a phenomenon, the simulation from a model in order to compare the result to the observation, ibid., 3; or the use of simplifying schemata, *HEA*, 14) or to create or incorporate analogies (*BC*, 12, 41).

These three types of instances – physics as the general paradigm, as the authority in science and as the source of pertinent analogies – were present through the whole work of Schumpeter. Yet this did not prevent him from stressing several times what he considered the misleading character of the physical metaphor: 'Analogy with the entirely different problems of physics is much more apt to be misleading than helpful' (*BC*, 32). In the same vein, he criticised Mitchell for his alleged overstatement of experimental procedures under the influence of the early physicist epistemology,[26] or Pareto for his illusions about the application of the method of physics (*TGE*, 189–190). He emphasised the differences between the field of economics and that of physics; since the former is more complex, there is no possibility of experiments,[27] it includes interpretative variables, and the scientist is under pressure to get socially useful results (ibid., 149, 189–190). This is certainly another example of the paradox.

Schumpeter knew that this paradigm dominated the main works of the neoclassicals, from Walras to Pareto and from Edgeworth to Fisher, and that it defined the contours of the marginalist revolution, with the sole and relevant exception of his own teacher, Menger. This is why Schumpeter dealt with this point from the opening pages of *HEA*, considering the general criticism of Hayek – a representative Austrian – of 'scientism', that 'uncritical copying of the methods of mathematical physics in the equally uncritical belief that these methods are of universal application and the peerless example of all scientific activity to follow' (*HEA*, 17). Along his discussion about this point, Schumpeter was ready to accept Hayek's argument against the incorporation of such a 'scientist bias', but argued that this was not a general case in economics and that only words were being transferred from physics.[28] On the other hand, following Schumpeter's argument, there were two essential reasons why physical concepts – 'borrowing words and nothing else' – made their appearance in economics: first, mathematics was developed sooner in physics and exact sciences[29] and, second, the analogies were supposedly very useful for teaching, since students understand a physical analogy more easily than its economic counterpart. The final argument by Schumpeter was that the presence of common concepts and methods only testified that economists and physicists have the same type of brains and act similarly when faced with theoretical problems (*HEA*, 18), and consequently:

> This does not involve any mechanistic, deterministic or other '-istic' errors, or any neglect of the truth that 'to explain' means something different in the natural and in the social sciences, or finally any denial of the implications of the historical character of our subject matter.
>
> (*HEA*, 18)

The whole passage indicates very clearly that, while accepting the general scientific paradigm of positivism and consequently the role of physics both as forerunner of scientific rigour and as a model for pedagogic analogies, Schumpeter resisted the idea that economic concepts and methods were derived from physics. He did so because of the Austrian influence still present in his writings, because he was certainly aware of the uncritical exaggeration of the neoclassical tradition, namely by Fisher, and possibly because his own research indicated that the available physical concepts were unable to encapsulate the economic reality of movement and change. But the author also accepted important exceptions, since some concepts and not only mere words ('equilibrium', 'potential') were incorporated under autonomous contents for each science.

This interpretation accounts for all the instances previously identified: in the general epistemological stance, Schumpeter certainly praised the authority and clarity of physics; but when concrete economic concepts were at stake, he denied any significant influence from physics, even when such a claim was wrong, as the case of the Comtian definition of statics and dynamics, below, will prove.

The argument about the concept of equilibrium is again very useful to illustrate this point. Schumpeter defined equilibrium by the twin properties of existence and stability: 'If the relations … are such as to determine a set of values of the variables that will display no tendency to vary under the sole influence of the facts included in those relations per se, we speak of equilibrium' (*HEA*, 969). Schumpeter immediately denied that this definition was related to physics in any way (ibid., 970). His definition of equilibrium was also presented as the core of the economic science:

> For our system is logically self-contained only if this is the case [being totally endogenously determined]: we can be sure that we understand the nature of economic phenomena only if it is possible to deduce prices and quantities from the data by means of those relations and to prove that no other set of prices and physical quantities is compatible with both the data and the relations. The proof that this is so is the Magna Carta of economic theory as an autonomous science, assuring us that its object is a cosmos and not chaos.
>
> (BC, 41)

In other words, economics became a science after establishing its Magna Carta – the Walrasian system – but, what is still more relevant to the present purpose, equilibrium was defined as the creation of order, derived from a set of variables that exhibit no tendency to create change. Of course, if this was really a 'self-contained process', then the Law of Conservation of Energy could easily be translated into the system and we arrive in the wonderful world of marginalist economics, where all relevant information is included in the system itself. But then Schumpeter added that there was something else, since this real process was nevertheless incomplete: the main argument of *BC* was that there is also another set of endogenous variables, the innovative processes, that adds movement and mutation to this orderly picture. In a word, we have two classes of endogenous variables: those that are well-behaved and those that are unpredictable, which create irreversible processes of change. Equilibrium exists, and so does disequilibrium: the system is intrinsically morphogenetic.

This is why Schumpeter did not follow the entire physical metaphor, although his determination to safeguard the notion of Walrasian equilibrium in the new synthesis also prevented him from avoiding or completely rejecting this metaphor. As a consequence, Schumpeter defined two separate theoretical domains, one where the equilibrium paradigm was used and another where it was not relevant.

Biology and dilettantism

With his detailed discussion of the analogy with physics, Schumpeter proved to be aware of the importance and problems of the metaphoric re-description. This section deals with a body of analogies used in Schumpeter's work, based on the biological concepts that appear in two different frameworks: in the general sense of the development process and in the concrete sense of the analysis of the circular flow. They are obviously very different in nature and in scope.

In *TED*, Schumpeter commented on two comparisons, one with the circular flow and the other with development, and rejected both. First, the circular flow could be conceived of as the process of blood circulation, but no growth and decline were allowed in the case of circular flow, unlike in the case of the organism (*TED*, 1961, 45). Nevertheless, three years later he came back to this topic, acknowledging that even for Quesnay – a physician, writing as an economist – the process of circular flow could not exactly repeat itself every time, since there is a relation between society and the incorporation of energy and materials from nature: 'This point of departure was in itself an obvious one, it was bound to be specially familiar to Quesnay because of the analogy to the nutritional process of organic bodies' (*EDM*, 54–55).

In Schumpeter's system, the analogue for this nutritional process was growth, under the impulsion of capital accumulation and population increase. The equilibrium can therefore be considered either a stationary process or an organic adaptive process (*BC*, 35), but it does not explain the cycle.

Second, Schumpeter argued that the process of development is different from the growth of a tree, since it is not continuous (ibid., 144; the tree metaphor was associated with Smith, Mill and Marshall and rejected by Schumpeter 1951, 233). The cycle – and the whole 'organic' process of capitalist development[30] – should be explained by another phenomenon, that

> process of industrial mutation – if I may use a biological term – that *incessantly* revolutionises (FN: 'Those revolutions are not strictly incessant; they occur in discrete rushes which are separated from each other by spans of comparative quiet') the economic structure from within, *incessantly* destroying the old one, incessantly creating a new one. This process of Creative Destruction is the essential fact about capitalism. It is what capitalism consists in and what every capitalist concern has got to live in.'
>
> (*CSD*, 83, original emphasis)

This is indeed a rather exceptional statement since, as a general case, Schumpeter also rejected in the strongest terms any attempt to incorporate a biological metaphor into economics.[31] In 1911, he wrote:

> Here [in the class of 'metaphysical' tendencies], too, belong all kinds of evolutionary thought that center in Darwin – at least if this means no more than reasoning by analogy.... But the evolutionary idea is now discredited in our field, especially with historians and ethnologists, for still another reason. To the reproach of unscientific and extra-scientific mysticism that now surrounds the 'evolutionary' ideas, is added that of dilettantism. With all the hasty generalisations in which the word 'evolution' plays a part, many of us lost patience. We must get away from such things.
>
> (*TED*, 1961, 43)

Almost 40 years later, Schumpeter still held the same opinion and expressed it in the same terms. Writing in *HEA* about the 1870–1914 period, he emphatically described biological evolutionism as 'a field infected by ideological bias and by dilettantism to an extent that surpasses anything that even we economists are accustomed to' (*HEA*, 788). In spite of this, Schumpeter considered Darwin's *Origin of the Species* to be an important scientific achievement, comparable to the definition of the heliocentric system (ibid., 445, 445n.), and his historical sketch of the previous biological theories to be a crucial piece for the sociology of science, but he did not indicate any possible kind of influence of theses texts on social sciences: his sympathetic references were probably mainly due to ceremonial reasons. Nevertheless, it is clear that his purpose was to attack the influential and wide-spread Spencerian type of evolutionism, which combined 'naive laissez-faire' with a simplified version of Darwinism, leading to conclusions such as the 'silly' suggestion of abandoning sanitary regulations or public systems of education and health (ibid., 773). Schumpeter also cared to inform the reader of the introduction to *BC* that his assumption about the organicity of economic processes did not at all imply being a supporter of laissez-faire, the Spencerian type of translation of Darwinian competition (*BC*, vi). Therefore, the concept of 'industrial mutation' was rather exceptional and carefully chosen in order to emphasise the non-equilibrium properties of development and evolution. In this, Schumpeter was indeed closer to Marx than to Walras.[32]

Statics versus dynamics: positivist evolutionism

As previously indicated, the main reason for Schumpeter's feelings about the utility of the Walrasian system was its static nature, described as the first rigorous and yet partial analysis of the economy. This was considered a limitation rather than a mistake, since the dynamic side could always be added to this first picture of the theoretical system, as the 'classics' intended to do:

> The main concern of the classical system is to determine these constant rates, in other words to investigate the political economy in a state of equilibrium.... Yet this did not mean that the 'classics' followed the natural sciences either in form or in content. Thus they intended at first to present the 'static view' of the economy to which were later added certain statements about evolutionary tendencies – a 'dynamic view'. These expressions, as well as the actual separation of the two views, were introduced into economics by John Stuart Mill who derived the former from Comte.
>
> (*EDM*, 1914, 94)

All through his work, Schumpeter developed the same argument: since Stuart Mill took from Comte the distinction between statics and dynamics, and Comte was inspired by the zoologist De Blainville, the ultimate source of this metaphor was zoology and not mechanics. This was his argument in 1914, as indicated, but also in 1934 (Schumpeter 1935, 6), in 1939 (*BC*, 37) and still in his last writings, in *HEA*:

> Adopting, as he [Comte] tells us, the terminology of the zoologist H. de Blainville, he called the former [phenomena] Statics and the latter Dynamics. J.S. Mill, the author who introduced these terms into economic theory, was well acquainted with Comte's thought, and it is natural to assume that he took them from Comte, though he did not say so. If this was the case, then Mill was wrong in speaking of a 'happy generalisation' of a 'mathematical phrase'. Since many people who failed to appreciate the importance of that distinction have tried to stigmatise it as an illegitimate derivative of a mechanistic way of thinking, it is time to state the fact that, so far as there is sense at all in talking about borrowing – as regards to words that is, not as regards the distinction itself which forces itself upon us in any case – the ultimate lender was not mechanics but zoology.
>
> (*HEA*, 417)

This argument is historically imprecise, theoretically misleading and therefore wrong.

Comte and Blainville

The relationship between Comte and Blainville was complex and discontinuous. From 1829 to 1832 Comte attended a course on general physiology taught by 'his friend' Blainville at the Faculty of Sciences in Paris (Comte 1970 [1839], Vol. 3, 209). Blainville was by then the main disciple and successor of Lamarck, and his work was well known, even if it did not make any impression on the future development of biology. Yet it is very probable that it did influence the preparation of Comte's *Cours de Philosophie Positive*, which was to be published seven years after the end of that course on physiology. But shortly afterwards there was a violent rupture between the two men: Comte accused Blainville of 'brusque decadence' and 'fall' (Comte 1970 [1839], Vol. 7, 571; also 665), since he subordinated his vision of organic evolution to a theological principle. By that time, Mill's *Principles* had already been published (1848), and his correspondence with Comte had developed for a long period (the first letter by Mill was sent in November 1841; Mill, 1841, CW, Vol. 13, 488).

It is certain that the distinction between statics and dynamics was central to Comte's work, and Blainville possibly had some influence on it. But this influence was probably felt mainly as a confirmation of Comte's vision, which was by itself defined according to the new trends of the science of the time and quite well established. Comte argued precisely this point, saying that both he and Blainville were inspired by D'Alembert, who treated mathematically the problem of reducing dynamics and statics to the same status (Comte 1970

[1839], Vol. 8, 442). And this was the conception inherited by Comte, who argued that progress should be subordinated to the static conception of order, abstracting from time and representing the 'fundamental unit toward which tends our nature'[33] (Comte 1970 [1839], Vol. 4, 3).

As Comte argued extensively in the book, which was so influential in Mill's work, he derived his concepts of statics and dynamics from 'rational mechanics', treating the static case as a particular form of the dynamic one (Comte 1970 [1839] Vol. 1, 480, 482, 491, 565). Of course, the physical metaphor makes possible this derivation of a static system as a particular case of the dynamics, but the biological metaphor does not, this crucial difference separating the concrete use of both inspirations.

From this conception followed that the 'social organism' was to be treated simultaneously from the point of view of statics (the fundamental nature) and dynamics (its evolution; ibid., Vol. 4, 430, 498; Vol. 8, 1). In any case, progress should be subordinated to order and dynamics to statics (ibid., Vol. 8, 2; Vol. 9, 3). Blainville's and Lamarck's general views of zoological evolution supported this approach, since they were characterised by a strictly gradualist and therefore mechanical evolution through a defined and teleological scale of animals: the 'natural' evolution of the animal world is precisely the analogue of Comte's account of the stages of thought (theological, metaphysical, scientific), which was the basis of his theory of history.

The conclusion is by now obvious: the Comtian linkage of Mill's distinction between statics and dynamics did not lead to any evolutionary conception but at most to a pre-evolutionary mechanical and teleological zoology, or more exactly to the generally admitted scientism of the epoch. Furthermore, this leads to a conception of the relation between dynamics and statics that states that both processes exist in nature and are closely related. Following this intuition and in spite of Schumpeter's claims, mechanics would rule economics.

In this sense, the 'classical' programme formulated by Schumpeter and consisting of static analyses, to which dynamical tools should be added later on, closely corresponded to Comte's programme. Schumpeter himself accepted this programme, and this was the substantial reason for his high praise of Walras. In this sense, he could not emancipate himself from positivism.

John Stuart Mill

Comte strongly influenced the evolution of John Stuart Mill, and this was indeed the main reason for the latter's rupture with the Benthamite School (Mill 1841, CW, Vol. 13, 488). It was, in fact, from Comte that Mill drew the distinction between statics and dynamics, the first being the study of the 'conditions of existence of the society' or the 'stationary society' and the second the study of 'the laws of its continuous movement' or the 'progressive state of wealth' (Mill 1841, Vol. 13, 695–696, 1882, 88–89). Both types of analyses were considered to correspond to real processes, in this sense to 'natural' processes (ibid., 100). In other words, Mill interpreted the Comtian conceptions of statics and dynamics as two simultaneous approaches of reality, order, which subsumes motion, and dynamics, which includes statics: the progression of wealth should also lead to a final stationary society (1848, 746f.).

But, as Mill argued in his *Autobiography*, the acceptance of Comte's gradualist law of social evolution was compatible with the pervasive and dominant scientism and with his own previous vision, which was inspired by physics[34] and not by biology[35]:

> This doctrine harmonised with my existing notions, to which it seemed to give a scientific shape. I already regarded the methods of physical science as the proper models....
>
> (Mill 1841, *CW*, Vol. 1, 173; also 75)

It is very important to note that Schumpeter acknowledged and specifically stressed this passage in *HEA*, in order to underrate it and to defend his previous interpretation:

> Thus, most economists, J.B. Say and J.S. Mill in particular, thought altogether too much of the analogy with the physical sciences, which the latter declared to be the 'proper model' for economic theory – a point for critics to fasten on but actually irrelevant, since no practical use was made of it.... We have already observed that the introduction of the terms Statics and Dynamics does not involve any such use, that is, any borrowing of a method from any physical science. Nor do economists borrow from mechanics when they employ the term equilibrium any more than does a bookkeeper who 'balances' an account.
>
> (*HEA*, 537)

Schumpeter's insistence on the 'zoological missing link' of the concepts contradicts his consideration, in the same *HEA*, presenting physics as the most exact and developed of all sciences and explaining his lack of interest in the biological metaphor. What is essential for the moment is that this argument is wrong: the ultimate inspiration for Mill's distinction between statics and dynamics was not zoology but an extreme positivist version of nineteenth-century scientism, inspired by mechanics, which considered evolution to be a special case of a gradualist and deterministic process. Mill, the 'classics' and Schumpeter received and accepted the *vision* that both static and dynamic processes are to be found in nature and that statics is a special case of dynamics.

This argument is relevant to the comprehension of Schumpeter's acceptance and reverence of Walras, and in fact to the definition of his own research programme with the aim of completing or constructing the missing dynamic side of Walras, without noticing any incompatibility or contradiction in this process.

Schumpeter's evolutionism

Schumpeter's evolutionism was not based on Darwinism or, in general, the biological metaphor, which only played a minor role, if any, in his system. But it was still an evolutionary conception, since it was based upon two central concepts: first, the economy was defined as an 'organic'[36] whole, propelled by a process of development with mutations and, second, this defined a non-mechanistic and historical view of capitalism as creation and destruction. Since the concept of 'mutation', that change arising from innovation in the core of the system, was previously discussed, this section will now turn to the concept of the organic system.

Here is how Schumpeter presented the concept, criticising the biological analogy:

> In the first place, we notice the idea that society, being an 'organic' system and not a 'mechanical' one, can be fruitfully analyzed in terms of an analogy with biological organisms such as the human body.... But the obvious puerility of this idea must not blind us to the fact that emphasis upon the 'organic nature' of the economic process may be but the means of conveying an eminently sound methodological principle – as it was, for instance, with Marshall. Theorists – especially of the 'planning' type – often indulge in the deplorable practice of deriving 'practical' results from a few functional relations between a few economic aggregates in utter disregard of the fact that such analytical set-ups are congenitally incapable of taking account of deeper things, the more subtle relations that cannot be weighted and measured.... 'Organic' considerations are perhaps the most obvious antidote – though in themselves hardly an adequate one – against such uncivilised procedure.
>
> (*HEA*, 788–789)

Besides the polemic bias, this is a clear indication of the nature of Schumpeter's thought: organic considerations were supposed to be essential in order to avoid the useless biological analogies and hence to provide an overall method for the economic inquiry: the solution of a system of equations was unable to represent complex or 'more subtle' relations. This explains his approach to causality in economics (*BC*, 7) and to the analysis of its features (Schumpeter 1949, 313). Evolutionism, then, was for Schumpeter simply the consideration of organic evolution in real time, or of historical and irreversible processes of change:

> Social phenomena constitute a unique process in historic time, and incessant and irreversible changes are their most obvious characteristic. If by

Evolutionism we mean not more than recognition of this fact, then all reasoning about social phenomena must be either evolutionary in itself or else bare upon evolution. Here, however, evolutionism is to mean more than this. One may recognise the fact without making it the pivot of one's thought and the guiding principle of one's method.... [James Mill's] various systems were not evolutionary in the sense that his thought in any of those fields turned upon evolution. And it is this that shall be the criterion of evolutionism for us, both as regards philosophy ... and as regards any 'scientific field'.

(*HEA*, 435–436)

It is possible to conclude that Schumpeter defined the social process as an intrinsic dynamic disturbance of equilibrium through the creation of novelty – the innovative mutation – and this was precisely what defined his evolutionary framework. It included stationary processes of equilibrium, the place of Walras, but also forces and processes moving towards disequilibrium, the place of Marx. And it was organic, since both processes were considered to be compatible and since all the relevant variables were considered to be endogenous to the system, which itself generates movement and change. Moreover, this particular combination was the very specificity of economics, and so Schumpeter believed that his general and historical approach was the only one able to integrate both the statics of general equilibrium and the dynamics of disequilibrating forces: in a synthesis, the unscientific bias of the physical and the biological analogies would be prevented, since those analogies took the part as the whole and thus developed dilettante or simplistic views.

This dilemma was obvious on several occasions in Schumpeter's work. The cold reception of *BC* in the scientific community was certainly one of the indications of the increasing difficulty for Schumpeter to maintain his profile as a mainstream economist while developing what was considered extravagant or esoteric research. Since Schumpeter had been the chairman of the founding meeting of the Econometric Society – he was at the time of the publication of *BC* its vice-president and was to become its president the next year – he was as a consequence expected to contribute to quantitative economics and to the mathematical formalism he praised so often. He did not and, in fact, in the whole scientific community only Frisch received the book with enthusiasm (Swedberg 1991, 271n.).

A couple of years after that book, *CSD* turned the tide and became the bestselling success in Schumpeter's career, although this also proved that he could be more read and discussed outside academia than among his own peers. Paradoxically again, this proved that the general public could understand or discuss his doomsday predictions, but the economists were not ready to understand their wrongs and the danger of taming innovation under the successful giant bureaucratic corporations and the interventionist state.

This methodological indication, combined with the definition of economics as the study of irreversible processes of change, plus the organic vision of evolutionary societies, defines the main conclusion of this section: since Schumpeter incorporated some essential traits of the historical view of economics as he invaded the new territory of historical mutation in the economies, Schumpeter was not a neoclassical economist; but at the same time he was not able to cease considering himself to be one, since he did not wholly reject neoclassical economics, as he was not ready to emancipate himself from the equilibrium paradigm and even tried to incorporate it along with the historical forces of mutation. This was Schumpeter's Paradox, as it was met in the previous discussion about the role of the Walrasian system in his brand of economics.

Cycles and crises

Three main points should be emphasised here. First, this schema considered the stationary process or the equilibrium conditions to be a special case of the dynamic movement, specifically that corresponding to the discrete points where the movement is null (*BC*, 70–71, 963). This quite closely matches the mechanical Mill-Comte definition of the distinction between 'statics' and 'dynamics', and thus of the possibility of conducting a static analysis, the 'bare bones of economic logic', 'cleaning the ground for rigorous analysis' (*BC*, 68).

Second, the existence of equilibrium was stated, and its stability was defined as the real processes of absorption of change and of disturbance:

> The thing that matters to us is nevertheless this tendency [towards equilibrium] considered as an actual force, and not the mere existence of ideal equilibrium points of reference.... We wish to distinguish definite periods in which the system embarks upon an excursion away from equilibrium and equally definite periods in which it draws towards equilibrium.
>
> (*BC*, 69–70)

Or also, without room for doubt:

> Common sense tells us that this mechanism for establishing or re-establishing equilibrium is not a figment devised as an exercise in the pure logic of economics but actually operative in the reality around us.
>
> (*BC*, 47, in the same sense also 56)

In this sense, the mechanism of equilibration provided the resistance to change in the economic system, namely the defence of established business and institutional traditions: it was the creation of order subsuming the creation of novelty,[37] for example, imitation restoring equilibrium after innovation. Equilibrium or order would be the moment of the formation of prices, while development or disorder is the evolutionary process: in Schumpeter's emphatic words, 'fluctuations must be fluctuations around something' (*BC*, 69).

Third, this did not imply that equilibrium was considered to be the desirable situation. In the first approximation, it was considered to be the situation where the promises of the boom were fulfilled, that is, where the availability of consumption goods increased for the whole community (*TED*, 1961, 161). But in the second approximation this was certainly more complex, since the system was described as in permanent turmoil, and its change – the disequilibrium processes – was the only form of progress. From this point of view, Schumpeter clearly opposed the 'classics' and the general equilibrium paradigm and even condemned their incapacity to incorporate real economic evolution: as he stressed in *EDM*, at the very same time that the first modern industrial crises were exploding, the 'classicals' still argued for Say's Law and rejected the theoretical possibility of disequilibrium, against all easily available evidence (*EDM*, 150). The main achievement of Juglar, by contrast, was precisely to define a new agenda for research indicating the problem, describing it empirically and presenting an explanation (Schumpeter 1927, 287).

In other words, the tendency towards novelty that moves the economic system forward depends on the ability of the entrepreneur to challenge equilibrium, as otherwise the economic agents with no entrepreneurial spirit would only be 'miserable figures':

> What a miserable figure he is, this economic subject who is always looking so anxiously for an equilibrium. He has no ambition and no entrepreneurial spirit; in brief, he is without force and life.
>
> (*DW*, quoted in Swedberg 1991, 29)

In Schumpeter's theory of the cycle, the motion of the system was analysed under a steady-state representation, then the possibility of change was introduced as an independent and separable dimension, since both correspond to social processes that can be isolated. In other words, Walras indicated a convenient approach to discussing one of the processes (*BC*, 47), but this was not enough, since evolution should also be explained: for Walras the needs were given, while for Schumpeter the real economic processes created new needs and led to deep transformations. The Schumpeterian research programme consisted of the bold task of providing the dynamic counterpart of the Walrasian schema in order to create a general theory.

This implied that some sort of logical separability was possible between the problems of growth and cycle, since growth was reduced to the monotonic trend of capital accumulation through savings and to population increase, both being added to an equilibrating process. Of course, this did not solve the statistical problem of the assessment of the trend and cycle, since he does not define a real trend of equilibrium – only a number of discrete equilibrium points, two for each cycle – and since the cyclical process by itself displaces the centre of gravitation upwards.

And, moreover, the three-cycle schema implied that the equilibria of the shorter cycles were defined in the artificial representation of the trend line of the larger cycles, and that the single true equilibrium occurred at the very beginning of a Kondratiev wave, when prosperity was to commence and the equilibria of the three types of cycles coincided. All other points are 'neighbourhoods of equilibrium', therefore unstable due to a new very structural reason: the dynamics of evolution in the larger cycles over-determined the shorter ones even when they were in the neighbourhood of equilibrium in their own motion. This was a form of representation of the feedback mechanisms in action in real economies but added singular difficulties to the mathematical treatment of the model – and Schumpeter certainly had these in mind when he accepted that his theories were very hostile to mathematical formalism.[38]

The end of capitalism or simply stagnation

The final lines that Schumpeter wrote or lectured in 1949 (he would die at the beginning of 1950) in which he again discussed the theme of 1942, the victory of socialism, all have a coincidental symbolic and challenging meaning. That is what I discuss in the final section.

His last public attendance was replacing Mitchell at a 1949 NBER conference on business cycles, which became a skirmish for a major confrontation between the empirical economists and the econometricians (that was part of the debate that came to be known to be about 'measurement without theory')[39] and, to the astonishment of some of his colleagues, he defended a middle ground incorporating non-measurable historical features in order to understand economic evolution. But in writing, his last words were dedicated to adding to *CSD* or to discussing the danger of stagnationism, both in theory and deeds. That was the case of his last chapter of *History of Economic Analysis*, which he left unfinished and untyped, dedicated to 'Keynes and modern macroeconomics', and that of the very last paper he wrote, the 'March into socialism' (Schumpeter, 1950), which is reproduced at the end of the editions of *CSD*, since it prolongs the argument of the book.

Schumpeter's bitter opposition and envy in relation to Keynes is a well-known fact,[40] and for instance in *CSD* he was not shy to claim his surprise at the 'astounding fact that the theory in question [Keynes's] is not simply laughed out of court', for it only reproduces a 'salesman mentality' (*CSD*, 394). As for what matters for this last section of the chapter, both these final papers address the question of stagnation; this is what will be briefly discussed.

Keynes' *General Theory* constitutes the 'greatest literary success of our epoch', Schumpeter concedes, although he points out the self-centred character he attributes to the author: 'he felt himself to have led economics out of 150 years of error into the land of definitive truth' (*HEA*, 1170, 1172). One of the points of this revelation would be the curse of stagnation, as 'Keynes must be credited or debited, as the case may be, with the fatherhood of modern stagnationism' (ibid., 1172). Stagnation, as the result of the fading out of the inventive and innovative characteristics emerging out of competition, was part of Schumpeter's argument about the danger of the collapse of capitalism. But he charged Keynes, no less than the author of the 'greatest literary success' in economics, of leading the camp of the stagnation hypothesis. This polemic bias, a common feature of Schumpeter, imposed on him a suffering position, since he accepted that, although rejecting Keynes's ideas, this might prove right, even if for the wrong reasons.

The stagnation theory itself was developed, according to *HEA*, 'under the brilliant leadership of Professor Alvin H. Hansen, who amplified and expanded the doctrine of the mature or stagnating economy in part on different grounds than Keynes', referring to Hansen's 1938 speech as the newly elected President of the American Economic Association.[41] And, although Schumpeter disagrees both in theory and in history, he is ready to accept the danger, since 'capitalist evolution tends to peter out – i.e. to settle down into a condition that might be just as well described as "stagnation" – because the modern state may crush or paralyze its motive forces.'[42]

In his 'March into socialism', Schumpeter concludes on an even more sombre note:

> Marx was wrong in his diagnosis of the manner in which capitalist society would break down; he was not wrong in the prediction that it would break down eventually. The Stagnationists are wrong in their diagnosis of the reasons why the capitalist process would stagnate; they may turn out to be right in their prognosis that it will stagnate – with sufficient help from the public sector.
>
> (*CSD*, 430)

It is not clear from this text why Schumpeter thought this could happen, and why he matched the perspectives of the end of capitalism and that of its stagnation – which are obviously different. Apparently, the wrongdoings of the state could precipitate either one of the alternatives, either automatising innovations (the 'motive forces' of capitalism) or imposing stagnation (from whatever governmental misjudgement or misconduct).

Leaving aside other interpretations of the last sentences of this 'March into socialism', we may find in Schumpeter's previous discussions on stagnation, or equilibrium, some hunches on what he may have thought in his last weeks, as expressed by this unfinished paper.

In particular, Schumpeter's vision on this permanent tendency towards the dislocation of the centre of gravity of the system and the complex interaction of the different cycles account for an original form of instability, created by the system itself. Schumpeter's theory was a system of self-generating complexity and instability, where the equilibrium concept really played only a subsidiary role. But, as I argued before, Schumpeter was not prepared to break with the Walrasian half of his theory, for philosophical rather than for theoretical economic reasons, and this is part of his paradox. The rationale for this refusal can be discovered in his general view of science and the definition of his own place in economic theory.

This leads to a complex and paradoxical position: for in some cases the equilibrating properties and even the stasis of equilibrium are presented as real features of the real economies and in other cases as simply figments of imagination; for in some cases a stationary case or stagnation is possible, although essentially disturbed by the motive forces of growth through frequent innovation; and, as in *CSD*, in some cases the monopolies may propel inventiveness, as they have the means for research, whereas in most cases the bureaucratic management and the lack of self-interested motivation that the owners used to have would condemn the firms to havoc. The contradictory picture emerging from this landscape is that there is no stagnation, given innovation; but then successful capitalism, generating big anonymous concentrations of capital, may tame innovation and therefore create threatening conditions for the end of capitalism itself. Therefore, what are missing in this picture are articulated economic and sociological analyses, in order to understand the balance of forces for change and for conservation, and that endeavour was the original promise of *Capitalism, Socialism and Democracy*. He did not deliver on that agenda.

An author frequently misread by Schumpeter, Michal Kalecki, provided an explanation for this curse of stagnation that persists as one of the most powerful analyses of the contradictions of late capitalism. For Kalecki, the degree of market power is crucial for establishing wages and profits and therefore both profitability and accumulation. In this framework, aggregate demand is a consequence of the structure of the distribution of income, and the market power itself is influenced by the social relationship of forces, as we have a political business cycle. The social strategies matter in the Kaleckian analysis. Furthermore, technical innovation moves competition and defines the possible entry of new firms, challenging the market power of those already established. Finally, financing plays a role, as 'the size of the firm thus appears to be circumscribed by the amount of its entrepreneurial capital both through its influence on the capacity to borrow capital and through its effect on the degree of risk' (Kalecki 1971, 106).

Josef Steindl pursued this line of investigation on the business cycle, namely in his *Maturity and Stagnation in American Capitalism* (1952), discussing the role of finance, debt and capacity utilisation, hypothesising that it is accumulation that leads to investment. The oligopoly profits, then, may create the conditions for stagnation, as

> the internal accumulation therefore tends to exceed the amount required for the expansion of capital equipment in these industries. The flow of the 'surplus' funds into other industries is impeded by the additional effort required for entering new lines which weakens the incentive to invest for the owners of these funds.
>
> (Ibid., 55)

Steindl points out that 'the conclusion is that the maldistribution of profits and internal savings consequent on the growth of oligopoly will have a depressing effect on the rate of real capital accumulation' (ibid., 127), and therefore

> stagnation didn't come over-night. Preceding it there had been a long process of secular change, which passed almost unnoticed, because memories are short and comparisons over long periods are difficult to make. Hardly anybody during the 'New Era' was aware of the fact that the annual rate of growth of business capital then was only half of what it had been thirty years earlier.
>
> (Ibid., 166)

Although technical innovation plays a role in this model, the introduction of market power and the credit system lead the author to a view diverging from Schumpeter and proposing another interpretation of the dangers of stagnation.

A curious question is: would Schumpeter, had he lived some more years and attentive as he was to the problem of credit creation, have developed his theory on the stalemate of giant corporations and modern capitalism in this sense? But, of course, we cannot have the answer for that. In any case, later historical events proved that innovation was, as Schumpeter intuited, a major driving force for change and evolution, as it also proved that stagnation may emerge in spite of flows of new technical capabilities, as Schumpeter feared.

In any case, here we have the paradox and eventually the justification for this book and the different interpretations of *Capitalism, Socialism and Democracy* you are offered: Schumpeter is one of the most modern of all economists because he felt, studied and discussed contradictions and tensions in the evolution of the developed economies. In that sense, Allen is right again: he had a paradoxical life and career, produced paradoxical ideas and books, had a career of failure which was, as a whole, a great success.

Acknowledgements

I thank Leonardo Burlamaqui and other reviewers for their comments, while remaining solely responsible for this chapter. Some of the material of this chapter was discussed in previous works of the author.

Notes

1 Schumpeter's book are indicated, for simplicity, as *DW* (1908, *Das Wesen und der Hauptinthalt der Theoretischen Nationalokonomik*), *TED* (1911, *Theory of Economic Development*, using the revised edition of 1926), *EDM* (1914, *Economic Doctrine and Method: An Historical Sketch*), *BC* (1939, *Business Cycles*), *CSD* (1942, *Capitalism, Socialism and Democracy*), *HEA* (1954, *History of Economic Analysis*, posthumous), and *TGE* (*Ten Great Economists: From Marx to Keynes*, posthumous reprint of essays).

2 Schumpeter to Frisch, 25 February 1933. All letters are quoted either from the Schumpeter Archive at Harvard or from the Frisch Archive at Oslo University.

3 Schumpeter to Haberler, 20 March 1933.

4 Schumpeter to Day, 2 May 1933.

5 It is fair to say that none of his closer students rallied around the Nazis and that his former secretary and mistress in Germany, Maria Stockel Bicanski, joined the underground. The Nazis shot her.

6 Schumpeter's last years were marked by long periods of depression, probably motivated by the turn of world events, especially World War II, which was destroying Europe, and certainly by the dramatic loss of his second wife and child in 1926 (Allen 1991, Vol. 1, 236). Unlike him, for instance, his friend and colleague Ragnar Frisch was a committed socialist whose political views stood opposite to Schumpeter's, and he suffered for his choices as he spent a year in a concentration camp as the Nazis invaded Norway. Yet, these differences neither prevented nor affected their life-long relationship. (As one reviewer noted, both Swedberg and McCraw share a less critical interpretation of these remarks and argue Schumpeter never had sympathies for the Nazis).

7 Louçã, 2007, for a detailed account of these discussions.

8 Frisch to Schumpeter, 12 November 1932.

9 Schumpeter to Frisch, 3 December 1932.

10 Frisch to Schumpeter, 11 January 1933.

11 Schumpeter to Cowles, 6 May 1937. In another episode, and while Schumpeter was quarrelling with Frisch over the nomination of Marschak, Keynes had asked his opinion about the suitability of Emil Lederer, a German economist, for the job of correspondent of the *Economic Journal*. Schumpeter advised against him:

> Now you have asked about him I find it much easier to do so: he is a party man of a type which obeys orders without asking a question. And in all matters which can be brought into any relation at all with politics he is absolutely unable to see except through party glasses. I hope you will believe me if I say that it is not his belonging to the socialistic party which caused my qualms. I should have felt exactly the same difficulty about any other strong party man who reacted on the party type in this particular manner.
>
> (Schumpeter to Keynes, 3 December 1932)

This tends to suggest that the political stance (Lederer was a member of the Social-Democratic Party in Germany) was more valued by Schumpeter than any other criterion.

12 It is also fair to say that this was not the end of the story: later on, when Marschak could not find a suitable job, Schumpeter wrote letters of recommendation to Columbia (12 March 1939) and to Berkeley (6 April 1939).

13 Schumpeter to Mitchell, 19 April 1933.

14 Schumpeter to Day, 2 May 1933.

15 As the reader will notice, my conclusion and interpretation in this matter differ from those of other authors in this book.

16 Samuelson was one of those who noted that Schumpeter loved to take the 'unpopular side' in disputes (Samuelson 1951, 49–50, 50n.).

17 Schumpeter indicates that he had introduced, since 1912, the concept and importance of innovation for economic analysis (ibid., 292). More on this in the next section.

18 He states rather strongly that 'practically every nonsense that has ever been said about capitalism has been championed by some professed economist' (*CSD*, 144). The cold reception to his magnum opus, the previous book, *Business Cycles*, certainly did not promote his sympathies towards the academic economic communities.

19 Schumpeter never allowed a new edition of the book, of which only 1,000 copies were printed in this edition (and which was reprinted only in 1970 in Germany)

and did not even take a copy with him when leaving Europe for the USA in 1932. He never explained the reasons for the rejection of this book (Swedberg 1991, 30).

20 This gave him a very peculiar position in the economics of Austria. The 1908 book emphasised the importance of Pareto and Walras and Schumpeter's distance in relation to Austrian economics (Witt 1993, XIII). Witt explained this feature by his early wishes of getting a specific standing: 'It is no secret, of course, that Schumpeter wanted to achieve a standing of his own and thus tended to distance himself from standard Austrian positions from the very beginning' (Witt 1995, 84). Nevertheless, he was clearly on the 'theoretical' or marginalist side: in 1906 Schumpeter published his first two papers on those lines. One was a paper on the role of mathematics ('pure theory') in economics, where he approvingly quoted Jevons: 'If Economics is to be a science at all, it must be a mathematical one' (in Allen 1991, Vol. 1, 56). The second one will be dealt with later on.

21 The reason why Schumpeter waited 28 years to describe this important meeting – why he did not do it in the biographic article about Walras the following year, or in 1911 when presenting his research, or yet in 1914 when arguing about the history of economic method, and did it in a preface to a book which was only accessible to Japanese readers at the time – was never explained, but it is certainly a curious detail. The reason why he did so in 1937, just when he had finished the writing of *Business Cycles*, is nevertheless clear: by that time, the development of his system of thought had shocked several times with the limitations of the static analysis and the stationary Walrasian processes, as *BC* explicitly acknowledged.

22 Schumpeter's concept of capital was defined as a flexible resource, distinct from the technical structure of the production process (Oackley 1990, 38). It belongs to the circular flow, and is 'that part of the social product of preceding economic periods which maintains the production of the current period' (*EDM*, 54). Thus, there are two sources of accumulation, one being the circular flow and another the development process, which is moved by innovation.

23 Thus, the upper and lower turning points, traditionally the centre of the polemics about causality in cycle theory, were not the main concern of Schumpeter.

24 In the first edition of *TED*, Schumpeter used the distinction 'circular flow'/'development'; in the second edition (1926), these were replaced by statics/ dynamics. But, from 1934, as indicated in the preface to the English edition of *TED*, 'in deference to Professor Frisch', and also in *BC*, Schumpeter used the distinction between static and dynamic *forms of analysis*, and stationary or development *processes in nature* (Schumpeter 1939, 6).

25 While preparing his *TED*, Schumpeter summarised his views:

> First, the economic processes divide into two different and also in practice clearly discernible classes: static and dynamic. Second, the latter constitutes the pure economic evolution, that is, those changes in the model of the economy which arise from itself. Third, the economic evolution is essentially a disturbance of the static equilibrium of the economy. Fourth, this disturbance provokes a reaction in the static masses of the economy, namely a movement towards a new state of equilibrium.
>
> (Schumpeter 1910, quoted in Andersen 1994, 41)

26 The criticism did not challenge the importance of the physical analogies, but rather its general implication that Schumpeter feared could launch a new and useless Methodenstreit:

> on those few and well-timed occasions when he is looking for formal analogy to the procedure of physical science, he seems to overstate the importance of the experimental, and to understate the importance of the theoretical side of their work.
>
> (Schumpeter 1930, 152)

27 At least once, Schumpeter concluded that the impossibility of experimentation in economics might suggest another procedure also copied from physics, where such impossibility is sometimes the case: a model should be defined, in order to generate a series and then to compare it to the real observations (Schumpeter, 1935, 3). This suggested some form of proof by simulation.

28   As regards the question of principle, there cannot be the slightest doubt that Hayek is right … in holding that the borrowing by economists of any method on the sole ground that it has been successful somewhere else is inadmissible…. Unfortunately this is not the real question. We have to ask what constitutes 'borrowing' before we can proceed to ask what constitutes illegitimate borrowing…. Similarly, the concepts and procedures of 'higher' mathematics have indeed been first developed in connection with the physicist's problems, but this does not mean that there is anything specifically 'physicalist' about this particular kind of language. But it also holds for some of the general concepts of physics, such as equilibrium potential or oscillator, or statics and dynamics, which turn up of themselves in economic analysis just as do systems of equations: what we borrow when we use, for example, the concept of an 'oscillator' is a word and nothing else.

(*HEA*, 17–18)

29 In another place in *HEA*, Schumpeter argued again:

Finally, the reader should also observe that the conceptual devices sketched have nothing to do with any similar ones that may be in use in the physical sciences…. Since the physical and mechanics in particular were so much ahead of economics in matters of technique, these conceptual devices were consciously defined by physicists before they were by economists so that the average educated person knows them from mechanics before he makes the acquaintance in economics, and hence is apt to suspect that they were illegitimately borrowed from mechanics. Second, such devices being unfamiliar in a field where a looser conceptualisation prevailed, some economists, I. Fisher in particular, thought it a good idea to convey their meaning to the untutored mind by way of the mechanical analogy. But this is all.

(*HEA*, 965). Is this all?

30 In a letter written in the early 1940s, Schumpeter argued that the organic nature of his thought was responsible for the difficulty of formalisation: 'there is nothing in my structures that has not a living piece of reality behind it. This is not an advantage in every respect. It makes, for instance, my theories so refractory to mathematical formulations' (quoted in Andersen 1994, 2).

31 This 'biological term' was used for the first time in 1941, in the Spanish preface to *TED* (Schumpeter 1944, 15).

32 Schumpeter's main argument was that the nature of the economic reality was a disequilibrating process, just as Marx conceived it (*HEA*, 77, 774n.; *CSD*, 83). In the Japanese preface, this was indicated when he argued that Marx was, with Walras, the main source of his thought, and that unlike the latter, he discussed dynamical processes of change.

33 Marshall criticised Comte's distinction between order and progress, equivalent to that distinction between statics and dynamics, in the 1907 preface to the Principles (Marshall 1907 in 1890, 47–48). Schumpeter's attitude was consistently different: more on it later on.

34 Mill fully assumed the importance of the physical metaphor for the definition of the proper method in sciences:

Now Induction is mainly finding the causes of effects; and in endeavouring to give an account of the manner of tracing causes and effects in the physical sciences, I soon saw that in the more perfect of those sciences we ascend, by generalisation from particular instances to the tendencies of causes considered singly, and then reason downward from those separate tendencies, to determine the action of the same causes when combined.... My practice being to study abstract principles in the best concrete instances I could find, the Composition of Forces, in Dynamics, occurred to me as the most complete of the logical process I was investigating.

Nevertheless, Mill was aware that the principle of the addition of causal implications could not be extended to all sciences:

On examining what the mind does when it applies the principle of Composition of Forces, I found that it performs a simple act of addition. It adds the separate effect of the one cause to the separate effect of the other, and puts down the sum of the separate effects as the joint effect. But is it a legitimate process? In dynamics and in the other branches of mathematical physics it is; but in some other cases, as in chemistry, it is not.

(Mill, 1841, *CW*, Vol. 1, 166)

35 Mill studied Darwin's *On the Origin of Species* and was impressed by the achievements of evolutionist biology, but considered it to provide no more than a fascinating hypothesis. In an 1860 letter, he wrote: 'It [Darwin's book] far surpasses my expectations. Though he cannot be said to have proved the truth of his doctrine, he does seem to have proved that it may be true' (Mill, 1841, *CW*, Vol. 15, 695). And nine years later he wrote in another letter:

Darwin has found (to speak Newtonially) a *vera causa*, and has shown that it is capable of accounting for vastly more than had been supposed; beyond that, it is but the indication of what may have been, though it is not proved to be, the origin of the organic world we now see.

(Mill, 1841, *CW*, Vol. 17, 1553–1554)

36 Of course, the 'organic' argument may be a trivial declaration of the self-containedness of a system. In this case, the 'organicity' of the system is fully identified with its mechanistic character, that is, a 'natural' system that excludes purposive action. The word is used in this chapter in a distinct sense, indicating the indirect influence of the biological metaphor: an organic system includes complex and indeterminate interactions and feedbacks including with the environment, as it is an open system. This is the Schumpeterian concept of an organic whole.

37 Rosenberg interprets Schumpeter's position on the circular flow as a theoretical description, as opposed to the real processes of change in capitalism (Rosenberg 1994, 43), and Swedberg interprets it as an ideal-type (Swedberg 1991, 32). But the previous quotations refute this interpretation: for Schumpeter, the circular flow was a real process, *simultaneous* with development, and a complete theory should integrate both dimensions in the same framework.

38 One of the main reasons for the sense of failure Schumpeter felt in his last years was his incapacity to develop a formal model for his theories. His own diary proves that he worked almost daily and helplessly with systems of equations, at least since 1934 when preparing *BC*, and afterwards looking for a general equilibrium model accounting for the time path of the variables (Allen 1991, Vol. 2, 8, 142, 177, 190, 227). But he suspected that the available differential and difference equations were unsuited to define an evolutionary system including social relations and complex behaviours. Furthermore, his colleagues, such as Goodwin, witnessed his difficulties with mathematics.

39 The young Richard Goodwin, then at Harvard, recognised that 'it was a great shock to me' (quoted in Swedberg 1991, 176).

40 I discussed this point in some detail in Louçã 1997.
41 Schumpeter compares Keynes' and Hansen's approach to the Ricardo–Mill theory of the advent of a stationary state, for Keynes insisted on the pressure of the reduction of population and of the 'human effort' (*HEA*, 1173). This seems to be too far-fetched.
42 *HEA*, 1173fn. In *CSD* he had used a very similar expression, fingering the state for the damping out of innovation.

References

Allen, R. (1991). *Opening Doors: The Life and Work of Joseph Schumpeter*. New Brunswick, NJ: Transaction Books.

Andersen, E.S. (1994). *Evolutionary Economics: Post-Schumpeterian Contributions*. London: Pinter.

Bottomore, T. (1992). *Between Marginalism and Marxism: The Economic Sociology of J.A. Schumpeter*. Hemel Hempstead, UK: Harvester Wheatsheaf.

Comte, A. (1970). *Oeuvres d'Auguste Comte*. Paris: Anthropos, 1839.

Kalecki, M. (1971). *Selected Essays on the Dynamics of the Capitalist Economy, 1933–1970*. Cambridge: Cambridge University Press.

Louçã, F. (1997). *Turbulence in Economics: An Evolutionary Appraisal of Cycles and Complexity in Historical Processes*. Cheltenham, UK: Edward Elgar.

Louçã, F. (2007). *The Years of High Econometrics*. London: Routledge.

Marshall, A. (1907). Introduction. In: A. Marshall (1890), *Principles of Economics: An Introductory Volume* (8th edn. 1920). London: Macmillan.

Mill, J.S. (1841). *Collected Works of John Stuart Mill*. Toronto: University of Toronto Press-Routledge.

Mill, J.S. (1848). *Principles of Political Economy with Some of Their Applications to Social Philosophy* (1909 edn.). London: Longmans.

Mill, J.S. (1882). *Auguste Comte and Positivism*. London: Trubner.

Oackley, A. (1990). *Schumpeter's Theory of Capitalist Motion: A Critical Exposition and Reassessment*. Cheltenham, UK: Edward Elgar.

Rosenberg, N. (1994). Joseph Schumpeter: Radical economist. In: Y. Shionaya and M. Perlman (Eds.), *Schumpeter in the History of Ideas* (pp. 41–57). Ann Arbor, MI: University of Michigan Press.

Samuelson, P. (1951). Schumpeter as a teacher and economic theorist. In: S. Harris (Ed.), *Schumpeter: Social Scientist* (pp. 48–53). Cambridge: Harvard University Press.

Schumpeter, Joseph. (1911). *Teoria do Desenvolvimento Económico*. São Paulo: Abril (*TED*).

Schumpeter, J. (1914). *Economic Doctrines and Method: A Historical Sketch* (1954 edn.). New York: Oxford University Press.

Schumpeter, J. (1927). The explanation of the business cycle. *Economica*, December, 286–311.

Schumpeter, J. (1930). Mitchell's business cycles. *Quarterly Journal of Economics*, 150–172.

Schumpeter, J. (1935). The analysis of economic change. *Review of Economic Statistics*, 17(4), 2–10.

Schumpeter, J. (1937). Preface to the Japanese edition of *Theorie der Wirtschaftlichen Entwicklung*. In: R.V. Clemence (Ed.), *Essays on Economic Topics of J.A. Schumpeter* (pp. 158–163). New York: Kennikat Press, 1951.

Schumpeter, J. (1939). *Business Cycles*. New York: McGraw.

Schumpeter, J. (1942). *Capitalism, Socialism and Democracy* (1992 reprint). London: Routledge.

Schumpeter, J. (1944). Prologo a la Edicion Española, *Teoría del Desenvolvimiento Económico* (1957). Ciudad de Mexico: Fondo de Cultura Económica.

Schumpeter, J. (1949). The historical approach to business cycles. In: R.V. Clemence (Ed.), *Essays on Economic Topics of J.A. Schumpeter* (pp. 308–315). New York: Kennikat Press, 1951.

Schumpeter, J. (1950). *The March into Socialism*. Cambridge, MA: Harvard University Press, included in J. Schumpeter (1942), *Capitalism, Socialism and Democracy*. London: Routledge, 1992.

Schumpeter, J. (1951). *Essays on Economic Topics of J.A. Schumpeter* (R.V. Clemence Ed.). New York: Kennikat Press.

Schumpeter, J. (1954). *History of Economic Analysis* (1994 edn.). London: Routledge.

Schumpeter, J.A. (1961). *The Theory of Economic Development*. Oxford: Oxford University Press, 1911, 2nd edition, 1926.

Schumpeter, J. (1997). *Ten Great Economists: From Marx to Keynes*. New York: Francis & Taylor, 1952.

Steindl, J. (1952). *Maturity and Stagnation in American Capitalism*. Oxford: Blackwell.

Streissler, E. (1994). The influence of German and Austrian economics on Joseph A. Schumpeter. In: Y. Shionoya and M. Perlman (Eds.), *Schumpeter in the History of Ideas* (pp. 13–38). Ann Arbor, MI: University of Michigan Press.

Swedberg, R. (1991). *Joseph A. Schumpeter: His Life and Work*. Cambridge: Polity Press.

Swedberg, R. (1992). Introduction. In: J. Schumpeter (1942), *Capitalism, Socialism and Democracy* (pp. ix–xxi). London: Routledge, 1992.

Walras, L. (1883). *Compêndio dos Elementos de Economia Política Pura* (1983 edn.). São Paulo: Abril Cultural.

Witt, U. (1993). *Evolutionary Economics*. Cambridge: Cambridge University Press.

Witt, U. (1995). Schumpeter versus Hayek: Two approaches to evolutionary economics. In: G. Meijer (Ed.), *New Perspectives on Austrian Economics* (pp. 81–101). London: Routledge.

4 Individual, society and order

A Schumpeterian trinity

Beniamino Callegari

Introduction

In the opening chapter of *Capitalism, Socialism and Democracy* (2011, *CSD* from now on), Schumpeter explains the enduring success of Marxism not with its scientific merit, but with the 'supreme art [displayed] in ... preaching in the garb of analysis and analyzing with a view to heartfelt needs' (2011, 6). Schumpeter describes Marxism as a religion, a statement not meant to disqualify Marxism from debate; on the contrary, it is presented as highest praise. While Marx became a prophet during his lifetime, Schumpeter failed in his objective to conquer and reform the world of economics: always influent but never dominant, his work falling into a 'dusty oblivion' (Johnson 1951, 139) in the wake of his passing. It would take decades for economists to rediscover Schumpeter, an outcome he quietly accepted as shown by his farewell address to his students in Bonn: 'Unlike politics and business, immediate success should not matter in science ... I for my part accept the judgement of future generations' (Haberler 1950, 372). He expected to be brought back into prominence on the grounds of his magnum opus, *Business Cycles* (Schumpeter 1939), as a scientist and a scholar. Instead, he was moulded into a post-mortem prophet of innovation (McCraw 2009), lifted into thin air by the diaphanous wings of his 'little book of essays' (Allen 1991, 89).

The necessity of prophetic attire has been explained by Schumpeter himself in discussing Marxism and hardly bear repetition. A more interesting question would be why the resurrection was accomplished through *CSD* – flimsy support in the eyes of its own author. And to a certain extent, Schumpeter is not wrong: compared to *Business Cycles* (Schumpeter 1939), *CSD* certainly lacks in rigour, discipline and, most importantly, analysis. Sharp descriptions of complex theories, situations and historical events are often presented with little in the way of justification that would satisfy grim academic standards, leaving readers intrigued, but not necessarily satisfied. Yet, the simple fact of its enduring success points to greatness (Schumpeter 2011, 3), which demands explanation. *CSD* is the only book in which Schumpeter explicitly mixes his economic, political and sociological theories, crafting something that is 'no longer a mere proposition about the logical properties of a system of abstractions; it is the stroke of a brush that is painting the wild jumble of social life' (ibid., 46). It is precisely the book where Schumpeter is so close to Marx that descriptions of the latter can be applied to the former, which propelled the rise of Schumpeter as a prophet.

But the scientific merits of *CSD*, while downplayed by the author, should not be minimised. It is here that the Schumpeterian system reached its maximum extent, showcasing both the full breadth of its applicability and its inherent limits. It is here that the consequences of the rise of large oligopolistic firms for economic development are clarified, that the innovation process is described outside the capitalist setting, that the conditions for institutional regime change are specified. Even more importantly, it is here that the concept of order is fully integrated in the pre-established skeleton of Schumpeter's economic theory, centred around the conflict between individual and society. The resulting theoretical framework can be described as a Schumpeterian trinity, whose elements are indissolubly linked and cannot be fully comprehended in isolation. In this chapter I will describe the resulting Schumpeterian theoretical system and the contribution of *CSD*, its significance for present analysis and its role in shaping the current research agenda. The first step is to establish the dialectical foundations of Schumpeter's analysis of economic evolution.

Static foundations

Schumpeter laid the foundations of his system in the aptly named *The Nature and Essence of Economic Theory* (2010), his first book. In this work, he carefully described his understanding of the strong points and weaknesses of then-current theory, made the case for a new theory based on different assumptions, and identified its main objects of study: internal, discontinuous change, capital, profits, interest and money. Most importantly for our current discussion, he adopted his personal interpretation of methodological individualism,[1] further explored in a later article dedicated to the subject (Schumpeter 1909). The individual is the starting point of Schumpeterian economic theory: in this, and in little else, common ground can be found with the school described by Schumpeter as 'modern', and now commonly identified as neoclassical.

As argued by Hodgson (2007), it would be unwise to attribute to Schumpeter the position commonly associated with the term 'methodological individualism' today. The idea 'that all social phenomena resolve themselves into decisions and actions of individuals that need not or cannot be further analysed in terms of superindividual factors' (Schumpeter 1954, 888) is described by Schumpeter as 'sociological individualism' and immediately rejected as untenable. Schumpeterian 'methodological individualism' implies exclusively the necessity to start economic analysis from the level of the individual, and nothing more. Political individualism is explicitly rejected as an entirely separate assumption (Schumpeter 2010, 58), and no metaphysical claim is made:

the adjective 'methodological' is used to signal that the adoption of the individualist position is purely instrumental. Its adoption is required by the choice to base economic analysis on the value principle, what today would be called subjective theory of value (Schumpeter 1909, 215). Since wants can be felt only by individuals, and since they are affected by individual endowments, the individual must be the starting point.

But the wants of the isolated individual are not identical to those of the same individual inside a society: 'all utilities are changed when he lives within society, because of the possibility of barter' (ibid., 219). As later restated by Arrow (1994), the fundamental economic phenomenon, the act of exchange, necessarily implies a role for social structures in economic analysis. But barter is not the only social force influencing and shaping individual preferences, leading Schumpeter to state that individual demand curves are in fact *formed* by social structures. Schumpeterian individualism starts with the individual, but the individual is a social construct. Additionally, besides individuals, it is possible to identify uniquely social elements which, while necessarily emerging from individual interactions and processes, cannot be reduced to them. A straightforward example is prices, which, although based on individual values, cannot be reduced to them, their existence being confined to the social, rather than individual level (Schumpeter 1909, 217).

Values and prices provide a useful example of the Schumpeterian methodological structure. 'Society forms individuals and directly influences their economic value' (ibid., 232): social structures affect individuals. At the same time, socialised individual values influence, although not entirely determine, the price system (Schumpeter 1917–1918), a social structure. Social forces, while predominant, are not sufficient to entirely overwrite individual phenomena. At the same time, there is no logical precedence that can be assigned: individual and social phenomena coevolve in constant interaction. Consequently, economic analysis cannot be based on an either purely individual or social basis: it must be structured on two distinct yet interacting levels. This specific interpretation of methodological individualism, originally developed in order to analyse and criticise static economic theory, will form the basis of Schumpeterian evolutionary analysis, through the introduction of the crucial idea of conflict.

The idea of conflict emerges from the analysis of its opposite, the equilibrium condition, initially defined by Schumpeter as the state in which 'the acts of exchange stop' (Schumpeter 2010, 137). This isolated definition can be misleading: equilibrium is not a state of individual inaction. From the timeless perspective typical of static economic theory (Carvalho 1983), equilibrium is a state in which all acts of exchange for the indeterminate future, including productive activities, have been publicly settled. From a mechanical time perspective, equilibrium consists in the ordered execution of individual, yet mutually consistent, publicly known, and previously agreed plans, each consisting of a precise exchange schedule. The missing tendency 'for further changes' (Schumpeter 2010, 137) must therefore be interpreted as a lack of tendency for changes in plans, not necessarily in action. The actual content of individual plans is entirely irrelevant: as long as individual plans are executed according to mutual expectations, equilibrium is maintained.

The circular-flow model developed by Schumpeter (1934) is a particular state of equilibrium, characterised by endless repetition of the same acts of exchange on the part of all individuals. This follows from an additional assumption of strictly static conditions, introduced in order to isolate and describe with precision the process of economic development. This assumption, however, is purely instrumental and has no bearing on the results; the essence of economic development lies not in changes in actions, but in changes in plans and the knowledge thereof. From the Schumpeterian methodological individualism perspective, equilibrium might be defined as a condition in which individual variables have no direct impact on economic outcomes: the individual dimension is entirely subsumed in the social one. And yet this definition, while necessary to underline a crucial equilibrium property, cannot be accepted in its entirety:

> to substitute for the many Individual values the idea of a Social value cannot lead to more than an analogy. This analogy is separated from reality by a great gulf, – by the fact that values, prices, and shares in the social product all depend on, and are dominated by, the original distribution of wealth.
>
> (Schumpeter 1909, 222)

There's the rub.

Under equilibrium, social structures subsume individual phenomena, but the maximum extent of this process is governed by the institutional setting implicitly or explicitly assumed by the modeler. The assumption of perfect competition, for example, allows the unique determination of the price structure and the implied disappearance of an independent causal role of individual values (ibid., 228). Social price subsumes individual value. An opposite effect is reached by the assumption of private property. Since the distribution of wealth is established only at the individual level, its causal relevance in the explanation of economic outcome cannot disappear: consequently, the equilibrium condition will never entail an absolute maximisation of social welfare, but only the maximum satisfaction 'which can be attained *under those circumstances*' (Schumpeter 1909, 229, emphasis in the original), set by original individual endowments. It should be stated, in passing, that a formalised version of this proposition advanced by the young Schumpeter would form the basis of the Sonnenschein–Mantel–Debreu theorem.

The issue reveals the social/individual dichotomy's insufficiency as a platform for economic analysis. For the definition of the mechanisms governing their interactions hinges on the definition of a minimum set of institutional rules relative to control of resources. A model economy 'characterised by private property and controlled by private initiative' (Schumpeter 1939, 223) will not maximise social welfare under any compatible assumption, because endowments will never be exclusively controlled by social structures. Conversely, a general equilibrium model of a communistic society with 'direct control of all means of production' (Schumpeter 1909, 216) would feature the absolute maximisation of social welfare. The term general equilibrium model should be sufficient to establish both the exclusively abstract nature of this proposition and its limited application to conditions of absence of economic development. Yet it should be sufficient to establish (1) the necessity of institutional considerations for economic analysis, and, consequently, (2) the non-universal nature of economic theory.

The minimum set of institutional rules was identified by Schumpeter with the term regime. This third element completes the Schumpeterian economic system for equilibrium analysis. The regime determines the maximum extent of equilibrium, defined as the absorption of individual phenomena under social phenomena in causal determination of economic outcomes. Economic theory then consists in identifying the assumptions required for reaching such equilibrium, describing the mechanisms through which individual phenomena are absorbed by social phenomena, and finally indicating how social and potentially individual phenomena determine economic outcomes. The initial Schumpeterian contribution was entirely methodological in nature: his objective was not to add to theory, but rather to create an internally consistent foundation for analysis in order to shed light on the numerous controversies of his time. It was the unsatisfactory result yielded by this approach that propelled him towards theoretical reform.

The lack of satisfaction was due to the fact that, under equilibrium, Schumpeter found no substantial role for key phenomena, such as capital, profits, interest and money. It is not that equilibrium theories for these phenomena could not be advanced, it is that they are not necessary (cf. Hahn 1965; Arrow and Hahn 1971; Lucas 1984). It would then follow that they could be modelled only through ad hoc assumptions introducing frictions and imperfections in the basic model. This Ptolemaic solution was defended by Schumpeter as a conditionally valid scientific approach (Schumpeter 2010, 38). 'But when we find a principle that does not require an auxiliary hypothesis and that produces a neat, pure, homogenous system that generates many valuable findings … it would simply be stupid to reject it' (ibid., 39). Schumpeter thought that the best solution was not to add new assumptions, but to drop the assumption of the absence of economic development. If the resulting system could generate an independent role for capital, profits, interest and money, the approach would then be vindicated.

From the present perspective, it might seem as if we are preparing the ground for the paradoxical statement that Schumpeter introduced economic development in his theory only to analyse other economic phenomena. I want to reassure the reader that this is far from the truth. The main object of study of Schumpeter was the process of economic development, and there is little reason to challenge this article of faith: the prophetic garb remains untarnished. What the present reconstruction should be sufficient to demonstrate, however, is that any theory of economic development that does not include significant explanatory roles for capital, profits, interest and money could hardly be described as Schumpeterian, for the purpose of clarity, if nothing else. Having established the static roots of Schumpeterian theory, it is now possible to move on to its actual dynamic content.

Dynamic development

The question facing Schumpeter was how to model economic development as an interaction between individual and society in a given regime. The first problem was conceptualisation. Economic development was incompatible with equilibrium, and the latter consisted in the predominance of the social over the individual for the determination of economic outcomes. This suggested that economic development could be conceptualised as the process through which individual phenomena determine economic outcome *in contrast* with the social element. It implies an element of conflict, unsurprisingly missing in models of general equilibrium, which brings Schumpeterian theory closer to the other conflict-based economic theory, Marxism. Yet there is an important difference. Marx based his theory around two fundamental conflicts: the class conflict, driving the historical dialectical progress, and the conflict between capitalists, taking the form of adversarial competition and creating the conditions for breakdown and proletarian revolution. The former is a conflict between social classes, a concept missing from Schumpeter's economic theory,[2] while the latter is a conflict between individuals. The key Schumpeterian conflict is instead between the individual and social structures.

Social structures constrain the ability of the individual to act, essentially stripping it[3] of its agency and determining its behaviour. Agents are reduced to passively reacting to given stimuli: a passive response (Schumpeter 1947a). Individual agency is in fact incompatible with a condition of equilibrium, in which agents act on the basis of common knowledge of present and future conditions, and therefore of the actual behaviour of all other agents. The complete knowledge conveyed by the market implies the annihilation of agency. Since the adaptive behaviour is optimal behaviour under given conditions, the individual failing to adapt would be automatically sanctioned through wealth loss: sustained 'irrational' behaviour would lead to indigence and consequent loss of ability to interact economically with other agents. In this system, qualitative change can take place only through exogenous shocks, followed by a timeless process of social absorption.

The point of departure of Schumpeterian theory is in placing the exogenous shock not at the social, but the individual level: this is the creative response, which 'cannot be predicted by applying the ordinary rules of inference from the pre-existing facts' (ibid., 150). Economic development begins not as a shock to the economic system's fundamentals, but in the ability of the individual 'to decide in favor of untried possibilities' (Schumpeter 1939,

99), that is, according to circular flow's logic, of possibilities not integrated in current individual plans, actions and resulting prices. The creative response requires not only the ability to imagine new possibilities, but also to evaluate their economic consequences without the support of market mechanisms and to act effectively on this basis. The individual ability to imagine economic possibilities and consequences is introduced by Schumpeter as horizon (Schumpeter 1939, 99), corresponding to the idea of forming expectations.

'Carrying out a new plan and acting according to a customary one are things as different as making a road and walking along it' (Schumpeter 1934, 85). Schumpeter strongly underlines the difficulties involved in the creative response, always an exceptional endeavour. This is because it necessarily involves conflict between the creative individual and the society. This element of conflict is precisely what differentiates Schumpeterian entrepreneurship from speculation. In the latter case, the individual also acts on the basis of its horizon in contrast with current social values, but it does so by anticipating the working of the economic system in reaction to future or imminent shocks. This requires the individual to possess 'a model of the model' (Minsky 1996). The Schumpeterian entrepreneur needs to temporarily substitute itself to the social mechanisms, to bring about the possibilities currently excluded by the economic system, encountering rational resistance in the process. Superficially, the conflict appears to be between individuals, as other agents reject or ignore the creative individual. But in fact, the conflict is between creative and adaptive response: between creative individual behaviour and social routines implied by common knowledge and the related price system.

Integrating the possibility for exceptional individual agency to modify social values through conflictual processes involving gains and losses in the Schumpeterian platform gives us a synthesis of Schumpeterian economic theory before *CSD*. The process of economic development gives rise to various conflicts between corresponding individual/social phenomena, whose descriptions identify the various theories comprising the Schumpeterian system, presented in the following synthetic table for explanatory purposes:

Table 4.1 attempts a schematisation of the notoriously complex Schumpeterian system, by organising the arguably most important concepts according to the appropriate level. The dotted line indicates the aspect of conflict, whose description provides the kernel of the various theoretical elements listed in the third row. Intentional lack of borders between columns reflects the fact that the Schumpeterian system, as the name suggests, forms a coherent whole, with each element interacting with every other. The Schumpeterian theory of the business cycle, for example, is a natural consequence of the Schumpeterian theory of innovation and relies on all the individual and social elements mentioned. Similar descriptions can be made for each part of the Schumpeterian system.

Not represented is the regime, the set of assumptions describing the relevant institutional features of the economy under analysis. While the

Table 4.1 Schumpeterian system

Individual	Behaviour	Horizon	Endowments	Values	(Relational) Credit
Society	Routines	Knowledge	Commodities	Prices	(General) Money
Theory	Theory of entrepreneurship	Theory of innovation	Business-cycle theory	Price theory	Credit theory of money

fundamental motive for the various individual/society conflicts can be stated in universal terms, the development of precise theoretical propositions regarding their resolution mechanisms strictly requires and applies to a specific regime. For example, the mechanisms involved in the creative-destruction process apply to a regime of competitive capitalism and cannot be assumed to be operative under any other institutional configuration. The regime is not visually represented because it is exogenous, derived from sociological and legal analysis of the relevant socioeconomic system under study. Two limitations of Schumpeterian theory follow.

First, the model described by Schumpeter, developed for a regime of competitive capitalism, was already obsolete at the time of writing (Schumpeter 1928, 362) and should be discarded for any analysis of the present or the recent past. Second, the exogenous nature of the regime, combined with its fundamental importance, relegates theoretical development to the rear-view mirror. Any theoretical proposition is context-dependent and therefore will apply with any certainty only to past periods. The Schumpeterian system could describe the economic consequences of an endogenous process of development, but the development of the theoretical system itself remained fundamentally exogenous until 1942. The scientist Schumpeter was satisfied with this situation. But the prophet Schumpeter required something more.

Evolutionary order

In using competitive capitalism as the primary regime for theoretical development in both *The Theory of Economic Development* (1934) and *Business Cycles* (1939), Schumpeter was consciously developing a theory applicable primarily to his past rather than his present. His objective was not to provide an analysis of then-present issues, perhaps with a view towards policy intervention, or justification of specific political stances, but to illustrate the relevance and viability of economic development's analysis for the progress of economics. To this purpose, given the institutionally limited applicability of theoretical propositions, the best approach was to focus on the past, securing the opportunity to judge the theory's adherence to established facts. Once the principle is settled, it would then be possible to extend the field of applicability by deriving theoretical propositions consistent with present regimes. Schumpeter intended to establish the method and the object of study, rather than specific theoretical propositions.

CSD provided Schumpeter with the opportunity, motive and justification to leave its scientific precinct and explore the present situation for the distinctively unscientific purposes of speculating about the future, a task he described in *History of Economic Analysis* in the following terms:

> It is as unreasonable to expect the economist to forecast correctly what will actually happen as it would be to expect a doctor to prognosticate when his patient will be the victim of a railroad accident and how this will affect his state of health.
>
> (Schumpeter 1954, 13)

Paradoxically, it was by renouncing any scientific pretence that Schumpeter developed his methodological system further, by abandoning the pure economic theory approach that Schumpeter had adhered to before.

CSD integrates sociological and political elements that had been previously discussed by Schumpeter in dedicated essays (Schumpeter 1918, 1951) but always separately from his main contributions in economic theory. Even *Business Cycles* (Schumpeter 1939) does not comprise any explicit sociological or political theorisation, although several suggestive hints can be extracted from the extensive historical analysis presented therein. With *CSD*, all the Schumpeterian pieces come together at the same time, in rich, vital prose, illustrating the multidisciplinary nature and internal coherence of the Schumpeterian system. But *CSD* is a book of essays, not a book dedicated to theoretical development, such as *The Theory of Economic Development* (Schumpeter 1934). It is not a description, but an application of theoretical propositions. The problem is that Schumpeter applies an extended and updated version of his theory, which has not been fully described before.

The analytical task left to the *CSD* reader is, therefore, to reverse-engineer the underlying theoretical propositions and assumptions from their application to a specific case. It is only then that *CSD* can be appreciated, not only for its message and its style, but for its undeniable scientific merit. It is precisely to this aim that a sketch of the pre-*CSD* Schumpeterian system has been offered: to pinpoint changes and additions brought by *CSD* and integrating them with Schumpeter's previous theoretical development efforts. Based on the Schumpeterian system's description presented above, it can be argued that *CSD* makes essentially two major contributions, the first to the analytical structure, by modifying a crucial element of the methodological approach, and the second in terms of theoretical propositions, by extending the contents of the theory itself to the conditions of trustified capitalism.

The first contribution consists in the expansion of the concept of regime, an exogenous set of institutional rules, in the more general idea of order, including the socio-political conditions required for its preservation. The definition of a specific regime, a necessary preliminary step for theoretical development, implied precise boundary conditions for the analysis: the resulting theoretical propositions could not be applied to socioeconomic systems characterised by different regimes. But institutional rules do change over time. When the specific regime under analysis is entirely in the past, the boundary conditions are explicit and pose no analytical challenges. But when theory is applied to the present, Schumpeterian methodology provides no guidelines to discover how, or when, regime-change will take place, therefore potentially invalidating previous theory-based inferences. The application of pre-*CSD* Schumpeterian theory to the analysis of the present is therefore potentially misleading, as it might result in the application of theoretical propositions inconsistent with the actual regime.

This was precisely the problem faced by Schumpeter in *Business Cycles* (1939). The theoretical propositions developed under the competitive capitalism regime proved to be at least partially inadequate for the analysis of then-contemporary events, forcing Schumpeter to apply in his historical sections various theoretical elements entirely missing from previous chapters dedicated to theoretical development, such as the concept of profitless prosperity (ibid., 105, 408–410), used to explain the early US financialisation of the 1920s, yet barely mentioned before. This issue contributed to the rather cold reception received by the book, probably pushing Schumpeter to try a different approach when he returned to present analysis in *CSD*. To do so, however, it was necessary to integrate social and political elements, and particularly, the concept of social class.

Schumpeter started developing a theory of social class during the winter of 1910 and stated in 1927 that his work on this line of thinking was continuing and would be complete 'only years from now, if at all' (Schumpeter 1951, 101). In his sociological studies, Schumpeter expanded the individual/social dichotomy to accommodate a third intermediate level: the family. Social classes are actual social structures – and not merely creations of researchers (ibid., 105) –, whose existence is well-known and perceived by all individuals. Each family belongs to a specific class, and by virtue of its relationship with his/her family, each individual is class-born. While individuals belong to specific classes, social classes are formed by families, not individuals (ibid., 113). Families can occupy different strata inside their own class, depending on their relative performance; however, this performance is mostly dependent on exceptional individual success, rather than steady familiar superiority or objective conditions (ibid., 119).

Class barriers exist but are always and everywhere porous (ibid., 159), with families constantly entering and exiting social classes – social mobility is primarily a family matter (ibid., 125–127). Social classes are themselves organised in hierarchical fashion, although such hierarchy is constantly shifting (ibid., 134), for two primary causes. Given that each social class is associated with the performance of a definite social function, the position of each class 'depends, on the one hand, on the significance that is attributed to that function, and, on the other hand, on the degree to which the class successfully performs the function' (ibid., 137), although custom and tradition always introduce a lag in the process of change in relative class positions (ibid., 158). Since all class functions are socially necessary, their ranking is not functional, but based on the link between the social function and the practice of social leadership (ibid., 158). Social leadership is defined as the ability 'to decide, to command, to prevail, to advance' (ibid., 165) under conditions of novelty and consequently uncertainty. Through the successful practice of leadership, the individual, and his/her family manage to advance, gaining prestige and resources and entrenching their positions: when the process involves coordination between families and a mutually recognised bond, a class is born (ibid., 167). The problem of class follows from the process of entrenchment allowing a failing or functionless class to maintain its relative position, thus damaging the social interest (ibid., 166). Another potential social problem arises from the ability of successful ruling social classes to impose socially damaging agendas, at least in the short-term, as exemplified by the case of imperialist export monopolism (Schumpeter 1951).

This summary of the Schumpeterian theory of social class is sufficient to understand the concept of order introduced in *CSD*. The latter provides no indications that Schumpeter has reneged any previously held propositions, sometimes even restated to the letter (e.g. Schumpeter 2011, 14), which will therefore be assumed relevant for the argument developed here. The starting point of the process of reverse-engineering is afforded by the famous statement: '[capitalism's] very success undermines the social institutions which protect it, and "inevitably" create conditions in which it will not be able to live and which strongly point to socialism as the heir apparent' (ibid., 61). Our purpose will be to extract from the specific analysis of trustified capitalism general propositions to be integrated in the methodological platform developed above. The quote hints at the possibility for economic mechanisms to modify those social institutions allowing the same mechanisms to operate: if this was to be the case, institutional rules could be considered endogenous, and the concept of regime surpassed.

The bourgeoisie rose to prominence due to its business success (ibid., 73), its associated social function being the generation of profits (ibid., 74). Schumpeterian economic theory establishes that this entails the pursuit of economic development (Schumpeter 1934). Yet the celebrated description of oligopolistic competition clarifies that the social function of the bourgeoisie is not only the generation of profits, but also the creation and defence of rent through 'profit-conserving' strategies (Schumpeter 2011, 80): the expression of their success as a class is the rise of large oligopolistic firms, trusts and cartels. The pursuit of profit therefore implies and relies on rent-seeking behaviour; this 'tritest common sense' (ibid., 91) implies that competitive capitalism cannot fail to give way to trustified capitalism, as more and more sectors become organised around a few big concerns. These considerations point towards an important mistake in the Schumpeterian model of economic development under competitive capitalism. Schumpeter assumed that the

individual entrepreneurial function would operate exclusively for the generation of profits, which would be quickly eliminated by a social response – the
'suicidal stimulus of profits' (Schumpeter 1939, 105). *CSD* suggests that the
entrepreneurial function should be expanded to include the mechanism of
conversion of profits into rent, thus giving rise to the oligopolistic firm. It is
important to note that the fault lies in the model, not the theory, as the
lengthy description of the motives of the entrepreneur clarifies the importance of the legacy-building, which, in economic terms, can only be translated
into rent-seeking (Schumpeter 1934).

If entrepreneurial profits and rents were pursued by separate agents, no
significant problems would arise, as the entrepreneurs would steadily undermine the rentiers. However, when the entrepreneur is characterised as a
dynamic rent-seeker, each business cycle will lead to a progressive concentration of the productive sector. Thus, over time, the crucial assumption of
competitive capitalism, that innovative activities are pursued exclusively by
outsiders, will be undermined by the rise of large, innovative concerns, an
abstract translation in economic terms of the emergence of trustified capitalism. Under the latter, some of the previous theoretical propositions will
cease to be valid, and new ones will be required. The case reveals that it is
possible, although only under certain conditions to be presently discussed, to
model a regime change in purely economic terms. In fact, regime changes
could result endogenously from the normal working of the economic model.

According to Schumpeter, trustified capitalism is superior to competitive
capitalism, in terms of social welfare, as it provides a better basis for the
process of economic development, broadening access to required resources
and reducing the negative consequences through planning. Yet, trustified
capitalism is denounced by Schumpeter as an instrument of euthanasia of
the entrepreneur first, and the rentier later, '[expropriating] the bourgeoisie
as a class' (Schumpeter 2011, 134). This is achieved through two separate
mechanisms: the success of capitalism as an economic system eliminates the
functional basis of bourgeois dominance, while the success of capitalism as a
civilisation eliminates its extra-rational basis. The first mechanism can be
understood through the application of Schumpeterian economic theory. By
automatising and routinising the process of economic development, the role
of the individual ceases to be relevant, thus eliminating the kernel of
Schumpeterian theory. More specifically, the entrepreneurial horizon can
now be fostered and accommodated inside the borders of the large innovative firm, providing all the required resources for its implementation, eliminating the conflict between individual and system. Consequently,
Schumpeterian profits do not appear at all (Schumpeter 1939, 408–410),
with innovation gains taking the form of enduring rent. Over time,
however, the innovation process becomes entirely controlled by employed
managers and workers, with no functional role left for the rentier, thus
leading to the gradual disappearance of interest and the conversion of rents
into wages.

So far, it appears that this particular regime change could also potentially be modelled in purely economic terms, as before. But there is something more. The loss of social function threatens the dominant bourgeois position, just as the military function's decline accompanied the fall of the aristocratic class (Schumpeter 2011, 136). In the latter case, however, the process took centuries (Schumpeter 1951), because the aristocratic dominant position was upheld by extra-rational values that the feudal system explicitly diffused and supported. Capitalism, instead, is a rationalistic civilisation (ibid., 123), which effectively erodes and destroys all supporting extra-rational values. It follows that, once functionally replaceable, the bourgeois political regime would very quickly disappear, to be replaced by something else, which Schumpeter identifies with socialism, a regime with neither private property nor private initiative. The underlying general principle appears to be that the regime's socio-political features are associated with continued dominance of the ruling class. Hierarchical shifts imply regime changes that cannot be integrated in economic models.

It is now possible to define the concept of order in general terms. Given a specific socioeconomic system, order is defined as the relevant set of institutional rules required for the development of applicable Schumpeterian theoretical propositions. At a minimum, the order should identify (1) the ruling social class, (2) the conditions sustaining its dominant position, (3) the agents performing the entrepreneurial function and (4) the agents and instruments involved in the acquisition of the resources required for performing the entrepreneurial function. Prima facie, the concept of order might appear a marginal innovation over the previous idea of regime, simply clarifying and extending the minimum institutional set of assumptions required. Most importantly, however, the concept of order makes Schumpeterian institutional analysis dynamic, through the introduction of conflict. There is no theoretical reason to expect the four conditions to be coherent – there is no such thing as an institutional equilibrium. The concept of order implies the additional identification of potential long-term conflicts arising from the interactions between the conditions. At a minimum, monitoring the development of these conflicts provides the analyst with clear warning signs regarding the model's applicability. Additionally, conflicts between institutional conditions three and four can be made endogenous, thus allowing the model to remain relevant for the analysis of transition into a new order. In the relevant case of capitalist order, given the economic nature of the function supporting the bourgeois dominant position, and the limited relevance of extra-rational values, conflicts involving institutional condition two can also be endogenised.

Schumpeter forecast the advent of socialism through the application of his mature theoretical system to the analysis of trustified capitalism. Capitalism did not fall. The prophet did not deliver the kingdom.[4] But this prophetical failure remains a scientific success. Schumpeter attempted to do nothing more than to diagnose observable tendencies and to state what results would be, if these tendencies should work themselves out according to their logic. In itself, this does not amount to prognosis or prediction because factors external to the chosen range of observation may intervene to prevent that consummation; because, with phenomena so far removed as social phenomena are from the comfortable situation that astronomers have the good fortune of facing, observable tendencies, even if allowed to work themselves out, may be compatible with more than one outcome; and because existing tendencies, battling with resistances, may fail to work themselves out completely and may eventually "stick" at some halfway house.

(Schumpeter 2011, 422)

Schumpeterian methodology does not admit prediction beyond this very limited sense because of the integration of individual agency and the holistic view of the social process. Economic models, even when informed by institutional analysis, remain necessarily incomplete, for economic phenomena are never entirely determined by economic conditions alone (Schumpeter 1934, 58). Economics can provide a scientific analysis of trends, conditions and, crucially, causal mechanisms, but complete descriptions of actual events remain the domain of history: the role of economic theory is to support the creation of *histoire raisonnée* (ibid., 44).

With the substitution of regime with the broader concept of order, Schumpeterian economic theory reached its maximum extent. Yet this implied no break with established foundations. The economic dichotomy between individual and society is maintained: the family level, while central for sociological analysis, is not associated with any specific economic phenomena and does not figure in the description of any economic mechanism. Prediction is admitted exclusively as an incomplete description of current trends and their implied conflicts: forecasting remains outside of the scientific precinct. The role of economic theory remains the identification of potential causal mechanisms, but its direct application to the analysis of empirical materials is fruitless: economics is not the queen of social sciences (Lindenberg 1983), economics is the *ancilla* of history.

The resulting multidisciplinary approach

Throughout its development, the Schumpeterian system acquired a more and more definite multidisciplinary nature. Schumpeter was constantly engaged in economic, sociological and historical research at the same time, but at the beginning he tried as much as possible to keep his work in economic theory as 'pure' as possible, despite explicit recognition of the severe limitations inherent in such an approach. His mature works, however, show increasing acceptance of the need for integration across disciplines, as testified by *Business Cycles* (Schumpeter 1939) and *CSD*. This development was followed *pari passu* by increasing attention to epistemological and ontological issues. In *Nature and Essence of Economic Theory* (Schumpeter 2010) Schumpeter studiously avoids any metaphysical claim, sticking to purely methodological and instrumental discourses, and in *Theory of Economic Development* (1934) he goes as far as renouncing completely 'the armor of methodological commentaries' (Schumpeter 1934, 4). It is only in *Business Cycles* (Schumpeter 1939), *History of Economic Analysis* (Schumpeter 1954) and other later writings (Schumpeter 1949, 1951, 1984) that these issues are finally tackled.

Schumpeter makes precise distinctions between theory, models and explanatory hypotheses, identifying 'reckless or dilettantist hypothesis making' as the main reason responsible for 'the discredit into which theory has fallen' (Schumpeter 1939, 30). Derivation of empirical hypotheses is an auxiliary task belonging to the realm of applied studies rather than theoretical analysis. Schumpeter denies the appropriateness of the process of induction to economics; 'to assemble statistics, to treat them by formal methods, and to present the results as the solution of a problem' (ibid., 32) is an inappropriate procedure for the derivation of theoretical propositions. 'Nonsense Induction', logical operations void of sense but clothed in exact terms, are likely results. Empirical materials are also unfit to perform verification, which Schumpeter describes as 'Spurious'. Statistical findings cannot prove or verify theoretical propositions because 'one and the same behaviour of a time series can analytically be accounted for in an indefinite number of ways' (ibid., 33).[5] Neither can they be disproved, because 'a very real relation may be so overlaid by other influences acting on the statistical material under study as to become entirely lost in the numerical picture' (ibid., 33). In general, economic phenomena are subject to too many disturbances to 'fulfill the logical requirement of the process of induction' (ibid., 33). Statistical and historical facts have a different role to play, 'to induce the theoretical work and determine its pattern' (ibid., 32).

The inclusion of the creative response and uncertainty in the analysis prevents prediction:

> It is as unreasonable to expect the economist to forecast correctly what will actually happen as it would be to expect a doctor to prognosticate when his patient will be the victim of a railroad accident and how this will affect his state of health.
>
> (Ibid., 13)

Theory's main function is the identification of the tools of analysis, i.e. concepts and the propositions describing their relations, so-called theorems. A model identifies a specific set of analytic tools coherently framed in order to describe the distinct phenomena under study. The primary aim of theory is the description of causal mechanisms:

> Our mind will never be at rest until ... we have assembled in one model causes, mechanisms, and effects, and can show how it works. And in this

sense, whatever we may object, the question of causation is the Fundamental Question, although it is neither the only one nor the first to be asked.

(Schumpeter 1939, 34)

Economic theory has a purely explanatory role, but even that role is limited:

> … providing *a schema of possible modi operandi* that tells us which are the 'circumstances' to watch and which will produce which effects. This is where economic theory might come in to serve the historian – and not by offering sweeping explanatory hypotheses.
>
> (Schumpeter 1947b, 5–6, emphasis in the original)

The objective of economic theory is to provide conditional, and therefore incomplete, causal explanations of economic phenomena, based on a limited array of concepts, mechanisms and assumptions.

Due to its incompleteness, the direct application of pure economic theory to the analysis of empirical reality is misguided. The economic system is not an isolated machine but a set of interconnected social objects, mechanisms and phenomena whose separation from the rest of society exists exclusively in the eye of the economist. Yet the identification of a pure economic system provides a valuable basis for further analysis. Whereas economic phenomena are specific manifestations of broader social forces, their nature and interactions suggest internally consistent logics and mechanisms whose essence is revealed in artificial isolation. This is somewhat reminiscent of Pasinetti's 'separation theorem':

> we must make it possible to disengage those investigations that concern the foundational basis of economic relations – to be detected at a strictly essential level of basic economic analysis – from those investigations that must be carried out at the level of the actual economic institutions.
>
> (Pasinetti 2007, 275)

Similarly, it is possible to advance an interpretation of Schumpeterian theory close to the institutionalist interpretation of Keynesian theory advanced by Crotty (1990a). Whereas the actual theoretical content differs, their foundations appear to be close, and in some aspects identical.

Following Crotty, it is possible to identify in Schumpeter three distinct levels of analysis. The first level, pure economic theory, contains the descriptions of assumptions, concepts and fundamental principles built around the individual/society dichotomy. The results obtained at this level are not limited to any specific economic system and therefore universal in nature: yet, their incomplete and abstract essence prevents their direct application to any real context. The second level introduces the institutional elements identified by the concept of order: stylised descriptions of the institutions, agents and mechanisms involved in both adaptive and creative processes. The integration of sociological considerations allows the development of contingent models of economic development of increasing complexity, describing potentially real causal mechanisms. Lastly, there is a third, historical, level, integrating in the analysis exogenous factors, contingencies and missing actual social phenomena. The output of the third level of analysis takes the form of extensive historical case studies, in which heterogeneous empirical material is brought into contact with the theoretical apparatus, to demonstrate both the latter causal powers and the extent of the domain of historical happenstance: *histoire raisonnée*. These three levels identify the mature Schumpeterian approach to theoretical development.

The implicit order is fundamentally arbitrary and does not betray any methodological normative position. Both economic and institutional analysis require prior investigation of actual empirical phenomena, through historical and statistical analysis. 'No decade in the history of politics, religion, technology, painting, poetry and what not ever contains its own explanation ... you must survey a period of much wider span. Not to do so is the hallmark of dilettantism' (Schumpeter 1946, 3–4). The comprehension of institutional evolution requires an analysis of relevant adjacent systems to reveal potentially hidden real causes and forces supporting the current transient configuration. An analysis of the past allows an understanding of the mechanisms and processes of evolution, while an analysis of different contemporary systems leads to the identification of specific conditions operating in the evolutionary trajectory followed by the system under study. In general, the three levels are deeply interconnected, forming a coherent whole; separation is relevant mostly for hermeneutical purposes. The complete Schumpeterian system is developed over four major axes: economic theory, sociology, history and statistics[6] (Schumpeter 1954, 19).

The description above supports the position originally expressed by da Graça Moura (2002), namely that critical realism could be the key to the rationalisation of Schumpeterian theory. A first step in this direction was taken by Courvisanos and Mackenzie (2011) in their examination of the Schumpeterian concept of entrepreneurship. Present efforts are to be interpreted as a potential addition to this fruitful path. Strong similarities in goals, methods and assumptions can be identified. The main objective of scientific analysis is the development of causal explanations (Schumpeter 1939, 34; Lawson 2003), relying on real causal mechanisms involving interactions between individual agency and social structures. The following description of the realist transformational model of social activity could be easily extended to the Schumpeterian system here described: 'the individual and society, though irreducible to each other, are interdependent features of a socio-transformational process of linked or codevelopment' (Lawson 2003, 50). Contrary to the actualist position, Schumpeterian mechanisms do not correspond to the generalisation of empirical regularities (Schumpeter 1939, 33; Bhaskar 1978, 238). The economic system is not open, barring an application of the inductive method. Observable demi-regularities (Lawson 1997) are to be interpreted as signals of underlying mechanisms to be identified, defined and discussed by theoretical analysis.

The implied method of reasoning is neither induction nor deduction, but rather retroduction/abduction: to move from empirical observation to the description of a potential underlying causal mechanism, or mechanisms, ultimately leading to the observed empirical manifestation (ibid., 107–108). This crucial epistemological point is argued at length in *Nature and Essence of Economic Theory*:

> On the one hand, our theory is in essence arbitrary, and on this are based its system, its rigor, and its exactness; on the other hand, it fits the phenomena and is conditioned by them, and this alone gives it content and significance.
>
> (Schumpeter 2010, 533)

> To be sure, neither our 'assumptions' nor our 'laws' lie in the real world of phenomena ... But this does not preclude them from *fitting* the facts. How can this be? ... because in constructing our schema we proceeded, no doubt arbitrarily, but reasonably in that *we designed the schema with the facts in mind*
>
> (Ibid., 527, emphasis in the original)

While the validity of empirical generalisation is denied, it is possible to generalise from real mechanisms, theoretically identified, through the classification of required contextual conditions (Sayer 2010), identified in the Schumpeterian concept of order. These close analogies between Schumpeterian methodology and critical realism can be easily explained by their common goal, as 'critical realism accommodates the intentional actions of a human agent in society' (Courvisanos and Mackenzie 2011, 13). Schumpeter's ontological, epistemological and methodological positions have similarly developed to accommodate the analysis of the creative response.

While the comparison is suggestive, it would be anachronistic to classify Schumpeter as a critical realist. His approach to economics was *sui generis* and should be assessed on its own merits, including its manifest contradictions (da Graça Moura 2002). Yet, in the context of the interpretation proposed here, approximation to critical realism provides a powerful instrument to highlight the crucial Schumpeterian elements that have received less attention in contemporary economic analyses of innovation. It also works as a crude, yet effective, antidote to the general perception of Schumpeterian economics as Walrasian, or neoclassical, or even just consistent with the assumptions usually related to these schools. Instead, it suggests that Schumpeter and his analysis should be considered closer in assumptions, though not in content, to approaches consistent with the foundations of critical realism: the Keynesian and institutional schools (Fleetwood 2002; Lewis 2004). Further support for this hypothesis can be drawn from an analysis of the limitations and related opportunities for further development offered by the post-*CSD* Schumpeterian system.

The Schumpeterian system today: limits and opportunities

The Schumpeterian system's interpretation described thus far has been intentionally focused on the underlying solidity and coherence of Schumpeter's theoretical apparatus, a dominant opinion in the profession until the 1960s (e.g. Clemence and Doody 1950; Haberler 1950; Marget 1951; Stolper 1951; Wolfson 1958). The distinction between theory, institutional analysis and models allows for acknowledging superficial contradictions while defending the existence of a coherent and, most importantly, usable core, whose relevance might be challenged but not discarded without debate. However, at least three major limitations must be recognised, discussed and overcome if Schumpeterian theory is to become relevant for the present analysis. They are: the ambiguous role of the Walrasian equilibrium, the missing economic theory of the State, and the required preliminary work of institutional and theoretical adaptation to current realities.

The above analysis allows us to tackle the issue of the circular flow, the Walrasian starting point consistently used by Schumpeter for model-building (Schumpeter 1934, 1939). Its central position has led many to believe that this construct, and its underlying assumptions, play a large analytical role. The interpretation presented here rejects this position entirely. It is argued instead that Walrasian equilibrium plays a purely expository role, a temporary background that allows the reader to understand the basic mechanisms behind economic evolution, to be discarded through the progress of theoretical analysis and bound to play no role in explanation of actual empirical phenomena. As expressed by Elliott: 'Schumpeter's analysis of the circular flow in a deeper sense is not intended to be either descriptive or prescriptive; that is, it neither accurately describes actual capitalist economies nor provides normative benchmarks for evaluation of capitalist economic performance' (Elliott 1983, 282).

The Walrasian equilibrium is a theoretical closure allowing Schumpeter to derive a model from his theoretical set of concepts and mechanisms. A similar methodological stance has been discussed in depth, although without reference to Schumpeter, by Chick and Dow (2005). Provisional closures are introduced to generate models embedded in a more general, open theory. Such closures are necessarily distorting, as the outcome of the model will be partially unreal. It is therefore important to distinguish between theoretically valuable mechanisms, spurious results produced by the distorting closure and empirical phenomena. The downsides implicit in the approach are significant, yet both Chick and Dow (ibid.) and Schumpeter (1939, 68) claim that no better alternative is available for theoretical analysis. For Schumpeter, a complete economic theory is a contradiction in terms (Schumpeter 1934, 58): pure economic theory must be incomplete; yet, a model cannot be. The specific institutional closure provided by the order allows it to derive contextual causal mechanisms from the universal concept of the creative response, which is sufficient for theoretical exposition. But the generation of a complete model requires a similar closure for the realisation of the universal concept of the adaptive response, too.

Consequently, the Walrasian equilibrium is explicitly employed as 'a *description of an apparatus of response*' (Schumpeter 1939, 68, emphasis in the original). Notice that it is simply '*an apparatus*' rather than '*the apparatus*', no more than 'a first approximation which stops far short of what we need for an analysis of processes in an incessantly disturbed economic world' (ibid., 47). It provides a description of the adaptive response that, while unreal, is coherent with the fundamental features of the adaptive response, a passive adjustment taken at the individual level on the basis of socially determined prices. While individual agents ultimately generate the equilibrium through their actions, such actions are based on social data, due to the fundamental Walrasian assumption, 'that people react to existing prices only' (Schumpeter 1939, 53). Actual social values are not significant; they do not have any purpose for purely theoretical analysis, and the unreal qualities of this model prevent application to empirical phenomena. All that the Walrasian equilibrium provides to the Schumpeterian system is the existence of a social norm, the distance from which identifies the creative response; a purely theoretical closure, external to the universal set of 'tools of analysis', introduced for the specific purpose of generating a model.

The question, however, of why Walrasian equilibrium was chosen as the specific theoretical closure remains. It is possible to argue that the Walrasian system was used by Schumpeter because he saw it as the best systemic economic analysis of the adaptive response available at the beginning of the previous century, when Schumpeter's career started (Schumpeter 1954). But there is a more important reason behind that choice. Schumpeter focuses on what he perceived as the key missing element of economic analysis, namely the creative response, disregarding its counterpart, the adaptive response, being largely content to rely on established economic theory for the latter's representation. It could be argued that the adaptive response falls outside of the scope of Schumpeterian theory, as Schumpeter has not produced a description of its actual mechanisms, simply being content with an explicitly unreal description, useful only as a background for the working of the creative response – an expository strategy for which Schumpeter would later explicitly apologise, stating its true purpose: 'to bring out, by contrast, the contours of the phenomena of economic evolution' (Schumpeter 1939, 36 n. 1).

The problem is that the assumptions supporting the Walrasian equilibrium are incompatible with the mechanisms and conclusions of Schumpeterian theory. The establishment of a social norm in the form of a specific price vector shared by all agents, used as a unique basis for decision, requires previously occurring indeterminate repetition of identical outcomes, an outcome requiring the pre-existence of the same social norm it is intended to deliver: a paradox occurring due to the attempt to integrate the mechanical time of Schumpeterian theory with an essentially timeless construct (Carvalho 1983). But timeless identical repetition, the assumption required for the generation and maintenance of the Walrasian norm, is also incompatible with the main object of study of Schumpeter, economic development. Endless repetition requires a complete absence of creative response and, therefore, of uncertainty. Conscious of the issue, Schumpeter introduced a theoretically not justifiable ad hoc assumption that the creative response starts taking place only after an indeterminate long-term period absolutely dominated by the adaptive response. But this fix is insufficient.

When the creative response starts operating, the apparatus of response should cease to work. Timeless repetition is disrupted by historical evolution, eliminating any support for the re-establishment of a new social norm. The final phase of the Schumpeterian model sees a return to a, slightly changed, equilibrium, but this is inconsistent with the premises. Since timeless repetition has been breached, how is the new set of supporting social prices generated? Schumpeter does not discuss this point because the Walrasian closure he chose cannot accommodate such changes. The framework supports a theory of how the creative response upsets conventional evaluations expressed by the socioeconomic system but cannot effectively describe how the latter change in response. This is because the conventional basis of systemic evaluations follows, in Schumpeterian theory, from the necessarily mixed socioeconomic nature of the system, opposite the pure economic logic embodied by the Walrasian model, in which the implicit set of expectations is simply given as consistent with equilibrium: 'heroic theorising' (Schumpeter 1954, 968). This forces Schumpeter to introduce a nebulously defined 'neighborhood of equilibrium' concept (Schumpeter 1939, 71) as the final state of the system, a compromise forced by the fundamental inconsistency of economic development with Walrasian equilibrium (Wolfson 1958).

The adoption of the Walrasian equilibrium as theoretical closure allows Schumpeter to build a model, but the resulting conflicts in underlying assumptions lead to severe inconsistency. Since the closure does not play a substantial role at the abstract theoretical level, and Walrasian assumptions are in fact inconsistent with economic development, there are ample reasons to advocate its removal from the Schumpeterian system. Yet, an individual creative response still requires a norm to deviate from. Schumpeterian economic theory requires a description of how social norms emerge and survive in a world where the creative response is always possible, and a corresponding theoretical closure. While a coherent theoretical apparatus of response could be built *ex novo*, the Schumpeterian interpretation proposed here supports instead an integration between Schumpeterian and Keynesian theory. It is not the first time that such an integration has been proposed from either side. The earliest instances can be traced to a time when both Keynes and Schumpeter were still alive (e.g. Stolper 1943; Bennion 1943; Wright 1945). Isolated cries could still be heard in the 1950s: 'What a misfortune it is that twentieth century economics is not enriched by a Schumpeter-Keynes correspondence' (Smithies 1951, 163). Calls and efforts in this direction have been recently renewed (e.g. Sylos Labini 1983; Minsky 1990a; Goodwin 1991; Whalen 2001; Nasica 2002; Verspagen 2002; Bertocco 2006; Dosi, Fagiolo and Roventini 2010; Caiani, Godin and Lucarelli. 2014; Knell 2015; Mazzucato and Wray 2015), hence contributing to reducing the distance between the two traditions.

In particular, post-Keynesian mechanisms could provide a superior description of an 'apparatus of response' based on path-dependent institutions, conventions and monetary phenomena rather than timeless repetition. The introduction of such economic closure would allow the theorisation of interactions between conventional evaluations and the creative response, allowing the study of the impact of discontinuous changes on the former. The inclusion of Schumpeterian concepts would allow for a novel expansion of the analysis of stability under uncertainty, a key debate of the post-Keynesian tradition,[7] while at the same time vastly improving the least satisfying aspect of Schumpeterian theory. The explicit distinction between the two points of view is meant to express the need for integration to proceed as a discussion, rather than a hybridisation. The atmosphere of mutual respect in the presence of significant differences of opinion evoked by Stolper (1989) provides the most appropriate background. Keynesian theory does not 'complete' Schumpeterian theory, and vice versa; still, more extensive contact and exchange between the two traditions appears to be desirable from both sides.

The second limitation of Schumpeterian theory illustrates another avenue for integration and an important caveat. Both the pre-*CSD* concept of regime and the idea of an order imply the obsolescence of any original contingent element. As remarked above, this does not exclusively mean that the specific variant of capitalism used by Schumpeter as institutional closure is not appropriate for the analysis of any other relevant context. It also means that all Schumpeterian theoretical propositions developed under such institutional assumptions are to be discarded, if not confirmed by new, relevant institutional closures. Schumpeterian profits, competition-mediated disruption and bank-financing of innovation: all these elements and more must be acknowledged as transient constructs whose relevance is to be argued anew. The basis for such arguments must be present in institutional analysis. The burgeoning field of innovation studies has created a comprehensive knowledge basis for the current workings of the actual entrepreneurial function and its immediate institutional context. However, in order to move from actual description to a stylised Schumpeterian order, a similarly extensive description of the financial and monetary infrastructure is required, something that innovation studies in general, and the neo-Schumpeterian branch in particular, have disregarded, a problem recently acknowledged by Hanusch and Pyka (2007).

Again, the most appropriate solution appears to be integration with the Keynesian tradition, which has never lost sight of the importance of money and finance for the analysis of capitalism. In particular, it is possible to identify the work done, and influenced, by Hyman Minsky as a natural starting point for integration. As described by Knell (2015), despite starting his doctoral research work under Schumpeter, after graduating Minsky became a devoted proponent of Keynes. Very few references to Schumpeter could be found in Minsky's work until 1986, when, to celebrate the centenary of Schumpeter and Keynes, Minsky wrote an essay dedicated to the pair (Minsky 1986a). Schumpeter is unfavourably compared to Keynes; the Great Recession, he writes, prompted a 'magnificent' performance from Keynes, *The General Theory*. Schumpeter's response, *Business Cycles*, was 'banal,' a step backward in comparison to his earlier work. The tone is consistent throughout the article: Keynes is reactive and original, while Schumpeter is Ptolemaic; Keynes is a patriot working for the betterment of the world, Schumpeter is aloof, not involved in the civil and political struggle. Some merits are accorded to Schumpeter, e.g. monetary analysis, the focus on banking and the dynamic perspective. But there is no doubt that the comparison is unfavourable for Schumpeter. Yet, a few years later, something changed. Schumpeter and Keynes are now declared compatible; in fact, an integration of Schumpeter and Keynes 'improves our understanding of capitalist economies' (Minsky 1990a, 2). While some criticism remains, the tone of the article is markedly different. It is here that for the first time, Minsky, inspired by 'Schumpeterian insight', introduces his classification of the stages of capitalist financial development for the first time, an explicit reference to Schumpeter's regimes. The integration of institutional considerations in economic analysis is necessary because they 'change the relations between financial and real economic variables, which in turn changes the dynamic patterns of the economy' (ibid., 27).

The Minskyan definition of the capitalist regime, refined over a series of papers (Minsky 1990a, 1990b, 1991, 1993a, 1993b, 1996; Gatti, Gallegati and Minsky 1994; Minsky and Whalen 1996) hinges on the relationship between finance and business. In particular, 'regimes are distinguished by differences between trade and industry, the capital intensity … and the balance of economic power between merchants and managers on one side and financial institutions and financial market operators on the other' (Minsky 1990a, 27). Gone is the Schumpeterian attention to the creative response, substituted by the traditional Keynesian theme of the relative influence of managers and financial agents on investment decisions, the focus of Chapter 12 of the *General Theory* (Keynes 1936). Notice that at the very same time Crotty criticises Minsky's previous work for conflating the concepts of managers and shareholders, arguing for a shifting balance of power to be determined through historical and institutional analysis (Crotty 1990b), Minsky's 'Schumpeterian insight' is leading him in the exact direction advocated by Crotty.

While the Minskyan definition of a capitalist regime is different from Schumpeter's, it is not incompatible. Minsky is concerned with the general relationship between production and finance; Schumpeter identifies the same relationship as pivotal, although in the specific context of the creative response. The two conceptualisations, while different, tend to overlap, although mismatches might emerge during transitional periods. It should be noted that the more general Minskyan approach might be required for the analysis of the coherent process of adaptive response to successful entrepreneurial projects. At the same time, a Schumpeterian focus on the systemic channels dedicated to enabling the creative response could strengthen the Minskyan analysis of an evolving financial economy. This later stage of the Minskyan contribution has heavily influenced two separate research agendas: the Post-Keynesian Institutionalist approach (Whalen 2013) and the 'Money View' approach (Mehrling 2010). The former has argued for a deeper, broader integration of institutionalist analysis in the Post-Keynesian tradition, directly acknowledging the potential role that Schumpeterian integration could play in the process. The latter has instead focused on a theory-laden analysis of both the micro and macro structures of financial markets, producing an in-depth, realist analysis of these crucial institutions and their development over time. Both these approaches are meaningful 'entry points' for a Schumpeterian/Keynesian integration: the first providing the ground for a fertile theoretical and methodological debate, the second a precious source for the derivation of a relevant institutional closure to make the Schumpeterian system useful for the analysis of today.

While largely consistent with the pre-*CSD* concept of regime, however, Minskyan and generally Post-Keynesian institutional analysis of capitalism does not integrate the socio-political concepts developed by Schumpeter under the concept of order. The consequences are in line with expectations. Minsky identifies several capitalistic variants, but his analysis does not extend, and in its current form could hardly extend, to the analysis of non-capitalistic systems. At the same time, just like the pre-*CSD* regime conceptualisation, the Minskyan regimes are rather static, a description of a given condition not containing any element to assess the possibility and conditions for regime change. If we do not intend to lose the methodological advances secured by *CSD*, it is necessary to expand the Minskyan regimes into order descriptions, by integrating both creative response considerations, and the relevant socio-political elements. This future task, a strict requirement from a Schumpeterian perspective, would also be consistent with the interest demonstrated by a large part of the Post-Keynesian community in the analysis of the conditions, consequences and prospects of the currently financialised society (e.g. Stockhammer 2004; Zalewski and Whalen 2010; Palley 2016; Mehrling 2017).

A third limitation concerns the role of the state in the theory of economic development. Schumpeter is almost silent on the subject, and almost no mention of the public sector can be found in his main works on economic theory (Schumpeter 1934, 1939). The reason is revealed in an early historical and sociological contribution, *The Crisis of the Tax State* (Schumpeter 1918). Schumpeter describes a capitalist economy as one in which production is organised by and for private interests; in this context, the nature of the state is that of 'an economic parasite' (ibid., 112), diverting resources from the private economy to a variety of uses. The state can transcend this role and 'become an entrepreneur itself' (ibid., 116), using its considerable resources to create and run economic activities. However, profits are not an aim of the state per se, but simply a potential source of purchasing power, similar to taxation. Therefore, Schumpeter is sceptical of the entrepreneurial state, arguing that as long as the aim is to raise money, taxing private enterprise is likely to be a superior alternative to direct state entrepreneurship. From this perspective, the guiding principle must be to adopt a modus operandi that minimises the disruption of private interests, the drivers of economic development.

Revisiting the topic 30 years later, Schumpeter (1948) described this perspective as Gladstonian, consistent with laissez-faire liberalism, and adapted to a competitive capitalism regime that did not exist anymore. The new state emerging from the World Wars intended to use its policies to extensively affect economic activities while maintaining the broader capitalist framework. Schumpeter was a vocal critic of such developments but, crucially, not on economic grounds. He admitted that state intervention might lead to lower unemployment, subdued economic cycles and a gradual reduction of inequality, and that all this could be achieved without substantially injuring the development potential (Schumpeter 1950). What he lamented instead was the passing away of 'a scheme of values, an attitude toward life, a civilisation – the civilisation of inequality and of the family fortune' (ibid., 450). Economic praise and the socio-cultural condemnation of state intervention in the post-war era is found in other contributions; for example, in Schumpeter (1949) the British state is praised for its direct investments, and further planning and regulations are encouraged in order to achieve the desired economic objectives, despite severe criticism of the underlying 'laborite creed'. The clearest example is offered in Chapter XVI of *CSD*, in which an economic system entirely run by a centralised bureaucracy is described as not only possible, but also potentially superior, on pure economic rounds, to a trustified capitalism order.

The lack of an explicit discussion of the role of the state in the process of economic development is therefore not a silent indictment of the inability of the state to perform that role, but rather an omission justified by the Gladstonian view adopted by Schumpeter in the earlier stages of his career. The institutional closure of the competitive capitalism regime implies a marginal state, whose parasitic role can be initially ignored for theoretical purposes. However, if the absent state is justifiable in the analysis of a specific institutional configuration, its absence from the theoretical core appears as an important limitation to be remedied. And yet the situation is not so clear cut, because the Schumpeterian State is among the 'denizens of the world of commercial society' (Schumpeter 2011, 169): it exists only within the confines of an institutional regime of private property and private initiative, and 'should not be allowed to intrude into discussions of either feudal or socialist society' (ibid.). Therefore, while an integration of the Schumpeterian theory of the state in the general Schumpeterian system might be desirable, it should take place at the specific level of institutional analysis rather that at the general level of economic principles.

In Schumpeter's original conceptualisation, the state is a special configuration of the monopoly of violence arising in response to the development of Individual economic interest. It is 'a machine ... that ... opposes individual egotism as a representative of the common purpose' (Schumpeter 1918, 110). Essentially, the state takes care of tasks related to the common good that an individualistic economy, and therefore an individualistic society, would not perform. The state resorts to direct and indirect coercion in order to maintain the commonwealth in an individualistic system[8]; how the common purpose is defined, articulated and pursued depends on specific historical trajectories. The legitimisation of a private sphere of individual wants and aims implies the simultaneous emergence of a separate public sphere: the state. Both the state and the individualist economic system are born from the fission of the organic community, where only the common interest was recognised. This peculiar definition of the state implies a definite limit to the exercise of its faculties. While the monopoly of violence theoretically gives the state unlimited power of coercion, the state exists only if its coercive actions are consistent with the continued existence of private interests; from a Schumpeterian perspective, a totalitarian state is a contradiction in terms: 'If socialism became a reality through the conquest of the economy by the power of the state, the state would annul itself by its very expansion' (ibid., 109). Of course, an entity that alternative definitions could identify as 'state' would still exist, but the Schumpeterian state would have disappeared.

This definition of state makes its introduction in the theory of capitalist economic development, as opposed to the general theory of economic development, a sheer necessity, as the underlying individualistic economic system implies its existence. How does it interact with the other constituting theoretical elements? As the carrier of the public interest, the State is by definition detached from the individualistic rationality of the private economic system. At the same time, its actions are constrained by the need to maintain the working of the private sphere. The universalistic tendencies of conventional expectation will necessarily integrate the state and its actions in the working of the price system. Therefore, even if moved by entirely different interests, the state's actions can still be understood under the framework of the adaptive and creative response.

While the power of coercion gives the state significant latitude to ignore conventional expectations, there is a limit to the actual ability to exercise such power. Successful creative response forces the revaluation of economic resources and income redistribution; an exceedingly entrepreneurial state risks undermining confidence in conventional expectations and the related ability of the private sector to invest. This is the theoretical root behind Schumpeter's diffidence towards the New Deal and, in general, towards novel expansions of state activities (Schumpeter 1950). The main problem, however, does not lie in the expansion of the state in itself, but rather in the new, unexpected and untested ways in which it might be manifested – not the quantitative expansion of the budget, but rather the concomitant qualitative changes. Bold new economic policies might be successful in meeting their stated objectives, while simultaneously undermining the capability for private investment; the mechanism works through confidence and expectation, rather than through the displacement of physical resources. Even so, the negative side effect is temporary and results not from actual policy content but from the expectation gap. However, combined successful implementation and disappointing performance might lead to a continuous expansion of the public agenda, thereby making it impossible for confidence to recover and steadily eroding the economic relevance of the private sphere. This is the limiting case of the entrepreneurial state, whose continuous successful novel activities ultimately transform society away from an individualistic to a socialist system. Its purely theoretical nature is underscored by the difficulty inherent in identifying valid historical examples.

The Gladstonian perspective adopted by Schumpeter in his early works provides an excellent example of the opposite limiting case of the passive state. The objective of Gladstonian finance (Schumpeter 1954, 401) is to remove fiscal obstructions to private activity, and consequently minimise public functions. By steadily curtailing government intervention, a source of uncertainty for market evaluations is eliminated, hence boosting confidence. The resulting minimal state takes care of the public interest indirectly, through the growth of income resulting from the unhampered work of private agents. The success obtained by this historical experiment was not a specific application of the general virtue of laissez-faire, but instead the result of special contextual circumstances. Public interests were served, not by the normal working of private agents, but by the unprecedented period of shared growth that took place in England at the time. The Gladstonian state is reliant on continuous economic expansion to meet its objectives, as without sustained growth it lacks the resources required to take care of the public interest. Due to an inconsistency with established expectations, its explicit commitment to a minimal size hampers the scope of any potential crisis intervention. The laissez-faire approach is able to strengthen the reach of conventional expectations and, during expansion, relative confidence, but cannot respond to crisis and depression without substantial changes.

From a Schumpeterian perspective, Minsky's 'Big Government' (1986b), the apparent opposite to the minimal state of Gladstone, appears as simply a development and refinement of the latter. Big Government adjusts its budget to validate corporate profit expectations, in order to maintain high levels of investment and employment through a subdued economic cycle. Contrary to the liquidationist view often associated with him (e.g. De Long 1990), similar Keynesian policies have been analysed and endorsed by Schumpeter on multiple occasions (1985, 1939, 2011). Like the Gladstonian state, Big Government aims toward the satisfaction of public interest through sustained economic growth by supporting conventional expectations and related confidence. The crucial difference lies in the Keynesian understanding of the frail nature of expectations and the resulting development of the resources and instrument required for the state to support and maintain the structure of conventional expectations when the private agents involved fail in this task.

Minsky's Big Government describes the working of a state that has integrated the short-term objective of Keynes's policy agenda: the stabilisation of the economic cycle and enduring full employment (Keynes 1936, 322). However, Keynes's long-term objective was nothing less than the euthanasia of the rentier, the elimination of interest income. This is what Schumpeter describes as the 'laborite creed' of the Keynesians. Despite its class connotations, Schumpeter acknowledges that the euthanasia of the rentier is not synonymous with socialism. The latter implies the elimination of the legitimised individualist economy and the reintegration of the public and private sphere into a new communal form. Instead, the euthanasia is consistent with the continued existence of a state and therefore an individualist economy, although, crucially, not with the survival of capitalism. Money would lose its ability to generate income for the owner, in short, to be capital; for Schumpeter, no other definitions of capital are admissible. The hypothetical resulting society is consequently described by Schumpeter as labourist, as opposed to socialist, whereas the aim of Minsky's Big Government is the continuation of capitalism in a stabilised form. The crucial policy of cheap money and the related control of the term structure of the interest rate through comprehensive debt management (Tily 2006, 2016) are correspondingly abandoned, together with the commitment to low and steadily reducing interest rates.

The weakness of this approach, described in Ferri and Minsky (1992), is the vulnerability to entrepreneurial activities. Constant qualitative change in economic processes can reduce the effectiveness of the instruments deployed by the state to validate expectations, forcing ever increasing interventions that could eventually run into economic or political obstacles. Even in the case of perfect implementation, the creative response's inevitability condemns Big Government to a progressive decline in the ability to respond. From a Schumpeterian perspective, the most evident sign of this issue is a 'perennial inflationary pressure' (Schumpeter 1950). This pressure creates difficulties for the financial sector and its ability to maintain profitability, thus leading to instability and the necessity for increased intervention. Ironically, the preservation of capitalism under stable conditions appears to be as challenging as the Keynesian project to supersede it. In the long-term, the only potentially effective Big Government appears to be an entrepreneurial state, able to creatively respond to the economic system's evolution, the only alternative being progressive delegitimisation and eventual regime change.

Schumpeterian entrepreneurship is a relative concept, defined in relation to existing conventional expectations. It does not identify any specific economic activity as 'entrepreneurial' in itself. Similarly, a Schumpeterian entrepreneurial state is not necessarily involved with the entrepreneurial function, the implementation of new viable economic combinations. The term identifies instead a state whose current policies are not consistent with ruling conventional expectations. Barring exceptional conditions, the situation must be temporary, as governmental activities will eventually modify existing expectations. Such changes might or might not undermine confidence in ruling conventions and their supporting agents, depending on the actual scope and nature of the activities involved.

Yet the integration of the state in the Schumpeterian theory of capitalist development must also take into account its potential consequences for the entrepreneurial process. From this point of view, we can identify two primary potential roles for the state. First of all, the state provides an alternative channel through which entrepreneurial agents can obtain the resources required for innovative activities. As a non-profit entity able to own, tax, borrow or create great amounts of resources, the state satisfies the requirement of partial financial autonomy and can effectively act to enable and support entrepreneurs. This support is not motivated by profit expectations, as gain cannot be the objective of a Schumpeterian state, but rather consistency with politically established public interests. Entrepreneurial activities might be fostered to improve the ability of the State to protect its citizens, or project its power. Another example is currently provided by the many state initiatives aimed at supporting the slow transition toward an environmentally sustainable economy.

Second, the state can adopt an explicit objective of economic transformation, engaging directly in the required entrepreneurial activities. A Schumpeterian analysis of the developmental state would focus on its exceptional characteristics in comparison to other agents: 1) the state could be entirely independent of financial interests in domestic activities, although the same cannot be said for any initiative involving resources under foreign control. In this case, the state might be hampered by profitability considerations and therefore lose many of its unique characteristics as an entrepreneurial agent, and 2) the power of coercion of the state allows it to perform and/or organise innovative activities outside the established innovation process. While individual entrepreneurs must still adhere to the conventions ruling the financing of the creative response, the developmental state is free to act unconventionally in an unconventional way. The state therefore has the ability to not only foster innovative activities, but also to consciously modify the current working of the innovation process if deemed to be inconsistent with the public interest. It follows that the state has the potential to be a conscious actor of Schumpeterian institutional regime change, although such a role likely requires an understanding of the centrality of innovation in the economic process that goes beyond a linear growth relationship. While the potentially disruptive nature of the developmental state has been obscured in the original contribution by the early Gladstonian view adopted by Schumpeter, the direction for future research sketched here appears promising. The above discussion shows that, yet again, constructive interaction with the Keynesian tradition might be a rewarding approach for both sides.

The above considerations, in addition to other numerous contact points highlighted by the researchers supporting the integration mentioned above, trace the broad contour, not of a 'fixed' Schumpeterian system, but of a debate between two traditions that, while separate, have never actually been distant. The limitations of the inherited Schumpeterian contribution suggest a programme of collaboration. A broad institutionalist interpretation, an example of which is provided here, presents a potential Schumpeterian starting point, as the discussion above identifies some natural Keynesian counterparts. In a situation in which modeling efforts in both traditions show promising signs of convergence (cf. Caiani *et al.* 2016, with Dosi, Fagiolo, Napoletano and Roventini 2013), a debate on the fundamental assumptions, methodological positions and theoretical propositions of the two systems would be a natural and required step in the co-respective development of the two traditions.

Conclusion

Reviewing Keynes's *General Theory* (1936), Frank Knight describes the attempted Keynesian revolution in these terms: 'fundamental assumptions [of economic theory] are rejected outright and others are substituted' (Knight 1937). Starting with his *Theory of Economic Development* (1934), Schumpeter ostensibly embarked on a similar operation. Yet, while Keynes took an explicit approach, Schumpeter clad his revolutionary attempt in conservative garb, unintentionally obscuring the more far-reaching consequences of his own work. While the Keynesian revolution was unfinished, or perhaps adulterated (Robinson 1962), the Schumpeterian revolution never truly started. The neo-Schumpeterian revival of the 1980s lifted a few concepts from the graveyard of economic ideas, adapting them to then-current debates, ultimately leading to what could be described as a Schumpeterian-neoclassical synthesis. It also inspired the emergence of what is today recognised as a new school of economic thought, evolutionary economics, whose theoretical and methodological achievements have enriched our understanding of economic change. Economists from both schools have adopted an image of Schumpeter as a prophet of innovation, an inspiring figure to be followed, from a safe distance.

What was left behind was the idea of the Schumpeterian system as a coherent, structured, extensive system of economic analysis, a system whose development reached its zenith with *CSD*. It was the scientific achievement that Schumpeter thought would guarantee his legacy. This short review has attempted to establish some of the reasons behind that confidence. It would perhaps not be an exaggeration to argue that the depth, scope and ambition of the Schumpeterian contribution, built over decades of economic, sociological and historical analysis deserve the qualification of being a paradigm. It is not, however, nor was it ever meant to be, a complete work, and perhaps nowhere do its limits stand so exposed as in *CSD*. Yet I would argue that these limits, and even its, perhaps inevitable, contradictions, are insufficient to condemn the whole edifice. Standing on its top, it is still possible to state

> [t]hat there are paths, on which one can press forward further, that the area, in which we work, has not been exhausted yet, that there is also a tomorrow for us – and not only a yesterday – a future and not only a past, this is all that we can claim with ease, but at the same time, also everything that we need.
>
> (Schumpeter 2010, 270)

Notes

1 Incidentally christening the famous methodological stance in the process.
2 Although crucially not from his sociological and political theory, nor from the final Schumpeterian synthesis reached in *CSD*.
3 The choice of neutral pronoun underlines the purely abstract nature of the Schumpeterian Individual described.
4 In keeping with established best practices.
5 See Schumpeter 2010, 466 for an earlier statement of the same argument.
6 The latter does not have a specific function in theoretical analysis but informs and supports all three levels.
7 A summary of its earlier development can be found in Rosser 2001.
8 There is a remarkable affinity between the Schumpeterian idea of the state as the necessary counterpart of the legitimised individualist economic system and Polanyi's conceptualisation of the pure, complete market as incompatible with the survival of human society (Polanyi 1944).

References

Allen, R.L. (1991). *Opening Doors: The Life and Work of Joseph Schumpeter*. New York: Transaction Publishers.
Arrow, K.J. (1994). Methodological individualism and social knowledge. *The American Economic Review*, 84(2): 1–9.
Arrow, K.J. and F.H. Hahn (1971). *General Competitive Analysis*. San Francisco, CA: Holden Day.
Bennion, E. (1943). Unemployment in the theories of Schumpeter and Keynes. *The American Economic Review*, 33(2): 336–347.
Bertocco, G. (2006). The characteristics of a monetary economy: A Keynes–Schumpeter approach. *Cambridge Journal of Economics*, 31(1): 101–122.
Bhaskar, R. (1978). *A Realist Theory of Science*. Hemel Hempstead, UK: Harvester Press.
Caiani, A., Godin, A., Caverzasi, E., Gallegati, M., Kinsella, S. and Stiglitz, J.E. (2016). Agent based-stock flow consistent macroeconomics: Towards a benchmark model. *Journal of Economic Dynamics and Control*, 69: 375–408.
Caiani, A., Godin, A. and Lucarelli, S. (2014). Innovation and finance: A stock flow consistent analysis of great surges of development. *Journal of Evolutionary Economics*, 24(2): 421–448.

Carvalho, F. (1983). On the concept of time in Shacklean and Sraffian economics. *Journal of Post Keynesian Economics*, 6(2): 265–280.

Chick, V. and Dow, S. (2005). The meaning of open systems. *Journal of Economic Methodology*, 12(3): 363–381.

Clemence, R.V. and Doody, F.S. (1950). *The Schumpeterian System*. Cambridge: Cambridge University Press.

Crotty, J.R. (1990a). Keynes on the stages of development of the capitalist economy: The institutional foundation of Keynes's methodology. *Journal of Economic Issues*, 24(3): 761–780.

Crotty, J.R. (1990b). Owner-manager conflict and financial theories of investment instability: A critical assessment of Keynes, Tobin, and Minsky. *Journal of Post Keynesian Economics*, 12(4): 519–542.

Courvisanos, J. and Mackenzie, S. (2011). Addressing Schumpeter's plea: Critical realism in entrepreneurial history. Paper presented at the Eighth AGSE International Entrepreneurial Research Exchange Conference, Swinburne University of Technology, Melbourne, Australia.

da Graça Moura, M. (2002). Metatheory as the key to understanding: Schumpeter after Shionoya. *Cambridge Journal of Economics*, 26(6): 805–821.

De Long, J.B. (1990). 'Liquidation' cycles: Old-fashioned real business cycle theory and the Great Depression. NBER Working Paper No. 3546. National Bureau of Economic Research.

Dosi, G., Fagiolo, G., Napoletano, M. and Roventini, A. (2013). Income distribution, credit and fiscal policies in an agent-Based Keynesian Model. *Journal of Economic Dynamics and Control*, 37(8): 1598–1625.

Dosi, G., Fagiolo, G. and Roventini, A. (2010). Schumpeter meeting Keynes: A policy-friendly model of endogenous growth and business cycles. *Journal of Economic Dynamics and Control*, 34(9): 1748–1767.

Elliott, J.E. (1983). Schumpeter and the theory of capitalist economic development. *Journal of Economic Behavior & Organisation*, 4(4): 277–308.

Ferri, P. and Minsky, H.P. (1992). Market processes and thwarting systems. *Structural Change and Economic Dynamics*, 3(1): 79–91.

Fleetwood, S. (2002). *Critical Realism in Economics: Development and Debate*. London: Routledge.

Gatti, D.D., Gallegati, M. and Minsky, J.P. (1994). Financial institutions, economic policy, and the dynamic behavior of the economy. Levy Economics Institute. Economics Working Paper Archive.

Goodwin, R.M. (1991). Schumpeter, Keynes and the theory of economic evolution. *Journal of Evolutionary Economics*, 1(1): 29–47.

Haberler, G. (1950). Joseph Alois Schumpeter★ 1883–1950. *The Quarterly Journal of Economics*, 64(3), 333–372.

Hahn, F. (1965). On some problems of proving the existence of an equilibrium in a monetary economy. In F. Hahn and F. Brechling (Eds.), *The Theory of Interest Rates* (pp. 126–135). London: Macmillan.

Hanusch, H. and A. Pyka (2007). *Elgar Companion to Neo-Schumpeterian Economics*. Cheltenham, UK: Edward Elgar.

Hodgson, G.M. (2007). Meanings of methodological individualism. *Journal of Economic Methodology*, 14(2): 211–226.

Johnson, H.G. (1951). Reviewed work: *The Schumpeterian System* by R.V. Clemence and F.S. Doody. *The Economic Journal*, 61(241): 139–141.

Keynes, J.M. (1936). *The General Theory of Interest, Employment and Money*. London: Macmillan.

Knell, M. (2015). Schumpeter, Minsky and the financial instability hypothesis. *Journal of Evolutionary Economics*, 25(1): 293–310.

Knight, F.H. (1937). Unemployment: And Mr. Keynes's revolution in economic theory. *The Canadian Journal of Economics and Political Science/Revue canadienne d'Economique et de Science politique*, 3(1): 100–123.

Lawson, T. (1997). *Economics and Reality*. London: Routledge.

Lawson, T. (2003). *Reorienting Economics*. London: Routledge.

Lewis, P. (2004). *Transforming Economics: Perspectives on the Critical Realist Project*. London: Routledge.

Lindenberg, S. (1983). Utility and morality. *Kyklos*, 36(3): 450–468.

Lucas Jr, R.E. (1984). Money in a theory of finance. *Carnegie-Rochester Conference Series on Public Policy*, 21: 9–46.

McCraw, T.K. (2009). *Prophet of Innovation*. Cambridge, MA: Harvard University Press.

Marget, A.W. (1951). The monetary aspects of the Schumpeterian system. *The Review of Economics and Statistics*, 33(2): 112–121.

Mazzucato, M. and Wray, L.R. (2015). Financing the capital development of the economy: A Keynes-Schumpeter-Minsky synthesis. Levy Economics Institute of Bard College Working Paper No. 837.

Mehrling, P. (2010). *The New Lombard Street: How the Fed Became the Dealer of Last Resort*. Princeton, NJ: Princeton University Press.

Mehrling, P. (2017). Financialisation and its discontents. *Finance and Society*, 2(2): 138–150.

Minsky, H.P. (1986a). Money and crisis in Schumpeter and Keynes. In H.-J. Wagener and J.W. Drukker (Eds.), *The Economic Law of Motion of modern Society: A Marx-Keynes-Schumpeter Centennial* (pp. 112–122). Cambridge: Cambridge University Press.

Minsky, H.P. (1986b). *Stabilising an Unstable Economy*. New Haven, CT: Yale University Press.

Minsky, H.P. (1990a). Schumpeter: Finance and evolution. In: A. Heertje and M. Perlman (Eds.), *Evolving Technology and Market Structure: Studies in Schumpeterian Economics* (pp. 51–73). Ann Arbor, MI: University of Michigan Press.

Minsky, H.P. (1990b). Money manager capitalism, fiscal independence and international monetary reconstruction. In: M. Szabo-Pelsoczi (Ed.), *The Future of The Global Economic and Monetary System* (pp. 209–218). Budapest: Institute for World Economics of the Hungarian Academy of Science.

Minsky, H.P. (1991). Financial crises: Systemic or idiosyncratic. Levy Economics Institute Working Paper No. 51.

Minsky, H.P. (1993a). Finance and stability: The limits of capitalism. Levy Economics Institute Working Paper No. 93.

Minsky, H.P. (1993b). Financial structure and the financing of the capital development of the economy. Hyman P. Minsky Archive. Paper 479.

Minsky, H.P. (1996). Uncertainty and the institutional structure of capitalist economies: Remarks upon receiving the Veblen–Commons Award. *Journal of Economic Issues*, 30(2): 357–368.

Minsky, H.P. and Whalen, C.J. (1996). Economic insecurity and the institutional prerequisites for successful capitalism. *Journal of Post Keynesian Economics*, 19(2): 155–170.

Musgrave, R.A. (1992). Schumpeter's crisis of the tax state: An essay in fiscal sociology. *Journal of Evolutionary Economics*, 2(2), 89–113.

Nasica, E. (2002). Financing economic activity: Schumpeter vs Keynes. In: R. Arena and C. Dangel-Hagnauer (Eds.), *The Contribution of Joseph Schumpeter to Economics* (pp. 251–256). London: Routledge.

Palley, T. (2016). *Financialisation: The Economics of Finance Capital Domination*. London: Palgrave Macmillan.

Pasinetti, L.L. (2007). *Keynes and the Cambridge Keynesians: A 'Revolution in Economics' to be Accomplished*. Cambridge: Cambridge University Press.

Polanyi, K. (1944). *The Great Transformation: Economic and Political Origins of our Time*. New York: Farrar & Rinehart.

Robinson, J. (1962). The General Theory after 25 Years (review of Harry Johnson's *Money, Trade and Economic Growth*). *Economic Journal*, 72: 690–692.

Rosser, J.B. (2001). Alternative Keynesian and Post Keynesian perspective on uncertainty and expectations. *Journal of Post Keynesian Economics*, 23(4): 545–566.

Sayer, A. (2010). *Method in Social Science* (revised 2nd edn.). London: Routledge.

Schumpeter, J. (1909). On the concept of social value. *The Quarterly Journal of Economics*, 23(2): 213–232.

Schumpeter, J.A. (1917–1918). *Das Sozialprodukt und die Rechenpfennige: Glossen und Beiträge zur Geldtheorie von heute*. Tubingen: Archiv für Sozialwissenschaft und Sozialpolitik. Reprinted in: J.A. Schumpeter, *Ten Great Economists: From Marx to Keynes*. New York: Francis & Taylor, 1952. English translation in *International Economic Papers* 1956, 148–211.

Schumpeter, J.A. (1918). The crisis of the tax state. In: R. Swedberg (Ed.), *Joseph A. Schumpeter, the Economics and Sociology of Capitalism*. Princeton: Princeton University Press, 1991.

Schumpeter, J.A. (1928). The instability of capitalism. *The Economic Journal*, 38(151): 361–386.

Schumpeter, J.A. (1934). *The Theory of Economic Development: An Inquiry into Profits, Capital, Credit, Interest, and the Business Cycle*. Cambridge, MA: Harvard University Press.

Schumpeter, J.A. (1939). *Business Cycles: A Theoretical, Historical and Statistical Analysis of the Capitalist Process*. New York: McGraw-Hill.

Schumpeter, J.A. (1946). The decade of the Twenties. *The American Economic Review*, 36(2), 1–10.

Schumpeter, J.A. (1947a). The creative response in economic history. *The Journal of Economic History*, 7(2): 149–159.

Schumpeter, J.A. (1947b). Theoretical problems of economic growth. *The Journal of Economic History*, 7(S1): 1–9.

Schumpeter, J.A. (1948). Wages and tax policy in transitional states of society. In: R. Swedberg (Ed.), *Joseph A. Schumpeter, the Economics and Sociology of Capitalism*. Princeton, NJ: Princeton University Press, 1991.

Schumpeter, J.A. (1949). English economists and the state-managed economy. *Journal of Political Economy*, 57(5): 371–382.

Schumpeter, J.A. (1950). The march into socialism. *The American Economic Review*, 40(2): 446–456.

Schumpeter, J.A. (1951). *Imperialism and Social Classes: Two Essays*. New York: Meridian Books.

Schumpeter, J.A. (1954). *History of Economic Analysis*. New York: Oxford University Press.

Schumpeter, J.A. (1984). The meaning of rationality in the social sciences. *Journal of Institutional and Theoretical Economics*, 4: 577–593.

Schumpeter, J.A. (1985) [1926/1927]. Die Arbeitslosigkeit. In: C. Seidl and W. Stolper (Eds.), *Aufsätze zur Wirtschaftspolitik* (pp. 729–732). Tübingen: Mohr.

Schumpeter, J.A. (2010) [1908]. *The Nature and Essence of Economic Theory*. New Brunswick, NJ: Transaction Publishers.

Schumpeter, J.A. (2011) [1942]. *Capitalism, Socialism and Democracy*. New York: Harper and Brothers.

Smithies, A. (1951). Schumpeter and Keynes. *The Review of Economics and Statistics*, 33(2), 163–169.

Stockhammer, E. (2004). Financialisation and the slowdown of accumulation. *Cambridge Journal of Economics*, 28(5): 719–741.

Stolper, W.F. (1943). Monetary, equilibrium, and business-cycle theory. *The Review of Economic Statistics*, 25(1): 88–92.

Stolper, W.F. (1951). Reflections on Schumpeter's writings. *The Review of Economics and Statistics*, 33(2): 170–177.

Stolper, W.W. (1989). Spiethoff, Schumpeter und Das Wesen des Geldes: Comments and additions. *Kyklos*, 42(3): 435–438.

Sylos Labini, P. (1983). Nuovi aspetti dello sviluppo ciclico dell'economia. *Moneta e Credito*, 36(144): 379–395.

Tily, G. (2006). Keynes's theory of liquidity preference and his debt management and monetary policies. *Cambridge Journal of Economics*, 30(5): 657–670.

Tily, G. (2016). *Keynes's General Theory, the Rate of Interest and 'Keynesian' Economics: Keynes Betrayed*. New York: Palgrave Macmillan.

Verspagen, B. (2002). Evolutionary macroeconomics: A synthesis between neo-Schumpeterian and post-Keynesian lines of thought. *The Electronic Journal of Evolutionary Modeling and Economic Dynamics*, 1007.

Whalen, C.J. (2001). Integrating Schumpeter and Keynes: Hyman Minsky's theory of capitalist development. *Journal of Economic Issues*, 35(4): 805–823.

Whalen, C.J. (2013). Post-Keynesian institutionalism after the Great Recession. *European Journal of Economics and Economic Policies*, 10(1): 12–27.

Wolfson, R.J. (1958). The economic dynamics of Joseph Schumpeter. *Economic Development and Cultural Change*, 7(1): 31–54.

Wright, D.M. (1945). The future of Keynesian economics. *The American Economic Review*, 35(3): 284–307.

Zalewski, D.A. and Whalen, C.J. (2010). Financialisation and income inequality: a post Keynesian institutionalist analysis. *Journal of Economic Issues*, 44(3): 757–777.

Part II

New dimensions

5 (Re)introducing finance into evolutionary economics

Keynes, Schumpeter, Minsky and financial fragility

Mariana Mazzucato and L. Randall Wray

Introduction: a Schumpeter–Keynes–Minsky foundation

This chapter discusses the role that finance plays in promoting the capital development of the economy, with a particular emphasis on the current situation of the United States and the United Kingdom.[1] In order to do so, the link between profits and investment will be analysed both at the micro and at the macro level. The analysis is based on a synthesis of the main contributions of three of the twentieth century's greatest economists: J.M. Keynes, Josef A. Schumpeter and Hyman P. Minsky.

Following Minsky, we define both 'finance' and 'capital development' very broadly. In the modern economy, a wide range of financial institutions, including commercial banks, investment banks and shadow banks, are in the business of accepting IOUs (I-owe-yous or liabilities) as assets. They typically issue their own IOUs to finance their positions in the assets. The assets might be held, or they are commonly sold – often after packaging in the process known as securitisation.[2] What are thought of as nonfinancial corporations now engage in such practices, providing finance not only to purchasers of the output from their nonfinancial lines of business but also creating financial arms that compete with financial corporations.[3] The 'capital development' of the economy includes private investment in plant and equipment, but also public infrastructure and what is termed human capital investment (education and job-specific training). Minsky's use of the term 'capital development' is not too dissimilar to Schumpeter's use of the term 'economic development', although Minsky placed less emphasis on the role played by innovation in the nonfinancial sector – as discussed below.

The capital development of the economy advances in two ways – and the US and the UK are failing in both across most categories (see below). First, we can improve the quantity and quality of investments (in private, public and human 'capital') that promote the capital development using state-of-the-art knowledge, techniques and processes. Since new investment in physical capital as well as in human development will generally utilise the newest knowledge, techniques and processes, new and replacement investment will usually promote the capital development of the economy.

Second, quality can be improved through Schumpeterian innovation and 'creative destruction': new technologies come along that 'destroy' the productivity of old technologies (not always in a physical sense but in a profitability sense). Schumpeter did not just mean physical investments in plant and equipment but also new ways of doing things – what is usually defined as process innovation. For Schumpeter, economic development can be the result of innovation, characterised as the carrying out of new combinations of materials and productive forces or productive means. It includes the introduction of a new type or quality of commodity, the introduction of a new method of production, opening of a new market, conquest of a new source of supply of raw materials or intermediate goods, or carrying out of a new organisation of industry (e.g. the creation or destruction of monopoly power[4]). This innovation is the product of the entrepreneur (or, in his later writings, the entrepreneurial state), who swims against the stream, putting inventions into practice.

Schumpeter emphasised that innovation must be distinguished from invention; in many cases, the entrepreneur commercialises inventions that have not been applied because they represent a break with routine. The innovation needs to break habits, to break down the resistance of groups threatened by the use of the invention, and to get the necessary cooperation of capitalists, managers, workers and consumers. This is the role of the entrepreneur (or entrepreneurial corporation), a role that cannot be a profession, nor can there be a class of entrepreneurs.

In an increasingly globalised economy, innovation is critical to retaining and expanding market share. Innovation is the result of both public and private investment, with the former often leading the latter through mission-oriented investments that create animal spirits in the business sector (Mazzucato 2016). In the 1950s, a large and relatively closed economy (like that of the USA at the time) could rely on investment that improved the quantity and quality of the nation's means of production – the first path to improving capital development discussed above. However, with relatively open economies today, innovation has become critical for retaining market share and creating the opportunities for future investment. Innovation has both a rate and a direction, and the direction of innovation determines also the direction of growth (Mazzucato and Perez 2015).

Like all production, innovation must be financed, so finance is central to the innovation and growth process. Indeed, this is why Schumpeter called the banker the 'ephor' of the exchange economy (Schumpeter 1934, 74). In a capitalist society, 'credit is essentially the creation of purchasing power for the purpose of transferring it to the entrepreneur' (Schumpeter 1934, 107). The banker produces 'the commodity "purchasing power" that makes it possible to carry out the new combinations associated with innovation' (Schumpeter 1934, 49, 74). The idea is that innovations cannot be financed out of savings that do not yet exist. The banking ephors need to provide finance first, to let the innovation proceed. The innovations then are rewarded with profits (allowing the finance to be repaid) even as they destroy competitors. Thus, innovation requires use of money as a 'claim ticket' on productive resources without use of money as a 'receipt voucher' for sale of commodities or services (Bellofiore 1985, 1992). Just as the circular flow is broken by innovation, the neutrality of money is broken by entrepreneurial activity; indeed, economic development – as Schumpeter defined it – requires non-neutrality of money.

For Schumpeter,

> the money market is always, as it were, the headquarters of the capitalist system, from which orders go out to individual divisions and that which is debated and decided there is always in essence the settlement of plans for further development.
>
> (Schumpeter 1934, Ch. 3)

Yet in recent decades finance has retreated from serving the real economy: the financial sector serves itself, and companies in the real economy have become 'financialised' to an important extent – to be discussed below.[5]

From Schumpeter, we borrow two insights: (1) it is critical to understand the innovation process in order to begin to analyse the dynamics of the capitalist economy, and (2) part of this understanding concerns the fact that innovation needs appropriate types of finance. In Schumpeter's view this is because innovation must be financed *before* it can generate revenues. While in his early work (Schumpeter 1934, originally published in German in 1912) Schumpeter focused on the need for finance to allow new entry (into the 'circular flow' through start-ups), in his later work (Schumpeter 1942) he focused on the importance of internal finance for financing large R&D laboratories of established corporations. Either way, the point of finance is that it is tightly related to the ability to allow new things to happen.

From Keynes we borrow two central insights: the theory of effective demand and his argument that when the 'capital development of a country becomes the by-product of the activities of a casino, the job is likely to be ill done' (Keynes 1936, 159). Keynes's theory of effective demand can be stated succinctly as follows: firms hire the resources they think they will need to produce what they think they can sell. And that depends on the state of effective demand, which is a function of the 'animal spirits'. Entrepreneurial decisions are affected by fundamental or Knightian uncertainty. Most frequently, entrepreneurs cannot even decide which will be the most likely outcome of a particular investment decision simply because there is no way to know the probabilities attached to such decisions. It is also for this reason that Keynes believed in the state as the actor which could remove uncertainty and bolster confidence during troubled times.

What this means is that employment is not determined in labour markets – but rather by the level of sales expected. Indeed, the concept of animal spirits in Keynes is not only useful for behavioural finance (Shiller 2005), but also for Schumpeterian economists that have focused on entry and investment behaviour as being driven by the 'perception' of where the future technological and market opportunities are (Dosi and Lovallo 1997; Pavitt 1984; Mazzucato 2013a, 2013b; Dow and Dow 2011).

Keynes also argued that saving is not the source of finance, as he rejected the loanable funds theory that a flexible interest rate allocates a scarce supply of saving to investment. Keynes reversed the causation: spending creates income and it is the spending on investment that creates the income that is saved. This is why a decrease in the interest rate per se is not going to stimulate spending and investment, especially in the context of balance sheet recession (Koo 2011), in which those who are indebted are selling their assets instead of buying new ones. In circumstances similar to the debt deflation (Fisher 1933) that characterised the Great Depression of 1929, expansionary monetary policies have little effect on investing decisions, no matter how much liquidity is injected into the economy via asset purchase programmes, such as the Federal Reserve's quantitative easing.[6] We must look elsewhere to find the source of finance for investment because investment *precedes* saving both at the aggregate and even at the firm level.

Keynes's Chapter 12 (of the *General Theory*) details the second insight: 'speculation' can come to dominate over 'industry'. What Keynes meant is that the financial system (especially) might direct its efforts towards creating short-term profits generated by rising asset prices (speculation) rather than towards profits generated by productive activities that produce income flows. If we look to the stock market, for example, 'enterprise' would mean purchasing stocks with a view to the long-term prospects of the issuing firm. 'Speculation', however, would be indicated where share purchases are undertaken on the belief that others think share prices will rise. The goal is to buy just before prices rise, and to sell just before they fall. In the modern period, top management has the incentive and the capacity to boost stock prices through legal manipulation. A large share of compensation takes the form of stock options. To increase compensation, managers focus on policies to increase share prices, including use of share buy-backs, thus transforming themselves from entrepreneurs into rentiers.

From Minsky we borrow the recognition that the dynamics of the capitalist system are not necessarily stabilising, and that when finance is brought into the analysis, the dynamics become much worse. Minsky stood orthodoxy's 'invisible hand' metaphor on its head: market forces are destabilising, but the instability can be contained by institutions, including regulation and supervision. This is particularly true where capital equipment is expensive and long-lived, so that investing firms need external finance that commits them to future debt service. Use of external finance helps to fuel a boom, as optimistic expectations (shared by investing firms and their banks) raise investment and thus aggregate demand, accelerating investment. On the other hand, once pessimism sets in, investment collapses, lowering sales and making it impossible to service the debt built up in the boom phase.

Minsky broadened Schumpeter's view – it is not just innovation that has to be financed, as a portion of investment (whether innovative or not) is typically externally financed.[7] Indeed, all spending must be financed – out of income flows, sales of accumulated assets, or borrowing. As also Marx and Keynes said, the main objective of a monetary production economy is not to sell products and services, but to create more money – i.e. M-C-M' with M > M'. What Minsky made explicit is that the source of finance matters – using external finance makes the financial structure more fragile. He also extended Keynes's 'investment theory of the cycle' to include a 'financial theory of investment'. By viewing money as being endogenously created[8] by financial intermediaries, he provided the alternative to the loanable funds theory that Keynes had rejected.

For all these reasons, we need to understand the role played by finance in allowing spending to proceed. Finally, we must heed Minsky's warning that 'stability is destabilising', and that mainly has to do with the innovations in finance that are encouraged by the appearance of stability.

Financing Schumpeterian innovation

A framework for analysis of the capital development of the economy can be developed based on the Schumpeter-Minsky approach that is concerned with evolution of the structure of the economy over time – those factors that disturb equilibrium and can spur growth.

Minsky (1975) developed the 'investment theory of the cycle and the financial theory of investment' to put the Keynesian model in the context of the business cycle. The first part of this is Keynesian, the second brings in Schumpeter's 'ephor'. Over the cycle, the structure of the economy and most importantly the structure of its finance changes in a manner that makes it fragile. All of this is the best-known part of Minsky's approach to financial regimes – what he called hedge, speculative and Ponzi structures.

According to Minsky, 'Schumpeter's banker financed the creative part of creative destruction', but it is necessary to wed this view of banking with Keynes's theory of asset pricing (Minsky 1990, 56) and also with Keynes's view about the role played by 'animal spirits' – i.e. expectations about future profitability that have an impact on current investment decisions both at the firm level and at the economy-wide level. The innovative investment requires not only that, from the perspective of the innovator, the demand price exceeds supply price, it also requires that the banker's risk aversion is overcome. In order for an expansion to proceed, portfolio preferences must be such that the banker is willing to take a position in liabilities issued by entrepreneurs even as the bank must issue its own liabilities to finance this position. Up to some point banks can do this while conforming to normal practice (regarding the liabilities issued to finance the position). Expansion of balance sheets beyond this, however, requires the revision of banker rules of thumb, changes of conventions regarding prudent behaviour, and even the creation of new financial instruments – in short, financial innovations.

Financial innovation is thus the 'monetary' counterpart to Schumpeter's 'new combinations', which will require finance so they may be carried out. These financial innovations require a change in the perception of what is possible.[9] Minsky argued that every prolonged expansion will lead to innovations in finance; such innovations are endogenously induced by success. So long as investment continues to increase, profits increase (as in the Kalecki profits equation that Minsky referred to – although Schumpeter would not have agreed)[10] and encourage greater leveraging of prospective income flows. This leads to a self-fulfilling prophecy, as dependence on external finance increases the size of the circular flow such that incomes are even greater than expected so that margins of safety for the next round of spending can be reduced.

Innovations, whether by bankers or by industrialists, can create market power and change the allocation of aggregate profits such as to reward innovation (Minsky 1990, 56). Prospective monopoly profits are incorporated in demand prices of assets – the same capital asset is worth more to the firm with greater market power – and in the market (or equity) price of the firm with market power. This firm can service more debt because sales prices are higher and more secure. Those who recognise this are able to use prospective monopoly profit share to support liabilities that give them controlling ownership in the firm. This recognition was behind the merger and buy-out waves in the US, which dwarfed any previous wave of concentration and must qualify as a wave of Schumpeterian innovation. In other words, the financial innovation – the LBO (leveraged buy-out) – financed a merger wage that changed the environment within which nonfinancial firms operated, increasing market power. Financial innovations can be conducive to capitalist development but they also might be regressive. In fact, many of the recent financial innovations did not contribute to capital development. Policy reform is necessary to redirect finance to serve this public purpose.

Part of the explanation for the burst of financial innovations that allowed greater leverage and lower margins of safety can be traced to the 'perfection' of lender-of-last-resort interventions by the central banks in the post-war period. Each time a financial innovation was tested by a crisis, the Fed and other major central banks intervened to validate it. In fact, the Fed is only the most visible guarantor of private financial instruments; in the US, the government (whether the Treasury or one of many governmental agencies) stands behind one-third of all privately issued liabilities. (In the Great Financial Crisis (GFC) that safety net expanded – the total volume of loans originated by the Fed in response to the GFC accumulated to nearly $30 trillion).

Clearly, individuals can reduce margins of safety if the government's safety net is extended to cover virtually all liabilities of those with market power. The preference for liquidity is reduced, and prices of assets whose return comes from taking illiquid positions are higher. In this way, government back-stops for behemoth financial institutions can potentially lead to rising concentration outside the financial sector, and to destructive financial innovation that directs efforts to that sphere rather than to productive investments.

Financialisation of the economy does not promote capital development

The past quarter century witnessed the greatest explosion of financial innovation the world had ever seen. Financial fragility grew until the economy collapsed into the global financial crisis. At the same time, we saw that much (or even most) of the financial innovation was directed outside the sphere of production – at complex financial instruments related to securitised mortgages, at commodities futures and at a range of other financial derivatives.

We begin with the observation that the financial *system* evolved over the post-war period from one in which closely regulated and chartered commercial *banks* were dominant, to one in which financial *markets* dominated the system (Figure 5.1). During this period, the financial system grew relatively to the nonfinancial sector, rising from about 10% of value added and a 10% share of corporate profits to 20% of value added and reached 40% of corporate profits in the USA (see below). This was to a large degree because instead of finance financing the capital development of the economy, it was financing ... itself.

Figure 5.2 shows a similar trend for the UK, as an index for gross value added by the financial sector spikes sharply just before the crisis (climbing much faster than the index for aggregate value added).

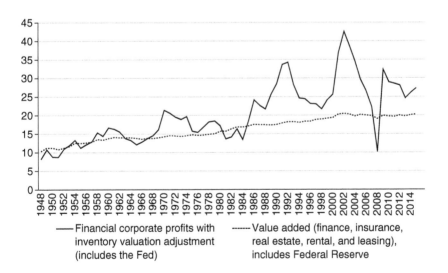

Figure 5.1 US financial sector share of corporate profits and value added, US (1955–2010).

Source: Bureau of Economic Analysis.

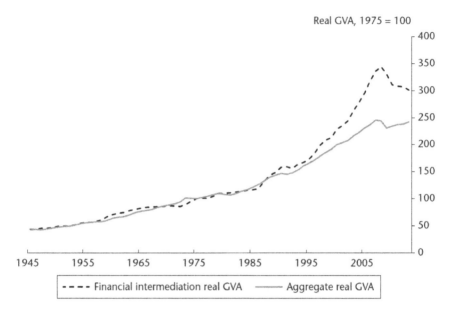

Figure 5.2 Gross value added (indices 1975 = 100), UK 1945–2013.

Source: Alessandri and Haldane 2009 (2009–2013, data extended by authors with data from the Bank of England).

The origins of the financial crisis and the massive and disproportionate growth of the financial sector began in the early 2000s when banks increasingly lent to other financial institutions, largely via wholesale markets. That is, rather than lending to nonfinancial firms and households (to finance purchases of output), while issuing deposits (that would be used for payments), financial institutions increasingly lent to hedge funds, private equity and other financial institutions to buy assets. This lending by financial institutions to other financial institutions grew rapidly in the US from nearly zero in the early post-war period to 125% of GDP just before the crash. This can be called financial layering – the layering of debt on debt by the financial sector.

In addition, the maturity of the assets they held shortened as they avoided longer-term loans to business and households in favour of marketable mortgages that could be securitised as well as very short-term loans (increasingly overnight loans) to financial institutions. They further magnified return on equity by raising leverage ratios and multiplied their capital gains through speculative purchases using funds borrowed in very short-term markets (such as commercial paper), endangering their liquidity and solvency. The risks escalated, but were severely underpriced. The result was that banks' assets ballooned, but success was based on outcomes unlikely to be realised.

Further, as has been noted by many commentators, the nonfinancial sector became highly *financialised* by other measures, including debt ratios as well as proportion of income generated by financial activities (even industrial power-houses like GM and GE created financial arms that generated much of their profits, and most large firms began to treat cash balances as a financial asset to generate revenue). In the United States the total debt ratio (including debt of governments, households, and firms, plus the debt of financial institutions to other financial institutions) reached 500% of GDP before the GFC.

This combination of financial layering (debt-on-debt), financial leveraging (rising debt-to-income ratios) and reliance on extremely short-term finance proved deadly for the financial sector: as delinquencies on home mortgages rose, financial institutions suddenly realised that debt ratios were too high so they tried to liquidate assets. At the same time, they refused to roll over short-term loans to one another (on the rational belief that such lending had become risky). There was a simultaneous run to safety (government bonds), a credit crunch (cutting-off lending) and a Fisher-type debt deflation process engendered by the rush to liquidate assets.

Not only did the rising financialisation expose the economy to the danger of a crash, but it also hindered the capital development of the economy even before the crash. If we apply a broad definition, to include technological advance, rising labour productivity, public and private infrastructure, innovations and advance of human knowledge, the rate of growth of capacity has seemingly slowed. In many basic areas the US and the UK are falling behind: universal education, health improvements, public and private infrastructure, and poverty alleviation.

Evidence for the UK shows that financialisation has had a negative impact on capital accumulation. The distribution of dividends not only decreases available liquidity but also has a further negative behavioural effect on the rate of growth of physical capital. At the macro level, this translates to lower productivity of the economy and a shift from manufacturing towards financial services. In the 1970s, the share of manufacturing in value added was equal to 31% whilst the financial activities (Financial Intermediation and Real Estate – FIRE) accounted for only 13%. Since 1991, in the UK, the share of FIRE has surpassed manufacturing, and as of 2013 the financial sector represents 31.2% of the total value added, whilst that of manufacturing dropped to 9.8% (Tori and Onaran 2015).[11] Similar findings are reported in a previous publication by the Bank for International Settlements (BIS), which warns about the detrimental effects of an overly developed financial sector (Cecchetti and Kharroubi 2012). More recently, even some economists from the International Monetary Fund (IMF) shared their concerns about an excessive focus on financial liberalisation pursued by those economies that implemented the Washington Consensus recipe (Ostry, Prakash and Furceri 2016).

The US is no different from the UK. When deciding where to allocate funds, non-financial corporations tend to invest in financial assets rather than in R&D, human capital and physical accumulation. Instead of facilitating the development of the main business activity, finance is crowding out real investment (Orhangazi 2008; Stockhammer 2004). Such perverse outcomes were at play even before the great financial crisis erupted in August 2007, so that they can be considered one of the causes – if not the main one – that led to the financial meltdown of the American economy.

The American Society of Civil Engineers' (ASCE) infrastructure report card awarded an overall D+ in 2013 to the US, estimating that $3.6 trillion of infrastructure investments would be needed by 2020. Almost none of the infrastructure needed to keep America competitive in the global economy received a grade above a D (Table 5.1)

Further, even as the financial sector experienced serial booms (and busts), the infrastructure situation generally worsened across most of these categories, as the estimate of the spending required nearly tripled over the years, rising from $1.3 trillion in 1998. Although the grades have risen slightly in recent years, this is mostly due to private investment in infrastructure, which is a welcome trend but insufficient. As the 2013 report notes:

> We know that investing in infrastructure is essential to support healthy, vibrant communities. Infrastructure is also critical for long-term economic growth, increasing GDP, employment, household income, and exports. The reverse is also true – without prioritising our nation's infrastructure needs, deteriorating conditions can become a drag on the economy.[12]

Unlike Schumpeter, Minsky did *not* see the banker merely as the ephor of capitalism, but as its key source of instability. This comes from his understanding of finance as having a dynamic of its own – beyond a medium of exchange or as the enabler for economic development – an insight that is consistent with Marx's theory of capitalism.[13] Furthermore, due to the financialisation of the real economy, the picture is not simply one of runaway

Table 5.1 ASCE's 2013 report card for America's infrastructure

Water and environment		Transportation		
Dams	D	Aviation	D	A = Exceptional
Drinking Water	D	Bridges	C+	B = Good
Hazardous Waste	D	Inland waterways	D–	C = Mediocre
Levees	D–	Ports	C	D = Poor
Solid Waste	B–	Rail	C+	F = Failing
Wastewater	D	Roads	D	
		Transit	D	
Public facilities				
Public parks and recreation	C–	Energy		
Schools	D	Energy	D	

Source: American Society of Civil Engineers.

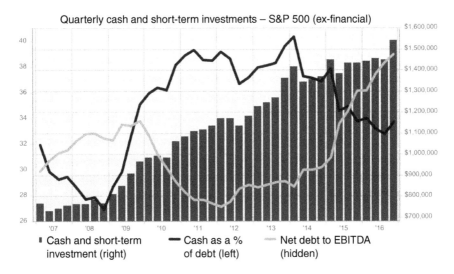

Quarterly cash and short-term investments – S&P 500 (ex-financial)

■ Cash and short-term investment (right)   ▬ Cash as a % of debt (left)   ▬ Net debt to EBITDA (hidden)

Figure 5.3 Investments by S&P 500 corporations (excluding financial firms).

Source: *A $1.3 Trillion Opportunity Staring Investors Right in the Face*, blog entry by Nathan Slaughter available at www.streetauthority.com/research/3/item/9734.

finance and an investment-starved real economy, but one where the real economy itself has retreated from funding investment opportunities: rather, either hoarding cash or using corporate profits for speculative investments such as share buybacks (Lazonick 2013). Financialisation is rooted in predation; Matt Taibbi has famously argued that Wall Street behaves like a giant blood-sucking vampire squid.[14] According to a recent financial newsletter, the S&P 500 companies (excluding banks and other financial institutions) were sitting on $1.3 trillion as of the third quarter of 2013, up by 13.5% from the previous year[15] (Table 5.3).

Financial investments (purchasing financial instruments for their own sake) – as opposed to productive investments (e.g. in R&D) – became key sources of profit for a great proportion of American corporations (Krippner 2005). In some industries like pharmaceuticals and oil and gas, firms are investing more in share buybacks and paying dividends than in R&D and innovation (Lazonick and Tulum 2011; Lazonick and Mazzucato 2013a). This sort of dysfunctional 'financialisation' is not the 'finance for development' that Schumpeter had in mind.

The modern evolutionary economics approach to financing capital development

For Schumpeter, finance is fundamental for understanding how technological change occurs. In his analysis, the banker played the most important role, but this task can now also be played by various types of shadow banks, including private equity partnerships and business angels. Perez (2002) argues that the inertia that characterises incumbents, and what she calls 'production capital' more generally, requires *finance* capital to lead new revolutions (venture capitalists and banks willing to take on risk), with production capital only taking the lead once the new technological paradigm is deployed.

Yet 'finance capital' tends to only enter after a long gestation period in which it is public funds that invest in the areas of highest capital intensity and highest technological and market risk. In general, the lessons from biotech, nanotech and clean-tech are that there is a shortage of risk capital in high-risk areas, with many pioneering projects and radical ideas unable to cross the 'valley of death', never making the shift from R&D laboratories to markets. This is because radical innovation is not just risky but deeply *uncertain* (Knight), because the price and performance of new technologies cannot be known in advance, nor can the specific consumer preferences and practices. If implemented, radical new technologies also amplify uncertainty over rates of return on traditional technologies, to which investors may already be exposed, creating an 'innovators' dilemma' for financial investors as well as non-financial corporations. As traditional banking was replaced by 'originate to distribute' shadow banking, the relationships that are required to build confidence sufficient to supply credit to entrepreneurial activities seems to have disappeared. It is very hard to see how liabilities of innovators can be pooled to serve as collateral behind high risk securities – especially since most 'managed money' is subject to fiduciary rules on asset quality.

Venture capital, for example, is doing with green-tech what it did with the biotech 'revolution': waiting for the government to first make the major investments on which it can later ride the wave. Currently it is only public-sector funds that are funding the riskiest and the most capital-intensive projects in green technology. Venture capitalists are increasingly targeting incremental innovations in established technologies to improve energy efficiency, moving away from more radical forms of innovation for energy production. As more pension-fund and other institutional finance flows into venture capital funds, potentially increasing their scope to finance early-stage innovation, these funds have become more risk-averse by refocusing on later stages, so failing to realise that potential. This may have been compounded by the increased scope, through financial markets, for making high and relatively safe returns through restructuring and re-trading existing assets (corporate equity and property) rather than creating new assets of highly uncertain long-run value. Even when venture capital is effective in helping some of Europe's most innovative and successful companies (those listed on Europe's 'new' stock markets) overcome credit constraints, and thus to be born in the first place, it has a limited effect on their ability to raise equity capital, grow, and create jobs (Bottazzi and da Rin 2002).

Finance and innovation are characterised by feedback: different types of innovations (and firms) require different types of finance, but we need to explore what type of finance is received, and how that affects the patterns of innovation (O'Sullivan 2004). For example, while venture capital (VC) was initially thought to be a good substitute (for innovative firms, at least) to seeking finance from risk-averse banks, as VC has increasingly been focused on an early 'exit' via an IPO, this has affected the investment patterns in sectors like biotech. Innovation is collective, uncertain and cumulative (Lazonick and Mazzucato 2013b). This defines the type of finance it needs: long term, committed, patient finance. This is the type of finance that is missing, and it is increasingly hard to find in the private sector (Mazzucato 2013a). The theoretical distinction of corporate-financing sources holds that traded share, venture capital and retained profits would provide liquidity for exploring new technological paradigms, while long-term bank loans should be more easily channeled into firms characterised by learning processes. However, the financialisation of the economy has blurred the difference between the two institutional settings. Market selection forces are weak in market-oriented systems such as the UK and the USA, just as in credit-based economies such as Germany, France and Japan. By shifting the focus from a 'retain and invest' strategy to a 'downsize and distribute' strategy, financialisa- tion has also affected the behaviour of large firms. Managers were too eager in reaping the benefits of short-term investments, and they coherently imple- mented what was more convenient for them: maximising shareholder value (Dosi, Revest and Sapio 2016; Lazonick 2013). At the aggregate, this resulted in a slowdown in capital accumulation, affecting both US and UK firms (Stockhammer 2004; Orhangazi 2008; Tori and Onaran 2015). It is also important to determine whether the goals of a firm with respect to innova- tion change when VC enters. Few VC-funded projects are successful, and those that are tend to attract a large share of the funding. Does this mean that many potentially viable innovations are left behind?

It is often thought that what prevents the capital development of the economy or the take-off of green technologies is a shortage of money: there is not enough finance. In reality there is *too much* finance, but it is the wrong type. There is not enough patient long-term committed finance (Lazonick 2013). And it is also not true that there is too little 'supply' of finance; it is often that there is not enough 'demand': i.e. not enough high-growth innov- ative companies wanting to invest in innovation (Mazzucato 2013b).

Corporate profit flows are much larger than investment[16] – indicating that at least in today's environment there is no significant shortfall of funds, at least among the big corporations. In any case, there is evidence that 97% of the firms that seek finance get it (Nightingale and Coad 2014). The problem is whether the missing 3% include a high concentration of the innovative firms that the economy should be targeting. And the answer is that there is evid- ence (Bottazzi, Secchi and Tamagni 2008) that innovative firms are penalised by credit markets precisely because they embody higher risk and, in par- ticular, uncertainty (as innovation is characterised by true Knightian uncer- tainty). Moreover, there is no strong relationship between profitability and growth, so that the latter has not to be necessarily fed by profits (Dosi 2008; Dosi *et al.* 2016). What orthodox economics miss is that financing decisions are different from spending decisions, and that savings are not needed in order to invest. What innovative firms are looking for is a way to obtain credit without having anything to offer other than a promise to repay the loan once profits will be realised. The 'ephor' therefore has to assess the entrepreneurs' creditworthiness, as the latter cannot offer assets to be pledged against liquidity.

The role of the state in financing innovation

The reluctance of venture capital, and private banks, to fund early stage developments, is highlighted by Mazzucato (2013a), where it is argued that in many technological revolutions key early-stage funding has come not from private 'entrepreneurs' or private finance capital but from the state. Block and Keller (2011) argue that this leading role of the state has had to remain 'hidden' for political reasons, creating a decentralised network of state agencies. Ironically, this has made the US one of the most interventionist economies in the world, notwithstanding its usual portrayal as the 'market model' to follow.

Figure 5.4 below shows the important role that public agencies (in orange) have played across the entire innovation chain, from blue-sky research funded by agencies like the National Science Foundation to more applied research being done by agencies like the National Institutes of Health and ARPA-E in

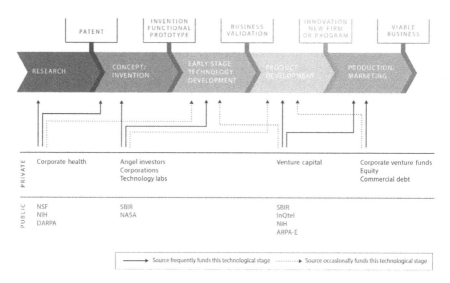

Figure 5.4 Public financing of innovation across the entire innovation chain.

Source: author's insertion of public funding in figure from Auerswald and Branscomb 2003.

the Department of Energy. As venture capitalists have become increasingly short-termist (seeking to exit via an IPO or buyout in three years), early stage risk finance for companies is increasingly coming from public agencies like the Small Business Innovation Research Program (SBIR), or the guaranteed loan scheme of different agencies.

Such mission-oriented investments, like putting a 'man on the moon' or fighting climate change, are not driven by the need to simply 'fix' market failures but more about shaping and creating new markets. Through these kinds of mission-oriented investments, the state has led in the development of key 'General Purpose Technologies' (Lipsey, Carlaw and Bekar 2005; Bresnahan 2010), such as the US 'mass production' system, aviation technologies, space technologies, information technology, internet technologies and nuclear power. Indeed, as shown in Mazzucato (2013a), all the technologies that make the iPhone 'smart' were publicly funded: the internet, GPS, touchscreen display and SIRI. In each case it was not just funding innovation or creating the right conditions for it – i.e. directly or indirectly fixing a market failure – but also envisioning the opportunity space, engaging in the most risky and uncertain early research, and overseeing the commercialisation process. Far from the often-heard criticisms of the state potentially 'crowding out' private investments, such bold 'mission oriented' public investments (amongst decentralised public actors) created new opportunities that private initiative later seized (Mazzucato 2013b).

Such investments are also very high-risk. The fact that innovation is inherently uncertain (in the Knightian sense) means that for each success, there are many failures. This is just as true for private venture capitalists (VC) as it is for public investments. Most recently this has been shown by the guaranteed loans of the US Department of Energy, to companies like Solyndra (a failure, with a $500 million guaranteed loan) and Tesla S (a big success, with a $465 million guaranteed loan). Indeed, for each Tesla there are many Solyndras. But rather than bashing government for its failures, it might be more useful to consider how to structure the investments as a portfolio, with the successes being able to cover the failures and the next round. Just like private VC.

Indeed, while private VC earns a direct return from the successes to cover the failures and the next round of investments, public funds often do not. Why should the state earn a return beyond taxation, through equity or perhaps retention of a 'golden share' of the IPR (as argued in Mazzucato 2013a)? Some might say that the government needs the money to continue to finance innovation. But that cannot be correct – the sovereign government cannot run out of its own currency. Sovereign governments frequently – even virtually always – run budget deficits. Governments typically budget spending and set tax policy with some view as to what the budget balance ought to be; however, the budgetary outcome (deficit, surplus, or balance) is not discretionary and will not be known until the end of the fiscal year. Indeed, the view that government 'pays for' its spending through tax receipts misunderstands how the government actually spends – a topic beyond the scope of this project.[17]

Given that the innovation process is collective, cumulative, tacit and uncertain, and given that most path-breaking technologies were privately appropriated by corporations only after public agencies developed them, it makes sense for public investment in innovation to earn a return that should be redistributed via progressive tax policy. It is common for certain types of infrastructure projects to match costs against anticipated receipts – toll bridges are an example. This imposes a test on the usefulness of the project: are users willing (and able) to pay for the benefits they receive from the bridge?

Another reason why governments should earn a return from investments in path-breaking technologies is politics. Given that innovation is by its very nature highly uncertain, most projects will not succeed. While the voters are willing to accept failures by private innovators, it is much harder for them to accept numerous failures of government-funded projects. If, for example, 90 or even 99 projects fail for every success, voters are likely to find that to be an unacceptable risk. However, if they can understand that the one highly successful project earns returns that cover all the losses of 90 or 99 projects, they can see the benefits of funding risky innovations.

For these reasons, it makes sense for government to share in the rewards of financing innovations – in the same way that it generates revenue from building toll bridges. By setting aside a revolving fund of finance for innovation, perhaps initially funded by government expenditure but then funded by sharing the rewards from the few successful projects, government holds managers accountable and can assure the voters of the worth of the programme. With such a 'trust fund' out of which innovative projects are funded, and into which the rewards of risk-taking flow, government can be a patient source of finance for innovation. Government does not need to get the quick returns that impatient finance demands; it can therefore finance stages of the innovation process that private finance avoids.

However, to ensure that the revolving fund is replenished it is necessary to ensure that the private beneficiaries – say, Apple, for example – share the rewards with government. This should be the task accomplished by progressive taxation, as it is the public sector, and not the private one, to ultimately create value. It would also be a step toward Keynes's 'euthanasia of the rentier', an economic policy by which nearly every source of rent is annihilated or strongly discouraged by the government.

Considering patient finance reframes the debate about financial reform. It is not about 'increasing' the quantity of finance, but transforming its quality. What is needed, is finance that is less speculative, more committed towards long-term goals (Mazzucato 2013a). Long-term committed finance has proven difficult to find in the private sector, not only due to the risk aversion of banks (leading to VC policies), but also because increased financialisation has allowed investors to make 'easy' profits. The first problem requires the public sector to enter and be courageous enough to directly fund innovation, which private finance does not do (this is the entrepreneurial state's role); the second requires the tax system to be reformed so that longterm investments (key for value creation) are rewarded over short-term speculative investments (that are focused on value extraction). This latter objective must include tax reform: raising the capital gains tax (making it less profitable to make short-term investments), and also adding a financial transaction tax (penalising quick speculative trades).

But where will the money come from to support a larger government role?

The retreat of private finance from nurturing the real economy has triggered state investment banks (SIBs) to increase their role around the world (Mazzucato and Penna 2014). These banks offer the much-needed counter-cyclical credit, as well as credit aimed at capital development (e.g. infrastructure). Also, increasingly, they fund the cutting edge of innovation. Indeed, in 2012 SIBs offered $80bn to the renewable energy sector, much more than private agents (BNEF 2014). The China Development Bank, Germany's KfW and Brazil's BNDES are three particularly strategic SIBs that carry out mission-oriented policies that have been leading investors in renewables. (As we will explore in the next section, this is consistent with Keynes's call for socialisation of investment; cf. Keynes 1936, 346.)

Key to thinking about financing innovation is the question: where does money come from?[18] And does it matter? Money is not just a medium of exchange, greasing the wheels of commerce, but is also a central driving force, since capitalism is essentially a credit-driven system – or as Minsky put it, capitalism is a 'financial system'. In considering the wherewithal that the public sector has to invest in innovation, attention to money creation is fundamental. Indeed, countries in the OECD differ radically in terms of whether innovation financing occurs directly or indirectly, with the latter being primarily through tax incentives. It is the nations that have structured public finance to directly finance innovation that have also succeeded in increasing business expenditures in R&D. This is because private business tends to enter the innovation game only *after* it sees clear returns in sight (technological and market) opportunities (Dosi and Lovallo 1997). Hence it is countries where different types of public sector institutions have been able and willing to directly finance innovation that have been able to achieve innovation-led growth (Mazzucato 2013a).

Mazzucato and Penna (2014) studied the enhanced roles that state investment banks play in the economy; in their typology of SIBs, they identify four distinct roles: a countercyclical role; a developmental role; a venture-capitalist role; and a mission-oriented role. While historically SIBs have been a key source of finance for capital development, in recent decades they have diversified their roles and increased their investments, thus countering the trend whereby private finance retreated from financing the real economy. Particularly for transformative ambitions (such as creating a sustainable energy system), SIBs became the major source of finance, representing an important alternative to 'old' mission-oriented funding mechanisms and to private finance. Mazzucato and Penna (2014) conclude that SIBs represent a concrete institutional mechanism that can help reform the 'dysfunctional' financial system from within. Furthermore, through the use of an array of financing tools – standard loans, income contingent loans, equity, grants – SIBs are able to reap the reward for their investments, therefore socialising not only the risks and uncertainties, but also the rewards.

During the aftermath of the great financial crisis, the most important role seems to be the countercyclical one. Investment in strategic sectors such as manufacturing and key enabling technologies (KETs) could rebuild productive capacity, sustain aggregate demand, crowd in private investment and help to solve pressing problems such as Britain's trade deficit. In the context of open economies and freedom of financial flows, it is not enough to implement financial stimuli without worrying about the composition of the economy's productive structure. Investing in sectors that can potentially compete at an international level will avoid the subsequent increase in imports that otherwise would widen the trade deficit. When public investment is directed at new sectors developing radical innovations, the Keynesian 'multiplier effect' is much larger than when governments 'dig ditches and fill them up again'.[19]

This is one link between Schumpeter and Keynes, which can be further enhanced by taking into account Minsky's 'Big Government, Big Bank' as well as his concern about achieving full employment by granting an equitable distribution of output. SIBs can provide a concrete answer to the question 'for whom should the game be fixed and what kind of output should be produced' (Minsky 1975, 164). It is just a matter of assigning to such public institutions the role of investor of last resort, rather than merely recurring to central banks acting as lender of last resort.

The other link between the three great economists is that opportunities – i.e. expected profits – drive investment, and not the other way around. There are many times during which private actors may be affected by speculative myopia. Entrepreneurs could not invest in particular sectors of the economy, not because there are no ways to improve them, but just because profits are considered too low or too difficult to reap. It is no surprise that a slump is transformed into a supposedly inevitable 'secular stagnation' (Summers 2014). Without a leading public sector willing to bear the risk of shaping new markets, financial crises affect not only the sphere of circulation, but also the production process, thus becoming not just an accidental feature of capitalism but a permanent one. Insisting on decreasing short-term interest rates and on forcing private banks to accept central banks' liquidity via the quantitative easing will not solve the impairment of the transmission mechanism of monetary policy. Changes in the official interest rate affect the rate of substitution between short-term finance and long-term finance. However, financing decisions are different from both saving and spending decisions. In fact, when studying the behaviour of aggregate corporate investment from 1952 to 2010 in the USA, Kothari, Lewellen and Warner find that 'investment grows

rapidly following high profits and stock returns but, contrary to standard predictions, is largely unrelated to recent changes in market volatility, interest rates,
or the default spread on corporate bonds' (Kothari *et al.* 2014). As Claudio
Borio, Head of the Economic and Monetary Department of the Bank for International Settlements puts it: 'Spending of any form, whether on pre-existing
real or financial assets, or on goods and services for investment or consumption
purposes, requires *financing*, not saving' (Borio 2014, emphasis added).[20]

Reconstituting the financial system to support capital development

What changes might encourage innovation and reorient it towards the long-
term capital development of the economy? We need to improve the national
innovation system, which requires participation by financial institutions,
venture capitalists, government, universities and academic researchers, shop-
floor workers, engineers, users and industry research consortia. These are
linked through organisational relations, not through markets, where innovation is promoted through building a culture that promotes security of all the
stakeholders that create value. The current system of value extraction
increases the insecurity and uncertainty of the innovation process because
most of the stakeholders are poorly rewarded, including government, workers
and even users.

Most importantly, patience needs to be rewarded. Early IPOs, stock repurchases and M&A deals that are designed to downsize the labour force and
strip assets for quick sale all reward impatience – pump and dump, quick
capital gains over income from production, and fees for VCs over returns to
long-term investors. Government needs to play a bigger role in providing
patient finance and ensuring markets for products. Capital gains tax rates
should be raised to eliminate the incentive for speculative behaviour. Mission-
oriented finance as well as to-the-asset financing would tie financial success to
successful product creation.

Over the past three or four decades we have had substantial policy convergence around the globe, as nations opened their economies to trade and
'capital flows'. This required substantial deregulation and de-supervision to
allow domestic banks to compete with international banks. This was at least
in part due to the Washington Consensus, and the justification was that this
would result in a convergence, as developing nations grew faster to catch up
with the rich nations. However, the outcome was greater divergence, as the
poor got poorer and middle-income nations got trapped (Reinert 2007).
Within at least some of the rich nations the result was also divergence as the
richest got richer and almost everyone else lost in relative terms, and even in
real terms as real wages fell. Domestic growth was uneven, with the biggest
gains in the FIRE sector and in Big Pharma.

We need policies that support innovation, enhancing the government's
role in many of the stages required to see innovation through to fruition. By

itself, that will not be enough. We need to change the environment in which decisions are made by top management of financial institutions: eliminate support of and actively discourage speculation; raise the capital gains rate significantly to reduce the incentive for 'short-termism'; reorient finance away from the financial sector; encourage patient finance; force banks to improve underwriting; reduce the fragility of the financial structure; and promote good governance of financial institutions.

As McCulley puts it, private liquidity is highly 'endogenous', and the ex-ante liquidity is always greater than the ex-post liquidity.[21] For that reason, bank credit can be highly destabilising. This is the core of Minsky's FIH (financial instability hypothesis). Minsky argued that reducing concentration plus forcing banks to retain risk can reorient banks back to relationship banking. There is a critical role for government to play in re-regulating and re-supervising financial institutions. There are no magic formulas (capital ratios, living wills, skin in the game), however. Banks must be supervised by trained and committed professionals from the regulatory agencies.

Innovation policy will not work unless the financial system is reformed to provide more patient long-term committed capital to high-growth innovative firms. This is because what is missing is not simply 'finance' (indeed, there is plenty of it) but the right kind of finance. Similarly, corporate governance should be restructured to make sure that profits of firms are reinvested in the real economy, rather than in financialised practices like share buybacks, which have escalated exponentially since the late 1990s. In this sense innovation policy and financial policies must go hand in hand.

The collective, uncertain and cumulative nature of innovation means that what is required is not just any type of finance but long-term committed finance – which is no longer provided by private venture capital that is increasingly exit driven and short-termist. It is also necessary to realise that there is not only a problem of the supply of finance, but also the demand for finance, i.e. there is a deficiency of high-growth innovative companies seeking finance. We propose the following reforms to allow the financial system to better support innovation:

1   Innovation policy must target the entire innovation chain, from early-stage seed financing to commercialisation. This is not about 'Death Valley' problems or lack of finance, but about providing early-stage patient long-term committed capital at the start of the chain, and following it up with support throughout.
2   Mission-oriented policies are required to crowd in business investment, creating animal spirits endogenously. Without innovation opportunities, an increase in finance does not lead to real investment.
3   Given the high risk involved in providing finance to particular companies (as received by Tesla, Solyndra, Apple, Compaq, Intel), it is essential for some of the returns from the 'upside' to be retained by the public funding agencies. While it can be argued that the state does not need to seek

profits, the reality is that the political support for such investments is much easier to gain when they are seen as part of a portfolio with the government socialising not only the risks but also the rewards.

4   Currently there is much 'piggy-back' riding by private venture capital on forms of public seed finance like the Small Business Innovation Research programme. If SBIR-type grants precede private VC financing, there should be a more concrete way to make sure that the returns earned by VC are proportionate to the actual risk they take, rather than the risk others – including most importantly government and shareholders – take (first).

5   Impatient finance should be taxed heavily, hence forms of financial transaction taxes should be used to provide more incentives for long-termism.

6   While the US system of innovation has a decentralised system of public-sector organisations that provide funding for mission-oriented innovations, this system resulted in socialisation of risks and privatisation of returns. There is therefore a role for public banks (e.g. SIBs) to play in the capital development of the economy, because they are able to reform this system from within through concrete financial mechanisms that help rebalance the risk reward nexus.

Long-run growth is a result of private and public-sector actors working together dynamically, and symbiotically. What we have today is an increasingly financialised private sector, hoarding cash and/or spending profits on boosting stock prices instead of long-run areas like R&D and human-capital formation of employees; and a public sector too fearful to invest in long-run areas due to the (ideological) pressure to keep government debt to GDP ratios low. Yet it is precisely long-run investments that create the growth of the future, which increases the denominator of the debt ratio. Indeed, the countries suffering most in Europe today are those that had modest deficits but very few investments in areas like R&D, and hence had low growth (thus increasing only the numerator and not the denominator of the debt ratio).

Past periods of sustained long-run growth have been results of mission-oriented public spending, which have created new markets around information technology, biotechnology, nanotechnology and – today – green technology (Mazzucato 2013a). This is not only about investments in technology but also in associated policies that allow innovations to be fully deployed, affecting the productivity of all sectors. Indeed, without the policies of suburbanisation, the mass production revolution would not have been fully deployed.

What is required today is a similarly ambitious policy centred around, for example, the green economy, where the public sector can invest in those areas of high capital intensity and high technological risk that the private sector is too fearful to touch, as well as in associated policies that make it more desirable for consumers to change their consumption patterns and lifestyle (Mazzucato and Perez 2015).

It is essential to realise that tax incentives create little additionally. Business does not invest until it sees future growth opportunities, regardless of today's current costs (affected by tax or interest rates). For that reason, relying on tax subsidies or low interest-rate policy has little pay-off in terms of boosting long-term growth. On the other hand, future technological and market opportunities have been strongly correlated with ambitious and entrepreneurial state sector involvement. Government needs to play an active role – not merely a passive role that relies on tweaking market incentives. The bottom line is that money manager capitalism (on steroids) is a new 'animal' without 'animal spirits'. It will not deliver sustainable growth. It has to be radically reformed. But that will mean politics and political coalition building.

Notes

1 London and New York are the most important financial centres; the Euro area has also experienced similar problems, made more complicated by the unusual monetary arrangements (each member state is responsible for its own financial institutions but with limited fiscal and monetary policy independence).
2 In securitisation, a large number of similar financial assets – such as home mortgages – are bundled, with a debt instrument issued against them. The income flows associated with the underlying assets (mortgage interest and principle payments, for example) are passed through to the security holders according to an agreed structure.
3 Both General Electric and General Motors had huge financial arms that brought in much of their pre-crisis profits and created huge losses in the GFC. In the aftermath of the crisis, both are moving to reduce their financial sector footprint.
4 Minsky did emphasise the role played by market power in ensuring access to credit and hence in producing profit (see Minsky 1986, Chs. 7 and 11, for example).
5 A good example is the leveraged buy-out, where a corporation with little debt is viewed as a 'cash cow' that can be taken-over, heavily leveraged with debt, and then sliced and diced so that profitable pieces can be sold.
6 As Keynes warned: 'If ... we are tempted to assert that money is the drink which stimulates the system to activity, we must remind ourselves that there may be several slips between the cup and the lip' (Keynes 1936, Ch. 13). The remedy to a situation in which 'animal spirits' are weak is envisioned by Keynes in the following quote:

> The State will have to exercise a guiding influence on the propensity to consume partly through its scheme of taxation, partly by fixing the rate of interest, and partly, perhaps, in other ways. Furthermore, it seems unlikely that the influence of banking policy on the rate of interest will be sufficient by itself to determine an optimum rate of investment. I conceive, therefore, that a somewhat comprehensive socialisation of investment will prove the only means of securing an approximation to full employment; though this need not exclude all manner of compromises and of devices by which public authority will co-operate with private initiative.
>
> (Keynes 1936, 346)

7 See Minsky 1986, 1990, 1992a, 1992b, 1993a, 1993b, 1996; Minsky and Ferri 1991; Minsky, delli Gatti and Gallegati 1994; Wray 1991, 1993, 1994, 1995, 2009, 2010, 2012; and Papadimitriou and Wray 1998 for links between the approaches of Schumpeter and Minsky.

8 'Anybody can create money – the problem is to get it accepted' (Papadimitriou and Wray 2010); 'A bank is not a money lender that first acquires and then places funds … a bank first lends or invests and then 'finds' the cash to cover whatever cash drains arise' (Minsky 1975, 154, see Wray 2015b).

9 An example of a financial innovation is securitisation of home mortgages. While seemingly simple, the 30-year fixed rate self-amortising mortgage is actually a complex instrument. But the innovation of bundling and tranching appeared to create a new instrument with characteristics similar to government bonds. Another innovation was the creation of the credit default swap, which appeared to offer cheap insurance against losses without requiring issuers to hold loss reserves because they could hedge risks by taking offsetting positions.

10 Note that the statement that (all else equal) investment creates an equal amount of investment applies only at the aggregate level. No firm can be assured that it will receive profits equal to its investment. However, if firms in the aggregate are investing, profits will be higher, and many of the individual investments will be successful, encouraging more investment.

11 The authors use panel data based on balance sheets of publicly listed non-financial companies supplied by Worldscope for the period 1985–2013 (Tori and Onaran 2015).

12 www.infrastructurereportcard.org/a/#p/overview/executive-summary, accessed on 20 May 2014. Note that President Obama addressed the infrastructure problem in his 2015 State of the Union address, and Senator Bernie Sanders addressed the infrastructure deficit in his report, *Preview of the Congressional Budget Office Budget and Economic Report: Rebuilding the Disappearing Middle Class*, 24 January 2015.

13 Marx argued that orthodoxy sees production as C-M-C', starting with commodities to exchange for other commodities, with money only playing a role as a medium of exchange. Instead, he viewed capitalist production as M-C-M'; that is, Marx's argument is that production begins with money to produce commodities to be sold for more money. We might view modern finance as starting with money (M) to make more money (M') without the production of commodities.

14 www.rollingstone.com/politics/news/the-great-American-bubble-machine-20100405.

15 Source: Nathan Slaughter, www.streetauthority.com/research/3/item/9734.

16 Note from the Kalecki equation that aggregate profits can exceed investment since they can be generated by budget deficits and current account surpluses; they can also result if saving out of wages is negative and/or consumption out of profits is positive. (Accounting profits are not the same as NIPA profits. For example, firms can book 'goodwill', which raises the value of assets and generates accounting profits that do not show up in NIPA). In the case of the USA, current accounts are persistently negative (draining profits) but consumption out of profits is probably positive and saving out of wages were negative for much of the period from 1996 to 2006 (adding to profits). Budget deficits were very large after the crisis hit, but have been declining over the past few years; this will reduce the boost to profits in excess of investment. However, if the biggest corporations have substantial pricing power, they might be able to increase their share of a shrinking aggregate profits pie.

17 See Wray 2015a.

18 See Wray 2010 and 2015b for Minsky's views, and Wray 2015a for the Modern Money Theory perspective.

19 'The important thing for government is not to do things which individuals are doing already, and to do them a little better or a little worse; but to do those things which at present are not done at all' (Keynes 1926, 46).

20 This holds true both in a closed and in an open economy.

In a closed economy, saving is not a pre-requisite for investment, but materialises only once investment takes place if the necessary financing is available. In an open economy, by construction, a current account deficit somewhere must be matched by a surplus elsewhere. But countries running current account surpluses are *not* financing those running current account deficits.

(Borio 2014, emphasis in the original)

21 Paul McCulley, lecture at the Levy Economics Institute; available at www.econo-monitor.com/lrwray/2012/06/25/paul-mcculley-mmt-won-declare-victory-but-be-magnanimous-about-it/.

References

Bellofiore, R. (1985). Money and development in Schumpeter. *Review of Radical Political Economics*, 17(1–2): 21–40.

Bellofiore, R. (1992). Monetary macroeconomics before the General Theory: The circuit theory of money in Wicksell, Schumpeter and Keynes. *Social Concept* 2: 47–89.

Block, F.L. and Keller, M.R. (2011). *State of Innovation: The U.S. Government's Role in Technology Development.* Boulder, CO: Paradigm Publishers.

Bottazzi, L. and da Rin, M. (2002). Venture capital in Europe and the financing of innovative companies. *Economic Policy* 17: 229–269.

Bottazzi, G., Secchi, A. and Tamagni, F. (2008). Productivity, profitability and financial performance. *Industrial and Corporate Change*, 17(4): 711–751.

Borio, C. (2014). The international monetary and financial system: Its Achilles Heel and what to do about it. BIS Working Paper No. 456.

BNEF (2014). State bank finance database. Bloomberg New Energy Finance.

Bresnahan, T. (2010). General purpose technologies. In: *Handbook of the Economics of Innovation* (Vol. 2, pp. 761–791). Amsterdam: Elsevier.

Cecchetti, K. and Kharroubi, E. (2012). Reassessing the impact of finance on growth. BIS, Conference Draft, January 2012.

Dosi, G. (2008). Statistical regularities in the evolution of industries: A guide through some evidence and challenges for the theory. *L'industria*, 29(2): 185–220.

Dosi, G. and Lovallo, D. (1997). Rational entrepreneurs or optimistic martyrs? Some considerations on technological regimes, corporate entries and the evolutionary role of decision biases. In: R. Garud, P.R. Nayyar and Z.B. Shapira (Eds.), *Technological Innovation: Oversights and Foresights.* Cambridge: Cambridge University Press, 1997.

Dosi, G., Revest, V. and Sapio, A. (2016). Financial regimes, financialisation patterns and industrial performances: Preliminary remarks. LEM Working Paper No. 25.

Dow, A. and Dow, S.C. (2011). Animal spirits revisited. *Capitalism and Society*, 6(2): 1–23.

Fisher, I. (1933). The debt-deflation theory of great depressions. *Econometrica: Journal of the Econometric Society*, 337–357.

Keynes, J.M. (1926). *The End of Laissez-Faire.* London: L&V Woolf.

Keynes, J.M. (1936) [1964]. *General Theory of Employment, Interest and Money.* Orlando, FL: HBJ Publishers.

Koo, R. (2011). The world in balance sheet recession: causes, cure, and politics. *Real-World Economics Review*, 58(12): 19–37.

Kothari, S.P., Lewellen, J. and Warner, J.B. (2014). The behavior of corporate aggregate investment. MIT Sloan School Working Paper 5112–5114.

Krippner, G.R. (2005). The financialisation of the American economy. *Socio-Economic Review*, 3: 173–208.

Lazonick, W. (2013). The financialisation of the U.S. Corporation: What has been lost, and how it can be regained. *Seattle University Law Review*, 36: 857–909.

Lazonick, W. and Mazzucato, M. (2013a). Apple's changing business model: What should the world's richest company do with all those profits?' *Accounting Forum*, 37: 249–267.

Lazonick, W. and Mazzucato, M. (2013b). The risk-reward nexus in the innovation-inequality relationship: Who takes the risks? Who gets the rewards?' Special issue of *Industrial and Corporate Change*, edited by M. Mazzucato, 22(4): 1093–1128.

Lazonick, W. and. Tulum. Ö. (2011). US biopharmaceutical finance and the sustainability of the biotech business model. *Research Policy*, 40(9): 1170–1187.

Lipsey, R.G., Carlaw, K.I. and Bekar, C.T. (2005). *Economic Transformations: General Purpose Technologies and Long-Term Economic Growth.* Oxford: Oxford University Press.

Mazzucato, M. (2013a). *The Entrepreneurial State: Debunking the Public vs. Private Myth in Risk and Innovation.* London: Anthem Press.

Mazzucato, M. (2013b). Financing innovation: Creative destruction vs. destructive creation. *Industrial and Corporate Change*, 22(4): 869–901.

Mazzucato, M. (2016). From market fixing to market-creating: A new framework for innovation policy. Special Issue of *Industry and Innovation:* Innovation policy – can it make a difference?, 23(2): 140–156.

Mazzucato, M. and Penna, C. (2014). Market failure vs. mission oriented: A new framework to understand the rise of state investment banks. SPRU working paper.

Mazzucato, M. and Perez, C. (2015). Innovation as growth policy. In: J. Fagerberg, S. Laestadius and B. Martin (Eds.), *The Triple Challenge: Europe in a New Age.* Oxford: Oxford University Press. SPRU working paper version available at www.sussex.ac.uk/webteam/gateway/file.php?name=2014-13-swps-mazzucato-perez.pdf&site=25.

Minsky, H.P. (1975). *John Maynard Keynes.* New York: Columbia University Press.

Minsky, H.P. (1986). *Stabilising an Unstable Economy.* New Haven, CT: Yale University Press.

Minsky, H.P. (1990). Schumpeter: Finance and evolution. In: A. Heertje and M. Perlman (Eds.), *Evolving Technology and Market Structure: Studies in Schumpeterian Economics* (pp. 51–74). Ann Arbor, MI: The University of Michigan Press.

Minsky, H.P. (1992a). The capital development of the economy and the structure of financial institutions. Levy Institute Working Paper Series no. 72.

Minsky, H.P. (1992b). Commentary. In: F.M. Scherer and M. Perlman (Eds.), *Entrepreneurship, Technological Innovation, and Economic Growth: Studies in the Schumpeterian Tradition* (p. 363). Ann Arbor, MI: The University of Michigan Press.

Minsky, H.P. (1993a). Finance and stability: The limits of capitalism. Working Paper no. 93. Annandale-on-Hudson, NY: The Jerome Levy Economics Institute.

Minsky, H.P. (1993b). Schumpeter and finance. In: S. Biasco, A. Roncaglia and M. Salvati (Eds.), *Markets and Institutions in Economic Development: Essays in Honour of Paolo Sylos Labini* (pp. 103–115). New York: St. Martin's Press.

Minsky, H.P. (1996). Uncertainty and the institutional structure of capitalist economies. Levy Institute Working Paper Series no. 155.

Minsky, H.P., delli Gatti, D. and Gallegati, M. (1994). Financial institutions, economic policy and the dynamic behavior of the economy. Working Paper no. 126. Annandale-on-Hudson, NY: The Jerome Levy Economics Institute.

Minsky, H.P. and Ferri, P. (1991). Market processes and thwarting systems. Working Paper no. 64. Annandale-on-Hudson, NY: The Jerome Levy Economics Institute.

Nightingale, P. and Coad, A. (2013). Muppets and gazelles: Political and methodological biases in entrepreneurship research. *Industrial and Corporate Change*, 23, 113–143.

Orhangazi, Ö. (2008). Financialisation and capital accumulation in the non-financial corporate sector: A theoretical and empirical investigation on the US economy: 1973–2003. *Cambridge Journal of Economics*, 32(6): 863–886.

Ostry, J.D., Prakash, L. and Furceri, D. (2016). Neoliberalism: Oversold? *IMF Finance & Development*, 53(2): 38–41.

O'Sullivan, M. (2004). Finance and innovation. In: J. Fagerberg, D.C. Mowery and R.R. Nelson (Eds.), *The Oxford Handbook of Innovation* (pp. 240–265). New York: Oxford University Press.

Papadimitriou, D.B. and Wray, L. R. (1998). The economic contributions of hyman minsky: varieties of capitalism and institutional reform. *Review of Political Economy*, 10: 199–225.

Papadimitriou, D.B. and Wray, L.R. (2010). Introduction: Minsky on money, banking and finance. In: D.B. Papadimitriou and L.R. Wray (Eds.), *The Elgar Companion to Hyman Minsky*. Cheltenham: Edward Elgar.

Pavitt, K. (1984). Sectoral patterns of technical change: towards a taxonomy and a theory. *Research Policy*, 13(6): 343–373.

Perez, C. (2002). *Technological Revolutions and Financial Capital: The Dynamics of Bubbles and Golden Ages*. Cheltenham, UK: Edward Elgar.

Reinert, E.S. (2007). *How Rich Countries Got Rich … and Why Poor Countries Stay Poor*. London: Constable.

Schumpeter, J.A. (1934) [1912]. *The Theory of Economic Development: An Inquiry into Profits, Capital, Credit, Interest, and the Business Cycle*. Cambridge, MA: Harvard University Press.

Schumpeter, J.A. (1942). *Socialism, Capitalism and Democracy*. New York: Harper and Brothers.

Shiller, R.J. (2005). *Irrational Exuberance*. New York: Random House.

Stockhammer, E. (2004). Financialisation and the slowdown of accumulation. *Cambridge Journal of Economics*, 28(5): 719–741.

Summers, L.H. (2014). US economic prospects: Secular stagnation, hysteresis, and the zero lower bound. *Business Economics*, 49(2): 65–73.

Tori, D. and Onaran, Ö. (2015). *The Effects of Financialisation on Investment: Evidence from Firm-Level Data for the UK*. Greenwich Political Economy Research Centre.

Wray, L.R. (1991). Saving, profits, and speculation in capitalist economies. *Journal of Economic Issues*, 25(4): 951–975.

Wray, L.R. (1993). The origins of money and the development of the modern financial system. Working Paper No. 86. The Jerome Levy Economics Institute.

Wray, L.R. (1994). Government deficits, liquidity preference, and Schumpeterian innovation. *Economies et Sociétés*, 9 (January/February): 39–59.

Wray, L.R. (1995). If free markets cannot efficiently allocate credit, what monetary policy could move us closer to full employment? *Review of Political Economy*, 7(2): 186–211.

Wray, L.R. (2009). The rise and fall of money manager capitalism: A Minskian approach. *Cambridge Journal of Economics*, 33(4): 807–828.

Wray, L.R. (2010). What do banks do? A Minskian analysis. Levy Institute Public Policy Brief No. 115.

Wray, L.R. (2012). The Great Crash of 2007 viewed through the perspective of Veblen's theory of the business enterprise, Keynes's monetary theory of production and Minsky's financial instability hypothesis. In: E.S. Reinert and F.L. Viano (Eds.), *Thorstein Veblen: Economics for an Age of Crises* (pp. 303–316). London: Anthem Press.

Wray, L.R. (2015a). *Modern Money Theory: A Primer on Macroeconomics for Sovereign Monetary Systems* (2nd edn.). New York: Palgrave Macmillan.

Wray, L.R. (2015b). *Why Minsky Matters: An Introduction to the Work of a Maverick Economist*. Princeton, NJ: Princeton University Press.

6 Innovative enterprise and sustainable prosperity

Taking up the Schumpeterian challenge

William Lazonick

> What we have got to accept is that [the large-scale business enterprise] has come to be the most powerful engine of [economic] progress.... In this respect, perfect competition is not only impossible but inferior, and has no title to being set up as a model of ideal efficiency.
>
> (Schumpeter 1950, *Capitalism, Socialism, and Democracy*, 106)

Investment in productive capabilities[1]

We want an economy that generates stable and equitable growth – or what I call 'sustainable prosperity.' We want productivity growth that makes it possible for the population to have higher standards of living. We want stable employment opportunities that enable people to remain productive for some four decades of their working lives while providing them with enough savings for adequate incomes over some two decades of retirement. And we want an equitable sharing of income among those whose work efforts and financial resources contribute to the nation's productivity.

Since the 1980s, the US economy has experienced unstable employment, inequitable income and sagging productivity – the opposite of sustainable prosperity. The purpose of this chapter is to argue that a critical first step in attaining sustainable prosperity in the United States, or any other national economy, is to change the intellectual understanding of academics, policy-makers and the informed public about how a modern economy operates and performs. I argue that we cannot pursue a coherent set of public policies to generate stable and equitable economic growth unless we reject the neoclassical theory of the market economy and replace it with an economic theory that focuses on how organisations, including households, governments and businesses, invest in productive capabilities, with a theory of innovative enterprise at its core.

Sustainable prosperity requires innovative enterprise. The essence of innovative enterprise is investment in productive capabilities that can generate goods and services that are higher-quality and/or lower-cost than those that were previously available. The innovative enterprise tends to be a *business enterprise* – a unit of strategic control that over time must make profits to survive. But, in a modern society, business enterprises are not alone in making investments in the productive capabilities required to generate innovative goods and services. Household families and government agencies also make investments in productive capabilities upon which business enterprises rely. Working in a harmonious fashion, I call these three types of organisations – household families, government agencies and business enterprises – 'the investment triad'.

Household families invest in the education of the young with a view to providing them with the knowledge that they will need to function as productive adults, who will then use the income from productive employment to have families of their own. Critical determinants of household investments in productive capabilities are the relation between spouses as providers of household care and income, the quality of education that the young are able to receive and the number of years over which they receive their education. A productive society requires the presence of the supportive family.

Government agencies support the investments in productive capabilities by household families by providing schooling that households, each acting on its own, could not afford. A well-financed primary, secondary and tertiary education system is a necessary condition for a modern society to embark on a path of sustained development through which most of the population can attain higher standards of living (Lazonick 2009, Ch. 5). Government agencies can also be charged with investing in the creation, through basic and applied research, of new scientific and engineering knowledge that would otherwise not come into existence. As a critical component of investment in productive capabilities, government agencies are involved in providing services for public and personal health. In addition, we rely on government agencies to invest in physical infrastructure, such as transportation systems, communication systems, energy systems and water and waste systems. Taken together, the investments in productive capabilities, both human and physical, by government agencies manifest the presence of the developmental state.

Business enterprises make use of the knowledge and infrastructure provided by government agencies and the human capabilities provided by household families as foundations for making further in-house investments in human and physical capabilities that can generate goods and services that these businesses can sell on product markets. In high-tech fields, business enterprises may have to make specialised investments in in-house capabilities to absorb the high-tech knowledge that investments by government agencies have created. In many cases, government agencies make strategic investments in knowledge creation through business enterprises in the forms of research contracts and subsidies. Of particular importance, it is typically through on-the-job experience in business enterprises as well as government agencies that masses of individuals, building on their formal educations, accumulate the productive capabilities that enable them to contribute to the innovation process. The development and utilisation of these productive capabilities are the essence of the innovative enterprise.

The investment triad enables innovative enterprise to function as a foundation for sustainable prosperity. Stable and equitable growth occurs when the investment strategies of households, governments and businesses interact as supportive families, developmental states and innovative enterprises. Households and governments interact through investments in education. Governments and businesses interact in the development of the high-tech knowledge base. Businesses and households interact through the employment relation. The quality of these interactions in the development and utilisation of productive capabilities is of critical importance to the productivity of resources that are invested in the innovative enterprise.

Business enterprises provide adults in household families with employment that, with sufficient productivity, should enable them to support their families. Through formal and on-the-job training, business enterprises also invest in the knowledge of some or all of the people whom they employ. These enterprises then have an incentive to retain the people whom they have trained. They generally do so through pay increases and promotions to jobs that require superior functional capability and greater hierarchical responsibility. Indeed, it is primarily through in-house pay increases and promotions for valued employees in stable employment relations in innovative enterprises that households' living standards increase over time. It is through the employment relations of productive enterprises, not labour-market supply and demand, that we get the thriving middle class that is the social substance of stable and equitable growth.

In short, the investment triad puts in place the productive capabilities that are essential to a prosperous economy. Investments in the knowledge base by household families, government agencies and business enterprises must be financed. Investments in educating the labour force are generally funded by some combination of after-tax household incomes supplemented by household debt and government tax revenues supplemented by debt issues at local, state and federal levels. To some extent business enterprises finance the education of the labour force through corporate taxes, philanthropic contributions based on business fortunes, and direct payments to employees for the education of themselves or their children as part of the employment relation.

Ultimately, however, the ability of household families and government agencies to afford investments in productive capabilities requires the utilisation of the knowledge and skills that have been developed through these investments. And in a modern society, to ensure the utilisation of the knowledge base that has been developed, we rely primarily on its employment by business enterprises that, to survive, must produce and sell competitive – that is, high-quality, low-cost – products. The innovative enterprise is central to the triadic social system that enables the attainment of sustainable prosperity.

In the next section of this chapter, I contrast the investment-triad perspective, with its focus on organisations – supportive families, developmental states and innovative enterprises – as the microfoundations of sustainable prosperity, with the neoclassical economics theory that views the operation of markets as the microfoundations of the most efficient economy. I show that the neoclassical perspective, which is taught by tens of thousands of economics

PhDs to millions of students around the world every year, rests on the absurd proposition that the most unproductive firm is the foundation of the most efficient economy – an ideal of economic organisation known as 'perfect competition'. Indeed, the neoclassical theory of markets as omnipotent in the allocation of economy's resources depends on a theory of the firm that portrays the ideal business enterprise as impotent. As we shall see, the neoclassical theory of perfect competition has as its roots a firm that has the characteristics of an overcrowded sweatshop in which workers are unable and unwilling to be productive.

Economics is in need of a theory of innovative enterprise to replace the neoclassical theory of the firm, and thereby recognise the centrality of organisations to the economy's operation and performance, while exploding 'the myth of the market economy' (Lazonick 1991a, 2003, 2016b). The third section of this chapter outlines the theory of innovative enterprise (TIE) as a conceptual framework for analysing whether, how and under what conditions the investment triad supports or undermines the attainment of stable and equitable growth. Drawing on the experience of the US economy over the past 70 years, I make use of TIE to analyse how during the first three decades of this period, the United States moved towards stable and equitable growth under a 'retain-and-reinvest' corporate resource-allocation regime whereas from the late 1970s on, under a 'downsize-and-distribute' regime, unstable employment, inequitable income and sagging productivity have characterised the US economy (Lazonick and O'Sullivan 2000).

In the fourth section of this chapter, I place intellectual blame for the US failure to achieve sustainable prosperity since the 1970s on a particular brand of neoclassical economics known as agency theory, with its ideology that the business corporation should be run to 'maximise shareholder value' (MSV). Far from being a theory of value creation, MSV has legitimised predatory value extraction from US business corporations. Effected through massive distributions of corporate cash to shareholders and incentivised by the stock-based pay of senior corporate executives, MSV has resulted in the (largely legal) looting of the US business corporation. I argue that MSV has undermined innovative enterprise and the operation of the investment triad, and with it the possibility of achieving sustainable prosperity in the United States.

In the final section of this chapter, I argue that, as a conceptual guide to formulating policies to get the US economy on a sustainable-prosperity trajectory, innovation theory must replace agency theory. I contend that the eradication of MSV ideology is a necessary condition for enabling an economy's business enterprises to contribute to, rather than thwart, the achievement of sustainable prosperity. To provide the intellectual rationale for specific proposals (elaborated elsewhere; Lazonick 2016a) to stop the looting of the business corporation – including banning stock buybacks, compensating senior executives for their contributions to the value-creating enterprise, placing representatives of households as workers and taxpayers on corporate boards and reforming the tax system so that it recognises and supports the investment triad – I call for innovation theory to replace agency theory in our conceptualisation of how the economy operates and performs.

The theory of the firm and economic performance

The investment-triad perspective views organisations, not markets, as the microfoundations of sustainable prosperity. Comparative-historical study reveals that developed markets in products, finance, labour and land are outcomes, not causes, of economic development (Lazonick 1991a). Product competition assumes the existence of business enterprises that have developed the capabilities to produce goods and services of a quality that buyers want and need that can be sold at prices that buyers are willing or able to pay. Developed markets in stocks and bonds depend on the existence of business enterprises with the capability to issue and pay yields on these securities. Employment opportunities that can be accessed via labour markets assume the existence of business enterprises and government agencies that have developed the capability to employ labour productively. A market for land exists because households, governments and businesses have invested in the infrastructure of a particular locality.

For the sake of continued innovation, the organisations on which the economy depends for investments in productive capabilities need governments to regulate these developed markets once they have emerged (see, for example, Lazonick 1990, 2017a). As demonstrated repeatedly in the history of American capitalism, in the absence of regulation, developed markets tend to disrupt and undermine the organisational processes that enable investment in productive capabilities. Here are just a few examples from the history of the United States:

- In the 1920s, industries such as textiles, coalmining and agriculture, characterised by large numbers of competitors, were 'sick' because of cutthroat competition, even though the firms in these industries had access to the most advanced technologies in the world. A major role of 1930s New Deal government intervention was to implement regulations and programmes that helped to make these industries healthy.
- Today, with the prices of medicines largely unregulated in the United States despite government-funded research, government-granted monopoly patents and government-subsidised demand, pharmaceutical companies have become prime sources for predatory value extraction, undermining their capabilities to engage in drug innovation.
- The 1982 deregulation of the practice of stock repurchases by the US Securities and Exchange Commission through Rule 10b-18 has resulted in more than three decades of looting of corporate treasuries by well-positioned stock-market traders, including senior executives, resulting in the concentration of income at the top and the destruction of middle-class employment opportunities.

- Inadequate minimum wages that result from overcrowded labour markets have left hardworking families in poverty, even when the heads of households are holding down two full-time jobs.
- The 'free-market' approach to college tuitions and student loans has made higher education unaffordable to most working-class households, in a nation that had once been in the forefront of free or low-cost public higher education.
- We need only look back to the financial crisis of 2008–2009 to see the vast devastation visited on household families by government failure to regulate housing markets.
- Devastating destruction occurs through 'natural' disasters caused by the failure to regulate industries whose processes and products contribute to climate change.

The TIE approach to understanding the operation and performance of the economy, including the interactions of households, governments and businesses as investors in productive capabilities, stands in stark contrast to the neoclassical focus on market coordination of economic activity. The neoclassical theory of the market economy poses a profound intellectual barrier to analysing and understanding the organisational foundations of economic development. Neoclassical economists assume that an advanced economy is a market economy in which millions of household decisions concerning the allocation of the economy's resources are aggregated into prices for inputs to and outputs from production processes. Any impediments to this process of market aggregation are deemed to be 'market imperfections', and any undesirable social outcomes from the process are deemed to be 'market failures'.

Developed markets are of utmost importance to our economy and society; they can allow us as individuals to choose the work we do, for whom we work, where we live, and what we consume. Insofar as we have market choices, however, it is because the economy is wealthy, and it is wealthy because of the household, government and business organisations that constitute the investment triad. If market processes cannot explain investment in productive capabilities, then the theory of the market economy cannot explain the wealth of nations. If economists want to devise public policies to shape the processes and influence the outcomes of investment in productive capabilities, we need to construct an economic theory of 'organisational success.' At its centre is a theory of innovative enterprise.

Yet it is the theory of the market economy that dominates the teaching of economics and the 'well-trained' economist's mindset on how the economy operates and performs. The theory of perfect competition, which is the neoclassical economist's ideal of economic efficiency, views the firm as impotent and the market as omnipotent in allocating the economy's resources. By the neoclassical theory's key assumptions, the firm in perfect competition is, as I will explain, an unproductive firm. Yet neoclassical theory posits the firm in perfect competition as the microfoundation of an economy in which the allocation of resources results in the ideal of economic efficiency, even if that ideal is difficult or impossible to attain.

If, thus put, neoclassical logic concerning the relation between firm productivity and economic performance sounds absurd, that is because it is. Seventy-five years ago, Joseph Schumpeter, with his focus on innovation as the fundamental phenomenon of economic development, confronted the myth of the market economy when he argued that 'perfect competition is not only impossible but inferior, and has no title to being set up as a model of ideal efficiency.' The reason: large-scale enterprise is 'the most powerful engine of [economic] progress and in particular of the long-run expansion of total output' (Schumpeter 1950, 106).

The neoclassical theory of the firm in perfect competition cannot explain why for well over a century very large firms have dominated the US economy (Lazonick 2012). In 2012 (the most up-to-date statistics that include revenues), 964 companies that had 10,000 or more employees in the United States, with an average workforce of 33,542, were only 0.017% of all US businesses. But these 964 companies had 9% of all establishments, 28% of employees, 31% of payrolls and 36% of receipts. For 1,909 companies with 5,000 or more employees, these shares were 11% of establishments, 34% of employees, 38% of payrolls and 44% of receipts.[2] How these large companies allocate the resources under their control has profound implications for employment opportunities, income distribution and productivity growth in the United States.

The neoclassical answer must be that these large firms represent market imperfections, also known as monopolies or oligopolies. But that does not explain the productive power of these large firms. Nor does it explain, intuitively at least, why, as the neoclassical theory posits, an economy dominated by very large numbers of small unproductive firms would yield the most efficient economy. This intellectual puzzle is solved when we realise that the neoclassical theory is utterly illogical. The theory of the unproductive firm as the foundation of the most efficient economy dominates the thinking of economists because it serves to make the market omnipotent and the firm impotent in the allocation of the economy's resources. In effect, this ideological tenet, which is held dear by both liberal and conservative economists, obviates the need to consider the role of the investment triad, including the innovative enterprise, in achieving superior economic performance – that is, stable and equitable growth.

Let's go back to basics to see why 'perfect competition' is illogical. As conventionally defined, perfect competition exists when a very large number of identical firms in an industry each has such a small share of total industry output that each firm, acting on its own, can choose to produce its profit-maximising output without influencing the price of the industry's product. Each of these identical firms is constrained to be very small by the assumption that at a very low level of the firm's output relative to industry output, increasing average variable costs (AVC) overwhelm decreasing average fixed costs (AFC), so that the firm faces a U-shaped cost curve in deciding how much output to produce. It follows mathematically that the firm maximises profits at the output at which marginal revenue equals marginal cost. Thus, we have the theory of the optimising firm that holds centre stage (and generally the only stage) in virtually every introductory economics textbook used worldwide.[3]

The model for the modern 'principles' textbook, created by Paul Samuelson, was *Economics: An Introductory Analysis*, first published in 1948 and reissued in 18 subsequent editions (with Samuelson as the sole author through the twelfth edition, published in 1985). The large corporation was not unknown to Samuelson. In the first edition, he observed that

> a list of the 200 largest nonfinancial corporations reads like an honor roll of American business, almost every name being a familiar household word.... In manufacturing alone, the 100 most important companies employed more than one-fifth of all manufacturing labor and accounted for one-third of the total value of all manufactured products.
>
> (Samuelson 1948, 125)

After commenting that 'their power did not grow overnight', Samuelson states: 'Large size breeds success, and success breeds further success.'

How did these large corporations attain these dominant positions, and why did the top 100 manufacturers achieve high labour productivity relative to all manufacturers? The existence of very large, highly productive firms should have led economists to search for a theory of innovative enterprise as a foundation of economic analysis.[4] Yet Samuelson's scientific papers (which are virtually all mathematical, devoid of empirical content) and his famous 'principles of economics' textbook in its successive editions promulgated the theory of the unproductive firm in perfect competition as the ideal of economic efficiency.

Perfect competition idealises the very small firm, its growth constrained by rising AVC as it expands output. It is assumed that at a very low level of output (for the firm to remain very small), the increase in AVC outweighs the decline in AFC so that average total costs rise, giving the firm's cost curve its U-shape. But why do AVC rise to such an extent that they outweigh declining AFC? Current textbooks do not supply an explanation. For example, N. Gregory Mankiw, in *Principles of Microeconomics*, simply states that the cost curve is U-shaped – representing 'cost curves for a typical firm' (Mankiw n.d., 259) – and illustrates this 'principle' with made-up numbers for a hypothetical coffee shop in which AVC increase from $0.30 for one cup of coffee to $12.00 for ten cups, with rising AVC surpassing declining AFC after six cups (ibid., 254). Similarly, Paul Krugman and Robin Wells, in *Essentials of Economics*, argue that a 'realistic marginal cost curve has a 'swoosh' shape' (Krugman and Wells 2017, 189) and give the example of a salsa maker whose AVC rise from $12.00 for one case of salsa to $120.00 for ten cases, with rising AVC surpassing declining AFC after three cases (ibid., 185). In both the Mankiw and Krugman/Wells textbooks, the 'explanation' for the U-shaped cost curve – and hence the unproductive firm that is the ideal of economic efficiency – is simply the made-up numerical example!

We can, however, find an explanation for the U-shaped cost curve in the early editions of Samuelson's textbook.[5] In the first through fifth editions of *Economics*, Samuelson explained the U-shaped cost curve by assuming that (as is typically the case) labour is the firm's main variable-cost input and that as the employment of labour increases as the firm expands output, the average productivity of labor falls because of, in Samuelson's words, 'limitations of plant space and management difficulties.' As the professor put it (with my emphasis) in the fifth edition of *Economics*, published in 1961 (with wording only slightly different from that in the first edition):

> After the overhead has been spread thin over many units, fixed costs can no longer have much influence on average costs. Variable costs become important, and as *average variable costs begin to rise because of limitations of plant space and management difficulties, average costs finally begin to turn up.*
> (Samuelson 1961, 524)

There it is: the explanation of the most important 'principle' of the neoclassical theory of the firm – and I would argue, of neoclassical economics more generally – buried away on page 524 of an 853-page textbook. The theory of the firm in perfect competition in turn provided the foundation for Samuelson's 'grand neoclassical synthesis' of microeconomics and macroeconomics, which continues to dominate economics teaching and thinking. But Samuelson's two cryptic sentences provide far more of an explanation for the U-shaped cost curve than Mankiw and Krugman/Wells (as but two examples from the crowded field of Samuelson-clone introductory economics textbooks) have to offer.

So, what do those sentences mean? When I used the fifth edition of Samuelson, *Economics* in my very first economics course in 1964, I was told that what Professor Samuelson was arguing was that as more workers are added to the workplace as variable inputs as the firm expands output, their average productivity falls because of overcrowding that causes them to bump into one another ('limitations of plant space') and because the increase in the number of workers to be supervised makes it more difficult for the employer to prevent workers from shirking ('management difficulties'). The resultant decline in labour productivity as output increases causes AVC to rise. In other words, Samuelson's explanation for the U-shaped cost curve was that a rise in AVC occurs because workers *can't* work and *won't* work.

Moreover, the cost curve gets its U-shape when the rise in AVC is so large that it overwhelms the fall in AFC. The rise in total unit costs, reflecting declining productivity as the firm expands its output, then constrains the growth of the firm, and rather than confront 'limitations of plant space' and 'management difficulties', the neoclassical employer just optimises subject to these 'given' constraints. In sharp contrast, the innovative enterprise would confront 'limitations of plant space' by investing in more spacious plant and 'management difficulties' by creating incentives for workers to supply higher levels of productivity. These investments and incentives would add to the firm's costs, but if the innovating firm can increase its productivity sufficiently by making these expenditures, it could possibly outcompete the optimising firm, as shown in Figure 6.1. So much for the neoclassical ideal of economic efficiency!

Just a minute (I can hear the well-trained neoclassical economist saying). What about the neoclassical theory of monopoly that one can also find in virtually every introductory economics textbook, with its demonstration that, compared with perfect competition, the monopolist, maximising profits subject to a downward-sloping demand curve, restricts output and raises the product's price? Isn't that proof of perfect competition as the ideal of economic efficiency?

No, it is not. There is a logical flaw in the neoclassical monopoly model that yields the 'results' – restricted output, higher price – that neoclassical ideology requires. As shown in Figure 6.2, it is assumed that the monopolist maximises profits subject to the same cost structure as the perfect competitors.

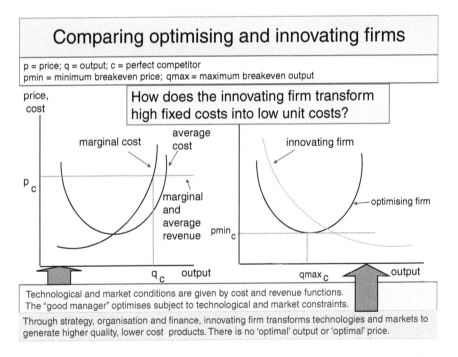

Figure 6.1 The innovating firm transforms the cost structure that the optimising firm takes as a 'given' constraint.

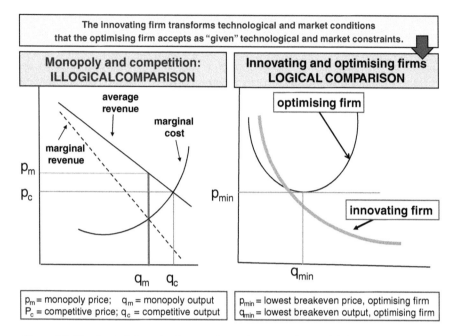

Figure 6.2 The logical flaw in the neoclassical monopoly model that seeks to prove that 'perfect competition' is the ideal of economic efficiency.

But then how did the monopolist become a monopolist? In the theory of innovative enterprise, the firm grows large, and outcompetes perfect competitors, by transforming the cost structure – by, for example, investing in a more spacious plant to prevent overcrowding, creating positive incentives for employees to expend more work effort or launching an R&D initiative that may yield a higher-quality product. Compared with perfect competitors, who follow the neoclassical directive to optimise subject to given constraints, the innovating firm increases output and, by driving down AFC as it expands output, can lower prices to consumers while still increasing its profits. For the prosperity of the economy, that's a big plus. For neoclassical theory, however, that's a big minus.

Note also that in his explanation of the U-shaped cost curve, Samuelson writes (with my emphasis) that because of limitations of plant space and management difficulties, 'average costs *finally* turn up.' Samuelson inserted (probably instinctively) the word 'finally' because if average costs do not turn up, the firm will grow larger and destroy the possibility of 'perfect competition' as an ideal and 'constrained optimisation' as the decision rule for the 'profit-maximising' firm. Samuelson's theory requires that the firm that is the 'ideal of economic efficiency' remain small and unproductive. If the economy is dominated by firms in which, to use Samuelson's own words, 'large size breeds success, and success breeds further success,' then perfect competition as the 'ideal of economic efficiency' disappears, and 'constrained optimisation' may not be the management practice that achieves superior economic performance.

Yet even Paul Samuelson was aware that the real-world economy can be dominated by large firms that are highly productive. In Chapter 2 ('Central problems of every economic society') of the fifth edition of *Economics*, Samuelson first discusses 'Increasing costs' and 'The famous law of diminishing returns' (both subheadings) and provides a table with a numerical example that bears the heading 'Diminishing returns is a fundamental law of economics and technology' and the caption 'Returns of corn when units of labor are added to fixed land.' On the next page, however, he has the subheading 'Economies of scale and mass production: a digression,' with the explanation: 'Economies of scale are very important in explaining why so many of the goods we buy are produced by large companies … They raise questions to which we shall return again and again in later chapters.'

Samuelson made his 'honor role of American business' remark, cited above, 100 pages later. But it would be an exaggeration to say that the professor kept his promise to 'return [to this central problem of every economic society] again and again.' After all, for Samuelson the actual importance of economies of scale to the productive economy was just 'a digression' from his obsession with 'the famous law of diminishing returns' as a 'fundamental law of economics and technology'.

It may be, however, that, in the course of revising *Economics* in the early 1960s, Professor Samuelson gave this glaring contradiction between neoclassical ideology and economic reality some deeper thought and came to realise the absurdity of arguing that the unproductive firm is the ideal of economic efficiency. If so, he resolved the problem, not by renouncing the neoclassical theory of the firm and calling for the construction of a theory of innovative enterprise – drawing upon, for example, Edith Penrose's seminal contribution *The Theory of the Growth of the Firm*, published in 1959, and Alfred Chandler's pioneering historical research documented in his 1962 book *Strategy and Structure* – but rather by simply excising from the sixth and subsequent editions *of Economics* the sentences quoted above about overhead being spread thin, limitations of plant space, and management difficulties. Henceforth, Samuelson would just refer to the 'famous law of diminishing returns' to justify the nonsense that the unproductive firm is the ideal of economic efficiency. And, over the subsequent generations, economists such as N. Gregory Mankiw and Paul Krugman, among other PhD economists, have published textbooks that reproduce this nonsense as a principle of economics, taught routinely to students and requiring neither introspection nor explanation.

The problem with perfect competition as the ideal of economic efficiency is not just that millions upon millions of economics students have been and continue to be miseducated about the role of the business enterprise in the economy. The bigger problem is that the 'well-trained' PhD economists who are supposed to be the educators (including those to whom so-called Nobel Prizes in economics have been meted out) spout the inanity that the unproductive firm is the ideal of economic efficiency and in so doing portray the 'ideal' firm as a powerless entity that does not, and should not, interfere with the market coordination of the allocation of resources. In my own teaching, I call this view of the world 'sweatshop economics' because the overcrowded and unmotivated firm that Samuelson describes as the microfoundation of ideal efficiency has the characteristics of a sweatshop. I make the point that if such firms actually dominated the economy, we would, in a nation such as the United States, all be living in poverty (Lazonick 2016b).

Meanwhile, the 'well-trained' economist views the highly productive firms that grow large, and perhaps even dominate the industries in which they operate, as massive 'market imperfections' that impede the purported efficiency of market resource allocation. In the real economic world, however, the innovative enterprise is a powerful entity that, by transforming the technological, market and competitive conditions that it faces, succeeds in generating the higher-quality, lower-cost goods and services that raise productivity. Far from being a market imperfection, by confronting and transforming the 'neoclassical constraints,' the innovative enterprise provides the productive foundations for achieving sustainable prosperity.

As I argue in the next section of this chapter, through the very process of developing and utilising productive capabilities, the innovative enterprise tends to provide more stable employment, more equitable incomes, and higher productivity than the 'uninnovative' enterprises with which neoclassical economists are enamoured. For society as a whole, the innovative enterprise is the linchpin of the investment triad, making it possible for household families, through stable and equitable employment, to be supportive, and for government agencies, through access to tax revenues from households and businesses and by servicing the needs of households and businesses, to be developmental.

For the sake of sustainable prosperity, the academic discipline known as economics needs to rid itself of the myth of the market economy – from the Samuelson-clone introductory textbooks to the ubiquitous mathematical models that typically bear no relation to reality (and which often reflect utter ignorance of how an actual economy functions and performs). It is high time to take up the Schumpeterian challenge and build a useful analysis of economy and society around a theory of innovative enterprise. We will then understand how and why the ideology that companies should be run to 'maximise shareholder value' subverts innovative enterprise and, with that subversion, our quest for stable and equitable economic growth.

From retain-and-reinvest to downsize-and-distribute

The theory of innovative enterprise (TIE) that I have constructed through decades of research and teaching provides an analytical perspective on the microfoundations of sustainable prosperity. There is no way in which an economy can attain stable and equitable growth unless its major business enterprises focus on investing in productive capabilities for the sake of generating innovative products. Beginning with a characterisation of the innovation process as uncertain, collective and cumulative, TIE articulates three 'social conditions of innovative enterprise' – strategic control, organisational integration and financial commitment – that can support the innovation process. Armed with TIE, we can then consider the impacts of the innovation process on employment stability, income equity and business productivity. We can ask whether the dominant characteristics of the nation's major business enterprises support or undermine the attainment of stable and equitable growth in the economy as a whole.

TIE is an analytical framework for understanding how a business enterprise can generate a product that is higher-quality and/or lower-cost than products previously available, and thus be a source of productivity growth. The innovation process that can generate a higher-quality, lower-cost product is uncertain, collective and cumulative (Lazonick 2015b).

- Uncertain: When investments in transforming technologies and accessing markets are made, the product and financial outcomes cannot be known; if they were it would not be innovation. Hence the need for strategy.
- Collective: To generate higher-quality, lower-cost products, the enterprise must integrate the skills and efforts of large numbers of people with different hierarchical responsibilities and functional capabilities into the learning processes that are the essence of innovation. Hence the need for organisation.
- Cumulative: Collective learning today enables collective learning tomorrow, and these organisational learning processes must be sustained continuously over time until, through the sale of innovative products, financial returns can be generated. Hence the need for finance.

TIE identifies three social conditions – strategic control, organisational integration and financial commitment – that can enable the firm to manage the uncertain, collective, and cumulative character of the innovation process.

- Strategic control: For innovation to occur in the face of technological, market and competitive uncertainties, executives who control corporate resource allocation must have the abilities and incentives to make strategic investments in innovation. Their abilities depend on their knowledge of how strategic investments in new capabilities can enhance the enterprise's existing capabilities. Their incentives depend on the alignment of their personal interests with the company's purpose of generating innovative products.
- Organisational integration: The implementation of an innovation strategy requires integration of people working in a complex division of labour

into the collective and cumulative learning processes that are the essence of innovation. Work satisfaction, promotion, remuneration and benefits are important instruments in a reward system that motivates and empowers employees to engage in collective learning over a sustained period of time.

- Financial commitment: For collective learning to cumulate over time, the sustained commitment of 'patient capital' must keep the learning organisation intact. For a startup company, venture capital can provide financial commitment. For a going concern, retained earnings (leveraged, if need be, by debt issues) are the foundation of financial commitment.

The uncertainty of an innovative strategy is embodied in the fixed-cost investments required to develop the productive capabilities that may, if the strategy is successful, result in a higher-quality product. But an innovative strategy that can eventually enable the firm to develop superior productive capabilities may place the innovating firm at a competitive disadvantage (as indicated for low levels of output in Figure 6.1 above) because such strategies tend to entail higher fixed costs than the fixed costs incurred by rivals that choose to optimise subject to given constraints. As an essential part of the innovation process, the innovating firm must access sufficient markets for its products to transform high fixed costs into low unit costs (see Figure 6.1), and, thereby, convert competitive disadvantage at low levels of output into competitive advantage at high levels of output.

These higher fixed costs derive from both the size and the duration of the innovative investment strategy. The innovating firm will have higher fixed costs than those incurred by the optimising firm if, as is typically the case, the innovation process requires the simultaneous development of productive capabilities across a broader and deeper range of integrated activities than those undertaken by the optimising firm. But in addition to, and generally independent of, the size of the innovative investment strategy at a point in time, high fixed costs will be incurred because of the duration of time that is required to transform technologies and access markets until they result in products that are sufficiently high-quality and/or low-cost to generate returns. If the size of investments in physical capital tends to increase the fixed costs of an innovative strategy, so too does the duration of the investment required for an organisation of people to engage in the collective and cumulative – or organisational – learning that, to transform technologies and access markets, is the central characteristic of the innovation process.

The high fixed costs of an innovative strategy create the need for the firm to attain a high level of utilisation of the productive resources that it has developed – what are generally called 'economies of scale'. Given the productive capabilities that it has developed, the innovating firm may experience increasing costs because of the problem of maintaining the productivity of variable inputs as it employs larger quantities of these inputs in the production process. But rather than, as in the case of the optimising firm, take increasing costs as a given constraint, the innovating firm attempts to transform its access to high-quality productive capabilities at high levels of output. To do so, it invests in the development of that productive capability, the utilisation of which as a variable input has become the source of increasing costs. To overcome the constraint on its innovative strategy posed by reliance on the market to supply it with inputs – which is what a variable factor of production entails – the innovating firm integrates the supply of that factor into its internal operations.

The development of the productive capability of this now-integrated factor of production adds to the fixed costs of the innovative strategy. Previously this productive resource was utilised as a variable factor that could be purchased incrementally at the going factor price on the market as extra units of the input were needed to expand output. Having added to its fixed costs in order to overcome the constraint on enterprise expansion posed by increasing variable costs, the innovating firm is then under even more pressure to expand its sold output in order to transform high fixed costs into low unit costs.

In effect, to restate Adam Smith's first principle of economics enunciated in *The Wealth of Nations* (Smith 1904, Ch. 1, 'On the division of labour'), economies of scale are limited by the extent of the market. The firm's higher-quality product enables it to access a larger extent of the market than its competitors, although learning about what potential buyers want and convincing potential buyers that the firm's product is actually 'higher-quality' add to the fixed costs of the innovation strategy. Hence the fixed costs of the innovative strategy depend on investments in not only transforming technology but also accessing markets, with an increase in fixed costs requiring an even larger extent of the market to convert high fixed costs into low unit costs. A potent way for an innovating firm to attain a larger extent of the market is to share some of the gains of this cost transformation with its customers in the form of lower prices.

As, through the development and utilisation of productive capabilities, the innovating firm succeeds in the conversion of high fixed costs into low unit costs, it in effect 'unbends' the U-shaped cost curve rather than, as in the theory of the optimising firm, take internal diseconomies of scale as a given constraint (see Figure 6.1 above). By reshaping the cost curve in this way, the innovating firm creates the possibility of securing competitive advantage over its 'optimising' rivals which, as instructed by the economics textbooks, take increasing costs as a given constraint.

To sum up: in my elaboration of TIE, I use the distinction between fixed costs and variable costs to argue that an innovating firm that experiences rising variable costs as it seeks to expand output will recognise the need to exercise control over the quality of the variable input, the use of which is decreasing productivity. To do so the innovating firm will integrate the production of that input into its internal operations, thus seeking to transform variable costs into fixed costs as part of its innovative strategy. This strategic move will place the innovating firm at a competitive disadvantage at low levels of output (as in Figure 6.1), increasing the imperative that it attain a large market share to drive down unit costs. Moreover, there are often high fixed costs of accessing that market share (branding, advertising, distribution channels, a salaried sales force, etc.), and indeed in some industries the fixed costs of accessing a large market share are greater than the fixed costs of investing in the transformation of production technologies.

Along with investments in plant and equipment, investment in productive capabilities entails training and retaining employees. It may also possibly entail sustaining learning relationships with firms that act as suppliers of inputs and distributors of outputs if these services are performed by legally independent enterprises. The theory of the optimising firm views labour as a variable cost, a commodity that is added to and subtracted from the production process as required by the expansion or contraction of output. In fact, however, when a company enhances the productive capability of an employee, either through formal or on-the-job training, that employee's capability takes the form of a fixed-cost asset that both can enhance the quality of the product that the innovating firm has to sell and increase the need to attain a large extent of the market to transform high fixed costs into low unit costs. When the firm succeeds in both, it generates a higher-quality, lower-cost product than was previously available. Innovation and the growth of the firm go hand in hand.

Investment in productive capabilities, including those of its labour force, drive innovation and the growth of the firm. To retain and motivate the employees that the firm has hired and trained, the innovating firm generally offers these employees higher pay, more employment security, superior benefits and more interesting work, all of which add to the fixed cost of the asset that an employee's labour represents. The innovating firm improves its employees' living conditions, but it can afford, and indeed profit from, the increased labour expense when that labour's productive capability enables the firm to gain a competitive advantage by generating high-quality, low-cost products.

The innovating firm shares the gains of innovation with its employees by making investments in what I have called their 'collective and cumulative careers' (Lazonick, Moss, Salzman and Tulum 2014; Hopkins and Lazonick 2014). Under such circumstances, increases in labour incomes and increases in labour productivity tend to show a highly positive correlation – an interconnection that, I argue, was prevalent in US business enterprises in the decades after World War II when, for white males at least, the 'career with one company' was the employment norm (Lazonick 2015c).

When successful, the innovating firm may come to dominate its industry, but its output is far larger and its unit costs, and hence potentially its product price, far lower than they would be if a large number of small firms had continued to populate the industry. Indeed, one might even find this transition from competition to dominance manifested by the transformation of a large number of overcrowded sweatshops with alienated labour into a small number of spacious factories with highly motivated labour! The overall gains from innovation will depend on the relation between the innovating firm's cost structure and the industry's demand structure, while the distribution of those gains among the firm's various 'stakeholders' will depend on their relative power to appropriate portions of these gains (Lazonick 1990, 2015b).

What is important in the first instance is that, as a result of the transformation of technological and market 'constraints', there are gains to innovative enterprise that can be shared. In expanding output and lowering costs, it is theoretically possible (although by no means inevitable) for the gains to innovative enterprise to permit, simultaneously, higher pay, more stable employment, and better working conditions for employees; a stronger balance sheet for the firm; more secure paper for creditors; higher dividends and stock prices for shareholders; more tax revenues for governments; and higher-quality products at lower prices for consumers. Innovative enterprise provides a foundation for achieving sustainable prosperity.

TIE explains how, in the rise of the United States to global industrial leadership during the twentieth century, a 'retain-and-reinvest' allocation regime enabled a relatively small number of business enterprises in a wide range of industries to grow to employ tens, or even hundreds, of thousands of people and attain dominant product-market shares. Companies retained corporate profits and reinvested them in productive capabilities, including first and foremost collective and cumulative learning. Companies integrated personnel into learning processes through career employment. Into the 1980s, the norm of a career-with-one-company prevailed at major US corporations. A steady stream of dividend income and the prospect of higher future stock prices based on innovative products gave shareholders an interest in 'retain-and-reinvest'.

In the immediate post-World War II decades, the beneficiaries of a retain-and-reinvest corporate resource-allocation regime were mainly white males. For minorities and women, access to more stable employment and more equitable income was bolstered by the Civil Rights Act of 1964 and the Equal Employment Opportunity Commission launched the following year. As a bellwether of progress in upward mobility, by the 1970s hundreds of thousands of blacks with no more than high-school diplomas were attaining middle-class status through employment in unionised semi-skilled operative jobs in mass-production industries such as automobiles, steel and electronics manufacturing (Lazonick, Moss and Weitz 2016b). White males, however, maintained privileged access to intergenerational upward mobility from blue-collar jobs to white-collar jobs as the sons of blue-collar workers obtained higher educations followed by 'career with one company' employment in business corporations. In the 1970s, females (disproportionately white) with college educations also gained significantly increased access to career employment in business corporations, although their upward mobility was impeded by the persistence of the ideology that, when children arrived, they would give up or interrupt their careers to assume the traditional middle-class 'stay-at-home-mother' role.

Then, however, from the late 1970s, and continuing to the present, for masses of Americans, including white males, the quantity and quality of employment opportunity that could support upward mobility eroded, while the distribution of income grew increasingly unequal. That, despite the fact that over the past 40 years or so, the real gross domestic product per capita has doubled in the United States (https://fred.stlouisfed.org/series/A939RX-0Q048SBEA). By the first half of the 1980s, some acute observers of blue-collar employment perceived that the US income distribution was taking a 'great U-turn' (Harrison and Bluestone 1986; Harrison, Tilly and Bluestone 1986). In historical retrospect, we now know that, since that change in direction in the early 1980s, the United States has continued down the road to extreme income inequality and the erosion of middle-class employment opportunities. TIE provides a framework for analysing this historic change in direction of US economic performance – essentially the end of the national quest for sustainable prosperity – by focusing on the transformation of the dominant regime of corporate resource allocation from retain-and-reinvest to downsize-and-distribute.

Under retain-and-reinvest, the corporation retains earnings and reinvests them in the productive capabilities embodied in its labor force. Under downsize-and-distribute, the corporation lays off experienced, and often more expensive, workers and distributes corporate cash to shareholders (Lazonick and O'Sullivan 2000). Since the beginning of the 1980s, employment relations in US industrial corporations have undergone three major structural changes, summarised as 'rationalisation', 'marketisation' and 'globalisation', that have eliminated existing middle-class jobs in the United States. The failure of the US economy to replace these jobs with new middle-class employment opportunities cannot, however, be attributed to these changes in employment relations alone. Exacerbating the rate of job loss and limiting investment in new career-employment opportunities has been the financialisation of the business corporation, manifested by massive distributions of corporate cash to shareholders.

From the early 1980s, rationalisation, characterised by plant closings, terminated the jobs of high-school educated blue-collar workers, most of them well-paid union members. From the early 1990s, marketisation, characterised by the end of a career with one company as an employment norm, placed the job security of middle-aged white-collar workers, many of them college-educated, in jeopardy. From the early 2000s on, globalisation, characterised by the accelerated movement of employment offshore to lower-wage nations, left all members of the US labour force vulnerable to displacement, whatever their educational credentials and work experience.

Initially, these structural changes in employment could be explained as business responses to changes in technologies, markets and competition. During the onset of the rationalisation phase in the early 1980s, the plant closings were a reaction to the superior productive capabilities of Japanese competitors in consumer-durable and related capital-goods industries that employed significant numbers of unionised blue-collar workers. During the onset of the marketisation phase in the early 1990s, the erosion of the one-company-career norm among white-collar workers was a response to the dramatic technological shift from proprietary systems to open systems, integral to the microelectronics revolution; a shift that favoured younger workers with the latest computer skills, acquired in higher education and transferable across companies, over older workers with many years of company-specific experience. During the onset of the globalisation phase in the early 2000s, the sharp acceleration in the offshoring of jobs was a response to the emergence of large supplies of highly capable, and lower-wage, labour in developing nations such as China and India which, linked to the United States through inexpensive communication and transportation systems, could take over US employment activities that had become routine.

Once US corporations transformed their employment relations, however, they often pursued rationalisation, marketisation and globalisation to cut current costs rather than to reposition their organisations to produce innovative products. Defining superior corporate performance as ever higher quarterly earnings per share (EPS), companies turned to massive stock repurchases to 'manage' their own corporations' stock prices. Trillions of dollars that could have been spent on investment in productive capabilities in the US economy over the past three decades have instead been used to buy back stock for the purpose of manipulating stock prices.

Figure 6.3 shows net equity issues (new stock issues minus stock taken off the market through stock repurchases and M&A activity) of US nonfinancial

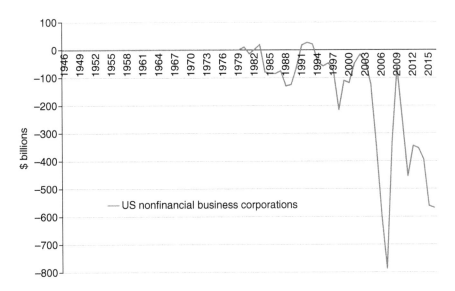

Figure 6.3 Net equity issues, US nonfinancial corporations, 1946–2016.

Source: Board of Governors of the Federal Reserve System, Federal Reserve Statistical Release Z.1, 'Financial Accounts of the United States: Flow of Funds, Balance Sheets, and Integrated Macroeconomic Accounts', Table F-223: Corporate Equities, 8 June 2017, at www.federalreserve.gov/releases/z1/current/.

corporations from 1946 through 2016. Over the decade 2007–2016 net equity issues of nonfinancial corporations averaged $412 billion per year. In 2016 net equity issues were $586 billion. Over the past three decades, in aggregate, dividends have tended to increase as a proportion of corporate profits. Yet in 1997 buybacks first surpassed dividends in the US corporate economy and, even with dividends increasing, have far exceeded them in recent stock-market booms (Lazonick 2015a, 2016a).

Using the data in Figure 6.3, the first data column of Table 6.1 shows the amounts of net equity issues by nonfinancial corporations, decade by decade, from 1946 to 2015, in 2015 dollars. For the first three decades after World War II, net equity issues were moderately positive in the corporate economy as a whole. In the following decades, however, net equity issues became increasingly negative (even after adjusting for inflation). As a gauge of their growing importance in the economy, the second data column of Table 6.1 shows net equity issues as a proportion of GDP.

As shown in Figure 6.4, since the early 1980s, major US business corporations have been doing stock buybacks on top of (and not instead of) making dividend payments to shareholders. Figure 6.4 shows dividends and buybacks for 236 companies that were in the S&P 500 Index in January 2016 that were publicly listed from 1981 through 2015. At the beginning of the 1980s, buybacks were minimal, and from 1981 through 1983 buybacks for these 236 companies absorbed only 4.3% of net income, with dividends representing 49.5%. The buyback proportion of net income increased to 18.8% in 1984 and 30.8% in 1985, while the dividend proportions were 42.5% and 52.4%. Thereafter, by ten-year periods, the buyback proportions of net income increased from 25.8% in 1986–1995 to 42.9% in 1996–2005 and 49.5% in 2006–2015, while dividend payouts over these decadal periods were 50.7%, 39.0% and 39.1%, respectively. Even though dividend payout ratios were

Table 6.1 Net equity issues by non-financial corporations in the US economy, by decade in 2015 dollars, and as a per cent of GDP

	Net equity issues, US non-financial corporations 2015 $ billions	Net equity issues as % of GDP
1946–1955	143.2	0.56
1956–1965	110.9	0.30
1966–1975	316.0	0.58
1976–1985	−290.9	−0.40
1986–1995	−1,002.5	−1.00
1996–2005	−1,524.4	−1.09
2006–2015	−4,466.6	−2.65

Sources: Net equity issues data is the same as in Figure 6.4, adjusted to 2015 US dollars, using the consumer price index in Council of Economic Advisors, *Economic Report of the President 2017*, January 2017, Table B-10, at www.presidency.ucsb.edu/economic_reports/2017.pdf.

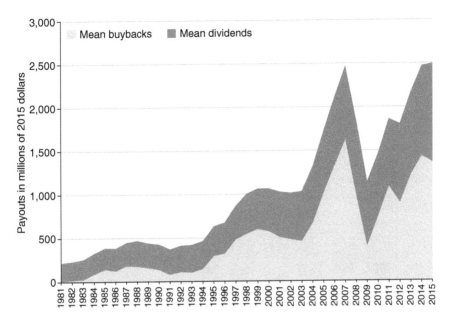

Figure 6.4 Mean cash-dividend and stock-buyback distributions in 2015 dollars for 236 companies in the S&P 500 Index in January 2016 that were publicly listed from 1981 through 2015.

Source: Standard and Poor's Compustat database; calculations by Mustafa Erdem Sakinç and Emre Gomeç of the Academic-Industry Research Network.

lower in 1996–2005 and 2006–2015 than in 1986–1995, total payout ratios to shareholders rose from 76.5% to 81.9% to 88.6% over these three periods. Most recently, the total payout ratios for these 236 companies were 97.0% in 2014 and 106.2% in 2015.

Over the past three decades, US stock markets, of which the New York Stock Exchange and the National Association of Securities Dealers Automated Quotation (NASDAQ) exchange are by far the most important, have enabled the extraction of trillions of dollars from business corporations in the form of stock buybacks. Of course, some companies do raise funds on the stock market, particularly when they are doing initial public offerings (IPOs). But these amounts tend to be relatively small, swamped overall by stock repurchases, which have been partially responsible for the hugely negative net equity issues of nonfinancial corporations shown in Figure 6.1. Moreover, when the most successful startups become major enterprises, often employing tens of thousands of people, they too tend to become major repurchasers of their own shares.

Why are companies doing these massive distributions to shareholders? In an article, 'Profits without prosperity', that I published in *Harvard Business*

Review in 2014 (Lazonick 2014a), I argue that the stock-based remuneration of senior executives who exercise strategic control over resource allocation in these US business corporations incentivises them to manipulate their companies' stock prices. That is the only logical explanation for this buyback activity. Standard & Poor's ExecuComp database provides the numbers needed to determine how much money the highest-paid corporate executives in the United States take home in total and the proportion of their total compensation which is stock based. Figure 6.5 shows the average total compensation of the 500 highest-paid executives in the ExecuComp database for each year from 2006 through 2015. It ranges from a low of $15.9 million in 2009, when the stock markets had crashed, with stock-based pay (realised gains from stock options and stock awards) making up 60% of the total, to a high

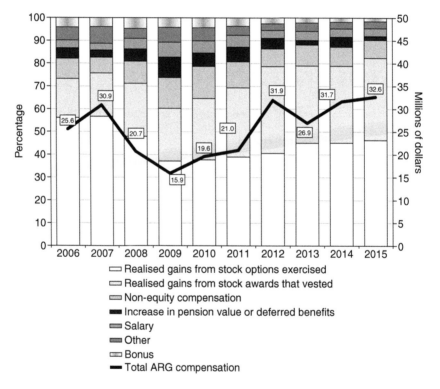

Figure 6.5 Mean total direct compensation, 500 highest-paid named executives in the United States, for each year, 2006–2015.

Source: Standard & Poor's ExecuComp database, retrieved 11 October 2016. Calculations by Matt Hopkins of the Academic-Industry Research Network.

Note
The following extraordinarily highly-paid outliers, with $1 billion or more in total compensation, have been removed: 2012, Richard Kinder, Kinder Morgan, $1.1 billion, and Mark Zuckerberg, Facebook, $2.3 billion; 2013, Mark Zuckerberg, $3.3 billion.

of $32.6 million in 2015, with stock-based gains making up 82% of the total. US corporate executives are incentivised to boost their companies' stock prices and are amply rewarded for doing so. In SEC-approved stock buy-backs, they have at their disposal an instrument to enrich themselves. In their massive, widespread and ubiquitous use of this instrument, they have been participating in the legalised looting of the US business corporation.

This stock-based pay of US corporate executives is a major reason for the extreme concentration of income that has occurred since the 1980s among the richest households in the United States.

Based as well on data from household federal tax filings, Figure 6.6 shows the share of income in the hands of the 0.1% of all households with the highest incomes, including capital gains, from 1916 through 2011. In 1975, the share of the top 0.1% was 2.56% of all US incomes, the lowest proportion over the entire 96-year period. The highest proportion was 12.28% in 2007, just before the financial crisis. In the crisis, the share of the top 0.1% declined, but bounced back with the recovery. In 2012 (not included in Figure 6.6), the share of the top 0.1% was 11.33%, the fourth-highest proportion recorded.[6] Clearly, from the late 1970s on, on a dramatic scale, there was a

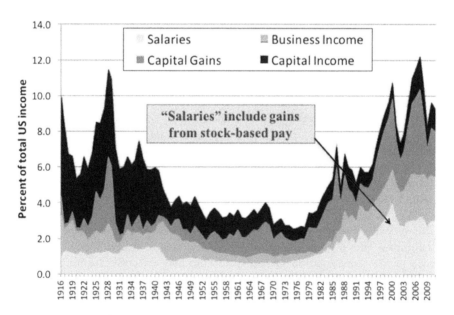

Figure 6.6 Share of total US incomes of the top 0.1% of households in the US income distribution and its components, 1916–2011.

Source: http://topincomes.parisschoolofeconomics.eu/#Database: United States, Top 0.1% income composition.

Note
The category 'salaries' includes compensation from the realised gains on exercising stock options and the vesting of stock awards.

reversal in the trend towards a somewhat falling share of income of the top 0.1% that had occurred in the decades after World War II.

Note that in Figure 6.6, a large part of the explosion of the share of the top 0.1% has been in the form of 'salaries'. As indicated, these 'salaries' include realised gains from stock-based pay – stock options and stock awards – that show up in the summary statistics of an executive's Form 1040 tax returns (the source of these data) as 'Wages, salaries, tips, etc.' Since 1976 virtually all of the realised gains from stock-based pay has been taxed at the ordinary income-tax rates and hence is not included in the 'capital gains' portion of the incomes of the top 0.1% as shown in Figure 6.6.

Federal tax returns include information on a filer's occupation and, through an employer identification number (EIN) on Form W-2, the type of business sector that provides the taxpayer with his or her primary employment income. Jon Bakija, Adam Cole and Bradley Heim accessed federal tax return data for selected years from 1979 to 2005 to analyse the occupations of federal taxpayers at the top of the US income distribution. They found that

> executives, managers, supervisors, and financial professionals account for about 60 percent of the top 0.1% of income earners in recent years, and can account for 70 percent of the increase in the share of national income going to the top 0.1% of the income distribution between 1979 and 2005.'[7]

For 2005, they found that, of taxpayers whose incomes (including capital gains) placed them in the top 0.1%, executives, managers, and supervisors in non-finance businesses made up 41.3% of the total, while financial professionals (including management) were another 17.7%. Of the 41.3% who were non-finance executives, managers or supervisors, 19.8% were salaried and the rest were in closely held businesses (ibid., 38). Besides the 6.2% of the top 0.1% who were 'not working or deceased', the next largest occupational groups were lawyers with 5.8%, real estate with 5.1%, and medical with 4.1%.

We can use the Standard & Poor's ExecuComp database, which compiles data on executive pay that is in SEC Form DEF 14A – the proxy statement that a company files prior to its annual general meeting of shareholders – to get an idea of the representation of high-paid corporate executives among the top 0.1% of households in the income distribution. In 2012, for example, the threshold income including capital gains for inclusion in the top 0.1% of the income distribution was $1,906,047.[8] From the ExecuComp proxy statement data on 'named' top executives (the CEO, CFO and three other highest-paid executives), in 2012, 4,339 executives (41% of the executives in the Execu-Comp database that year) had total compensation greater than this threshold amount, with an average income of $7,524,168. Of that amount, 64% were realised gains from stock-based compensation, with 32% derived from the exercise of stock options and the other 32% from the vesting of stock awards.

The number of corporate executives who, in 2012, were members of the top 0.1% club was, however, far higher than 4,339 for two reasons. First, total corporate compensation of the named executives does not include other non-compensation income (from securities, property, fees for sitting on the boards of other corporations, etc.) that would be included in their federal tax returns. If we assume that named executives whose corporate compensation was below the $1.91 million threshold were able to augment that income by 25% (to pick a plausible number) from other sources, then the number of named executives in the top 0.1% in 2012 would have been 5,095.

Second, included in the top 0.1% of the US income distribution were a potentially large, but unknown, number of US corporate executives whose pay was above the $1.91 million threshold, but who were not named in proxy statements because they were not the CEO, CFO or one of the three other highest-paid executives, as required by SEC regulations. For example, of the highest-paid IBM executives in 2012 named in the company's proxy statement, the lowest paid had a total compensation of $9,177,663. There were presumably many other IBM executives whose total compensation was between this amount and the $1.91 million threshold for inclusion in the top 0.1%. These 'unnamed' executives would have been among the top 0.1% in the income distribution.

Therefore, top executives of US business corporations – industrial as well as financial – are very well represented among the top 0.1% of the US income distribution, with much, and often most, of their compensation income coming from the realised gains from exercising stock options and the vesting of stock awards. When this mode of compensating top executives is combined with the fact that Wall Street has, since the 1980s, judged the performance of corporations by their quarterly stock prices, the importance of stock-based pay in executive compensation is clear. Stock-based pay gives top executives powerful personal incentives to boost, from quarter to quarter, the stock prices of the companies that employ them. In stock buybacks, these executives have found a potent, and SEC-approved, instrument for stock-market manipulation from which they can personally benefit, even if the stock-price boosts are only temporary.

Most household income comes from working in paid employment, with the business sector accounting for about 81% of all US civilian employment. Figure 6.7 shows the relation between the cumulative increase in hourly labour productivity and the cumulative increase in real hourly wages in the business sector of the US economy from 1948 to 2015. From the late 1940s to the mid-1970s, rates of increase in real wages kept up with rates of increase in labour productivity – an indicator of 'shared prosperity'. Beginning in the second half of the 1970s, however, the productivity growth rate began to outstrip the wage growth rate, and over the ensuing decades the gap between the two grew wider and wider, as shown in Figure 6.7.

I submit that the widening gap between productivity increases and wage increases reflects the intensification of the looting of the US business corporation.

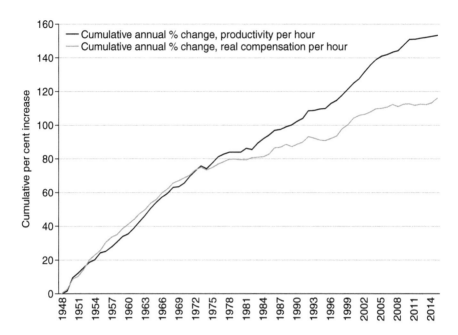

Figure 6.7 Cumulative annual per cent changes in productivity per hour and real wages per hour, 1948–2015.

Source: US Bureau of Labor Statistics, *Current Population Survey* (Nonfarm business labor productivity; Median usual weekly earnings – in constant (1982–1984) dollars).

Figure 6.8 appeared in a *New York Times* article, 'Our broken economy, in one simple chart.' Based on data in household federal tax filings, in 1980, there was a negative correlation between a household's superior position in the income distribution and its income gains since 1946. In sharp contrast, in 2014 compared with 1980, this correlation was positive, and enormously positive for the top 0.1% of the income distribution. From the perspective of the theory of innovative enterprise, Figure 6.8 charts the transition since the 1980s from retain-and-reinvest to downsize-and-distribute as the dominant norm of US corporate resource allocation. And justifying this looting of the US business corporation has been the neoclassical economics ideology, rooted in the theory of the unproductive firm as the foundation for the most efficient economy, that, for the sake of superior economic performance, business enterprises should be run to 'maximise shareholder value'.

As shown in the next section of this chapter, from the 1980s on neoclassical economists known as agency theorists, also mired in the theory of the unproductive firm, argued that US business corporations should use stock-based pay to incentivise senior corporate executives to distribute corporate cash to shareholders for the sake of the efficient allocation of the economy's

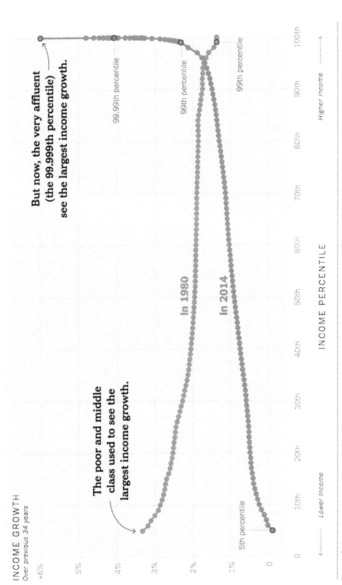

Figure 6.8 Per cent change in income growth during the previous 34 years, from 1980 to 2014, by percentile in the US income distribution.

Source: David Leonhardt, 'Our broken economy, in one simple chart', *New York Times*, 7 August 2017, at www.nytimes.com/interactive/2017/08/07/opinion/leonhardt-income-inequality.html.

resources. That is what agency theorists argued; extreme income inequality is what Americans got.

Agency theory and the looting of the US business corporation

Distributions of corporate cash to shareholders incentivised by the stock-based pay of senior executives are the clearest manifestations of the financialisation of the US business corporation.

Legitimising this financialised mode of corporate resource allocation has been the ideology that a business corporation should be run to 'maximise shareholder value' (MSV). Through their stock options and stock awards, corporate executives who make the resource-allocation decisions to distribute cash to shareholders are themselves prime beneficiaries of the focus on rising stock prices, earnings per share (EPS), and 'total shareholder return' (dividends plus stock-price gains) as the sole measures of corporate performance. While rationalisation, marketisation and globalisation have undermined stable and remunerative employment structures, the financialisation of the US corporation has entailed the distribution of corporate cash to shareholders through stock repurchases, often in addition to generous cash dividends. Over the past decade, at an accelerating rate, hedge-fund activists have joined senior corporate executives in the feeding frenzy in a process that can only be described as the legalised looting of the US business corporation (Lazonick and Shin 2017).

The dramatic change in trajectory from retain-and-reinvest to downsize-and-distribute that has occurred in the United States over the past four decades did not have to happen. Rather, it was imposed upon the US labour force by the adherence to a highly damaging and fallacious ideology of the relation between corporate governance and economic performance. The widespread acceptance of MSV ideology as a guide to US corporate governance from the 1980s on that resulted in the financialisation of the corporation represents a quintessentially neoclassical response to innovation and competition in the new global economy – a response rooted in adherence to the theory of the unproductive firm as the ideal of economic efficiency. In the name of MSV, US business executives favoured living off value created in the past rather than investing in productive capabilities that could create value in the future. The result was the U-turn of the US economy from a movement towards stable and equitable growth to instability, inequity and stunted productivity.[9]

We should not underestimate the role of the neoclassical theory of the market economy, as espoused by both the neoclassical conservative Milton Friedman and the neoclassical liberal Paul Samuelson, as well as their academic offspring, in sanctioning (even if out of ignorance and/or naïveté) the policies that, in the name of MSV, have resulted in the looting of the US business corporation. Beginning in the 1970s and with a vengeance in the

1980s, the United States as a society looked to 'market forces' to respond to changes in innovation and competition. Deregulation of product markets, financial markets and labour markets ensued. The neoclassical theory of the unproductive firm as the foundation of the most efficient economy under-pinned these free-market policy choices – with, not surprisingly, disastrous results in terms of employment opportunity and income distribution. What enabled these free-market principles to gain political traction and change the socioeconomic trajectory of the United States was the rise of a new ideology of corporate governance, rooted in the neoclassical theory of the unproduc-tive firm and propounded by agency theorists, who posited that, for the sake of economic efficiency, businesses should be run to 'maximise shareholder value'.

If 'the firm' is inherently unproductive, then the vast amounts of cash con-trolled by large corporations should be 'disgorged', as MSV's most vocal aca-demic critic, Michael C. Jensen, so crudely but evocatively put it,[10] to financial markets for reallocation to their most efficient uses. Never mind that agency theory, rooted in the neoclassical theory of the unproductive firm, has absolutely nothing to say about how business corporations grow large nor how 'the most efficient uses' to which the market is supposed to allocate resources come into existence. While the rise of MSV to its status as a hege-monic ideology of US corporate governance by the end of the 1980s repres-ented the triumph of the free-market Chicago School, the East Coast liberal Samuelsonian School shared with Friedman's Chicago School the same underlying, and intellectually debilitating, view of the unproductive firm as the ideal of economic efficiency. I know of no prominent Samuelsonian neo-classical economist, even the most progressive among them, who has been critical of MSV. Rather they have continued to spin their stories of imperfect markets and market failures while the looting of the business corporation has gone from bad to worse.

That having been said, the promulgation of MSV as a view of how the economy should operate and perform was the work of Milton Friedman's Chicago School of Economics. In September 1970, the *New York Times Magazine* published an article by Friedman, entitled 'The social responsibility of business is to increase profits' – an article which subsequently came to be viewed as the clarion call for the MSV version of agency theory. Friedman warns:

> In a free-enterprise, private-property system, a corporate executive is an employee of the owners of the business. He has direct responsib-ility to his employers. That responsibility is to conduct the business in accordance with their desires, which generally will be to make as much money as possible while conforming to the basic rules of the society, both those embodied in law and those embodied in ethical custom.
>
> (Friedman 1970)

Friedman concludes the article by quoting himself from his 1962 book *Capitalism and Freedom*:

> There is one and only one social responsibility of business – to use its resources and engage in activities designed to increase its profits so long as it stays within the rules of the game, which is to say, engages in open and free competition without deception or fraud.
>
> (Friedman 1970)

To produce profits, however, the firm must generate competitive – that is, high-quality, low-cost – products. On how a firm generates such products, Friedman's *Capitalism and Freedom* has nothing to say (Friedman 2002). Like Samuelson. Friedman rooted his free-market argument in the ideal of 'perfect competition' with its small unproductive firms. How does a business corporation 'make as much money as possible … in open and free competition without deception or fraud'? To answer that question, Friedman would have needed a theory of innovative enterprise.

The theory of innovative enterprise argues that, in a world of innovation and competition, if those who exercise strategic control over the allocation of corporate resources fail to invest in the productive capabilities that can generate innovative products, their firms will experience competitive decline. Indeed, Friedman's own advice to corporate executives that they should avoid 'social responsibility' proves this rule. At the top of Friedman's 'social responsibility' article as it appeared in *New York Times Magazine* was a photo of General Motors chairman James Roche, standing at the podium at the company's annual shareholder meeting that had taken place in May 1970, four months before the *Times* published Friedman's piece (presumably as a response to ongoing efforts to make General Motors socially responsible). The editorial description of the photo states that Roche was replying to members of 'Campaign G.M.,' an organisation that

> demanded that G.M. name three new directors to represent 'the public interest' and set up a committee to study the company's performance in such areas of public concern as safety and pollution. The stockholders defeated the proposals overwhelmingly, but management, apparently in response to the second demand, recently named five directors to a 'public-policy committee.' The author [Milton Friedman] calls such drives for social responsibility in business 'pure and unadulterated socialism,' adding: 'Businessmen who talk this way are unwitting puppets of the intellectual forces that have been undermining the basis of free society.'

Michael Olenick, who provided me with the pdf of the article as it originally appeared in the *New York Times*, with the photo of Roche and the editorialising on it, points out that, in historical retrospect, the demands of Campaign

G.M. for safer and less polluting cars were in effect demands for G.M. to engage in automobile innovation.[11] In the 1970s and beyond, the world leaders in producing these 'socially responsible' cars would be Japanese and European companies, leaving the 'profit-maximising' General Motors lagging further and further behind. What Friedman (and, quoting him, the *New York Times* editor) called 'pure and unadulterated socialism' proved to be the future of the automobile industry!

Meanwhile, Friedman and his MSV followers, themselves indoctrinated with the theory of the unproductive firm, instructed US corporate executives that they should do everything possible to resist such innovative strategies, perhaps making them, to turn Friedman on his head, 'unwitting puppets of the intellectual forces' of the absurd Friedman-Samuelson view that the unproductive firm is the ideal of economic efficiency. In effect, the neoclassical economists were advising corporate executives to, as Robert Hayes and William Abernathy would put it in a classic 1980 *Harvard Business Review* article, manage their way to economic decline.[12]

The neoclassical theory of the unproductive firm as the ideal of economic efficiency infused the agency-theory arguments in Michael C. Jensen and William H. Meckling's, 'Theory of the firm: managerial behavior, agency costs, and ownership structure,' the academic journal article published in 1976 that pioneered in applying agency theory to the separation of share ownership from managerial control, a dominant characteristic of the US business corporation since the early twentieth century (Jensen and Meckling 1976). On the business school faculty of the University of Rochester, an ultraconservative outpost of the Chicago School, Jensen and Meckling assumed that a public corporation should be run for the sake of its shareholders, as owners. They then posed the problem of the 'optimal' ownership structure that could get managers, as their agents, to serve the interests of the supposed principals.

Jensen and Meckling view the firm as a legal fiction that can be understood as a nexus of contracts. In this contractual relation, the agency problem for owners as principals is to provide incentives to managers to behave in a way that maximises profits for the owners. The 'agency costs' of the separation of ownership and control derive from the interaction of the parties to the contract as each seeks to maximise his own utility. Jensen and Meckling pose the agency problem as susceptible to a constrained-optimisation solution in which an 'equilibrium' (that is, an agreed-upon contract) is achieved. There is no notion in Jensen and Meckling that, by pursuing investment strategies to transform technologies and access markets, managers can lead firms that generate gains from innovative enterprise, obviating the need for a constrained-optimisation solution. Jensen and Meckling's 'Theory of the firm' lacks a theory of innovative enterprise.

Yet agency theory would have a profound influence on the real world of corporate resource allocation (see Lazonick and O'Sullivan 2000; Fox 2009; Fourcade and Khurana 2017). A critical point of departure[13] was the capture in 1981 of the US Securities and Exchange Commission (SEC) by free-market Chicago economists with the election of Ronald Reagan as President of the United States. Reagan's appointment of E.F. Hutton executive John Shad as chair of the SEC put the agency that was supposed to eliminate fraud and manipulation from the nation's financial markets under the leadership of a Wall Street banker for the first time since Joseph Kennedy had been the inaugural holder of that position in 1934–1935. Upon taking office, Shad immediately filled the post of 'chief economist' at the SEC, and picked for the position a 1975 Chicago economics PhD, Charles Cox, who, in a 1976 article in the *Journal of Political Economy* had applied the 'efficient markets hypothesis' to futures trading. In 1983, Shad managed to oust his nemesis, SEC Commissioner John Evans, a Nixon appointee, who believed that finan-cial markets needed to be regulated, and put Cox in Evans' place. Shad's new appointee as SEC chief economist, Greg Jarrell, was an outspoken 1978 Chicago business economics PhD who came to the SEC from a junior faculty position at the University of Rochester, home of Jensen and Meckling.

On 17 November 1982, the SEC promulgated Rule 10b-18, which gives a company a safe harbour against manipulation charges in doing open-market repurchases (Securities and Exchange Commission 1982). The safe harbour states that a company will not be charged with manipulation if, among other things, its buybacks on any single day are no more than 25% of the previous four weeks' average daily trading volume (ADTV). Under Rule 10b-18, moreover, there is no presumption of manipulation, should the corporation's repurchases exceed the 25% ADTV limit.[14] The adoption of Rule 10b-18 in 1982 was called a 'regulatory about-face' from previous SEC views on the detection and prevention of manipulation through open-market repurchases (Feller and Chamberlin 1984). Under Rule 10b-18, a publicly listed company can do hundreds of millions of dollars per day in open-market repurchases, trading day after trading day, for the sole purpose of giving manipulative boosts to its stock price.

As it happened, on 19 and 20 November 1982, within days of the adop-tion of SEC Rule 10b-18, Michael Jensen and Chicago economist Eugene Fama (inventor of the 'efficient market hypothesis' for stock-price determina-tion) held a conference, *Corporations and Private Property*, at the Hoover Insti-tution at Stanford University, ostensibly to commemorate the fiftieth anniversary of the publication of Adolf Berle and Gardiner Means' *The Modern Corporation and Private Property* (Moore 1983). In fact, with two joint articles by Fama and Jensen on 'Ownership and control' and 'Agency prob-lems and residual claims' (Fama and Jensen 1983a, 1983b), the Hoover Insti-tution conference agenda was to make shareholder-value ideology influential in the practice of corporate governance. That influence was assured when, in 1985, the president of Harvard University and the dean of Harvard Business School (HBS) convinced Jensen to leave Rochester to become an HBS pro-fessor.[15] Figure 6.9, taken from a paper that presents research on mentions of 'shareholder value' in the *Wall Street Journal* from 1965 to 2007, suggests that

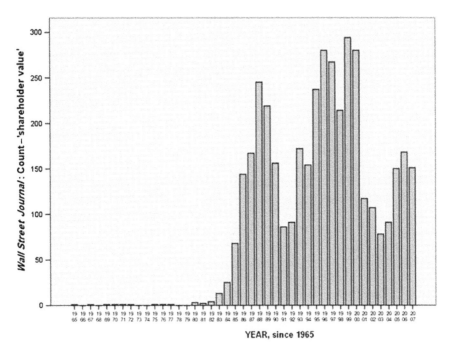

Figure 6.9 Mentions of 'shareholder value' in the *Wall Street Journal*, 1965–2007.
Source: Heilbron, Verheul and Quak 2014.

it was only in the mid-1980s that MSV became central to the public discourse on corporate governance.

In an article, 'Agency costs of free cash flow, corporate finance, and take-overs' that Jensen published in *American Economic Review* in 1986, he argued:

> Free cash flow is cash flow in excess of that required to fund all projects that have positive net present values when discounted at the relevant cost of capital. Conflicts of interest between shareholders and managers over payout policies are especially severe when the organisation generates sub-stantial free cash flow. The problem is how to motivate managers to dis-gorge the cash rather than investing it at below cost or wasting it on organisation inefficiencies.
>
> (Jensen 1986, 323)

In the 1980s and 1990s, Jensen advocated the use of stock-based pay to incentivise senior executives to 'disgorge' the so-called 'free cash flow' in the forms of buybacks and dividends (Jensen and Murphy 1990). Yet, it is the MSV argument itself that defines what cash flow is 'free' – even if it means laying off thousands of employees to do billions of dollars in buybacks to manipulate the company's stock price. Jensen's 'relevant cost of capital' is elevated by the shareholders' success in claiming that all profits should accrue to them, and the reinvestment of corporate cash is deemed to be 'below cost' when taxpayers and workers cannot be excluded from sharing in the gains of the value that they help to create. From the MSV perspective, reinvestment of corporate profits in a company that shares the gains of innovation with taxpayers and workers whose contributions of money and effort help to generate innovative products represents, for Jensen, 'wasting [corporate cash] on organisational inefficiencies'.

One way of solving the 'agency problem' is through what agency theorists call the 'market for corporate control', which seeks to use voting rights connected with shareholding to oust corporate executives who ignore the interests of shareholders. In practice, 'the market for corporate control' takes the form of proxy contests that seek to replace board members and senior executives, a process that, as Jang-Sup Shin and I recount (Lazonick and Shin 2017), was facilitated by the SEC in the 2000s by the rule that institutional investors (pension funds and mutual funds) must vote the proxies of the companies whose stocks they hold in their financial portfolios. Shin and I analyse the perpetrators of what we call 'predatory value extraction' as a concatenation consisting of senior executives as value-extracting insiders, institutional investors as value-extracting enablers and activist shareholders as value-extracting outsiders (ibid.).

In short, as articulated by Jensen and others, MSV is a theory of value extraction, posing as a theory of value creation (Lazonick 1994). MSV ideology is rooted in two misconceptions of the role of public shareholders in the US business corporation. The most fundamental error is the assumption that public shareholders invest in the productive assets of the corporation. They do not (Lazonick 2017a). They allocate their savings to the purchase of shares that are outstanding on the stock market, and they are willing to do so because the liquidity of the market enables them to sell those financial assets at any time they so choose. The erroneous MSV assumption that public shareholders invest in the productive assets of the company is then compounded by the fallacy that it is only public shareholders who make risky investments in the corporation's productive assets, and hence that it is only shareholders who have a claim on the corporation's profits, if and when they occur.

The agency-theory argument raises two critical and related questions: Why are public shareholders deemed to be the 'principals' in whose interests the firm should be run? And what contributions do public shareholders make to the value-creation process? The answers to these questions expose agency theory's logical and factual flaws.

Agency theory's answer to the first question is that only shareholders invest in the firm, while all other participants in the firm provide marketable inputs for which they are paid market-determined prices. Its answer to the second question is that, having invested in the firm, public shareholders take the risks of whether those investments will yield profits or losses, and hence, for the sake of economic efficiency, only shareholders have a claim on the firm's profits if and when there is a positive 'residual' of revenues over costs.

Public shareholders do not, as a rule, invest in the firm. They invest in shares outstanding by simply purchasing them on the stock market. And in purchasing shares on a liquid stock market such as the New York Stock Exchange or NASDAQ, public shareholders take little risk because they enjoy limited liability if they hold the shares while, at any instant and at a very low cost, they can sell the shares at the going market price.

Public shareholders are portfolio investors, not direct investors. The generation of innovative products, however, requires direct investment in productive capabilities. These investments in innovation are uncertain, collective and cumulative. Innovative enterprise requires strategic control to confront uncertainty, organisational integration to engage in collective learning and financial commitment to sustain cumulative learning. That is why, to understand the productivity of the firm, we need a theory of innovative enterprise.

When, as in the case of a startup, financiers make equity investments in the absence of a liquid market for the company's shares, they are direct investors who face the risk that the firm will not be able to generate a competitive product. The existence of a highly speculative and liquid stock market may enable them to reap financial returns – in some cases, even before a competitive product has been produced. It was to make such a speculative and liquid market available to private-equity investors, who were to become known as 'venture capitalists', that in 1971 the National Association of Security Dealers Automated Quotation exchange was launched by electronically linking the previously fragmented, and hence relatively illiquid, over-the-counter markets. NASDAQ became an inducement to direct investment in startups precisely because it offered the prospect of a quick IPO; one that could take place within a few years after the founding of the firm.

It is for that reason that venture capitalists call a listing on NASDAQ an 'exit strategy'. In effect, they are exiting their illiquid, high-risk direct investments by turning them into liquid, low-risk portfolio investments. If, after an IPO, the former direct investors decide to hold onto their shares, they are in precisely the same low-risk portfolio-investor position as any other public shareholder: they can use the stock market to buy and sell shares whenever they so choose.

But venture capitalists are not the only economic actors who bear the risk of making direct investments in productive capabilities. Taxpayers through government agencies and workers through the firms that employ them make risky investments in productive capabilities on a regular basis. From this perspective, households as taxpayers and workers may have, by agency theory's own logic, 'residual claimant' status: that is, an economic claim on the distribution of profits if and when they occur.

Through government investments and subsidies, taxpayers regularly provide productive resources to companies without a guaranteed return. As an important example, but only one of many, the 2016 budget of the US National Institutes of Health (NIH) was $32.3 billion, part of a total NIH investment in life-sciences research spanning 1938 through 2016 that added up to just under $1 trillion in 2016 dollars.[16] Businesses that make use of life-sciences research benefit from the public knowledge that the NIH generates. As risk bearers, taxpayers who fund such investments in the knowledge base, or physical infrastructure such as roads, have a claim on corporate profits if and when they are generated. Through the tax system, governments, representing households as taxpayers, seek to extract this return from corporations that reap the rewards of government spending.

In financing investments in infrastructure and knowledge, therefore, taxpayers make productive capabilities available to business enterprises, but with no guaranteed return on those investments. No matter the corporate tax rate, households as taxpayers face the risks that, because of technological, market and competitive uncertainties, the enterprise will not generate the profits that provide business-tax revenues as a return to households as taxpayers on their investments in infrastructure and knowledge. Moreover, tax rates are politically determined. Households as taxpayers face the political uncertainty that predatory value extractors – financial interests that 'take' far more than they 'make' (see Foroohar 2016) – may convince government policy-makers that unless businesses are given tax cuts or financial subsidies that will permit adequate profits, they will not be able to make value-creating investments. Politicians may be put in power who accede to these demands.

Workers regularly make productive contributions to the companies for which they work through the exercise of skill and effort beyond those levels required to lay claim to their current pay, but without guaranteed returns (Lazonick 1990, 2015b). Any employer who is seeking to generate a higher-quality, lower-cost product knows the profound difference in the productivity levels of those employees who just punch the clock to get their daily pay and those who engage in learning that allows them to make productive contributions through which they can build their careers, thereby putting themselves in a position to reap future returns in work and in retirement. Yet these careers and the returns that they can generate are not guaranteed, and under the downsize-and-distribute resource-allocation regime that MSV ideology – legitimised by agency theory – has helped put in place, these returns and careers have, in fact, been undermined.

Therefore, in supplying their skills and efforts to the process of generating innovative products that, if successful, can create value in the future, workers take the risk that, because of technological, market or competitive uncertainties, the application of their skills and the expenditure of their efforts will be in vain. Far from reaping expected gains in the forms of higher pay, more job security, superior benefits and better work conditions, workers may face cuts in pay and benefits if the firm's innovative investment strategy does not succeed, and they may even find themselves laid off. Workers also face the possibility that, even if the innovation process is successful, the institutional environment in which MSV prevails will empower corporate executives to cut some workers' wages and lay off others in order to extract value for shareholders, including themselves, that those workers helped to create.

As risk bearers, therefore, taxpayers whose money supports business enterprises and workers whose efforts generate productivity improvements have claims on corporate profits if and when they occur. MSV ignores the risk-reward relation for these two types of economic actors in the operation and performance of business corporations (Lazonick and Mazzucato 2013). Instead, based on agency theory, it erroneously assumes that shareholders are the only 'residual claimants'.

The irony of MSV is that the public shareholders whom agency theory holds up as the only risk bearers typically never invest in the value-creating capabilities of the company at all. Rather, they purchase outstanding corporate equities with the expectation that, while they are holding the shares, dividend income will be forthcoming, and with the hope that, when they decide to sell the shares, the stock-market price will have risen to yield a capital gain. Following the directives of MSV, a prime way in which the executives who control corporate resource allocation fuel this hope is by allocating corporate cash to stock buybacks to pump up their company's stock price.

Those holding onto their shares will receive cash dividends, while those wishing to sell their shares will stand a chance of reaping enhanced capital gains as higher stock prices are achieved through stock repurchases – if they are able to get the timing of the stock sales right. The assumption is that, via financial markets, shareholders will then reallocate at least a portion of their gains from dividends and stock sales to uses that are more efficient than those to which they would have been put, had the funds been retained by the company.

MSV implies that shareholders derive their gains by extracting value as a reward for taking the risk of contributing to processes that create value. Thus, when corporations pay dividends or do buybacks, MSV characterises these distributions as 'returning' capital to shareholders. For example, from 2012 through the second quarter of 2017, Apple spent $151 billion on buybacks and $54 billion on dividends under its 'Capital Return Program.'[17] Yet the only time in its history that Apple ever raised funds on the public stock market was in 1980, when it collected $97 million in IPO (Lazonick 2014b; see also Lazonick, Hopkins and Jacobson 2016a). How can a corporation return capital to parties that never supplied it with capital? The vast majority of those who hold Apple's publicly listed shares have simply bought outstanding shares on the stock market. They have contributed nothing to Apple's value-creating capabilities.

Proponents of MSV may accept that a company needs to retain some cash flow to maintain the functioning of its physical capital, but they generally view labour as an interchangeable commodity whose services can be hired, and fired, as needed on the labour market. And they typically ignore the contributions that households as taxpayers make to business-value creation.

Rooted in the neoclassical theory of the market economy, MSV assumes that markets, not organisations, allocate resources to their most efficient uses. Yet it is organisations – including not only businesses enterprises, but also government agencies and household families – that make the investments in productive capabilities that determine both the 'most efficient' uses that exist at a given point in time and the extent to which those 'most efficient' uses become more productive over time (Lazonick 2016b and references therein).

Once we debunk the myth that only shareholders take risk, therefore, the massive distributions that have been made to shareholders since the mid-1980s in the forms of buybacks and dividends raise questions about how much of the cash flow that both shareholders and managers have deemed to be 'free' has been the appropriation of funds that should have gone to masses of households as taxpayers and workers as returns on the investments of money and effort that they have made in the productive capabilities that have generated corporate profits (Lazonick 2017b).

Unfortunately, for lack of a theory of innovative enterprise, the vast majority of economists, be they liberal or conservative, adhere to agency theory's contention that, for the sake of economic efficiency, the purpose of the corporation is to 'maximise shareholder value'. Hence, they describe the trillions of dollars in cash flowing out of companies to the stock market as a 'return' of capital to shareholders, who will then reallocate financial resources to their most efficient uses. MSV, however, can explain neither how these 'most efficient uses' come into existence nor, in particular, the role of organisations in creating value in the economy (Lazonick 1991a, 2003, 2016b).

As we have seen, for about three decades after World War II, the United States consolidated its position as the world's leading economic power, driven by business enterprises that engaged in retain-and-reinvest. During these decades, the distribution of income became somewhat more equal, and a middle class of both high-school-educated blue-collar workers and college-educated white-collar workers thrived. Over the past four decades, in contrast, the United States has experienced extreme concentration of income among the richest households and the erosion of middle-class employment opportunities for the vast majority of the population (ibid.). These two economic problems are integrally related, as, under the influence of the mantra that companies should be run to 'maximise shareholder value', the resource-allocation regimes of business corporations have shifted from retain-and-reinvest to downsize-and-distribute (Lazonick and O'Sullivan 2000; Lazonick 2015a).

Eradicating shareholder value as an ideology of corporate governance

Why have agency theorists got it so wrong? Because, like neoclassical economists more generally, they lack a theory of innovative enterprise: a theory of how business organisations transform technologies and access markets to generate products higher in quality and lower in cost than those previously available. Yet these innovative products are the basis of economic growth. Moreover, based on comparative historical analysis, I contend that the ways in which innovative enterprises allocate resources and returns provide micro-foundations for not only economic growth but also the employment stability and income equity that are associated with a robust and expanding middle class (see Lazonick 1990, 1991a, 1998, 2003, 2007, 2009, 2010, 2015c; Lippert, Huzzard, Jürgens and Lazonick 2014).

If agency theorists have a coherent theory of the firm, it is the notion that the small, unproductive firm that optimises subject to given technological and market constraints provides the microeconomic foundation for the most effi-cient economy. As we have seen, hypothetical firms of this description play the leading role in the absurd theory known as 'perfect competition'. From such a neoclassical perspective, it is markets, not organisations, that allocate resources to their most efficient uses. From this perspective, the large corpo-rations that have dominated the US economy for over 100 years are massive 'market imperfections'. In line with this reasoning, if we want a more efficient economy, corporate executives should be incentivised, as Michael Jensen and his acolytes have told us, to 'disgorge the free cash flow'.

With its MSV ideology, agency theory is a theory of value extraction without a theory of value creation. It is not surprising, therefore, that Jensen's 1993 American Finance Association presidential address, 'The modern indus-trial revolution, exit, and the failure of internal control systems' (Jensen 1993), is, as the title states, all about *exiting* existing industrial investments, not about *entering* new ones. Jensen even interprets Joseph Schumpeter's notion of 'cre-ative destruction' as being about 'efficient exit', i.e. 'destruction' (ibid., 833), when in fact Schumpeter's entire theoretical orientation was towards the con-ditions for 'entry' through entrepreneurship and innovation: that is, towards the 'creative' part of the catchphrase, the part that called for making old ways of doing things obsolete (to which Schumpeter's 'destruction' refers; Schum-peter 2008, 81–85). To understand entry, one needs a theory of innovative enterprise, which is precisely what agency theory lacks.

The theory of innovative enterprise recognises roles of households acting as taxpayers, workers, consumers, savers and investors in the value-creation process, and hence provides an economic rationale for their claims on the extraction of value from that process. Through government agencies, house-holds as taxpayers make investments in physical infrastructure and human knowledge without which even, and perhaps especially, the largest business enterprises would not be able to generate competitive products. Hence, through the tax system, the body of taxpayers should get shares of corporate profits if and when they accrue. Through the employment relation, house-holds as workers supply business enterprises with skill and effort that are central to the processes of generating competitive products. Hence, through job stability as well as higher pay and benefits, workers should also share in profits if and when they accrue. Through demand for goods and services, households valorise the products that businesses generate. Hence, households should gain from the innovative capabilities of companies through the production of higher-quality, lower-cost products, which is indeed the purpose of the business corporation.

Finally, the theory of innovative enterprise permits the distinction between investors, who participate in the process of value creation, and savers, who derive incomes from the process of value extraction. Investors in value creation provide financial commitment to industrial enterprises to sustain the development and utilisation of productive resources, and hence should receive an equitable share of profits from the generation of competitive products if and when they accrue. In contrast, savers who, as value extractors, use their money to purchase outstanding corporate shares without in any way contributing to the value-creation process should get an income in the form of dividends after all other valid claims of value creators have been paid. In providing financial liquidity, the stock market permits this separation of ownership and control, making savers as passive shareholders able and willing to place their savings in securities in the hope that they will be able to obtain dividends or, if they choose to sell their shares, capital gains.

Innovative enterprise solves the agency problem. By incentivising and rewarding the real value creators, the innovative enterprise can mobilise the skill, effort and finance that, by generating high-quality, low-cost products, can improve the performance of the economy – defined in terms of stable and equitable economic growth. The application of innovation theory to corporate governance solves the 'agency problem' by setting up governance structures that induce individuals with varied hierarchical responsibilities and functional specialties to work together in business organisations towards the achievement of higher levels of productivity, embodied in higher-quality, lower-cost products. These value-creators share in the gains to innovative enterprise, and they collectively support tax payments as returns for governmental contributions to the value-creation process.

As I have argued elsewhere, the United States can start the transition from the value-extracting economy to the value-creating economy by banning stock buybacks, compensating senior executives for their contributions to the value-creating enterprise, placing representatives of households as workers and taxpayers on corporate boards and reforming the tax system so that it recognises and supports the investment triad (Lazonick 2016a). No progress will be made, however, as long as agency theory with its MSV ideology holds sway. By replacing agency theory with innovation theory, academics can contribute to the process of putting the United States and other nations on a path to achieving stable and equitable growth. The theory of innovative enterprise offers a relevant and rigorous analytical perspective that can educate academics, policy-makers and the informed public about how a prosperous economy functions and performs. We may then possess the collective intellectual capability to formulate polices that govern business enterprise for the sake of sustainable prosperity.

Acknowledgements

The research that underpins this chapter has been funded by the Institute for New Economic Thinking (see www.ineteconomics.org/research/experts/wlazonick); the Ford Foundation (project on Financial Institutions for Innovation and Development: www.fiid.org); the European Commission Horison 2020 Research and Innovation Programme under grant agreement No. 649186 (ISIGrowth: Innovation-Fuelled Sustainable and Inclusive Growth: www.isigrowth.eu/); and the Gatsby Foundation (project on Governing Financialisation, Innovation and Productivity in UK manufacturing: www.soas.ac.uk/news/newsitem121890.html). I thank Ken Jacobson and Jang-Sup Shin for comments on the material in this chapter.

Notes

1 Given the overarching perspective on innovative enterprise and sustainable prosperity that I provide in this chapter, most of the bibliographic references are to my own publications, in which the reader can find the sources for my arguments.

2 United States Census Bureau, 'Statistics of U.S. Businesses,' Data on 'U.S., NAICS sectors, larger employment sizes' at www.census.gov/data/tables/time-series/econ/susb/susb-. Unlike the data for 2012, the latest data on firm size for 2014 do not include receipts (collected only every five years).

3 I would be pleased to be informed of any microeconomics textbook that contradicts this statement on the theory of the firm.

4 In the 1940s, economists could have built on Schumpeter's focus on innovation as the fundamental phenomenon of economic development, a proposition that he put forward in Schumpeter 1934. See Lazonick 1991b. By the 1960s, Samuelson could have found powerful explanations, both theoretical and historical, for the growth of the firm in Penrose 1959; and Chandler 1962. In its various editions over the decades, Samuelson 1948, 1961, never referenced these scholars or the body of research that their ideas have spawned.

5 I am grateful to Wynn Tucker for searching through the first edition of Samuelson 1948, to locate the explanation.

6 The World Wealth and Income Database, at http://topincomes.parisschoolofeconomics.eu/#Database: United States, P99.9 income threshold. For the latest data on the pre-tax share of the top 0.1%, not including capital gains, see http://wid.world/world/#sptinc_p99.9p100_z/US/last/eu/k/p/yearly/s/false/2.9295/12.5/curve/false.

7 Bakija *et al.* 2012. The quote is from the paper's abstract.

8 The World Wealth and Income Database, at http://topincomes.parisschoolofeconomics.eu/#Database: United States, P99.9 income threshold.

9 On stunted productivity growth, see Gordon 2016.

10 Jensen 1986 (the term 'disgorge' is used on pages 323 and 328).

11 I am grateful to Michael Olenick, a researcher at INSEAD, for making this point concerning Friedman's 1970 *New York Times* article. See Michael Olenick, 'Original Shareholder Value Article – Milton Friedman to GM: Build Clunky Cars.' Available at https://olen.com/2017/09/15/original-shareholder-value-article-milton-friedman-to-gm-build-clunky-cars/and 'Shareholder Value Theory: History.' Available at https://olen.com/2017/09/15/shareholder-value-theory-history/, *Olen on Economics* (no dates of publication provided).

12 Hayes and Abernathy 1980. For a parallel argument that I made in the 1980s concerning the stance of neoclassical economic historians in the debate on British economic decline, see Elbaum and Lazonick 1984.

13 The following summary is based on my research in progress with Ken Jacobson of the Academic-Industry Research Network.
14 www.sec.gov/divisions/marketreg/r10b18faq0504.htm. For the safe harbour to be in effect, Rule 10b-18 also requires that the company refrain from doing buybacks at the beginning and end of the trading day, and that it do all the buybacks through one broker only.
15 See McDonald 2017. For my early critiques of Jensen and agency theory from the perspective of the historical evolution of the US economy, see Lazonick 1992, 1994.
16 National Institutes of Health, 'Budget,' at www.nih.gov/about-nih/what-we-do/budget. See also Lazonick, Hopkins, Jacobson, Sakinç and Tulum 2017.
17 Fingas 2017; Apple Inc., 'Return of Capital and Cash Position,' Press Release, at http://files.shareholder.com/downloads/AAPL/4402228650x0x840254/7137D28 C-2E6E-4406-8435-ADAB52BB6F4C/Return_of_Capital_Timeline_Q217.pdf.

References

Bakija, J., Cole, A. and Heim, B.T. (2012). Jobs and income growth of top earners and the causes of changing income inequality: Evidence from U.S. tax return data. Working paper, April 2012. Available at https://web.williams.edu/Economics/wp/BakijaColeHeimJobsIncomeGrowthTopEarners.pdf.

Chandler, A.D., Jr. (1962). *Strategy and Structure: Chapters in the History of the American Industrial Enterprise*. Cambridge, MA: MIT Press.

Elbaum, B. and Lazonick, W. (1984). The decline of the British economy: An institutional perspective. *Journal of Economic History*, 44(2): 567–583.

Fama, E.F. and Jensen, M.C. (1983a). Separation of ownership and control. *Journal of Law and Economics*, 26(2): 301–325.

Fama, E.F. and Jensen, M.C. (1983b). Agency problems and residual claims. *Journal of Law and Economics*, 26(2): 327–349.

Feller, L.H. and Chamberlin, M. (1984). Issuer repurchases. *Review of Securities Regulation*, 17(1): 993–998.

Fingas, R. (2017). Apple to increase capital return program by $50B, extended for full year. *AppleInsider* 2 May. Available at http://appleinsider.com/articles/17/05/02/apple-to-boost-capital-return-program-by-50b-extended-for-full-year.

Foroohar, R. (2016). *Makers and Takers: The Rise of Finance and the Fall of American Business*. New York: Crown Business.

Fourcade, M. and Khurana, R. (2017). The social trajectory of a finance professor and the common sense of capital. *History of Political Economy*, 49(2): 347–381.

Fox, J. (2009). *The Myth of the Rational Market: A History of Risk, Reward, and Delusion on Wall Street*. New York: Harper.

Friedman, M. (1970). The social responsibility of business is to increase its profits. *New York Times Magazine*, 13 September.

Friedman, M. (2002). *Capitalism and Freedom* (40th anniversary edn.). Chicago, IL: University of Chicago Press.

Gordon, R.J. (2016). *The Rise and Fall of American Growth*. Princeton, NJ: Princeton University Press.

Harrison, B and Bluestone, B. (1986). *Corporate Restructuring and the Polarising of America*. New York: Basic Books.

Harrison, B., Tilly, C. and Bluestone, B. (1986). Wage inequality takes a great U-turn. *Challenge*, 29(1): 26–32.

Hayes, R.H. and Abernathy, W.J. (1980). Managing our way to economic decline. *Harvard Business Review*, July–August: 67–77.

Heilbron, J., Verheul, J. and Quak, S. (2014). The origins and early diffusion of 'shareholder value' in the United States. *Theory and Society*, 43(1): 1–22.

Hopkins, M. and Lazonick, W. (2014). Who invests in the high-tech knowledge base? Institute for New Economic Thinking Working Group on the Political Economy of Distribution Working Paper 6, September (revised December 2014). Available at http://ineteconomics.org/ideas-papers/research-papers/who-invests-in-the-high-tech-knowledge-base.

Jensen, M.C. (1986). Agency. costs of free cash flow, corporate finance, and take-overs. *American Economic Review*, 76(2): 323–329.

Jensen, M.C. (1993). The modern industrial revolution, exit, and the failure of internal control systems. *Journal of Finance*, 48(3): 831–880.

Jensen, M.C. and Meckling, W.H. (1976). Theory of the firm: Managerial behavior, agency costs, and ownership structure. *Journal of Financial Economics*, 3(4): 305–360.

Jensen, M.C. and Murphy, K.J. (1990). Performance pay and top management incentives. *Journal of Political Economy*, 98(2): 225–264.

Krugman, P. and Wells, R. (2017). *Essentials of Economics* (4th edn.). New York: Worth Publishers.

Lazonick, W. (1990). *Competitive Advantage on the Shop Floor*. Cambridge, MA: Harvard University Press.

Lazonick, W. (1991a). *Business Organisation and the Myth of the Market Economy* Cambridge, MA: Cambridge University Press.

Lazonick, W. (1991b). What happened to the theory of economic development? In: P. Higgonet, D.S. Landes and H. Rosovsky (Eds.), *Favorites of Fortune: Technology, Growth, and Economic Development since the Industrial Revolution* (pp. 267–296). Cambridge MA: Harvard University Press.

Lazonick, W. (1992). Controlling the market for corporate control: The historical significance of managerial capitalism. *Industrial and Corporate Change*, 1(3): 445–488.

Lazonick, W. (1994). Creating and extracting value: Corporate investment behavior and American economic performance. In: M.A. Bernstein and D.E. Adler (Eds.), *Understanding American Economic Decline* (pp. 79–113). Cambridge: Cambridge University Press.

Lazonick, W. (1998). Organisational learning and international competition. In: J. Michie and J.G. Smith (Eds.), *Globalisation, Growth, and Governance* (pp. 204–238). Oxford: Oxford University Press,.

Lazonick, W. (2003). The theory of the market economy and the social foundations of innovative enterprise. *Economic and Industrial Democracy*, 24(1): 9–44.

Lazonick, W. (2007). Varieties of capitalism and innovative enterprise. *Comparative Social Research*, 24: 21–69.

Lazonick, W. (2009). *Sustainable Prosperity in the New Economy? Business Organisation and High-tech Employment in the United States*. Kalamazoo, MI: Upjohn Institute for Employment Research.

Lazonick, W. (2010). Innovative business models and varieties of capitalism: Financialisation of the US corporation. *Business History Review*, 84(4): 675–702.

Lazonick, W. (2012). Alfred Chandler's managerial revolution: Developing and utilising productive resources. In: M. Witzel and M. Warner (Eds.), *Oxford Handbook of Management Theorists* (pp. 361–384). Oxford: Oxford University Press.

Lazonick, W. (2014a). Profits without prosperity: Stock buybacks manipulate the market and leave most Americans worse off. *Harvard Business Review*, September: 46–55.

Lazonick, W. (2014b). Numbers show Apple shareholders have already gotten plenty. *Harvard Business Review*, 16 October. Available at https://hbr.org/2014/10/numbers-show-apple-shareholders-have-already-gotten-plenty.

Lazonick, W. (2015a). Stock buybacks: From retain-and-reinvest to downsize-and-distribute. Center for Effective Public Management, Brookings Institution, April, 10–11. Available at www.brookings.edu/research/papers/2015/04/17-stock-buybacks-lazonick.

Lazonick, W. (2015b). The theory of innovative enterprise: Foundation of economic analysis. AIR Working Paper, August. Available at www.theAIRnet.org.

Lazonick, W. (2015c). Labor in the twenty-first century: The top 0.1% and the disappearing middle class. In: C.E. Weller (Ed.), *Inequality, Uncertainty, and Opportunity: The Varied and Growing Role of Finance in Labor Relations* (pp. 143–192). Ithaca NY: Cornell University Press.

Lazonick, W. (2016a). The value-extracting CEO: How executive stock-based pay undermines investment in productive capabilities. Institute for New Economic Thinking Working Paper 54, 4 December. Available at www.ineteconomics.org/research/research-papers/the-value-extracting-ceo-how-executive-stock-based-pay-undermines-investment-in-productive-capabilities.

Lazonick, W. (2016b). Innovative enterprise or sweatshop economics? In search of foundations of economic analysis. *Challenge*, 59(2): 65–114.

Lazonick, W. (2017a). The functions of the stock market and the fallacies of shareholder value. Institute for New Economic Thinking Working Paper 58, 20 July. Available at www.ineteconomics.org/research/research-papers/the-functions-of-the-stock-market-and-the-fallacies-of-shareholder-value.

Lazonick, W. (2017b). Innovative enterprise solves the agency problem: The theory of the firm, financial flows, and economic performance. Institute for New Economic Thinking Working Paper 62, 28 August. Available at www.ineteconomics.org/research/research-papers/innovative-enterprise-solves-the-agency-problem.

Lazonick, W., Hopkins, M. and Jacobson, K. (2016a). What we learn about inequality from Carl Icahn's $2 billion 'no brainer'. Institute for New Economic Thinking Perspectives, 6 June. Available at www.ineteconomics.org/perspectives/blog/what-we-learn-about-inequality-from-carl-icahns-2-billion-apple-no-brainer.

Lazonick, W., Hopkins, M., Jacobson, K., Sakinç, M.E. and Tulum, Ö. (2017). U.S. pharma's financialised business model. Institute for New Economic Thinking Working Paper 60, revised 8 September 2017. Available at www.ineteconomics.org/research/research-papers/us-pharmas-financialised-business-model.

Lazonick, W. and Mazzucato, M. (2013). The risk-reward nexus in the innovation-inequality relationship. *Industrial and Corporate Change*, 22(4): 1093–1128.

Lazonick, W., Moss, P., Salzman, H. and Tulum, Ö. (2014). Skill development and sustainable prosperity: Collective and cumulative careers versus skill-biased technical change. Institute for New Economic Thinking Working Group on the Political Economy of Distribution Working Paper 7. December. Available at https://ineteconomics.org/ideas-papers/research-papers/skill-development-and-sustainable-prosperity-cumulative-and-collective-careers-versus-skill-biased-technical-change.

Lazonick, W., Moss. P. and Weitz, J. (2016b). The equal employment opportunity omission. Institute for New Economic Thinking Working Paper 53, 5 December.

Available at www.ineteconomics.org/research/research-papers/the-equal-employment-opportunity-omission.

Lazonick, W. and O'Sullivan, M. (2000). Maximising shareholder value: A new ideology for corporate governance. *Economy and Society*, 29(1): 13–35.

Lazonick, W. and Shin, J.-S. (2017). *Rebalancing Value Creation and Value Extraction: How to Deactivate Hedge Funds and Recreate Sustainable Prosperity*. Report to the Korea Economic Research Institute, 31 May.

Lippert, I., Huzzard, T., Jürgens, U. and Lazonick, W. (2014). *Corporate Governance, Employee Voice, and Work Organisation: Sustaining High Road Jobs in the Automotive Supply Industry*. Oxford: Oxford University Press.

Mankiw, N.G. (n.d.). *Principles of Microeconomics* (8th edn.). Boston: Cengage Learning.

McDonald, D. (2017). Harvard Business School and the propagation of immoral profit strategies.' *Newsweek*, 14 April. Available at www.newsweek.com/2017/04/14/harvard-business-school-financial-crisis-economics-578378.html.

Moore, T. (1983). Introduction [to the Special Issue from the Conference on the Corporation and Private Property]. *Journal of Law and Economics*, 26(2): 235–236.

Penrose, E.T. (1959). *The Theory of the Growth of the Firm*. Oxford: Oxford University Press.

Samuelson, P.A. (1948). *Economics: An Introductory Analysis* (1st edn.). New York: McGraw Hill.

Samuelson, P.A. (1961). *Economics: An Introductory Analysis* (5th edn.). New York McGraw-Hill.

Schumpeter, J.A. (1934) [1911]. *The Theory of Economic Development*. Cambridge, MA: Harvard University Press.

Schumpeter, J.A. (1950) [1942]. *Capitalism, Socialism, and Democracy* (3rd edn.). New York: Harper.

Schumpeter, J.A. (2008) [1942]. *Capitalism, Socialism, and Democracy* (xth edn.). New York: HarperCollins.

Securities and Exchange Commission (1982). Purchases of certain equity securities by the issuer and others: Adoption of Safe Harbor. 17 November, *Federal Register*, Rules and Regulations, 47, 228; 26 November 1982: 53333–53341.

Smith, A. (1904) [1776]. *An Inquiry into the Nature and Causes of the Wealth of Nations* (5th edn.) (Edwin Cannan Ed.). London: Methuen.

7 Secular stagnation and creative destruction

Reading Robert Gordon through a Schumpeterian lens

Fred Block

Returning to Schumpeter's *Capitalism, Socialism and Democracy* after 75 years is not at all an antiquarian exercise. On the contrary, it is vitally important for anyone trying to understand our current political economic situation. Schumpeter sought to make sense of the turbulent decades that had produced World War I, the Bolshevik Revolution, the Great Depression and World War II. Schumpeter was, above all, a theorist of historical discontinuity; he did not see societies or economies moving along some smooth trajectory, but rather, he emphasised disruption, creative destruction and the likelihood of deep economic downturns.

In this sense, Schumpeter's approach contrasts sharply with the views that have dominated the social sciences since the 1950s. In parallel with the emergence of the United States as the dominant global power after World War II, the social sciences have generally emphasised continuity, linearity and stability. This is most evident in neo-classical economics with its focus on the propensity of market economies to achieve equilibrium, but similar themes are echoed across the social sciences. In sociology and political science, for example, much work emphasises path dependence – the tendency for social or political development to proceed along the same track that had been established sometime in the past.

However, it is now clear that the global financial crisis that exploded in 2008 has basically returned us to Schumpeter's world of discontinuity and disruption. Even ten years after the dramatic events that required a massive rescue of many of the world's leading financial institutions, the world economy has barely recovered its earlier dynamism. Central banks continue to use unconventional methods such as massive bond purchases and negative interest rates to avert another economic downturn. The term 'secular stagnation' that last flourished in the 1930s and early 1940s has returned as a diagnosis of this period of significantly slower global growth. Moreover, the presumption of global political and military stability that has been part of the post-World War II world has also been punctured. The ferocity of the Syrian Civil War, just 900 miles from Europe's southern border, and the Russian incursions into the Ukraine have raised the spectre of a broader military conflict.[1]

Since our conventional social science with its focus on continuity and stability cannot make sense of these dramatic shifts, we must return to the insights of scholars such as Schumpeter who sought to make sense of an epoch of discontinuities.[2] This chapter does this by elaborating a Schumpeterian critique of the important recent book by Robert Gordon, *The Rise and Fall of American Growth*. Gordon argues that the extraordinary century of US economic growth from 1870 to 1970 has ended, and we have entered a new period in which major headwinds make it highly likely that economic growth will continue to occur at a much slower pace than before 1970. While Gordon certainly recognises a major discontinuity, or break, in historical development, I will argue that had he used the intellectual tools that Schumpeter provided, he would have been able to develop a much more powerful explanation for that discontinuity.

This chapter is developed in four parts. The first part explains Schumpeter's view of long economic cycles and shows how that idea has been further developed by later scholars. The second part summarises the core arguments of Robert Gordon's book and lays out a critique. The third part brings Gordon into dialogue with Schumpeter and offers an alternative explanation for Gordon's findings. The final part is a conclusion.

Schumpeter and neo–Schumpeterian theories

In *Capitalism, Socialism and Democracy*, Schumpeter expressed his scepticism about theories of secular stagnation that were common in the 1930s and early 1940s. Schumpeter's Harvard colleague, Alvin Hansen (1938) was one of the most famous proponents of this line of analysis. But in his Chapter 10, Schumpeter takes direct aim at those who claim that capitalism faces a crisis because of the vanishing of investment opportunities. He characterises the view of his opponents as follows:

> According to this view, we have been witnessing not merely a depression and a bad recovery, accentuated perhaps by anti-capitalist policies, but the symptoms of a permanent loss of vitality which must be expected to go on and to supply the dominating theme for the remaining movements of the capitalist symphony....
>
> (Schumpeter 1950, 111)

Schumpeter also notes the similarities of this diagnosis to the views of an earlier generation of economic thinkers between 1873 and 1896 who also imagined that they were living through the end of the capitalist symphony. Schumpeter's argument grew out of his massive study, *Business Cycles* (1939), in which he sought to explain the development of capitalism from 1787 onwards. In that work, Schumpeter made use of the framework elaborated by the Soviet economist, Nicolai Kondratiev.

Kondratiev identified long economic waves of 40 to 50 years. At the beginning of each of these waves, a handful of key technological advances produced dramatic growth in productivity and self-reinforcing dynamism. However, after 20 to 25 years, dynamism would slow and the economy would face serious barriers and extended periods of stagnation or slow growth. This contractionary phase could last as long as 20 to 25 years, and then a new wave of expansion would occur.[3]

Schumpeter wedded this framework to his view of the disruptive role of the entrepreneur. Schumpeter starts with the economy operating at some kind of equilibrium, but quite suddenly innovators, often working simultaneously in different industries, introduce new products and new processes that compete directly with established business models. The disruption drives profits and capital towards the new groups and will also accelerate economic activity. However, it also forces economic actors around the economy to retool their plans as they attempt to respond to the disruption. The response is often excessive optimism resulting in too rapid an expansion of productive capacity. At some point, the bubble bursts and firms begin a rapid process of retrenchment, and the economy enters recession. Under certain conditions, the recession can become a depression, and, following Kondratiev, the resulting period of stagnant growth can continue for decades.

There are points in his analysis where Schumpeter suggests that changes in government policy are necessary to make possible a new period of expansion. For example, in his discussion of the first Kondratiev cycle from 1787 to 1842, he recognises that railroad building began in the 1830s, but he also emphasised that momentum was extremely limited:

> Comparative slowness of beginnings is accounted for also by the fact that the entrepreneurial task of breaking down the resistance of the environment proved astonishingly difficult. Impediments, such as constraint to pay tolls to canal companies in cases of competition, local jealousies obstructing necessary connections, and so on, were not overcome until much later.
>
> (Schumpeter 1939, Vol. I, 291)

Since railroad building was the big driver of the next Kondratiev cycle (1843–1897), it follows that railroad entrepreneurs were ultimately successful in changing the political environment to break down these constraints. In fact, he discusses at length the importance of government land grants as a mechanism that allowed railroad entrepreneurs to float the bonds that provided the immediate financing needed to pay for railroad construction.

Schumpeter also recognises that at certain points in history, it has been government officials who have played the entrepreneurial role of breaking down barriers to technological advances. For example, in discussing German economic development in the early years of the nineteenth century, he describes the entrepreneurial role of German princes in setting up some of the most advanced manufacturing and mining operations (Schumpeter 1939, Vol. 1, 284). In this sense, Schumpeter anticipated by almost 75 years Mazzucato's (2013) discussion of the 'entrepreneurial state'.[4]

A group of neo-Schumpeterian scholars have built on these insights to construct a somewhat revised theory of long waves that sees action by the public sector as critical to the start of a new period of expansion. One strand of this work is the social structures of accumulation perspective developed initially by David Gordon, Richard Edwards and Michael Reich in the United States (Gordon 1980; Gordon, Edwards and Reich 1982; see also Kotz, McDonough and Reich 1994 and McDonough, Reich and Kotz 2010).[5] Another strand is the work of Christopher Freeman and Francisco Louçã (2001) and of Carlota Perez (2003) developed at the Science Policy Research Unit at the University of Sussex in England.[6]

For both of these groups, Franklin Roosevelt's New Deal in the United States represents the paradigmatic example of government policy facilitating a new period of economic expansion – the 30 glorious years of economic growth after World War II.[7] The basic argument is that the 1910s and 1920s in the US were decades of economic expansion driven by electrification and the mass production of the automobile. Just as in Schumpeter's model, these entrepreneurial breakthroughs led to vastly exaggerated expectations that culminated in the 1929 crash and the Great Depression. The crux of the problem was that the US had developed the technologies of mass production without facilitating mass consumption. During the 1920s, wages of industrial workers lagged far behind productivity growth, and farm incomes also stagnated. Moreover, the US had not yet developed the infrastructure to extend credit to consumers, so purchasing power lagged far behind the capacity to produce (Block 2015).

Across a number of fronts, Roosevelt's New Deal carried out reforms that were intended to create a mass-consumption economy. One critical piece was the development of a new system of mortgage financing that made possible the accelerated process of suburbanisation after World War II. Another piece was made up of agricultural and labour policies that allowed both farmers and industrial workers to enjoy higher incomes that allowed them to participate more fully in a consumer-driven economy. There were also critical investments in infrastructure and ultimately the design of global institutions, including the IMF and the World Bank, to stabilise the global economy in the post-war period.

It was these Roosevelt era policies that laid the basis for the dynamism of the US economy from 1945 to 1969. Yet as the Kondratiev–Schumpeter argument suggests, an economic expansion based on the automobile and suburbanisation began to experience greater strains by the later 1960s and early 1970s. The results were the growing economic difficulties experienced by the US and the global economy in the 1970s that gave rise to intense debates over economic policy choices. In the US, these debates culminated in a 'right turn', as Ronald Reagan's administration launched a period in which the US sought to fix the economy by massive tax cuts for the wealthy and big corporations, a reduction in the burden of government regulation, and cutbacks in public programmes that benefited the poor and the middle class.

Analysts in the neo–Schumpeterian tradition have divergent views on how to characterise the four decades that started with Reagan's presidency. Some argue that there was a neo-liberal long-wave upturn based on the computer and biotechnologies that began in the early 1980s and ran out of steam by the middle of the 2000s. Others have suggested that the entire 40-year period since the mid-1970s should be understood as the downward phase of the long cycle that began right after World War II. As in other down phases, there have been significant technological advances, such as the computer revolution, but in the absence of the appropriate social and economic policies, those technological advances have not been sufficient to generate the dynamism that is characteristic of the expansion phase of a long wave. But adherents of both of these positions agree that significant new public-sector initiatives are required to facilitate a new period of expansion that takes advantage of computer technologies and renewable sources of energy.

In sum, the core Schumpeterian insight is that there is no inevitability to the coming of a new period of economic expansion after a depression. His view is radically different from the Hayekian view that the downturn cleanses the economy and pushes wages, interest rates and raw material prices down to a level where business people again see the potential of profit in new investment activity. On the contrary, in a depressed economy, entrepreneurial agency is necessary both in the form of businesses trying to exploit new technological possibilities and in actions, now typically undertaken by governments, to create the infrastructure and the social acceptance required to bring those new technologies to scale.

Critiquing Gordon's argument

Introduction

Robert Gordon's massive book, *The Rise and Fall of American Growth*, is important because it has arrived in the midst of a renewed debate about secular stagnation. While other analysts have developed theoretical arguments about stagnation, Gordon's book is an ambitious empirical study that seeks to analyse changes in the nation's standard of living over a century and a half. Gordon's argument is that the rapid improvement in the American standard of living that occurred between 1870 and 1940 was both unprecedented and impossible to replicate because it depended on a series of massive technological improvements – electricity, the automobile and indoor plumbing – that have not been equaled by any subsequent technological advance. Gordon argues that from 1940 to 1970, the economy continued to benefit from those breakthroughs and a few related ones, such as television and commercial aviation, but that from 1970 onwards, the improvements in the standard of living pale in comparison to the heroic period from 1870 to 1940.

Gordon does not ignore the computer, the internet and other advances in communications technology, but he argues that the slowdown in measured productivity growth in the twenty-first century indicates that technology is influencing a much more narrow slice of human life than in those earlier periods, and this means that we cannot expect the kind of dividends of economic growth that were experienced earlier. It follows that we have little choice but to reconcile ourselves to a period of slower economic growth. In this respect, his analysis is far more pessimistic than that of Larry Summers (2016), who has argued that the problem of secular stagnation can be solved by aggressive government spending on infrastructure.[8]

There is much to admire in Gordon's massive study. As with Thomas Piketty's (2014) influential book, *Capital in the Twenty-First Century*, which is rooted in actual data on the distribution of income and wealth over many decades, Gordon's work rests on a rigorous effort to document how technological change has transformed everyday life. Moreover, in much of the book, Gordon is deeply sceptical that official economic data – the estimates of GDP – adequately capture the magnitude of the changes. He stresses repeatedly that important qualitative changes, such as increases in life expectancy, reductions in the physical toll that work imposed on the body, as well as the convenience of indoor plumbing, are not reflected in the economic measures. Gordon also mobilises an encyclopaedic knowledge of the history of specific technologies, such as the telephone, the assembly line and a host of other critical innovations.

Gordon, a professor at Northwestern, also does not carry the ideological baggage of the nearby Chicago school of free-market economics. On the contrary, Gordon repeatedly emphasises the central role that the public sector has historically played in nurturing and supporting technological innovations. He explains, for example, that government efforts to advance war production during WWII literally doubled the economy's supply of machine tools and that huge investment contributed to the post-war prosperity. He also cuts against the grain of his discipline by arguing that New Deal labour reforms were a driving force in the rapid increases in manufacturing productivity in the 1940s and after.

Gordon is also wisely critical of certain distinct patterns of growth that characterise the US. While recognising that suburbanisation was central to US growth for decades after World War II, he argues that the particular way in which suburban development occurred in the US produced a range of negative consequences. These include sprawl, vast housing tracts that are distant from available retail services, and the hollowing out of once vital cities. He insists that many of these consequences could have been avoided with better planning, and he points to the superior land-use patterns that have characterised European cities.

Finally, Gordon's account of the scale of the transformation of the average standard of living in the century from 1870 to 1970 is fundamentally sound. He acknowledges that race and gender discrimination meant that not all of these advances were shared, but he is persuasive in insisting that the combination of electrification, the internal combustion engine and indoor plumbing represented a huge improvement in the quality of people's everyday life.

The measurement problem

Most of the problems with Gordon's book become apparent in the second half of the book, when he focuses on the period since 1970. Here, again, he acknowledges the limitations of GDP as a measure of economic output, but he argues that for the recent period, the distortions are significantly more modest because the national income accountants have made adjustments for quality improvements for such key items as automobiles and computers. He argues, for example, that huge improvements in the quality of lighting and of automobiles between 1910 and 1940, for example, had gone unnoticed and unmeasured in the official data. The consequence is that increases in prices were overstated and, hence, growth in output was understated. However, in recent decades, the statisticians have introduced new methods to capture qualitative improvements in key products, making both price indexes and measures of output change more accurate.

But Gordon completely ignores one of the most important changes in recent decades; the extraordinary proliferation in the variety of consumer goods available in any given category. The change is enormous from the early years of the century when you could order a new Ford car in any colour as long as it was black. Moreover, with the search capacity of the internet, consumers are able to find relatively quickly a precise match to what they are looking for. To be sure, not all of this de-standardisation of products is truly necessary, but it does raise huge measurement issues. First, the accuracy of price indexes based on a standardised basket of goods becomes problematic when most consumers are no longer buying a quart of whole milk but are divided across skim milk, 1% milk, lactose-free milk, soy milk, almond milk, each of which comes in a proliferation of types with prices that vary in different rhythms. Second, how does one account for the consumer's recently acquired ability to tailor his or her milk purchase to a very specific set of dietary and aesthetic needs? Is that not a gain in consumer surplus comparable to the enormous convenience of indoor plumbing? Moreover, while Gordon waxes rhapsodic about the lifestyle gains from electric light bulbs and the mobility facilitated by the automobile, he mostly ignores the convenience gains of ordering products over the internet and avoiding the drive to the mall.

And that is only the tip of the iceberg. Gordon ignores some of the key qualitative changes in economic output that have been realised with billions and sometimes trillions of dollars of investment. The United States has spent vast sums since the early 1970s on environmental projects including reducing air and water pollution, cleaning up toxic waste dumps and slowing the production of greenhouse gases. While Gordon earlier placed much emphasis on the qualitative gain derived from removing horse manure from city streets when cars replaced horses, he completely fails to recognise the consumer gain from these initiatives. Perhaps he needs to spend more time in Beijing during one of their air-pollution crises to be reminded of the value of being able to take a deep breath without a feeling of choking.

It is also surprising that Gordon as a fierce critic of US-style suburbanisation neglects the work done over the last 30 years to make large cities more like the great cities of Europe with cafés along the waterfront, attractive urban parks and other amenities that are appealing to both tourists and residents. The investment in these amenities is closely linked to the revitalisation of downtown areas, and one only has to spend a little time in New York, or Chicago, or San Francisco, or almost any other large city to see how many people are taking advantage of these amenities. Surely, the benefits that consumers receive are far more than what they pay out in hotel and restaurant bills.

Most critically, Gordon is intellectually inconsistent when he rushes past the gains in life expectancy at 60 that have occurred from 1970 to the present. In the first part of the book, he makes a big deal of the gains in life expectancy at birth that occurred between 1870 and 1970 that resulted largely from dramatic reductions in infant mortality. On page 463, however, he acknowledges that life expectancy at age 60 rose more than 33% from 1950 to 2008, but he does not linger on this fact. Here is the full story: in 1900–1902, the best estimate is that life expectancy at 60 was 14.76 additional years. By 1969–1971 that had risen to 18.34 years, but by 2011, it had increased to 23.12 years. In other words, during 70 years of Gordon's heroic period, the average increase was 3.6 years, but in the 40 years following 1971, the increase was 4.8 years (US Department of Health and Human Services 2015, Table 21). This is a significant acceleration in the improvement in life expectancy that occurred in Gordon's epoch of allegedly slow growth.

Moreover, as Gordon knows, we now have measures of quality-adjusted life years that assess the degree to which additional years of life are burdened by illness and disabilities (Stewart, Cutler and Rosen 2013). These indicators show continuing improvements in this measure in the period from 1987 to 2008. This means that much of that almost five-year improvement in life span over the last 40 years has not been marred by an earlier onset of dementia or other illnesses that destroy the quality of life. Is it not a monumental improvement in the standard of living that the average person now enjoys 4.8 additional years once they reach 60? Given the low rates of labour-force participation for those 65 and older, this means that a lot of people are, in fact, enjoying 'golden years' that were previously available only to a small slice of the human population.

To be sure, there is the distressing recent data reported by Case and Deaton (2015) about higher rates of mortality among prime-age white males, and we also know that some portion of the elderly are struggling to survive on Social Security checks that are pathetically small. So, the demographic data are not all upbeat. Nevertheless, Gordon's insistence that there is a difference between the standard of living and GDP measures rings hollow when he simply ignores the extraordinary achievement of extending the lifespan of people at age 60. While he is right that our health-care system is extraordinarily wasteful, one has to recognise that the trillions that we have spent have resulted in big improvement in quality-adjusted life years.

But the single biggest problem with Gordon's study is his reliance on trends in total factor productivity (TFP) in the period from 1970 to the present. TFP is a measure that tries to assess the size of annual increases in real GDP that occur independently of growth in quality-adjusted inputs of labour and capital. TFP is a residual; it is an estimate of the portion of output growth that can be explained by technological progress or growing sophistication in our knowledge of how to use resources efficiently to produce outputs. Much of Gordon's argument hinges on his Figure 17–2 (575) that shows TFP rising at 1.89% per year from 1920 to 1970 and then increasing at only 0.57% per year between 1970 and 1994, at 1.03% per year from 1994 to 2004, and then back down to 0.4% from 2004 to 2014.

Reliance on TFP assumes that GDP is an accurate measure of the growth in economic output, that the GDP deflator is accurately adjusting for changes in prices, and that the statisticians have developed appropriate measures of annual quality-adjusted changes in both labour and capital inputs. But these are heroic assumptions, given how dramatically economic output has changed over the past century. Gordon cites a consumer study from 1917 to 1919 in which households were spending 41.1% of their income on food and 17.6% on clothing as compared to 5.4% and 3.1% in 2014. In 2016, goods of any kind – durable and nondurable – represent only about a third of consumer purchases. But the problem is that the output of the service sector – education, health care, public services, retail services and financial services – are difficult to measure, and it is even more difficult to measure accurately the labour and capital inputs into the production process.

For example, national income accountants include the net interest earned by banks as one element of the value added of the banking sector (Christophers 2013). The theory is that one of the key services that banks provide to the economy is intermediation, that is, connecting savers to borrowers, and the net interest earned by banks is a reasonable proxy for the value of those intermediation services that do not have an actual price tag. This represents a large exception to the way that interest flows are generally treated in the national income accounts; in the case of nonfinancial corporations, the interest they earn is not included as part of their contribution to GDP on the assumption that it is a transfer of income from somewhere else. Moreover, making this exception for banks is problematic because many economists believe that banks are not fundamentally intermediaries; they are institutions that are authorised to create credit. It follows that net interest is a problematic measure for the value to the economy of banks' credit-creating role. But these measurement problems are not trivial because the US GDP data shows that the value-added provided by banking and insurance in US GDP almost doubled between 1970 and 2008 from 4% to 8%.

Comparable problems emerge for another sector that also grew very rapidly across that same period – the health-care industry. On the one side, most output of the health-care sector is measured in GDP in terms of the dollar value of the services that were paid for. But as anyone who has had an overnight stay in a hospital knows, the resulting hospital bills are a work of imaginative fiction, and usually both private insurers and Medicare pay only a small fraction of the amount requested. But this also suggests that anything that shifts the relative bargaining power of insurers and hospitals can produce not insignificant shifts in the dollar value of the services that hospitals provide. And then national income statisticians face the daunting task of trying to differentiate between inflation and quality improvements. If the cost of a coronary bypass increases 15% from year one to year two, but patient-recovery time is cut in half, what portion of the price change should be attributed to quality improvement? Notwithstanding Gordon's claim that national income accountants are now better at measuring quality improvements, the US statisticians are only beginning to tackle this problem (Hall 2015).

And here we get back to the improvements in life expectancy at 60 and the upward trend line in quality-adjusted life years. A more accurate measurement of GDP would attempt to adjust the dollars spent on health-care services to reflect the real gains in quality of health-care delivery. But the current data do not do that. Since health care is now reported to be 17.5% of GDP, the problem is considerable. Together, health and finance represent about a quarter of GDP, but other poorly measured sectors, such as education, government and retail services, mean that our measurement scheme works badly for more than half the economy.

Furthermore, there is the huge issue of the mismeasurement of the public sector and the nonprofit sector. Essentially, the national income accountants assume the output of this part of the economy to be equal to the main input – the cost of labour. This means that productivity gains are impossible because output is just defined as being equal to the labour input. But since the weight of government and the nonprofit sector is much larger today than in 1940, this procedure pretty much assures that there will be a downward bias in economy-wide measures of productivity. But here again, there are strong reasons to believe that society's investment in government has produced returns that are completely unmeasured in GDP (Daly 2014).

The TPM is a measurement of a residual – the portion of economic growth that cannot be explained by changes in capital and labour inputs. However, our basic measure – GDP in real terms – of how much the economy has grown between 1970 and the present is flawed because we do not have good ways to measure the output of the service economy. It follows that the elaborate calculations involved in figuring out the TPM are a highly unreliable foundation for reaching the kind of conclusions that Gordon reaches.

The standard defence that Gordon suggests and that has been widely used by economists is that even if there is some bias in the official data because of poor measurement of the service sector, this is only a problem if the bias is increasing significantly over time. This defence is plausible when one compares output over shorter periods of time, such as five or ten years. Over such intervals, it seems implausible that quality improvements in health care, for example, would be so dramatic as to offset a finding that real GDP growth had slowed to 1.7% per year from an earlier growth of 3%. But the focus of Gordon's study is on comparing changes in consumption over much longer time periods, such as the four decades from 1970 to 2010. Over that period, for example, the purchase of services increased from half to two-thirds of personal consumption expenditures. Should one rely on that same data, when service output is poorly measured in GDP? Gordon's dependence on these dubious numbers represents a disappointing departure from the strong commitment to empiricism that has characterised much of his scholarly research.

Gordon's inadequate understanding of contemporary innovation

The most surprising weakness of Gordon's project comes towards the end of the book when he discusses solutions to the problem of slower growth. He states:

> The potential effects of pro-growth policies are inherently limited by the nature of the underlying problems. The fostering of innovation is not a promising avenue for government policy intervention, as the American innovation machine *operates healthily* on its own.
>
> (2016, 643, emphasis added)

One could write a whole book explicating everything that is wrong with this single sentence. First, the word 'healthily' is particularly jarring in a book devoted to the argument that a century of rapid technological advance ended in 1970. Gordon appears to be suggesting that even though the US innovation system is performing optimally, it is impossible to come up with any breakthroughs that compare to those of the late nineteenth century. But this suggested 'impossibility theorem' has nothing to do with history or economics; it is simply a metaphysical claim that is unconnected to data. It is like saying that human progress reached its peak with the discovery of fire and nothing can ever match that.

However, Gordon's own account provides evidence to challenge the claim that US business firms are making the optimal effort to push the innovation frontier. In his discussion of growing inequality, he points to the dramatic expansion of stock options in the compensation plans of corporate executives. This change is closely linked to the focus on maximising shareholder value, which has contributed to a pervasive short-term orientation among corporate executives. The focus on improving the share price next quarter means cutting back on investments that might contribute to corporate profits in five or ten years (Lazonick 2009). This has led many firms to cut back on their research and development expenditures. In fact, quite a few large firms have eliminated their corporate laboratories and now treat innovation as simply another input that they can purchase on the market.

There is also strong reason to believe that the offshoring of large segments of US manufacturing has undermined the innovative capacity of the US economy. The important MIT study (Berger 2013) provides powerful evidence that across the global economy, the firms that are most innovative are the ones where research and development efforts are located close to production facilities. Figuring out how to mass produce an innovative product is now the final stage in the R&D process; it requires research engineers and production engineers to work closely together, and this works best with physical proximity. It follows that the many US firms that have moved production facilities overseas have impaired their ability to produce new innovation products.

But the truly astonishing aspect of Gordon's sentence is the assertion that 'the American innovation machine operates … on its own.' Gordon appears to be ignorant of the overwhelming empirical evidence that almost all of the key technological innovations in the US since the end of World War II have relied heavily on government funding, government procurement, government support for research initiatives in universities and federal laboratories and, particularly since the 1980s, on a vast array of government programmes designed to help firms move innovations from the research laboratory into the commercial space (Block 2008; Block and Keller 2011; Mazzucato 2013; Weiss 2014).

In fact, there is good reason to believe that this sentence is not just a lapse but an indication of an appalling gap in Gordon's knowledge of recent history. Gordon begins his chapter on computers and the internet in 1960, so that he leaves out any mention of the government investments in computation in the US and the UK during World War II. He does not mention the Defense Advanced Projects Research Agency's huge role in pushing the computer field forwards from the late 1950s onwards, nor does he mention that almost all of the early procurements of mainframe computers were either for the Pentagon or the space programme (National Research Council 1999). He seems not to know that most of the key innovations of the personal computer were first developed at the Xerox-Parc laboratory paid for by government money (Fong 2001). And, of course, he does not mention Mariana Mazzucato's (2013) work showing how many of the innovations built into the iPhone had been developed in research efforts funded by the federal government.

Similarly, in his discussion of medical advances, he appears not to recognise that most of the successful new large molecule pharmaceuticals that have been developed in the last 30 years either came out of government laboratories or were the result of government-funded research (Vallas, Kleinman and Biscotti 2011). Moreover, almost all of the key advances in medical instruments and in imaging technologies have involved significant government involvement. Nor does he seem to know that the federal government is heavily involved in funding research on robotics and artificial intelligence and that government procurement has been a driver of advances in these fields.

Most critically, Gordon does not seem to know that the key locus of innovation in the US economy has shifted over the last generation to public-private collaborations organised through a wide variety of government programmes. One of the most important is the Small Business Innovation Research Program that provides roughly $2 billion a year to early-stage technology companies (Keller and Block 2013). This programme has nurtured far more successful firms than has the widely celebrated venture-capital industry that is generally reluctant to provide funds to firms that are years away from having a commercial product.

Collaborations between the federal laboratories, especially the Department of Energy laboratories that include Argonne, Lawrence Berkeley and the National Renewable Energy Laboratory also loom very large. In any given year, there are thousands of cooperative research and development agreements between big firms and the laboratories to do joint research to overcome key technological barriers. Sometimes, these collaborations are organised under the Work for Others programme where private firms pay the laboratories to do targeted research. Giant firms such as Intel, Exxon-Mobil and the pharmaceutical industry routinely make use of these services.

Finally, there has been a proliferation of government-funded research institutes that are organised to facilitate these public–private collaborations. On university campuses, there are dozens of NSF-funded Industry University Collaborative Research Centers and Engineering Research Centers (Currall, Frauenheim, Perry and Hunter 2014) devoted to solving technological problems faced by particular industries. The Department of Energy has also created many similar centres to address challenges such as developing advanced batteries and biofuels. More recently, the Obama Administration created 14 advanced manufacturing institutes to address the challenges of mobilising new manufacturing technologies, such as 3-D printing and the production of flexible and wearable electronics. As of late 2016, these institutes had 1,300 corporate partners and had initiated 240 separate research and development projects.[9]

The critical point here is that business firms both large and small are now enthusiastic participants in these collaborations. These firms are aware that they cannot effectively innovate on their own; it does not make sense for them to try to assemble in-house all of the scientific and engineering specialties that are required to develop new products or new processes. So, their strategy is to assemble smaller teams who then work with publicly funded scientists and engineers in efforts to overcome technological hurdles. Moreover, we see that firms are spending money on this strategy; thousands of firms, for example, pay dues to the NSF collaborative research centres to keep them going. We also see that major corporations are continuously lobbying on Capitol Hill in support of the government's science and technology spending.

It follows that Gordon is simply wrong that changes in government policy cannot influence the rate of innovation.[10] He should know that countries around the world have copied US efforts such as the SBIR programme precisely with the aim of accelerating their rates of innovation. It is also the case that this system of public–private collaborations in the US could be made significantly more productive with certain critical reforms. One still urgent problem, for example, is that many early-stage technology companies have great difficulty surviving in the years between receiving SBIR funds and developing a commercial product.

An empirical question

In fact, it is possible to assemble data showing that Gordon's pessimism about current technologies is off the mark. Here it is relevant to compare recent data to the heroic period from 1910 to 1929, when there were huge gains in manufacturing productivity as a result of electrification and improvements in factory organisation (Sklar 1992; David and Wright 1999; Field 2011). However, even in that period, there were only a handful of industries where productivity advances were so dramatic that quality-adjusted prices actually fell. Gordon shows that between 1910 and 1923, the quality-adjusted price of the Model T dropped from $722 to $196 – a 73% drop or an average price decline of 5.6% per year. After that, quality-adjusted prices actually rose slightly even though cars continued to be cheaper relative to disposable income. He also reports that the real price of a kilowatt-hour of electricity dropped by 6% a year between 1902 and 1929. He also cites William Nordhaus' (1997) research that shows that the quality-adjusted cost of a unit of lighting fell at 3.2% per year from 1910 to 1930 with the transition from carbon filaments to tungsten. The cost of long-distance phone calls also dropped about 66% between 1915 and 1930 or an annual decline of 4.4% (Gordon 2016, 185).

Since cars (and trucks), electricity, lighting and telephones were all general-purpose technologies that were widely diffused across the entire economy, these dramatic quality-adjusted price declines fuelled rapid adoption and broader gains in both productivity and living standards. But when one looks at the current period, one finds even more dramatic price declines for an even broader set of general-purpose technologies. Gordon (2016, 444–446) compares the computing power of a Cray-1 supercomputer in 1976 to a $449 Lenovo laptop in 2014 and calculates that the price decline over the period was at the rate of 41% per year.[11] He also cites work by Nordhaus (2007) suggesting that after 1980, the annual price decline was more like 64% per year. Gordon is moved to say that: 'The sharp contrast between the Cray-1 and today's most ordinary laptops represent progress so rapid that it is hard to grasp' (2016, 444).

But the reality is that price declines that are almost as dramatic have been occurring in the recent period in a range of different technologies. Byrne and Corrado (2015) estimate that for the last 20 years, prices of communications equipment have been falling at 11% per year. It appears that nobody has yet attacked the Herculean problem of measuring quality-adjusted prices of cellphone services over the last two decades, but given the competition among both handset providers and wireless service providers, it seems probable that consumer prices have been falling more rapidly than the 11% per year rate of decline for communications equipment.

Another recent study (Graetz and Michaels 2016) found that quality-adjusted prices of industrial robots declined by 80% between 1990 and 2005 or an annual rate of 5% per year. Between 1998 and 2013, the cost of installing solar-energy systems in the US fell by 6–8% per year, while the fall in prices of solar panels was even larger (Feldman *et al.* 2014). Nykvist and Nilsson (2015) report that the cost of lithium-ion battery packs for electric cars fell at an annual rate of 14% between 2007 and 2014, and there are reports that the declines have accelerated more recently. A study of LED light bulbs that represent a major advance over both incandescent and compact fluorescent bulbs shows that between 2011 and 2014, prices were declining at between 28 and 44% per year, and here also, there is every reason to believe that these declines are continuing (Gerke, Ngo, Alstone and Fisseha 2014). Finally, just between 2009 and 2015, the cost of wind power fell at close to 12% per year (US DOE 2016).

It is obvious that these price declines have not translated into the kind of dramatic measured productivity gains elsewhere in the economy that were visible in the 1920s. This is predictable since manufacturing has become a much smaller share of the whole economy. But two fundamental points follow from this evidence of a range of different products with significant quality-adjusted price declines. First, it calls into question the claim that there is somehow a slowdown in technological progress. On the contrary, since the computer is a general-purpose technology that influences every sector of the economy, it seems clear that the rate of technological advance is now more rapid than it was in the 1920s. Second, if we had in place in the United States the government policies required for a rapid transition to clean energy such as those employed in Germany and China, the falling prices of advanced batteries, LED bulbs, solar power and wind turbines could well start having more visible consequences for the larger economy.

Bringing Schumpeter back in

Gordon's account would be much richer had he drawn more heavily on the Schumpeterian tradition. He does employ several concepts that have links to Schumpeter and other scholars who have thought systematically about the rhythms of innovation over many decades. Gordon refers to three distinct Industrial Revolutions to characterise different periods of technological advance. The first, which happened in England in the early nineteenth century, does not figure in his story, but he talks about the cluster of innovations at the end of the nineteenth century that included automobiles and electrification as the Second Industrial Revolution. He then labels the advances in computers and communication that began with the first sales of mainframe computers in the late 1950s and have continued with the personal computer, the internet and mobile phones as the Third Industrial Revolution.

He also emphasises the closely related point that periods of innovation tend to occur in clusters. He notes that the key breakthroughs of developing the light bulb and a workable automobile occurred within months of each other in 1879. He also recognises that the 1920s and 1930s represented a key period of technological advance, as multiple breakthroughs occurred simultaneously. He employs the same idea when talking about advances in computerisation and communication in the last several decades.

But surprisingly, he only mentions Schumpeter once, and he never references the analysis of long waves of innovation that Schumpeter borrowed from Kondratiev. He also focuses almost entirely on changes in consumer goods, even though he has to acknowledge that much of the rapid economic advance of the 1920s through the 1940s was driven by the sharp improvements in the productivity of capital. As a result of these omissions, Gordon lacks a theoretical framework to help him to make connections among technological breakthroughs, the diffusion of new consumer and capital goods, and changes or lack of changes in the policy environment in which the economy operates.

This absence is particularly glaring in the final part of his argument. He uses the rather vague metaphor of headwinds to describe four distinct factors that make it unlikely that the US economy will soon again experience rates of economic growth comparable to those of the golden century from 1870 to 1970. The factors he identifies are certainly important, but giving them this label is confusing because for the pilot of an aircraft, headwinds are a given that cannot be altered. However, most of the items on Gordon's list are factors that could be changed with a transformation of the government policies that have been in place since the early 1980s. Moreover, in a brief postscript to the book, he argues for such a shift in policy.

Gordon's first headwind is the most important; it is the rising inequality of income and wealth in the US that has been well documented by Thomas Piketty (2014) and others. Since his focus is on the actual standard of living, he recognises that figures on the growth of average income per capita are insufficient at a time when almost all of the growth in income has gone to the top 1%. It is necessary to focus on the much slower rate of income growth for income recipients at the median. His second headwind is the far slower growth of average educational attainment that has occurred in the US since 1970. He draws on Goldin and Katz's (2008) finding that educational attainment increased by 0.8 years per decade from 1890 to 1970, but improvement since then has been negligible as dropout rates from high school remain high and the percentage of graduates going to college has been stagnant. His third headwind is a somewhat confusing demographic variable – the decline in work hours per person. The final headwind is the consequences of rising debt to GDP ratios in the two decades after 2020 that are projected because of the costs of health care and retirement benefits for the elderly.

As Gordon acknowledges, these headwinds could be overcome by a shift in public policies. Gordon argues for reducing inequality, investing more in public education and changing the tax system to raise more revenue. (The demographic problem would presumably be solved if these other measures worked to accelerate the rate of growth.) But his brief postscript makes these proposals seem like an afterthought rather than real advocacy. He seems to understand that his own diagnosis of the problem as secular stagnation has already doomed the progressive policy solutions that he favours.

The problem is that in US politics, the belief that the economy is going to grow slowly over the next two decades works to strengthen right-wing interests that insist that we need more austerity, not less. This has, in fact, been the story ever since the mid-1970s because of the rhetorical resonance of the right-wing economic diagnosis (Block 1996). A poorly performing economy has been used ever since as the justification for abandoning the more egalitarian policies of the New Deal era and passing tax cuts and other measures that have allowed the rich to get much richer. The same rhetorical move lies behind the disinvestment in public education that has produced stagnant levels of educational attainment.

So, regardless of Gordon's own political preferences, the evidence he has mobilised for slower growth will be used to argue that the nation cannot possibly afford to provide the funding for Social Security and Medicare that has been promised in current law. They will also insist that raising the minimum wage or placing a higher tax burden on the wealthy will prove counterproductive in a slow-growth context because such actions will discourage new hiring and new entrepreneurial initiatives.

Towards a more structural account

All of this is particularly unfortunate because if Gordon had made greater use of Schumpeterian and neo-Schumpeterian insights, he could have constructed an alternative narrative to secular stagnation that would actually provide support for the policy proposals that he has tacked on at the end of his book. This neo-Schumpeterian interpretation would have also helped him avoid the nostalgic argument in which a lost golden age is contrasted to the current period, where we are doomed to slow growth. This problematic frame forces Gordon to treat the extraordinary advances in computers and communication technologies as a minor sideshow. In a richer analysis, these advances can be recognised and seen as laying the foundation for a new period of dynamic growth.

A more dialectical approach would also better illuminate Gordon's core question of the changes in the standard of living in the period from 1970 to 2016. Gordon's account is that there has been slow growth for almost everybody, save the most affluent households. But when we factor in all of the qualitative elements that are poorly measured in GDP, we end up with a substantially more complex and nuanced picture. For one thing, sorting out the relative weight of qualitative gains versus qualitative losses is extremely difficult. On the one side, there are increases in quality-adjusted life years, environmental improvements, the huge benefits of computer-based connectivity and the enhanced amenities of urban areas. On the other, there is diminished social mobility, greatly increased insecurity of employment and income and the disappearance of millions of stable jobs that provided decent incomes.

Moreover, the benefits and losses have been distributed very unevenly regarding both geography and income groups. So, the benefits have been heavily concentrated in the largest metropolitan areas, and the negatives have been highest in rural areas and small towns. And generally, those in the top half of the income distribution have been winners, while the losers have been concentrated in the bottom half. But it is precisely this unevenness in the distribution of economic gains and economic losses that has fuelled the populist outrage that has dominated recent political debates in the US.

The irony is that much of Gordon's account of what happened between 1900 and 1970 fits the Schumpeterian model precisely. His description of the disruptive technologies of electrification and the automobile starting in the 1890s, but accelerating in the 1920s, is consistent with the neo-Schumpeterian story that mass production outran mass consumption. He also shows how New Deal reforms that increased worker purchasing power laid the basis for the three decades of expansion after World War II based on the automobile and suburbanisation.

What Gordon fails to see is that the period starting around 1970 shows the typical symptoms of a growth wave that has reached exhaustion. Growth based on suburban development had reached its limits as evidenced by ever longer commutes, wasteful use of energy and hollowed out city centres. At the same time, slower growth and fiscal crisis in the 1970s empowered the political right and produced the nation's extended experiment with 'free market' economics. According to the doctrine of Milton Friedman and his associates, measures such as tax cuts for the rich, reductions in antitrust actions, and slowdowns in the growth of government spending on nonmilitary programmes were supposed to reinvigorate the economy, but they had the opposite effect. Continuing fiscal crisis meant that levels of educational attainment in the US failed to rise. In fact, some of the slowdown in the growth in the standard of living after 1970 that Gordon documents was a direct consequence of misguided policies proposed by the right that were supposed to accelerate growth.

However, the Schumpeterian innovation process started up again in the 1980s and 1990s with the disruptive advances in computerisation, the internet and parallel advances in communications technology. All of these technologies could be traced back to earlier decades, but it was in the 1990s that they attained the scale needed to reshape perceptions across the whole economy. The result, once again, of this technological disruption was the predictable speculative boom of the late 1990s driven by exaggerated expectations about internet-based firms.

The problem, however, is that there are significant institutional barriers to a new period of expansion that could take full advantage of these technologies. So, what happened instead was an extremely anaemic economic recovery after the stock-market bubble burst in the early 2000s. And that anaemic recovery was heavily dependent upon a completely unsustainable boom in the building of single family homes that was facilitated by a rapid increase in mortgage lending, including the notorious expansion in subprime lending. When that mortgage bubble burst in 2007 and 2008, the result was the global financial crisis, which has been followed by another extended period of anaemic growth.

It is possible, however to anticipate what a new period of economic expansion based on these new technologies and a coordinated consumption economy might look like. The expected improvements in the standard of living could easily be substantial enough over 20 or 30 years that even Gordon would have to admit that they compared well with earlier heroic decades. Among the possible changes would be a shift to an environmentally sustainable model of economic growth that ended our dependence on fossil fuels. This would involve concentrating most of the population in urban areas, which would allow dramatic rewilding of a significant part of the continental land mass. There would be a dramatic expansion in desired leisure time, with the average workweek falling to 20 or 25 hours. The quality of jobs would also improve significantly, with the vast bulk of the labour force doing work that was intellectually challenging and provided intrinsic satisfactions. Finally, a rich urban lifestyle would be available to both urban dwellers and visitors. This would be facilitated by software apps that facilitate coordination, so that people could enjoy nearby parks, restaurants, cultural opportunities and ease of transportation from one part of the city to another. Finally, the combination of computers, improved communication and more leisure time would open up vast opportunities for lifelong learning for everyone.

There are, however, a series of very significant institutional barriers that block this type of economic expansion:

1   As in the 1930s, the maldistribution of income limits the ability of much of the population to participate in a new economy. There is still a yawning digital divide that excludes many people, and residential broadband services are inferior and more expensive than those in other developed nations. Moreover, maldistribution of income blocks the educational upgrading required for high-tech employment.
2   Public spending on infrastructure has been falling for a generation, so the resources to fund critically needed investments are lacking. This is particularly an issue for the pending transformation to renewable energy. The electrical grid needs to be modernised and charging stations must be built to support the electrification of cars and trucks.
3   There are no public policies to facilitate the upgrading of urban neighborhoods except through a process of gentrification that expels many long-term residents. This means that many of the benefits of dense, high-service urban life are confined to the upper middle class while others are pushed towards the urban periphery, where there are few services and employees face long commutes.

4   Another key improvement in the standard of living would be expanded leisure time, which did not come at the price of increased economic insecurity. However, this option is currently not available; employees who opt for reduced hours risk losing their jobs.

The point is that it is not secular stagnation or a slowdown in technological change that prevents us from realising these possibilities; it is rather institutional and political obstacles. While Gordon does propose reducing economic inequality, raising more funds through the tax system and spending more on infrastructure, he fails to recognise that a new reform effort, comparable in scale to the New Deal, could unlock the ability of current technologies to drive a major improvement in the standard of living (Block 2011). Had he engaged with Schumpeter and other theorists of long waves, he would have been able to recognise Schumpeter's central point that economic problems can ultimately be traced to particular institutions that require significant restructuring.

Conclusion

The core weakness of Gordon's book is its asymmetry. When he analyses the period from 1870 to 1970, his work is rooted in years of painstaking research, knowledge of the history of technology and great sensitivity to the qualitative changes experienced by much of the US population across that time period. But when he comes to the period from 1970 to the present, all of these strengths are lost. He substitutes aggregate statistics that are of dubious value for the careful analysis of different technological trajectories. His ignorance about the role of the US government in our current innovation system is a symptom of how little he has read about these more recent technological breakthroughs. And most importantly, he systematically ignores the substantial evidence of important qualitative improvements in the standard of living that have occurred since 1970, particularly the improvements in quality-adjusted years of life after age 60.

These weaknesses suggest that Gordon's core claim that current technological progress cannot compare to that of the first half of the twentieth century is an *idée fixe* rather than a hypothesis that he is willing to test against the data. We have shown, in fact, that there are a wider range of products today where quality-adjusted prices are falling on a year-to-year basis than in the 1910s and 1920s, and we have actually only scratched the surface with that argument. The dramatic cheapening of computer power makes it possible for a wide range of products to undergo quality-adjusted price declines. One can think of hearing aids, a wide variety of medical instruments, and machine tools as well as new applications that were previously unaffordable. In cities around the world, for example, bus and subway stops are now being equipped with displays that indicate when the next train or bus is expected to arrive.

However, it is a mistake to focus only on current technological advances that are closely linked to the computer. We are also living in a period of major advances in materials science that result from breakthroughs in nanotechnology. New composite materials make it possible to produce planes and automobiles that are lighter and yet stronger in resisting impact. There have already been new fabrics produced that are light-weight, protect from water and extreme cold and allow perspiration to escape. New composite building materials are also being developed that are strong, flexible and sustainable because they reduce energy use and do not require using scarce inputs. While these products are in the early stages of diffusion, as output expands, we can expect significant price declines.

But the fundamental critique of Gordon that has been advanced here is that he fails to build on the work of Schumpeter and others who stress the predictable discontinuities in the process of technological change. New technologies are disruptive, and they tend to break apart established institutionalised patterns. So, we have numerous examples in the history of technology where a cluster of innovations are introduced in a partial and halting fashion, while also sometimes generating excessive optimism and speculation. So it is to be expected that there will be periods of economic downturn when the old sources of growth no longer work and the new ones cannot get sufficient traction.

These periods, however, should not be viewed as examples of secular stagnation. They are rather symptoms of an institutional mismatch that keeps society from realising the potential of those new technologies. This is our current situation. Computerisation, automation, clean energy technologies and dozens of other breakthroughs make possible both a qualitative and quantitative improvement in the standard of living for people in the US and around the world. But achieving those gains requires a reform initiative on the scale of FDR's New Deal to reduce economic inequality, to raise new tax revenue, to make massive investments in infrastructure, to enact new social policies, to expand public input into urban and regional development, to create new economic institutions and to reform regulatory arrangements for many industries. If we are able to understand the economics of our current situation, we will be able to grasp the urgency of these political reforms.

Acknowledgements

I am grateful to the editors and to Larry Hirschhorn, Matthew Keller and Marian Negoita for feedback on an earlier draft.

Notes

1 To be sure, the Pax Americana has seen its share of wars, but up until recently, they were either brief, like the first Iraq War or Kosovo, or far away as with Vietnam and Korea.

2 Much of my own work has focused on another theorist of discontinuity, Karl Polanyi. Polanyi was Schumpeter's contemporary and was also born in Austria (Block and Somers 2014).

3 The problems in Schumpeter's theory of cycles are addressed in Burlamaqui's piece that is Chapter 2 of this volume. But as he notes, one can reject Schumpeter's effort to integrate three distinct cycles of different durations and still retain the idea that there are long waves organised around major technological innovations.

4 Schumpeter and the entrepreneurial state are addressed at length in Burlamaqui's chapter that is Chapter 10 of the current volume.

5 David Gordon, who died in 1996, was the brother of Robert Gordon. The parents, Robert Aaron Gordon and Margaret S. Gordon, were also economists.

6 For a related argument, see Atkinson 2004. Another scholar who has drawn on the Kondratiev framework is Immanuel Wallerstein, but he has been less focused on the role of the state in facilitating new periods of expansion.

7 Given that economic cycles operate differently in different parts of the world, there has been remarkable consistency among scholars using the long-wave framework in terms of dating the first four Kondratiev cycles (Goldstein 1988; Freeman and Louçã 2001). However, there is predictable disagreement about how to think of the last 20 or 30 years. Some analysts argue that a neoliberal expansion began around 1980 while others reject that view. McDonough (2010) reviews some of the disagreements within the social structure of accumulation perspective.

8 For useful critiques of secular stagnation and Gordon's broader argument, see Mokyr 2014, 2017. See also Sichel 2016.

9 On the advanced manufacturing institutes, see Bonvillian and Singer 2018.

10 For a careful analysis of the different rates of success of government innovation policies around the world, see Taylor 2016. See also Burlamaqui's Chapter 10 in this volume.

11 Gordon 2016, 444 acknowledges that the hedonic price index used in the official government statistics significantly understates the price decline for computer power. The same point is made in an analysis of semiconductor prices in Byrne, Oliner and Sichel 2015.

References

Atkinson, R. (2004). *The Past and Future of America's Economy*. Cheltenham, UK: Edward Elgar.

Berger, S. (2013). *Making in America*. Cambridge, MA: MIT Press.

Block, F. (1996). *The Vampire State*. New York: New Press.

Block, F. (2008). Swimming against the current: The rise of a hidden developmental state in the United States. *Politics & Society*, 36(2): 169–206.

Block, F. (2011). Crisis and renewal: The outlines of a 21st century New Deal. *Socio-Economic Review*, 9(1): 31–57.

Block, F. (2015). A neo-Polanyian theory of economic crises. *American Journal of Economics and Sociology*, 74(2): 361–378.

Block, F. and Keller, M.R. (Eds.) (2011). *State of Innovation: The U.S. Government's Role in Technology Development*. Boulder, CO: Paradigm.

Block, F. and Somers, M.R. (2014). *The Power of Market Fundamentalism*. Cambridge, MA: Harvard University Press.

Bonvillian, W. and Singer, P.L. (2018). *Advanced Manufacturing: The New American Innovation Policies*. Cambridge, MA: MIT.

Byrne, D.M. and Carrado, C.A. (2015). Prices for communications equipment: Rewriting the record. FEDS Working Paper 2015–069. Available at www.federalreserve.gov/econresdata/feds/2017/files/2017015pap.pdf.

Byrne, D.M., Oliner, S.D. and Sichel, D.E. (2015). How fast are semiconductor prices falling? National Bureau of Economic Research, Working Paper 21074.

Case, A. and Deaton, A. (2015). Rising morbidity and mortality in midlife among white non-Hispanic Americans in the 21st century. *Proceedings of the National Academy of Sciences* 112(49). Available at www.pnas.org/content/112/49/15078.

Christophers, B. (2013). *Banking Across Boundaries*. West Sussex, UK: Wiley-Blackwell.

Currall, S.C., Frauenheim, E., Perry, S.J. and Hunter, E.M. (2014). *Organized Innovation*. New York: Oxford University Press.

Daly, L. (2014). What is our public GDP? Valuing government in the twenty-first century economy. *Demos*. Available at www.demos.org/publication/what-our-public-gdp-valuing-government-twenty-first-century-economy.

David, P. and Wright, G. (1999). Early twentieth century productivity growth dynamics: An inquiry into the economic history of 'our ignorance'. University of Oxford, Discussion Papers in Economic and Social History 33.

Feldman, D., Barbose, G., Margolis, R., James, T., Weaver, S., Darghouth, N., Fu, R., Davidson, C., Booth, S. and Wiser, R. (2014). Photovoltaic System Pricing Trends. National Renewable Energy Laboratory/PR-6A20-625558.

Field, A.J. (2011). *A Great Leap Forward: 1930s Depression and U.S. Economic Growth.* New Haven, CT: Yale University Press.

Fong, G. (2001). ARPA Does Windows: The defense underpinnings of the PC Revolution. *Business and Politics*, 3(3): 213–237.

Freeman, C. and Louçã, F. (2001). *As Time Goes By: From the Industrial Revolution to the Information Revolution*. New York: Oxford University Press.

Gerke, B., Allison, F., Ngo, T., Alstone, A.L. and Fisseha, K.S. (2014). The evolving price of household LED lamps: Recent trends and historical comparisons for the U.S. market. Lawrence Berkeley National Laboratory #6854E.

Goldin, C. and Katz, L.F. (2008). *The Race Between Education and Technology*. Cambridge, MA: Harvard University Press.

Goldstein, J. (1988). *Long Cycles: Prosperity and War in the Modern Age*. New Haven, CT: Yale University Press.

Gordon, D.M. (1980). Stages of accumulation and long economic cycles. In: T. Hopkins and I. Wallerstein (Eds.), *Processes of the World System* (pp. 9–45). Beverly Hills, CA: Sage.

Gordon, D.M., Edwards, R. and Reich, M.R. (1982). *Segmented Work, Divided Workers*. Cambridge: Cambridge University Press.

Gordon, R.J. (2016). *The Rise and Fall of American Growth*. Princeton, NJ: Princeton University Press.

Graetz, G. and Michaels, G. (2016). Robots at work. London School of Economics, Centre for Economic Performance, Working Paper No. 1335.

Hall, A.E. (2015). Adjusting the measurement of the output of the medical sector for quality: A review of the literature. *Bureau of Economic Analysis Working Papers* 2015–5.

Hansen, A. (1938). *Full Recovery or Stagnation?* New York: W.W. Norton.

Keller, M.R. and Block, F. (2013). Explaining the transformation in the U.S. innovation system: The impact of a small government program. *Socio-Economic Review*, 11(4): 629–656.

Kotz, D.M., McDonough, T. and Reich, M. (Eds.) (1994). *Social Structures of Accumulation: The Political Economy of Growth and Crisis*. Cambridge: Cambridge University Press.

Lazonick, W. (2009). *Sustainable Prosperity in the New Economy?* Kalamazoo, MI: Upjohn Institute.

McDonough, T. (2010). The state of the art of social structure of accumulation theory. In: T. McDonough, M. Reich and D. Kotz (Eds.), *Contemporary Capitalism and Its Crises* (pp. 23–44). Cambridge: Cambridge University Press, 2010.

McDonough, T., Reich, M. and Kotz, D. (Eds.) (2010). *Contemporary Capitalism and Its Crises*. Cambridge: Cambridge University Press.

Mazzucato, M. (2013). *The Entrepreneurial State*. London: Anthem Press.

Mokyr, J. (2014). Secular stagnation? Not in your life. Vox, CEPR's Policy Portal, 11 August. Available at https://voxeu.org/article/secular-stagnation-not-your-life.

Mokyr, J. (2017). The past and the future of innovation: Some lessons from economic history. May. Available at http://conference.nber.org/confer//2017/AIf17/Mokyr.pdf.

National Research Council, Committee on Innovations in Computing and Communications. (1999). *Funding a Revolution: Government Support for Computing Research*. Washington, DC: National Research Council.

Nordhaus, W.D. (1997). Do real-output and real-wage measures capture reality? The History of lighting suggests not. In: T.F. Bresnahan and R.J. Gordon (Eds.), *The Economics of New Goods* (pp. 29–70). Chicago, IL: University of Chicago Press.

Nordhaus, W.D. (2007). Two centuries of productivity growth in computing. *The Journal of Economic History*, 67(1): 147–152.

Nykvist, B. and Nilsson, M. (2015). Rapidly falling costs of battery packs for electric vehicles. *Nature Climate Change*, 5: 329–332.

Perez, C. (2003). *Technological Revolutions and Financial Capital*. Cheltenham, UK: Edward Elgar.

Piketty, T. (2014). *Capital in the 21st Century* (Tr. by Arthur Goldhammer). Cambridge, MA: Harvard University Press.

Schumpeter, J. (1939). *Business Cycles* (2 vols). New York: McGraw-Hill.

Schumpeter, J. (1950) [1942]. *Capitalism, Socialism and Democracy* (3rd edn.). New York: Harper & Row.

Sichel, D. (2016). Two books for the price of one. *International Productivity Monitor*, Fall. Available at www.csls.ca/ipm/31/sichel.pdf.

Sklar, M.J. (1992). *The United States as a Developing Country*. New York: Cambridge University Press.

Stewart, S.T., Cutler, D.M. and Rosen, A.B. (2013). US trends in quality-adjusted life expectancy from 1987 to 2008: Combining national surveys to more broadly track the health of the nation. *American Journal of Public Health*, 103(11): e78-e87.

Summers, L. (2016). The age of secular stagnation. *Foreign Affairs*. Available at http://larrysummers.com/2016/02/17/the-age-of-secular-stagnation/.

Taylor, M.Z. (2016). *The Politics of Innovation: Why Some Countries Are Better than Others at Science and Technology*. New York: Oxford.

United States, Department of Energy. (2016). Revolution … now: The future arrives for five clean energy technologies – 2016 update. September. Available at www.energy.gov/revolution-now.

United States, Department of Health and Human Services. (2015). *National Vital Statistics Report* 64(11), 22 September.

Vallas, S.P., Kleinman, D.L. and Biscotti, D. (2011). Political structures and the making of U.S. biotechnology. In: F. Block and M.R. Keller (Eds.), *State of Innovation: The U.S. Government's Role in Technology Development* (pp. 57–76). Boulder, CO: Paradigm, 2011.

Weiss, L. (2014). *America Inc.: Innovation and Enterprise in the National Security State.* Ithaca, NY: Cornell University Press.

8 Schumpeter in the twenty-first century

Creative destruction and the global green shift

John Mathews

Introduction

Amongst the many virtues of Schumpeter's *Capitalism, Socialism and Democracy* (1942, *CSD*) is its Chapter 7 on 'The process of creative destruction'. In this short six-page exposition Schumpeter lays out his famous analysis of capitalism as a restless social and economic order that never is, and never can be, a stationary system. He paints a picture of capitalism as driven by 'gales of creative destruction' whereby innovation allows new players to enter markets and create new directions, financed by capitalist credit creation that puts the innovators on an equal footing with incumbents. The Schumpeterian analysis focuses on the evolutionary dynamics of the industrial system as it shifts from one technological trajectory to another. In the 75 years since his book appeared there have been numerous studies of industrial evolution and creative destruction in such sectors as automobiles, electronics and IT. While valuable, these studies shed little light on the dominant trend of our time, which is the rise of China, followed by India, as emerging industrial giants. In this chapter the insights generated by Schumpeter in *CSD* are applied to the rise of new green industries in China, with a focus on their evolutionary dynamics and potential to disrupt established fossil-fuel industries in the West.

Indeed, Western industrialism has achieved miracles, promoting unprecedented levels of prosperity and raising hundreds of millions out of poverty. Industrial capitalism is now diffusing east, where Japan was the first, followed by the four Tigers (Korea, Taiwan, Singapore and Hong Kong) and now China, all of them incorporating themselves into the global industrial world. India, Brazil and many others are expecting to follow the same course, which is best described as a Great Convergence. But as China, India and other industrialising giants grow, they are confronted with an inconvenient truth: they cannot rely on the Western industrial development model with its fossil-fuelled energy systems; resource throughput rather than circularity, and generic finance – for reasons to do with extreme spoliation of their own environment and energy security and resource security concerns as much as concerns over global warming.

By necessity, a new approach to development is already emerging in the East, with China leading the way in building green industry at scale. As opposed to Western zero-growth advocates and free-market environmentalists, it can be argued that a more sustainable capitalism is being developed in China – as a counterpart to its all-too-obvious black developmental model based on coal, oil and gas. In the words of Hu Angang, this alternative is the 'inevitable choice for China' – and by extension, one might say for other developing countries as well (see Hu 2006a, 2006b). The tension between the green development pathway and the black pathway is a defining feature of the next Great Transformation.

The core elements of this emergent industrial model are threefold: 1) the enhancement of energy security through basing energy systems on manufactured energy devices – rather than extracting and drilling for fossil fuels in increasingly tense geopolitical locations; 2) the enhancement of resource security through restructuring the economy along circular lines (the closing of industrial loops) rather than the traditional linear economy; and 3) the greening of finance to drive the transition. This new 'green growth' model of development, being perfected first in China and now being emulated in India, Brazil, South Africa (the BICS countries) and eventually by industrialising countries elsewhere, as well as by advanced industrial countries such as Germany and Korea, looks set to become the new norm in the twenty-first century. It is a model grounded in manufacturing and the diminishing costs associated with the learning curve that accompanies manufacturing, as Hao Tan and I put it in our 2014 article in *Nature*, 'Build energy security through manufacturing renewables' (Mathews and Tan 2014).

A Schumpeterian evolutionary dynamics approach to analysing these trends, as opposed to neoclassical comparative static approaches that are obsessed with comparative cost-based instruments like carbon taxes, promises to generate distinctive insights. Earlier sociotechnical transitions, as identified by Perez, Freeman, Berry, Louçã and others, have been characterised by an emergent pervasive technology that has falling costs and costs lower than incumbent technologies as well as applications across the economy. The case can be made that the characteristics of the current transition to renewable energy systems and circular economy constitutes a sixth such wave or surge of fresh development. Like its predecessors, it is already starting to wreak creative destruction in established industries – as is felt in the coal industry, gas and oil, electric-power generation and automobile industries as companies such as Tesla and BYD bring new technologies to the market and rewrite the rules of global competition.

While mainstream economists talk about the climate-change challenge framed in terms of costs and the role that carbon taxes could play in driving alternatives, the reality seems rather to be that the energy and resources transformation that is under way calls for major structural changes and state intervention, best described in Schumpeterian terms. China's renewable energy revolution and circular economy initiatives are driving cost reductions globally as well as in China and are creating business opportunities for new firms everywhere; this process may be viewed as the world's first case of a country breaking free of carbon lock-in by building its own domestic renewable energy industries and circulation of resources through state entrepreneurship.[1] As China grows its market for renewables and resource circulation processes (such as urban mining of materials), so its firms become more receptive to licensing advanced technologies from companies in advanced countries. These developments create complementarity between advanced firms in the West and Chinese mass producers – with the proviso that Chinese firms themselves are fast approaching the innovation frontier as well.

The test of Schumpeterian insights lies in their ability to shed light on contemporary industrial evolutionary dynamics. The global green shift that is under way is a case where the process calls for Schumpeterian insights in order to explain it adequately; it is a test case for the continued relevance of Schumpeterian evolutionary analysis and in particular the role of creative destruction in moving one technoeconomic system to another – or removing the vestiges of one system to create space for the new. The existence of these successive waves or surges of development is an empirical reality; the real issue is the framing of a theoretically sound explanation for their rise and fall that encompasses technological as well as financial and institutional dynamics. In the current case of the global green shift the role of China in driving the process gives it added interest and relevance.

Long waves in the global economy

The study of long waves in economic life has many antecedents, amongst which the most celebrated are those of the Russian scholar Nicolai Kondratiev, who did his principal research during the 1920s. Indeed, his major work as known in the West was his long paper published in the German *Archiv für Sozialwissenschaft und Sozialpolitik* in 1926.[2] Because he made the 'politically incorrect' finding that capitalism could go through evolutionary waves (in place of the terminal crisis favoured by the theorists of the Communist International) he was shot by Stalin's secret police. Today we are allowed to study the long-wave phenomenon with rather more political freedom.

Kondratiev's work was taken up by the doyen of business-cycle studies in the US, Wesley Mitchell, in 1929, and by Simon Kuznets at Harvard in his book on economic cycles, published in 1930. With these antecedents, it was Schumpeter who really championed Kondratiev, naming the wave that now bears his name in his 1939 masterwork, *Business Cycles*. So, it was Schumpeter who was really responsible for introducing K to the West – and thereby breathing life into the evolutionary-economics tradition.[3] And Schumpeter made an important addition to K's long-wave dynamics. K had delivered himself of the observation that each successive downturn saw a cluster of technological innovations being introduced (because the conditions favoured innovation). Schumpeter took this observation and turned it into a driving force behind why one wave succeeds another.

This observation (or hypothesis) has been elaborated on by modern scholars.[4] The central idea is that the economy is a dynamic, evolving system which moves through 50–60-year 'spurts', each driven by a new technoeconomic paradigm. It really is a scandal that so little work has been devoted to this central topic in economic analysis. The work itself seems to go through 'cycles', where there was an initial spurt triggered by Kondratiev himself and Schumpeter; then another cycle in the 1980s triggered by interest in an emerging fifth K-wave on the part of Perez and Freeman at SPRU and Ayres, Marchetti, Nakicenovic *et al.* at IIASA, plus others like Kleinknecht in The Netherlands, Berry in the US and Tylecote, Lloyd-Jones and Lewis in the UK. Now perhaps there will be a new spurt triggered by interest in a sixth wave emerging, based on greening trends, in the 2010s, together with an appreciation of the financial drivers of successive technological surges or waves.[5]

Schumpeter's greatest contribution perhaps was his inspired guess that the long cycles revealed in capitalism by Nicolai Kondratiev were triggered by clusters of technological innovations. This has resulted in informed scholars identifying the 'Kondratiev-Schumpeter' long-cycle evolutionary account of capitalism (e.g. Korotayev *et al.*) – or what the Danish scholar Andersen tellingly calls the 'engine of capitalism' after Schumpeter's own terminological innovation. Thompson (2014) looks to capture the same effect in the notion of technological clustering, which he suggests should be taken as the prime concept driving the evolutionary dynamics of the global business system. It is indeed a dynamic and disruptive account of evolution – not the incrementally progressive change assumed in mainstream neoclassical economics. As such it has great affinity with the punctuated-equilibrium perspective in biological evolution, introduced by Gould and Eldredge (1977), as an elaboration of the Darwinian approach, which now dominates the field. Let me call this the 'Kondratiev-Schumpeterian punctuated equilibrium' approach to evolutionary economics.

Five waves of industrial change

The industrial revolution ushered in a totally new period of economic evolution, one that is known as 'modern economic growth' (see Mokyr 2001, 2016). The pre-industrial agrarian economy, with its rises and falls in wealth and income governed by crops and the weather, plus pestilence and war, gave way to a quite different kind of economy, where systematic knowledge acquired by the scientific method became the basis of technologies and technological advance.[6]

Focusing on the technoeconomic drivers of change in our industrial system, we can draw from a Schumpeterian literature to identify five transitions in the period since the first transition, known as the Industrial Revolution – with a sixth putatively under way in the current period. The point is that each transition involves major social, technical, financial and business upheavals that go well beyond mere economic substitutions effected by relative price movements. In my own work on this topic I have identified two streams of literature as making a major contribution. There is the stream that focuses on the actual K-waves as measured using sophisticated statistical techniques – as done by K himself and subsequently by Berry and most recently by the Russians Korotayev and Tsirel – in work validated by Devezas (2012).[7] There is a stream that focuses on the institutional details of each shift in technoeconomic paradigm, with a clear focus on the 'reverse salients' involved and the struggles between the emerging technologies and business interests and the vested interests defending the status quo. A third stream of scholarship focuses on the financial dynamics, as elaborated by Minsky, Kregel and others.[8]

The key point is that the waves involving upturns and downturns in economic categories – from prices to GDP to industrial sectors – are an empirical reality, obvious to all who are prepared to look at the evidence. But what accounts for these waves is anything but obvious – in fact to find an adequate explanation must count as one of the greatest problems of the social sciences. Schumpeter himself started an extremely fruitful line of advance with his hypothesis that the successive waves are driven by spurts of new technoeconomic clusters. But then there is the issue of what drives the clustering of technological innovations. Schumpeter took what is arguably a wrong turn in imposing a deterministic, cyclical process on the historical data in his *Business Cycles*, in place of allowing the evolution to proceed in an open-ended fashion.

Let us look at the data first, prior to framing hypotheses. The most widely accepted dates for the five waves of technoeconomic change since the industrial revolution are those provided by Korotayev and Tsirel, as given in Table 8.1. Each successive wave with a clear upswing and downswing can be dated more or less as follows.

Table 8.1 Upswings and downswings in industrial capitalism, 1760–2011

Long wave number	Phase	Onset	Ending
1st	A: upswing	1780s	1810–1817
	B: downswing	1810–1817	1844–1851
2nd	A: upswing	1844–1851	1870–1875
	B: downswing	1870–1875	1890–1896
3rd	A: upswing	1890–1896	1914–1920
	B: downswing	1914–1920	1939–1950
4th	A: upswing	1939–1950	1968–1974
	B: downswing	1968–1974	1984–1991
5th	A: upswing	1984–1991	2008–2012?
	B: downswing	2008–2012?	?

Source: based on Korotayev and Tsirel (2010), 2, Tables 1, 2.

In brief, the initial surge was driven by new developments in water technology, both in terms of power (water wheels) and transport (canals), involving the factory mode of production itself and new sources of power such as steam. The first steam engine (or 'atmospheric engine') was demonstrated by Newcomen in 1712; it was put to use in pumping water out of coal mines. The Boulton and Watt partnership was created in Birmingham in 1775 as a means of exploiting Watt's patent on the steam engine with a separate condenser; the firm became a driving force as it expanded in the nineteenth century. The shift to the downswing occurred during the Napoleonic wars. The principal industry utilising the new water power and steam power was textiles, particularly cotton – the first 'carrier industry'.

A new wave was initiated by the development of steam power applied with greater efficiency to factory work and to transport, in the form of a moving locomotive. The new surge was carried by vast investments in railroads, as tracks were laid across Europe and the US after being pioneered in Britain. The key factors in the second wave were thus steam and iron, which were able to overcome the incumbent water-based systems as their costs declined, provoking the 'canal panic' of 1837. The Great Western Railway, founded in 1833, received its enabling Act of Parliament in 1835 and operated its first trains in 1838 – marking a significant moment in the second Kondratiev. In the US the Union Pacific Railroad was founded with the Act of Congress 1862 during the Civil War. This second industrial surge was examined closely by Schumpeter himself in his 1939 work *Business Cycles* – in what Andersen (2002) has called Schumpeter's proto-case of 'railroadisation'.

Moving closer to the modern era, a third wave of investment and technological change plus creative destruction was launched by both steel and electric power in the 1890s, in a new upswing terminating the long depression that lasted from the 1870s to the 1890s. The new electric motors were pitched against the incumbency of steam power and triumphed in the early years of the twentieth century because of falling costs and because of greater efficiency; the electric motors were able to harness power to machines wherever they were used, rather than from the central 'prime mover' that characterised the steam-powered workshop. It was the Bessemer process that transformed the world of iron into a world of steel – and it was the founding of a new steel company in the US by Andrew Carnegie in 1872, based on the Bessemer process that launched a new era and resulted in the formation of US Steel. In the new world of electric power, the greatest innovations were by Westinghouse and Edison and Tesla, resulting in the formation of major K3 firms General Electric and Westinghouse. In Germany, which was also rising to industrial leadership, the major K3 firms founded at the time were Siemens and AEG, which became the core of Germany's subsequent technological supremacy.

The heavy engineering of the 3rd K-wave proved to be a major impediment to its diffusion, and it proved no match for a fourth K-wave, which was launched in the early twentieth century with the arrival of the internal combustion engine (ICE) and the external combustion engine (diesel engine) as motive power for individual transport vehicles, based on the emergent oil industry as the source of fuel. This was the K-wave of oil, with the automobile as the lead industry and mass production as the lead organisational form. The origins of the K4 wave lay in the introduction of mass-production principles by Henry Ford in the automobile sector, perfected at the Highland Park (Michigan) plant in 1915, introduced during the downswing of the K3 wave. The introduction of this mass-produced car to the market was followed by unprecedented market expansion and cost reductions that flowered and diffused worldwide in the postwar boom (upswing of the K4 wave) – and that provide a glimpse of what is happening with green products such as renewable energy devices today.

The K4 wave is generally reckoned to have come to an end during the 1980s as financial crashes triggered new speculative booms – this time focused not on hardware like cars and white goods but on computers and information technology and the software that drove these new 'intelligent' devices. Early innovations were the transistor created as the first solid-state device in the 1960s and then the first 'chip' created by Intel in 1970, followed by the microprocessor in 1971. New fortunes in IT and software were created by completely new firms like Microsoft, Apple, Symantec and Oracle. The early investments were made in the downswing of the K4 period, only to bloom and flourish in the upswing of the K5 wave, in the late 1980s to the early 2000s.

This timing of successive waves dates our present period as the emerging downswing of the 5th K-wave, when investments in IT and knowledge industries continue to be made at scale but cannot be expected to carry the global economy to new levels of prosperity. Instead, investments in a new key factor are needed to do the job – and the best candidate for this new role is greening.[9]

Technoeconomic paradigms and their shifts

There are several sources that feed into this present exposition of a sixth wave transforming the global economy and shaping cities in a new urban geography. The first is Schumpeter himself and his fundamental conception of the evolutionary character of the capitalist system, or what he liked to call the evolution of the capitalist engine (a phrase picked up and utilised to great effect by his expositor, Esben Sloth Andersen, in his (2009) masterwork). The central concept in this stream of work is the notion of creative destruction and the long waves initiated by innovation (or clusters of innovative products and technologies). It is perhaps not widely appreciated that it was Schumpeter who really 'imported' Kondratiev and his long waves into Western economics – and gave the K-waves a conceptual underpinning in the form of technological innovation that they had not had in Kondratiev's own work.

Then there is the stream of work that elaborates on long waves and structural crises of adjustment, in which the work of Freeman and Perez (1988) is fundamental, with its central notion of the sociotechnical paradigm and the series of shifts in such paradigms culminating in the emergence of a fifth such shift in the 1970s and 1980s. This fundamental work introduced its taxonomy of innovations, as encompassing (1) incremental innovations (the most common); (2) radical innovations; (3) changes of technology system – where both radical and incremental technical innovations combine with organisational innovations; and (4) changes in 'techno–economic paradigm' – the most fundamental and far-reaching of all. It is viewed as having pervasive effects throughout the economy.

As elaborated by Perez in successive papers (Perez 1983; 1985) and by Freeman and Perez (1988) each successive TEP is characterised by a key factor or dominant cluster of technologies that have the characteristics that they feature:

1　clearly perceived low and rapidly falling costs;
2　almost unlimited supply over long periods; and
3　clear potential for incorporation of the key factor in products and processes throughout the economic system.

The crux of their paper was the demonstration that these characteristics at the time held most persuasively for IT and IT-related products, i.e. products of miniaturisation, electronics and digitalisation. Moving backward in time they argued that these characteristics held for the key factor of the 4W (oil) and (by extension) for mass production and the automobile. Further back the key factor of the 3W they argued to be low-cost steel (rather than electric power); and in the 2W low-cost steam-powered transport. Perez herself in her 1983 and 1985 papers referred to 'technological styles' as something that encompassed more than 'just' an innovation. By the 1988 paper she was happy to adopt the terminology 'technoeconomic paradigm' (TEP) and this remains the term of choice.[10]

In a manner closely similar to Freeman and Perez (1988), I wish to argue that in our own time an emergent paradigm shift is based on the key factor input of renewable energies and circular economic system (CERES) packaged together in eco-cities (or smart cities), where we see (1) drastically declining costs (and where the argument is that their costs are declining for fundamental reasons related to the fact that they are products of manufacturing); (2) unlimited supply of renewable energy sources (and recirculation of material inputs, potentially endlessly); and (3) demonstrated potential for incorporation in power systems, food production, water regeneration and in manufacturing and transport generally, i.e. right across the economy. In addition to key factors satisfying conditions of having low and descending relative costs, plus virtually unlimited supply and potential all-pervasiveness, Perez specifies that a new key factor should also demonstrate the potential to reduce costs of capital and other inputs into productive activities – which is clearly the case with the green-shift products and processes (see Perez 1983, 4).

If we include this fourth element as well, we see that it too fits the introduction of renewable energies and recursive materials systems since these elements have the demonstrated capacity to reduce costs for all other factor inputs (e.g. as water costs increase, due to scarcity, so water regenerated in renewable energy powered desalination systems becomes relatively much more cost effective).

The TEP based on fossil fuels is being superseded by RE-based power systems not because of perceived differences between 'green' and brown electric power (appealing to moral and ethical choices) but because the RE-based power is falling in cost relative to fossil-fuel-based power, and the RE-based power is finding wider and wider applications, e.g. in urban food production and urban water regeneration. If it is agreed that the mode of diffusion of a new TEP occurs through applications across multiple sectors, then we see a new green surge occurring driven by renewables and the circular economy, we find multiple applications of renewables across multiple sectors – including in food production and water regeneration, where urban-based innovations are emerging based on the capacity to supply virtually unlimited energy from solar and wind sources. This complex of IT-enabled renewable energy technologies constitutes a 'key factor' that enjoys steadily reducing costs (and prices) based on the fact that all the activities involved depend on the production of manufactured devices. Because of these falling costs associated with manufacturing experience curves, the 6W key factor may be seen as having widespread effects, bringing renewable electric power to ever-widening circles of users and enhancing their energy and resource security.

The 6W motive branches are those that are involved in the manufacture of renewable-energy devices (e.g. wind turbines and solar PV cells), energy-storage devices (e.g. lithium-ion batteries) and electric-grid devices (e.g. inverters, energy centres). The prosperity of these motive branches rises as the adoption of the 6W energy systems diffuses. Correspondingly the 6W carrier branches are the power-generation systems as well as electric-vehicle systems that utilise the key factor of renewable electric power. These, too, are products of manufacturing and reduce in cost (and then in price) as a result of the experience curve.[11]

Thus, we can identify 'induced branches' as those that are related to the diffusion of the carrier branches, such as the manufacture of EV-charging stations, battery-replacement stations for EVs and other such sectors that have no role in the fossil-fuel economy but constitute essential infrastructure in the 6W economy. We see then that *manufacturing* is the activity that is common to the key factor itself (renewable electric energy) and to the motive branches, the carrier branches and most of the induced branches (Mathews and Reinert 2014). What we need to demonstrate is that a surge exists in manufacturing activities related to renewable-energy and energy-storage devices that make the generation of renewable energy cost-competitive with traditional fossil-fuelled sources and ultimately more cost-effective than incumbent thermal sources. It is relative costs that account for the rise of a new surge and its supersession of an existing TEP – without having to posit an over-determined cyclical phenomenon. The missing element is the role played by finance, particularly state entrepreneurial finance – and here we see China playing a leading role in greening its financial system and giving full rein to development banks like the China Development Bank in driving investments towards green projects.[12]

The green shift of the twenty-first century as the 6th K-wave: the rise of China

Now there is a powerful argument linking the global green shift as a dominant technoeconomic development to the geopolitical shift that sees the rise of China as an industrial giant. Let us then review the evidence supporting the claimed shifts that are the dominant trends today – the shift in manufacturing east, and the green shift away from fossil fuels. They are in fact linked, at a profound level, because it is China that is driving the shift of manufacturing east, and as it does so, it finds that it has to drive the green shift, as well (Figure 8.1).[13]

Our starting point is the green shift that is currently under way in the industrial economies – including (and especially so) in the rising industrial giants, China and (to some extent) India. As China and eventually India build their vast manufacturing engines, so they discover the need to power them with energy sources – of which fossil fuels are the obvious and initially favoured candidates – just as has been the choice made by all previous rising industrial powers.

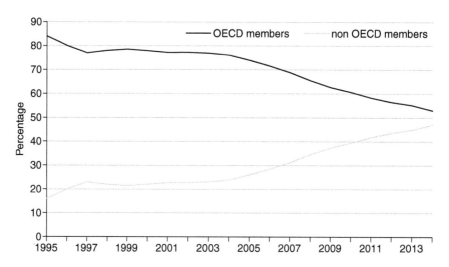

Figure 8.1 Manufacturing moving east.

Source: OECD Development Centre.

The green transition that is currently under way is the single most important feature of the current world, along with the rise of China as the world's premier manufacturing power. Indeed, the two features or processes are tightly linked, because China's rise is based on the building of a huge energy system to power the manufacturing system. China has discovered the limits to trying to build this energy system on the basis of fossil fuels alone. The limits are not so much commodity-supply limits of the kind investigated and popularised by the Club of Rome study of 1972 on *Limits to Growth*, but rather geopolitical limits as China finds that its quest for resources and especially fossil fuels around the world runs into problems involving economic blockades, trade wars, civil wars, revolutions and terrorism. Compelled by these factors, along with the terrible immediate environmental problems created by China's headlong rush to indus-trial maturity, China is finding that conventional energy and resource strategies ('business as usual') no longer work, and it is instead engaging in an alternative 'green growth' strategy that is proving to be very successful. This alternative is driven by reducing costs, market expansion and manufacturing innovation as China becomes a principal global player in installing renewable energy systems (such as wind power and solar photovoltaic cells) and in manufacturing the devices needed to capture the renewable energy sources.[14] China's green and black strategy is easily discerned when we look at longitudinal data on electric power generation (Figure 8.2).

The effect of this rapid expansion of fossil fuels input in China is well known – it is unbreathable air and undrinkable water, combined with rising

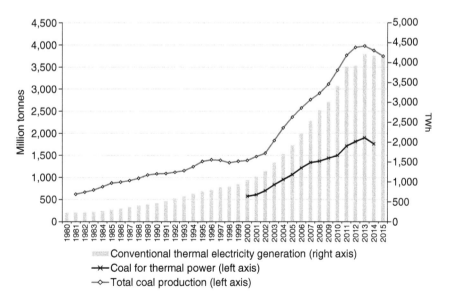

Figure 8.2 China's 'green and black' energy system, 1980–2015.
Source: Mathews (2016).

geopolitical tensions as China (and now India) scour the planet for fuels and resources. But China has stumbled on an effective remedy for these problems – renewable energies and urban mining or recirculation and regeneration of resources. The evidence demonstrating this shift is again clear and unequivocal. Consider Figure 8.3, which shows the rapid increase in proportion of electric power generated from water, wind and sun – rising from a low of 20% a decade ago to reach 34% in 2016 – a 14% shift in capacity in a decade. (The corresponding shift in electricity generated from WWS sources is also shown, rising from 15% to 25% over the same period.) This is an astonishing rate of change for such a huge system with its vast fossil-fuel infrastructure.

The conventional economic account of this green shift is to focus on switching from one energy system to another as a matter of substitution, where the price of one commodity/product versus another is determined in some equilibrium framework. Policy initiatives can be taken in such a framework by cost-moderating instruments like green taxes or market-mediated caps on emissions. Apart from the fact that such interventions have proven to be very weak when put into practice and stand little chance against the raft of subsidies that have historically supported the fossil-fuel system (oil and gas industry, coal industry, power-generation industry), these equilibrium-based instruments offer precious little insight into the workings of energy-industrial dynamics. But Schumpeter's approach, as exemplified in his major books (the

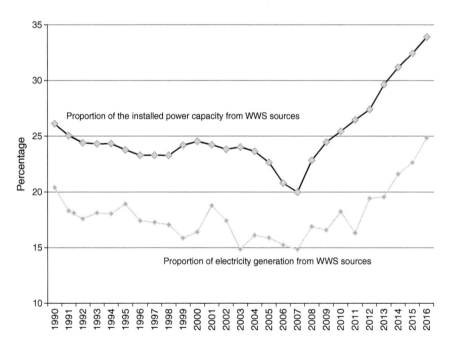

Figure 8.3 Greening of China's electric power system, 1990–2016.
Source: Globalgreenshift.

youthful *Theory of Economic Development* (1934) and the more mature *Business Cycles* (1939)) and briefly in his *CSD*, is far richer and promises to generate far more fruitful insights than the conventional approach.

If we start with the concept of creative destruction, we see that Schumpeter's approach in *CSD* would imply that the rise of a new cluster of renewable energy industries would be accompanied by the decline and fall of traditional industries, namely those based on fossil fuels. This is an evolutionary perspective, one that views the energy sectors as being in perpetual disequilibrium and shaken by waves of firms deploying new energy technologies taking over from those that cling to the prevailing technologies. The mode of supersession of one industrial cluster by another was always the focus of Schumpeter's analysis – as it needs to be in the case of the twenty-first-century shift in energy and resource systems.

Schumpeter himself took the trouble to exemplify his evolutionary analytical perspective by utilising the case of 'railroadisation' in the nineteenth century. This is what the current Danish Schumpeterian scholar Esben Sloth Andersen has called Schumpeter's principal case and reference point in describing the evolutionary dynamics of capitalism. Now we can take a similarly important case, around 100 years after Schumpeter's major scholarly interventions, in the form of the global greening shift that is having widespread creative destructive effects worldwide.[15]

Essentially, greening is a process of creative destruction – a destruction of the entire fossil-fuel industrial order and its supersession by an alternative energy and resources order based on renewable inputs. This is not the mere substitution of one or two products by different products – as in electric power produced from coal substituted by electric power produced by wind and sun. Rather it is a whole system transition or shift from one system based on fossil fuels to another system powered ultimately by renewables. A technoeconomic system transition implies taking cognisance not just of prices (as in the equilibrium-based mainstream economics perspective) but of other key factors including technologies (e.g. wind and solar power devices and their use to generate power, or EVs and batteries); infrastructure (electric power smart grid; EV charging stations); government policies (e.g. feed-in tariffs; public auctions of renewable energy concessions); finance in all its forms; and institutions and business models.

Correspondingly a Schumpeterian perspective on creative destruction focuses attention on the means of resistance waged by the incumbent firms and the technologies they support, as they strive to delay or block the supersession that is under way. It is an open-ended struggle whose outcome is anything but determined.

All these features can be seen in the current green shift that is diffusing worldwide. And just as there was a lead country with its lead firms driving previous technoeconomic shifts, so is there a lead country in the twenty-first century driving the shift to a green economy. In the nineteenth century there was the shift from mail coaches and canals to railroads, when the lead country was initially Britain, later followed by Germany and the USA. In the late nineteenth and early twentieth centuries there was the new wave sparked by electrification, where the lead country was the USA and to some extent Germany. In the twentieth century, as the fourth Kondratiev unfolded, based on oil, automobiles and mass production, the lead country was definitely the USA, and leading 4K firms like Exxon-Mobil, GE, GM and Ford were American. In the late twentieth-century, fifth Kondratiev based on IT/ICT, there has been a multipolar expansion with the lead shared at different times by US, EU and Japanese firms. Now in the twenty-first century we see the emergent sixth wave driven by applications of IT to energy and electric power, to food and water production and regeneration, and to the shaping of cities themselves as the envelopes of further technoeconomic advance.[16] China is emerging as the lead player as it moves rapidly from imitation to innovation.

China's greening of finance

As in other aspects of the greening of the economy, China is emerging as a leader in the financial aspects of the process. Take the role of the China Development Bank, which has extended lines of credit to Chinese solar photovoltaic (PV) companies like LDK and Yingli Solar, and to wind power companies like Goldwind, thus propelling them to leadership in the China market and subsequently to global dominance. Yingli, for example, enjoyed a $5.78 billion line of credit as of June 2011; LDK Solar received $9.1 billion; Suntech Power $7.6 billion, and Trina Solar $4.6 billion; while Sinovel Wind received a credit line worth $6.5 billion. All up, by 2010 Chinese firms had invested over $50 billion in clean energy, far surpassing the levels of any other country – largely financed by the China Development Bank and other 'policy banks' that provided the financial muscle behind the Chinese entrepreneurial state's green surge.[17]

While these preferential loans provided an initial impetus, China's green finance initiatives have since broadened and deepened.[18] Chaired by Dr Ma Jun of the People's Bank of China, the Green Finance Task Force issued its long-awaited report *Establishing China's Green Financial System* in April 2015 – making China the first country in the world to issue specific guidelines on the crafting of green securities.[19]

China is adopting a realist and pragmatic perspective on sources of green finance, viewing this as the driver of a technological transition. The 2015 report states that no more than 15% of all green investment can be expected to come from fiscal sources (i.e. tax-based investment). This means that the bulk of the financing – or 85% – is expected to come from the private sector, through various green finance channels (bank loans, green bonds, investment funds).

Ma Jun lists six core principles of greening of finance in his foreword to the report. These are what China's green financial system should move towards:

1   Building new channels for green investment, and not just restricting polluting investment;
2   Opening up new channels through new specialised green lending and investment institutions (such as a green bank), and not just relying on existing banking channels;
3   Steering private capital to the greening of industry, reducing reliance on administrative orders;
4   Ushering in a range of new green instruments such as green bonds, green stocks, green funds and green insurance, and not just providing green loans;
5   Changing the behaviour of financial institutions through financial and legal measures, with public funds aiming to leverage private funds up to tenfold; and
6   Providing necessary financial infrastructure that will enable green investments to thrive (such as green credit ratings, environmental impact data) rather than just offering administrative support for green investment.

This national strategy – the first of its kind to be explicitly drafted as such – underlines how seriously China is taking its role in greening its economy. The report proposes three major institutional innovations including the creation of green banks; the creation of green funds (i.e. green industry funds and public-private partnership arrangements); and a process of greening the existing development banks (such as the China Development Bank allocating part of its lending portfolio to targeted green investments). The report goes on to specify how China needs to develop specific green financial instruments, including 'discounted green loans' (i.e. offering bank loans at differential interest rates depending on whether projects meet green targets); permitting Chinese banks to issue green bonds, thus tapping into the debt securities market (and helping to grow it in China); and green IPOs, i.e. improving the mechanism through which firms' environmental performance is communicated and recognised in equity markets.

China's banks have since moved rapidly to issue a series of green bonds in pursuance of these goals. In October 2015, the Agricultural Bank of China (another development bank) issued a first green bond worth $1 billion. Then in January 2016 the Shanghai Pudong Development Bank issued a green bond worth 20 billion yuan (US$4.3 billion), designated for climate-related investments; then the Bank of China issued a green bond in July 2016 worth $3.03 billion. Chinese banks issued green bonds worth $36 billion in the year 2016 (compared with a global total of $81 billion), all targeted at institutional investors such as sovereign wealth funds, pension funds and insurance funds. Encouraged by these successes, individual companies are now starting to issue their own green corporate bonds.[20]

Thus, we have the situation where China is clearly paying as much attention to the financial as to the technological aspects of the current green surge, for the clear reason that it sees this surge as the means for bringing its industrialisation aspirations to a strong conclusion. This green surge is a product of China's state entrepreneurship crafted as a means of driving creative destruction of the incumbent fossil-fuel industry – but in a socially responsible manner, since the Chinese government sees its political future as tied to its being able to meet the rising economic aspirations of the Chinese people. This is a world away from the narrow concerns of neoclassical equilibrium-based analysis, as much as from any tightly deterministic notion of economic cycles succeeding each other in clockwork fashion.[21]

Schumpeterian analysis superior to that of neoclassical economics

My purpose in this chapter is to draw out the contrast between a neoclassical economics perspective and the Schumpeterian perspective on the global green shift. The neoclassical perspective, which for some incomprehensible reason still manages to maintain its dominance in academia, is based on microeconomic static reasoning, i.e. micro reasoning at a single point in time rather than macro dynamic analysis. Based on the prevailing equilibrium assumption, the insights offered are that as the price of some factor of production changes so its utilisation in the production function will shift. In the case of energy inputs, the neoclassical framework contrasts fossil-fuel-energy inputs with renewable-energy inputs in terms of their current prices. Based on an externally induced crisis (namely climate change) it generates a policy proposal to decarbonise energy inputs, through the medium of raising the prices of fossil-fuel inputs. The most straightforward way to do so is through a carbon tax – although there are other means of making fossil fuel inputs less attractive, such as cap and trade schemes, whereby producers are allocated a 'cap' on their allowable carbon emissions and are enabled to trade these allowances in a carbon market.

These schemes of one kind of 'environmental taxation' or another are discussed in a setting where an external threat is perceived and a moral duty to act to avoid the threat is posed. The problem is that the political resistance to such environmental taxes by vested interests is profound and determined, so much so that there has been precious little progress achieved globally in reducing carbon emissions over the 20-plus years of operation of the UN-sponsored Kyoto Protocol. And sometimes the moral imperative is posed with breathtaking arrogance – as when a political party in the advanced countries ignores the moral imperative incumbent on themselves and calls down divine punishment on governments in developing countries where fossil-fuel usage is rising, as a result of their implementing a strategy of industrialisation. India and China are the two countries that are receiving most of this opprobrium.

This neoclassical economics framework is entirely contingent, and frames the shift that is observable as a price-mediated substitution of one input by another, without any sense of where the system might be headed, or why.

The story told is simplicity itself. In the past there was an effective shift to fossil-fuelled energy inputs, powering a wave of wealth-enhancing industrialisation. Today the environmental costs of these are discovered and so economists advocate a carbon tax to induce price-guided substitution of energy inputs. The fact that they have been advocating the same policy for some 20-plus years with very little to show for their efforts is not – apparently – seen as a negative. It is put down to the fact that major substitutions are politically complex and difficult to achieve.

By contrast a Schumpeterian perspective puts the green shift in a plausible industrial and historical setting and frames realistic proposals as to how it may be achieved or accelerated. First, the green shift is viewed not as a unique occurrence but as the latest in a series of technoeconomic shifts – each one driven by the same kind of concatenation of events. The economy is viewed not as a series of static adjustments but as an evolving system. The driver of change is the technoeconomic character of the economy at a point in time, where long-term waves of development are observed empirically, and theory is developed to seek to account for these wave-like shifts. An existing technoeconomic paradigm (TEP) is ousted by a successor, whose existence can be validated by reference to the parallel shifts that have occurred in the past, together with the role of finance and state entrepreneurship in driving change from one TEP to another (as in China). The driver of change is investment (rather than relative prices), facilitated by state development banks in the first instance followed by a multitude of private firms flocking to the rising industries.[22]

From this perspective, the current green shift may be viewed as the sixth such transformation since the industrial revolution, where each period is characterised by a dominant technoeconomic paradigm that rises according to well-recognised dynamics and is in turn ousted by a successor. This historical perspective draws attention to the dynamics of the shift, looking to identify the motive forces (key factors) that are generated as well as their carrier industrial branches and their induced branches. The role of finance is underscored by the greening of finance, which is now a global phenomenon, driven by the emergence of a green financial sector in China.

When we combine geopolitical insights with those from industrial dynamics we get even closer to the present realities. In the case of the global green shift we have the simultaneous occurrence of a shift in manufacturing east (specifically to China in the first instance) plus the shift in terms of industrial dynamics to a post-fossil-fuel world. And these two trends are in fact deeply connected. As China industrialises (which it is pursuing in the name of enhancing wealth and income) so it finds it necessary to build a vast energy system to power its growth in manufacturing. It starts, of course, with fossil fuels – like all previous industrial powers. As it does so it comes across not just immediate environmental limits to expanding the scale of fossil-fuel usage (unbreathable air and soiled water) but geopolitical limits in the form of threats of war, revolution and terror as China penetrates regions of the earth that are less and less stable in search of fossil fuels (and resources) that are less and less accessible.[23] And so China looks actively for an alternative to fossil fuels in order to enhance its energy security – and an alternative to linear resource flows through recirculation as a means to enhance resource security. And as China makes the discovery that renewable devices and closing industrial loops are products of manufacturing, and as such generate increasing returns and can be performed anywhere, so its commitment to driving the emergent green surge both technologically and financially is deepened.

We have then an argument that starts with empirical realities, namely the observable green shift that is under way together with the shift eastwards in manufacturing and the energy choices (and resource choices) that are imposed on China to drive this industrial engine with some degree of energy security (and resource security). And we have a theoretical explanation for these shifts in terms of a clustering of green energy technologies that are becoming available (as the grip of fossil fuels is loosened) and are driven primarily by China as the optimal candidates for powering China's industrialisation. This is a powerful application of Schumpeter's conceptual apparatus applied in a new, twenty-first-century setting.

Notes

1 On carbon lock-in, see Unruh 2000; Unruh and del Rio 2012.
2 See Kondratiev 1926. This article was translated into English by W.F. Stolper and appeared in the *Review of Economic Statistics* in 1935. By that time Kondratiev was in prison in the Soviet Union, a victim of Stalin's purges. He was executed by firing squad probably in 1938. For a brief biographical treatment, see Grinin, Devezas and Koratayev 2012.
3 At the same time it has to be said that Schumpeter forced the Kondratiev swings into a tight cyclical framework that has done lasting damage to the study of long-range economic and industrial phenomena. For a critical treatment, see Burlamaqui's chapter in this collection.
4 Those scholars of note include Ayres, Berry, Devezas, Freeman, Gruebler, Lloyd-Jones, Lewis, Louça, Marchetti, Nakicenovic, Perez, Tylecote and others, as well as Russians Grinin, Korotayev and Tsirel, while Modelski has traced the long-wave concept back through 20 such waves occurring over the past 1000 years of globalisation. As a sampling of the work reported, see Allianz 2010; Andersen 2002, 2009; Ayres 1990a, 1990b; Freeman 1983, 1997; Perez 1983, 1985, 2002, 2010, 2015; Freeman and Perez 1988; Freeman and Louça 2001; Kleinknecht 1986; Korotayev and Tsirel 2010; Nefiodow 2006; Tylecote 1992; Lloyd-Jones and Lewis 1998; Berry, Kim and Kim 1993; and Gruebler and Nakicenovic 1991.
5 A business case for a new cleantech era is provided by Milunovich and Rosco 2008, while Wilenius and Casti 2015 continue the argument using the notion of 'X-events'.
6 It is fitting to describe the agrarian economy as Malthusian, since it was best described by Thomas Malthus at the very moment that it was disappearing in the early nineteenth century.
7 Devezas 2012 reports on a spectral analysis of the unfolding of global GDP growth rates, where cycles of periods 7.5 years, 15 years, 32 years (weak) and 52 years (strong) are clearly identified.

8 For expositions, see Burlamaqui 2015, Keidel and Burlamaqui 2016 or Burlamaqui and Kattel 2016.

9 Others, such as Nefiodow 2006 and the insurance firm Allianz 2010, have opted for biotech and personalised medicine, which I agree is a world-changing technological innovation but in my view is likely to see its flourishing in the next K-wave, after the conditions favourable to it are created by the emerging sixth wave.

10 For a general history of Perez' evolving concept of the TEP, see the chapters in the collection edited by Drechsler, Kattel and Reinert 2009.

11 See the argument spelt out in Mathews and Reinert 2014)

12 See the studies by Sanderson and Forsythe 2013, Keidel and Burlamaqui 2016 or Burlamaqui and Kattel 2016.

13 For my successive contributions on these themes, see Mathews 2011, 2012, 2013, 2015 as well as Mathews and Tan 2011, 2014, 2015, 2016).

14 On the falling costs of renewables, and in particular the falling costs of solar PV cells, see, for example, Bazilian *et al.* 2012.

15 See Andersen 2002 for his excellent contribution to Schumpeterian scholarship.

16 On cities as shapers of technological and financial trends, see, for example, Batty 2016 or earlier work by Bettencourt and West 2010.

17 See Sanderson and Forsythe 2013, 147–151. These scholars take the investment story up to 2012. There has been continuity of support since then. For example, Yingli Solar received a loan from CDB in June 2013 worth another $165 million; see the story at https://qz.com/77347/china-development-bank-makes-bet-on-yingli-as-a-solar-survivor/.

18 The following paragraphs are based on the chapter 'Greening of Finance' in Mathews 2017.

19 See the report at: www.cbd.int/financial/privatesector/china-Green percent-20Task percent20Force percent20Report.pdf.

20 On these trends, see the Climate Bonds Initiative, *Bonds and Climate Change: State of the Market 2016*, at www.climatebonds.net/resources/publications/bonds-climate-change-2016.

21 On the narrow concerns of equilibrium-based analysis, see for example Chen (2008); on a critique of deterministic economic cycles, see for example Burlamaqui (this volume).

22 From this perspective, the judgement of Nathan Rosenberg 1994 made a quarter-century ago that Schumpeter must be counted as a profoundly 'radical' economist, is surely justified.

23 See, for example, the discussion of China's efforts to fashion novel 'loans for oil' deals with such countries as Ecuador (Gholz, Awan and Ronn 2017).

References

Allianz Global Investors (2010). The sixth Kondratieff: Long waves of prosperity. Available at www.allianz.com/media/press/documents/kondratieff_en.pdf.

Andersen, E.S. (2002). Railroadisation as Schumpeter's standard example of capitalist evolution: An evolutionary-ecological account. *Industry and Innovation*, 9: 41–78.

Andersen, E.S. (2009). *Schumpeter's Evolutionary Economics: A Theoretical, Historical and Statistical Analysis of the Engine of Capitalism.* London: Anthem Press.

Ayres, R.U. (1990a). Technological transformations and long waves, Part I. *Technological Forecasting and Social Change*, 37: 1–37.

Ayres, R.U. (1990b). Technological transformations and long waves, Part II. *Technological Forecasting and Social Change*, 37: 111–137.

Batty, M. (2016). Creative destruction, long waves and the age of the smart city. In: R.D. Knowles and C. Rozenblat (Eds.), *Sir Peter Hall: Pioneer in Regional Planning, Transport and Urban Geography.* (pp. 81–98). New York: Springer.

Bazilian, M., Onyeji, I., Liebreich, M., MacGill, I., Chase, J., Shah, J., Gielen, D., Arent, Landfear, D. and Zhengrong, S. (2012). Re-considering the economics of photovoltaic power. White Paper 82, Bloomberg New Energy Finance, London. Available at www.bnef.com/WhitePapers/download/82.

Berry, B.J.L., Kim, H. and Kim, H.-M. (1993). Are long waves driven by techno-economic transformations? *Technological Forecasting & Social Change,* 44: 111–135.

Bettencourt, L. and West, G. (2010). A unified theory of urban living. *Nature,* 467 (21 October): 912–913.

Burlamaqui, L. (2015). Finance, development and the Chinese entrepreneurial state: A Schumpeter, Keynes, Minsky Approach. *Brazilian Journal of Political Economy* 35(4). Available at www.scielo.br/scielo.php?pid=S0101-31572015000400728&script=sci_arttext.

Burlamaqui, L. and Kattel, R. (2016). Development as leapfrogging, not convergence, not catch-up: Towards Schumpeterian theories of finance and development. *Review of Political Economy,* 28(2): 270–288.

Chen, P. (2008). Equilibrium illusion, economic complexity and evolutionary foundation in economic analysis. *Evolutionary and Institutional Economics Review,* 5(1): 81–127.

Devezas, T.C. (2012). The recent crisis under the light of the long wave theory. In L.E. Grinin, T.C. Devezas and A.V. Korotayev (Eds.), *Kondratieff Waves: Dimensions and Prospects at the Dawn of the 21st Century* (pp. 138–175). Volgograd: Uchitel.

Drechsler, W., Kattel, R. and Reinert, E. (2009). *Techno-Economic Paradigms: Essays in Honour of Carlota Perez.* London: Anthem Press.

Freeman, C. (Ed.) (1983). *Long Waves in the World Economy.* London: Butterworth.

Freeman, C. (1997). Schumpeter's *Business Cycles* and techno-economic paradigms. Science Policy Research Unit. Available at http://dcsh.xoc.uam.mx/eii/globelic-swp/SCHUMPETERS_BUSINESS_CYCLES_REVISITED.pdf.

Freeman, C. and Louçã, F. (2001). *As Time Goes By: From the Industrial Revolutions to the Information Revolution.* Oxford: Oxford University Press.

Freeman, C. and Perez, C. (1988). Structural crises of adjustment: Business cycles and investment behaviour. In: G. Dosi, C. Freeman, R. Nelson, G. Silverberg and L. Soete (Eds.), *Technical Change and Economic Theory* (pp. 38–66). London: Frances Pinter.

Gholz, E., Awan, U. and Ronn, E. (2017). Financial and energy security analysis of China's loans-for-oil deals. *Energy Research & Social Science,* 24: 42–50.

Gould, S.J. and Eldredge, N. (1977). Punctuated equilibria: The tempo and mode of evolution reconsidered. *Paleobiology,* 3(2): 115–151.

Grinin, L.E., Devezas, T.C. and Korotayev, A.V. (2012). Introduction: Kondratieff's ystery. In L.E. Grinin, T.C. Devezas and A.V. Korotayev (Eds.) *Kondratieff Waves: Dimensions and Prospects at the Dawn of the 21st Century* (pp. 5–22). Volgograd: Uchitel.

Gruebler, A. and Nakicenovic, N. (1991). Long waves, technology diffusion, and substitution. *Review* (Fernand Braudel Center), 14 (2): 313–343.

Hu, A. (2006a). Green development: The inevitable choice for China (Part 1). *China Dialogue.* Available at www.chinadialogue.net/article/show/single/en/134.

Hu, A. (2006b). Green development: The inevitable choice for China (Part 2). *China Dialogue.* Available at www.chinadialogue.net/article/show/single/en/135-Green-development-the-inevitable-choice-for-China-part-two-.

Keidel, A. and Burlamaqui, L. (2016). China Development Bank's strategy and its implications for Brazil. In L. Burlamaqui, R. Sobreira and M. Vianna (Eds.), *The Present and the Future of Development Financial Institutions: Theory and History*. Rio de Janeiro: MINDS.

Kleinknecht, A. (1986). Long waves, depression and innovation. *De Economist*, 134(1): 84–108.

Kondratiev, N.D. (1926). Die langen Wellen der Konjunktur. *Archiv für Sozialwissenschaft und Sozialpolitik*, 56: 573–609.

Kondratiev, N.D. (1935). The long waves in economic life. *Review of Economic Statistics*, 17 (November), 1065–1115 [originally published in 1926 in German in *Archiv für Sozialwissenschaft und Sozialpolitik*].

Korotayev, A.V. and Tsirel, S.V. (2010). A spectral analysis of world GDP dynamics: Kondratieff waves, Kuznets swings, Juglar and Kitchin cycles in global economic development, and the 2008–2009 Economic Crisis. *Structure and Dynamics*, 4 (1), e-journal. Available at http://escholarship.org/uc/item/9jv108xp.

Lloyd-Jones, R. and Lewis, M.J. (1998). *British Industrial Capitalism Since the Industrial Revolution*. London: UCL Press.

Mathews, J.A. (2011). Naturalising capitalism: The next great transformation. *Futures*, 43: 868–879.

Mathews, J.A. (2012). Green growth strategies: Korea's initiatives. *Futures*, 44: 761–769.

Mathews, J.A. (2013). The renewable energies technology surge: a new techno-economic paradigm in the making?' *Futures* 46: 10–22.

Mathews, J.A. (2015). *Greening of Capitalism: How Asia is Driving the Next Great Transformation*. Redwood City, CA: Stanford University Press.

Mathews, J.A. (2016). Competing principles driving energy futures: fossil fuel decarbonisation vs. manufacturing learning curves. *Futures*, 84: 1–11.

Mathews, J.A. (2017). *Global Green Shift: When Ceres Meets Gaia*. London: Anthem Press.

Mathews, J.A. and Reinert, E.S. (2014). Renewables, manufacturing and green growth: energy strategies based on capturing increasing returns. *Futures*, 61: 13–22.

Mathews, J.A. and Tan, H. (2011). Progress towards a circular economy in China: drivers (and inhibitors) of eco-industrial initiative. *Journal of Industrial Ecology*, 15(3): 435–457.

Mathews, J.A. and Tan, H. (2014). Manufacture renewables to build energy security. *Nature*, 513 (11 September): 166–168.

Mathews, J.A. and Tan, H. (2015). *China's Renewable Energy Revolution*. London: Palgrave-Macmillan.

Mathews, J.A. and Tan, H. (2016). Circular economy: Lessons from China. *Nature*, 331 (24 March): 440–442.

Milunovich, S. and Rasco, J. (2008). *The Sixth Revolution: The Coming of Cleantech*. New York: Merrill Lynch. Available at www.responsible-investor.com/images/uploads/resources/research/21228316156Merril_Lynch-_the_coming_of_clean_tech.pdf.

Mokyr, J. (2001). The Industrial Revolution and the economic history of technology: Lessons from the British experience, 1760–1950. *The Quarterly Review of Economics and Finance*, 41: 295–311.

Mokyr, J. (2016). *A Culture of Growth: The Origins of the Modern Economy*. Princeton, NJ: Princeton University Press.

Nefiodow, L.A. (2006). *The Sixth Kondratieff: The New Long Business Cycle of the World Economy* (6th edn.). Available at www.kondratieff.net/11.html.

Perez, C. (1983). Structural change and assimilation of new technologies in the economic and social systems. *Futures*, (10): 357–375.

Perez, C. (1985). Microelectronics, long waves and world structural change: New perspectives for developing countries. *World Development*, 13(3): 441–463.

Perez, C. (2002). *Technological Revolutions and Financial Capital: The Dynamics of Bubbles and Golden Ages*. Cheltenham, UK: Edward Elgar.

Perez, C. (2010). Technological revolutions and techno-economic paradigms. *Cambridge Journal of Economics*, 34: 185–202.

Perez, C. (2015). Capitalism, technology and a green global golden Age: The role of history in helping to shape the future. *The Political Quarterly*, 86 (S1): 191–217.

Rosenberg, N. (1994). Joseph Schumpeter: Radical economist. In: N. Rosenberg, *Exploring the Black Box: Technology, Economics and History* (pp. 47–61). Cambridge: Cambridge University Press.

Sanderson, H. and Forsythe, M. (2013). *China's Superbank: Debt, Oil and Influence. How China Development Bank is Rewriting the Rules of Finance*. New York: Bloomberg.

Schumpeter, J.A. (1934/1912). *The Theory of Economic Development: An Inquiry into Profits, Capital, Credit, Interest and the Business Cycle*. Boston, MA: Harvard University Press.

Schumpeter, J.A. (1939/1982). *Business Cycles* (2 vols). Philadelphia, PA: Porcupine Press.

Schumpeter, J.A. (1942/1950). *Capitalism, Socialism and Democracy* (with new introduction by Tom Bottomore). New York: Harper & Row.

Thompson, W.R. (2014). K-Waves, technological clustering, and some of its Implications. In: L.E. Grinin, T.C. Devezas and A.V. Korotayev (Eds.), *Kondratieff Waves: Juglar, Kuznets, Kondratieff* (pp. 164–180). Volgograd: Uchitel.

Tylecote, A. (1992). *The Long Wave in the World Economy: The Present Crisis in Historical Perspective*. London: Routledge.

Unruh, G. (2000). Understanding carbon lock-in. *Energy Policy*, 28: 817–830.

Unruh, G. and del Rio, P. (2012). Unlocking the unsustainable techno-institutional complex. In: G. Marletto (Ed.), *Creating a Sustainable Economy: An Institutional and Evolutionary Approach to Environmental Policy* (pp. 231–255). London: Routledge.

Wilenius, M. and Casti, J. (2015). Seizing the X-events: The sixth K-wave and the shocks that may upend it. *Technological Forecasting & Social Change*, 94: 335–349.

9 Domination, weak judgement and the dilemmas of contemporary Schumpeterian democrats

John Medearis

Joseph Schumpeter's mature democratic theory, summed up in *Capitalism, Socialism and Democracy* (2008), combined a qualified advocacy of minimal democratic electoral institutions with a behavioural account of voters as irrational and incapable of living up to the standards of 'classical' democratic theory. These distinct institutional and behavioural elements of Schumpeter's argument mutually supported and illuminated each other within the context of a historically-minded social vision, one that emphasised both the near-inevitability and the real desirability of elite rule over society. But in contemporary democratic theory, these elements of Schumpeter's later democratic thought have split off from each other, with scholars I shall term *institutional* Schumpeterians and others I shall term *behavioural* Schumpeterians each adopting only part of what was for Schumpeter an integral approach. At the same time, neither group of scholars follow their predecessor by situating their political analyses within a rich historical sociology of groups, classes, ideologies and conflict. And both schools of Schumpeterian democrats also reject their predecessor's elite political commitments in favour of more familiar democratic aims and affinities.

These scholars' partial approaches to drawing on their predecessor, I shall argue, cause notable strains and antinomies, weaknesses that undermine our ability to understand many contemporary challenges to democracy. The most prominent institutional Schumpeterian democrats, such as Adam Przeworski and Ian Shapiro, are motivated by justifiable worries about domination, and indeed understand democracy as a means of countering domination. But they have difficulty explaining why the minimal Schumpeterian democratic mechanisms they favour are the best or even a sufficient response to these concerns. If many forms of twenty-first-century domination are rooted in social and economic relations, as these scholars seem to recognise, it is likely that the democratic practices and endeavours needed to resist domination must transcend electoral devices for taming state power. Meanwhile, behavioural Schumpeterians like Christopher Achen and Larry Bartels focus most of their worries about contemporary democracy on a critique of citizen judgement. But in developing this critique, they have tended to treat political judgement in an implausibly dichotomous way, casting ideological thinking as the sophisticated, autonomous, but exceedingly rare antithesis of group-influenced pseudo-thought. This has the advantage of clarifying the grounds for their scathing view of most people's capacities for political judgement. But the polarised conceptualisation of judgement and the caustic view of citizens to which it leads makes it difficult for behavioural Schumpeterians to explain why they do not, like their predecessor, simply embrace democratic elitism. Moreover, the dichotomous account of judgement is in itself deeply suspect, and it makes behavioural Schumpeterians insensitive to serious ideological challenges to democratic life and practices.

My argument comprises three interrelated components or phases. The first involves establishing that there are, in fact, two different and distinct schools influenced by Schumpeter, characterised by selective borrowings from his democratic theory. The second phase involves critically analysing these approaches, demonstrating the weaknesses inherent to institutional and behavioural Schumpeterianism, which grow in each case out of the new purposes to which they try to put Schumpeter's ideas, as well as from attempting to secure one major element of his later democratic thought without drawing or relying on others. Institutional Schumpeterians cannot show that devices for limiting access to state power are sufficient for a robust democratic programme to resist the many contemporary forms of social and political domination at work today. Behavioural Schumpeterians' efforts to show that most voters are non-ideological, as they understand the term, are inherently dubious – and they leave their proponents unable, by definition, to identify specifically ideological challenges to democratic life.

The third phase of my critique, then, shows that these distinctive weaknesses of institutional and behavioural Schumpeterians, significant in their own right, also lead to a common inadequacy, a difficulty identifying and analysing an increasingly manifest challenge to Western democracies in the twenty-first century: the rise of populist and white nationalist movements and parties. What they have in common is that such movements aim to protect or extend the social position of racial or ethnic groups that have been traditionally dominant. Their threat to democratic life arises from the fact that they often seek to relegate members of other racial or ethnic groups to less valuable forms of citizenship, as well as from their frequent embrace of authoritarian policies and political tactics. Contemporary Schumpeterians' fundamental commitments unquestionably position them as foes of such political movements. And aspects of their approaches should attune them to the threat of populism and white nationalism – institutional Schumpeterians because of their commitment to non-domination and their concern about racial and ethnic allegiances that may predispose groups against compromise, behavioural Schumpeterians because they hold equality and sensitivity to the effects of group identity on political judgement in high esteem. But institutional Schumpeterians' narrow focus on limiting access to state power points them away from critically analysing the conflicting social relations of race and ethnicity that motivate populist and white nationalist movements. And behavioural Schumpeterians' analytic framework blinds them to the ways in which not weak political commitments but strong ones – robustly inegalitarian and authoritarian beliefs – may threaten contemporary democracy.

The Schumpeterian synthesis: institutional and behavioural theses entwined

Almost every political scientist knows this much about Schumpeter: first, that he disparaged voters' limited capacity for political judgement, and second, that he argued that democracy should be understood as nothing more than a minimalist institutional arrangement ensuring elite competition for popular support.

Schumpeter fashioned his behavioural thesis – his critique of voters' political judgement – as an attack on faith in what he called the 'will of the individual' (2008, 253). Like his contemporary behavioural followers, Schumpeter posited a demanding and very particular ideal standard of individual political judgement – mainly for the purpose of discarding the ideal as unrealistic in light of sobering, if stylised, evidence about voters. This ideal standard, which he attributed to the 'classical doctrine of democracy', required that an individual citizen possess durable political principles articulating 'what he wants to stand for' (253); that such individuals' attainment, possession and use of these principles be sufficiently autonomous that voter preferences could be regarded as the true 'ultimate data' of politics (254), immune to 'pressure groups and propaganda' (254); and that these principles be the premises upon which citizens could reach political conclusions 'according to the rules of logical inference' (253–254). In order to highlight some important elements of this complex ideal, I shall refer to these three assumptions, respectively, as stability, individual autonomy and deduction from abstract principles.

Schumpeter contended that the inability of most people to live up to this threefold standard was manifest – not just a matter of falling short but rather one of failing abjectly. Far from being built upon durable principles, most people's 'will' was little more than an 'indeterminate bundle of vague impulses loosely playing about given slogans and mistaken impressions' (2008, 253). At any given time citizens possessed just ephemeral 'phrases', 'wishes', 'daydreams' or 'grumbles' (261). In short, first, what I have termed stability was actually nowhere to be found, in Schumpeter's view. Nor, second, were abstract principles central to voters' reasoning, he thought. And the instability of most people's political preferences was aggravated by their inability to engage in reasoned deduction. Citizens' reasoning was far from rigorous, 'rational and prompt'; it could not be said to be derived in logical steps from firm principled premises (257). Their arguments were often 'infantile' – their thinking 'associative and affective' (262). And these two weaknesses, together, made democratic voters susceptible to 'dark urges' and manipulation by others (262). A variety of agents – 'professional politicians', advocates of 'an economic interest' and stage-managers of 'political shows' – all were 'able to fashion and, within very wide limits, even to create the will of the people' (263). The result, said Schumpeter, perhaps echoing Walter Lippmann, was a 'manufactured will', not a genuine one (263). So individual autonomy in political judgement was, like stability and deduction from abstract principles, no more than a political myth.

For Schumpeter, it was clear what inference one should draw from this critique of lay political judgement. Rather than a system in which 'the people itself decide issues through the election of individuals who are to assemble to carry out its will' (2008, 250), democracy could never be more than 'an institutional arrangement … in which individuals' – elite political professionals, not 'the people' – 'acquire the power to decide by means of a competitive struggle for the people's vote' (269). This, in a nutshell, was Schumpeter's institutional thesis. He insisted that elite 'competition for leadership' was the only realistic definition of democracy (271), the 'essence of democracy' (280), as he understood it. It would be a mistake, however, to assume he meant that such electoral competition fulfilled any democratic purposes and values as they had traditionally been understood. Modern elections could simply serve as a distinctive arena for the perpetual struggle between elite individuals and groups to serve as leaders. In short, democracy was really a particular way of accommodating 'the vital fact of leadership' (270), not of securing freedom and equality – or even free competition as it might be envisioned in classical economic theory. Schumpeter argued that it would be unrealistic to decry unfair, fraudulent competition or restraint of trade' in democratic politics (271). In saying that competition was the essence of democracy, he did not mean that it acted like an efficient market system for delivering to citizens what they wanted or needed – simply that the motivations and doings of rivalrous elites were essential in democracy. Indeed, satisfying the fleeting preferences of voters was incidental to this aim, at best (279, 282).

Given all this, it is not too much to say that for Schumpeter, democracy entailed elite domination of the rest of society as much as any other form of socio-political organisation. '[D]emocracy is the rule of the politician,' Schumpeter wrote (2008, 285). Not only did it require a great deal of 'voluntary subordination' (294), Schumpeter contended, it also was no more a formula for attaining 'personal' or 'individual freedom' than any other value 'enshrined in the classical doctrine' (271, 294, 302).

To fully appreciate Schumpeter's elite conception of democracy and its behavioural and institutional theses, it is necessary to view them in the context of what he would have termed his 'vision' of social structure and historical change (1989, 272).[1] We cannot fully make sense of them, that is, if we view the behavioural thesis as rooted solely in universal claims about human psychology, or the institutional thesis as constructed from claims about the properties of different political systems, abstracted from their social and historical context. Schumpeter's democratic theory was always rooted in a rich historical sociology of class, group and ideology. One key point is that Schumpeter thought that history showed all societies were led by classes whose special aptitudes made them indispensable in their time. This is the key assumption of his theory of class. Another is that Schumpeter thought capitalism in the twentieth century was in decline – slowly approaching replacement by democratic socialism – because the positions of two classes whose leadership was essential to capitalist society at its height, bourgeois entrepreneurs and the heirs of the feudal nobility, were being undermined by the spread of democratic ideologies. The elite theory of democracy found in *Capitalism, Socialism and Democracy* really lies at the intersection of these claims. For Schumpeter, democratic change was inevitable, but the dire limits of most voters' political judgement demonstrated that minimal democracy – elite competition for popular support – was the most robust form of democracy we should expect. So his behavioural thesis, one could say, underwrote his institutional thesis. Relatedly, Schumpeter's theory of class, holding that every society required leadership by a class with certain special aptitudes, showed why the modern 'rule of the politician' was not something to be regretted, but was in fact a necessary, even redeeming, feature of democracy. Since Schumpeter viewed democracy as just the most recent institutional incarnation of elite rule, one could also say that his institutional thesis rounded out and complemented his behavioural thesis. And these two theses interacted within a broad historical vision of social transformation and how conservatives should understand and respond to it.

It is important to emphasise a couple of aspects of this more complete picture of Schumpeter's elite theory of democracy and its conceptual roots. First, despite his derogation of the judgement of most citizens, Schumpeter did not claim, in contrast to some of his heirs, that ordinary citizens were incapable of ideological thought, or that their ideas and beliefs were insignificant. On the contrary, democratic ideology, for example, was widespread and significant and was relentlessly reshaping modern societies – in deleterious ways, Schumpeter thought. Second, Schumpeter did not think of the weak political judgement of ordinary people as representing a risk to democracy, a reason why actual democracy would always fall far short of some desirable ideal. In contrast to many of his heirs, he did not hold firm to democratic ideals of equality and freedom, even while arguing that citizens could not live up to the role assigned them by 'classical' democratic thinking. Nor, on the other hand, did he see democracy as a means of preventing domination, if we take domination to mean simply the overwhelming and essentially unchallengeable rule of one social group. Rather, for Schumpeter, it was the spread of democratic ideologies and practices that represented a risk to the traditional social order he deeply valued.

Domination and institutional Schumpeterians

Schumpeter's influence has run deep in political inquiry since World War II, but the sort of work I want to explore under the label of 'institutional Schumpeterians' is a relatively late development. Scholars such as Adam

Przeworski and Ian Shapiro are Schumpeterian and institutional because they favour a minimalist understanding of democracy as just an arrangement of political institutions that promotes electoral competition for power.

Crucially, however, they do not share Schumpeter's view that democracy has little to do with freedom, or his belief that elite pre-eminence is inevitable, and indeed desirable, in any society. In fact, these Schumpeterian theorists rely on versions of familiar democratic values to support minimalist democracy. They argue that democratic minimalism is the best defence against domination, viewed as a serious threat to equality, freedom and justice. But while their commitment to familiar democratic values is arguably admirable, it also puts them in the awkward position of adopting a Schumpeterian solution to a decidedly non-Schumpeterian problem. That is, having adopted resistance to domination as their goal, it is not clear that they can effectively advocate for Schumpeterian democratic minimalism, as against more robust versions of democratic practice.

One of the earliest to contribute to this literature was Adam Przeworski. At first glance, it appears that Przeworski's focus is something other than anti-domination, a more modest goal: the avoidance of political violence. But the centrality of anti-domination becomes clear with only a little examination of his argument. Przeworski understands minimalist democracy in explicitly Schumpeterian terms, as 'just a system in which rulers are selected by competitive elections' (1999, 23). His analysis begins with the 'obvious' assumption that 'resolving conflicts through violence' is an evil to be avoided (1999, 45). He notes that Karl Popper understood democracy to be, by definition, a system in which governments change without bloodshed (1999, 23). But for Przeworski the avoidance of violence is something more than an analytical truth contained within the clear meaning of democracy. Preventing bloodshed is, rather, for Przeworski a demonstrable property of minimal democracy as a self-perpetuating system. To show this, he draws on an earlier argument of his about democratic transition and consolidation: that, given the costs of violent confrontation, under minimal democracy rational political forces should calculate that they are better off accepting an electoral loss now, because of the prospect of future democratic wins later (1991, Ch. 2, 1999, 45–55). The danger of domination lies just below the surface of this argument, and there are a couple of ways to see this. First, although the only value explicitly acknowledged here is avoiding violence, it is pretty clear that the inherent good of alternating in office – which places temporal limits on potentially-dominating power – is built into this line of argument as well. Otherwise, a perfectly reasonable response to the possibility that changing governments will require bloodshed would be: don't change governments! Second, although Przeworski implies the issue just prevents 'conflicts' *in general* from being resolved through violence, the sort of conflict he has in mind is not just a generic one between equally-situated forces, but rather one between a challenger and an incumbent who controls the state's means of violence – an incumbent who, if not defeated, would confront few limits to the dominating exercise of that power. Third, at one point, Przeworski considers another procedure, besides alternating in office, that could potentially stave off violence: an agreement between conflicting parties to a 'distribution' of political goods and powers, the distribution that would have resulted from 'open confrontation' (1999, 47). But while such an agreement would fend off violent conflict, it would also put one party in the position of 'dictator' (1999, 47), something Przeworski clearly (if implicitly) wants to avoid.

Of course, it should not really be surprising that Przeworski, who grew up in communist Poland, would consider avoiding domination by a powerful state a key value of democracy. But this points to an important reservation about Przeworski's institutional Schumpeterianism: it has nothing to say about forms of domination that do not centre on the state. Yet Przeworski himself admits that even minimalist democracy rests on conditions that go beyond minimalist state or electoral institutions. '[E]lections alone are not sufficient' for achieving the purposes he lays out for them (1999, 55). He admits that an argument of the kind he mounts does not show that minimalist democracy is preferable to more robust varieties – only that minimalist democracy 'would be worth defending even if it could not be [improved]' (1999, 55).

These issues may be explored in greater depth in the work of Ian Shapiro, whose longstanding exploration of domination and democracy positions his work as the most thorough and explicit consideration of institutional Schumpeterianism as a doctrine of anti-domination. Like Przeworski, Shapiro argues that it is specifically electoral competition that secures minimal democracy's claim to be a bulwark against domination. '[T]he imperative to minimise domination', he wrote years ago, 'is best realised by competitive democracy of the sort proposed by Schumpeter' (2003, 58, 148). And this is still his position. State power is a natural monopoly, he argues, but electoral competition forces 'political parties to compete for temporary control' of it (2016, 78). Unlike Przeworski, whose commitment to anti-domination is almost disguised by his focus on avoiding political violence, Shapiro is explicit about his commitment to anti-domination, and reflects directly on the meaning and varieties of domination.

In part, his emphasis on resisting domination stems from Shapiro's Deweyan dislike of theory that spins out pure abstract ideals, such as freedom or equality. Those who value democracy, he argues, generally value it as a way to resist existing forms of domination. 'Democratic revolutions are usually undertaken less to implement abstract ideals than' – here Shapiro uses Dewey's words directly – 'to remedy evils experienced in consequence of prior political institutions' (2016, 62). And elsewhere he writes: '[T]he possibility of diminishing – if not eradicating – domination is often what draws people to democracy' (2003, 146). It follows generally from this 'reactive' approach to democratic theory that we should even be wary of placing too much emphasis on abstract definitions of domination. Nevertheless, he does write that domination involves 'the avoidable and illegitimate exercise of power that compromises people's basic interests' (2016, 5).

State-based domination is built into Shapiro's account of why minimalist, Schumpeterian democracy is the best way to stave off domination – his theory of state power as a monopoly that must not be allowed to be under anyone's control for too long. This emphasis on state power as a primary mode of domination is reinforced by Shapiro's insistence that political institutions, as distinct from institutions of civil society, are uniquely concerned with power.[2] Shapiro admits that power suffuses all social relations (2016, 32), but politics, he insists, is 'concerned in the last instance, as well as in the first, with managing power relations' because, in contrast to civil institutions, 'there is no overarching … good' that defines politics or political institutions (2016, 33).[3] The centrality of state domination is also integral to Shapiro's engagement with Robert Nozick, the point of which is to show that in the modern world, at least, 'domesticating the commanding heights of the state' is a continual challenge – because there is no point in asking, as did Nozick, whether there should be states. The state's potentially 'unaccountable power' is always already present, and always a primary political challenge (2016, 36). Finally, the prominence of state-based domination is woven into Shapiro's defence of majoritarianism, – about which, more below – since it is not clear how majorities are to be defined except by reference to all those subject to or contesting for state power.

Yet Shapiro is clear that domination by states and those who staff them – domination exemplified by 'fascism, communism, and more recent military and theocratic despotism', for example (2016, 62) – is not the only sort democrats have to worry about. Years ago, Shapiro was critical of liberals who fail to see that while 'governmental power is one potential site of domination', there are 'many others that permeate different domains of 'private' life' (1999, 32). And he devotes considerable attention, in his most recent work, to the argument that economic inequality fosters domination. Politicians, he notes, have more incentives to respond to the demands of the rich; the wealthy are better poised to exploit the complexity of political systems like that of the US; and absent controls, the wealthy can drown out other people's political speech (2016, 93–99). It is not clear in these passages whether Shapiro means that economic inequality constitutes or is associated with a distinctive form of domination – or just that it helps the wealthy prevent democratic mechanisms from working against state domination (2016, 93). But elsewhere he seems to describe modes of economic inequality that constitute dominant relations in themselves. He explores the idea of a global minimum wage as a means of 'combating domination', especially economic domination experienced in developing countries (2016, 126). And although he does not exactly specify the nature of this domination, his analysis touches on the association of very low wages with other sweatshop conditions and the non-transparency of many workplaces to outside scrutiny and the mismatch of power between capital and labour (2016, 124–130). Elsewhere, Shapiro explores the workplace as a potential site of private domination at greater length, noting that the 'unequally distributed knowledge and expertise, hierarchical organisation, and substantial exercises of power' that characterise most workplaces are at odds with the assumption of 'fully competent adults who are presumed sovereign over their interests' (1999, 143).

The absence of a more comprehensive sociology of domination, one not focused exclusively on the state – and especially the failure to explore at length the intersection of democracy and the social structures of racial or ethnic domination – expose a weakness in Shapiro's institutional Schumpeterianism. But this is not because he fails to recognise conflictive relations of race, ethnicity and religion. In fact, such relations constitute a crucial juncture in Shapiro's argument for minimalist, majoritarian democracy. To see how these issues arise for Shapiro, however, it is necessary to lay some groundwork. In *Politics against Domination*, Shapiro elaborates the case for minimalist, majoritarian democracy in three chapters in which he presents them as the best hedge against domination – and then defends majoritarianism against two types of frequently proposed limitations or supplements, ones meant in different ways to curb domination. The first proposed limitation is supermajority requirements – rules mandating that some or all legislation must be approved by more than a bare majority. Shapiro argues that supermajority proposals, in making change difficult, privilege the status quo, which is just as likely to be unjust and dominating as not (2016, 40). Supermajority requirements allow small numbers of people to impose their preferences on more numerous others, and so can actually foster domination. If so, then what actually does constrain majorities from dominating? Shapiro's answer has more to do with socio-political conditions than with state institutional mechanisms. He agrees with James Madison that the existence of multiple, cross-cutting cleavages among citizens can help – because they encourage constant political realignments, instead of rule of a particular majority without a foreseeable end. But cleavages of interest, outlook and ideology, he says, are not enough. For according to Shapiro, the Madisonian model only works if the shifting factions are wrangling over divisible goods, ones that 'can be divided and distributed [between them] in many different ways' (2016, 47). A focus on such divisible goods, then, encourages the kind of ever-evolving compromise that avoids domination.

Indivisible goods, by contrast, represent a serious challenge. For economists, any good is indivisible if it cannot be divided up and traded many different ways – if it is only meaningfully available or useful in large units or amounts. But Shapiro has in mind not so much economic commodities that come in large units, but rather political goods that people tend to view, for ideological or cultural reasons, in all-or-nothing terms. And the most prominent of these, he writes, are goods 'rooted in religion, race, and ethnic identities' (2016, 48). For example, he draws on the break-up of former Yugoslavia. As it tore apart into smaller nation-states likely to be dominated by a single ethnic group, people began to regard citizenship and ethnic supremacy as an all-or-nothing matter. They could foresee being either a member of a dominant ethnicity, a full citizen – or a second-class citizen at best, a non-citizen, dominated minority at worst (2016, 52). Elsewhere, Shapiro reviews the way in which Southern whites in the US used their power to maintain racial caste domination – hobbling social welfare programmes that might weaken it, while also blocking anti-lynching legislation and federal intervention in voting rights (2016, 73–74). Although he does not use the language of 'indivisible goods' in this instance, it is no stretch to cast racial dominance as such an all-or-nothing 'good' for many whites.

The core of Shapiro's argument for minimal, majoritarian democratic institutions is that electoral competition over state power can prevent any party from possessing the means of domination. Shapiro elaborates this argument, we have seen, through an engagement with those who favour supermajority requirements as an alternative means of battling domination. Majority rule 'minimizes the chances of domination when compared to the going alternatives' (2016, 44). So not just electoral competition, but electoral competition *for a majority*, is the key. The final element of his particular institutional Schumpeterianism is a rejection of generally republican arguments for dividing state power, again advocated as a means of staving off domination. The US constitution embodies a number of these divided-power devices. Yet there is almost no evidence, Shapiro argues, that they help reduce domination. For most of US history, the US Senate and Supreme Court have repeatedly been used as veto points by elites and reactionary forces to stave off democratic change, rather than as defenders of liberty (2016, 70–78). So again, the key is not dividing up the power of the state, but making sure no one possesses it fully for long.

Given all of what Shapiro says and suggests about domination, how adequate is his institutional Schumpeterianism for preventing it? A first step towards addressing this question is asking exactly what is meant by prevention. It could mean intervening to stop certain kinds of unjust acts. Or it could mean depriving political agents (as much as possible) of the social capacities needed to engage in those sorts of acts. Shapiro insists that 'merely having the capacity' to commit certain unjust acts should not count as domination (2016, 21).[4] But Shapiro's illustrations draw on the wrong intuitions about the sources of politically relevant power and vulnerability. For example, he asks: What about a bully who could beat up any child on the playground, but only beats up black children? Those not beaten up should not be seen as dominated, he writes. Unlike most cases of political interest, however, the dominating power Shapiro points to in this illustration is just the bully's physical strength, as opposed to any power held in virtue of his or her social position, or ability to draw on social norms and practices. And the choice of which children to oppress seems, in Shapiro's telling, to be simply a matter of the bully's individual choice. But in politically significant scenarios involving power, aggression and race, exactly who is subject to violent treatment is not generally a matter only of physical power and individual choice, but of social structure, racial ideology, human geography and criminal-justice policy. Police violence against African Americans in the US constitutes a single, prominent example. Under circumstances likes those pertaining in the contemporary US, it is not just those who are actually killed, manhandled or inappropriately frisked by police who are harmed, but also those who because of their race reasonably fear such treatment and inevitably must live differently as a result. When vulnerability to unjust treatment depends on the way social structures and shared beliefs distribute power and make people vulnerable to it, it is the social structures that must be changed in order to alleviate domination. And of necessity, that means not just intervening to stop or punish unjust acts, but making those acts impossible (or at least far less possible) by changing the social distribution of power. While never conceding terminological ground as to the definition of domination Shapiro, elsewhere, seems to admit the practical point at issue here when he writes that the goal is not just to intervene to stop certain acts, but to create a 'a world that no one can dominate' (2016, 6).

The example of police violence and race in the US brings us back to indivisible goods – to racial and ethnic conflict – and their relationship to a democratic programme of anti-domination. It appropriately sharpens the focus as we ask: What would be involved in creating a social world in which no racial domination, in particular, is possible? Shapiro's anti-domination programme, we have seen, is identical with his minimalist, majoritarian institutional framework – his institutional Schumpeterianism. Such a programme reduces the chance that those who hold state power will use it for any 'avoidable and illegitimate exercise of power that compromises people's basic interests' (2016, 5). But it does not have much to say about the social foundations of domination – in this case, enduring social relations of race and ethnicity – nor the way holding certain social positions may relate to occupying the state as a possible mechanism of domination. To be clear, Shapiro surely recognises and acknowledges these other sites or bases of domination – economic, social, racial and so on. It is just not clear how far electoral competition, per se, goes to addressing them. And this is no mere side-issue for Shapiro. Much of what he says about the efficacy of different mechanisms for making sure denizens of the state do not dominate points towards other sites of the phenomenon besides the state. Shapiro argues that Madison had only vague ideas about whom different parties and factions might represent (2016, 67–68), but he himself is clear that conflicts among parties with access to state power embody structural conflicts of interest extant in the broader society (2016, 83). This is clear in how he responds to the republican idea that the occupants of each branch will try to prevent domination by other branches. He notes that Southern democrats stood up to Franklin D. Roosevelt not in order to protect Congress from presidential encroachment, but to protect Southern racial hierarchy from federal intervention (69–70). And far from functioning routinely as a jealous check on domination by other branches, he notes, the Supreme Court's restraint of Congress has often served to protect racial caste or wealthy investors from democratic meddling (71–72). The Senate, too, rather than an exemplar of the use of deliberation to foil domination, has often shaped policy to deny protection to those 'at greatest risk for domination in the [American] South' (73).

These examples point to forms of domination other than runaway state power – and so to other domains and tasks for the politics of anti-domination besides the design of electoral institutions – and other practices for anti-domination politics besides participation in elections. Like the many forms of domination themselves, the forms of anti-dominating democratic action should be understood as plural and diverse, though unified by an 'orientation toward collectively managing crucial institutions, social relations, and forces in a way that strives for equality of power' (Medearis 2015, 140). Participation in voting and electoral competition are important, but a far wider array of democratic practices, including marching, mobilising, organising and protesting – practices deployed by movements around the world to transform and even upend enduring and unequal racial and ethnic relations – must surely be seen as equally essential to democratic anti-domination.

Sustained engagement with Shapiro's Schumpeterian institutionalism makes it easier to deal quickly with other examples of the genre. Nadia Urbinati sees her approach as transcending standard contrasts between Schumpeterian and participatory approaches to democracy, but she also says Schumpeter's 'classical formulation' is simply the 'best rendering of our system of government,' identifying what makes it 'democratic' (2006, 4, 14). And her approach neatly fits 'contemporary Schumpeterian institutionalism'. She views democracy in minimalist institutional terms, arguing that such democracy is the best defence against at least one crucial form of domination. What distinguishes Urbinati's contribution from Shapiro's is her focus on representation, as opposed to his electoral competition – as well as her view that the most worrisome and potentially dominating disfigurations of democracy involve enhancing the role of the public in the wrong way: populism, by over-emphasising popular mobilisation, and plebiscitarianism, by over-emphasising non-rational popular will (2014, Chs. 3–4). For Urbinati, the key to representation is that it slows the political process down, creating a temporal gap between 'judgement' and 'will'. (By contrast, she argues, populism and plebiscitarianism collapse the space between 'judgement' and 'will' dangerously.) But unless one believes that the primary contemporary threat of domination derives generically from hasty voters, and that delay generally favours those who oppose domination, it is difficult to see why we should see representative deceleration as a sufficient hedge. There is little doubt that contemporary populist movements present dangers to democratic values, but the threat is best understood in terms of the dominating social relations they seek to preserve or reinvigorate, and the inegalitarian and intolerant ideologies that motivate them, rather than abstract redescriptions of their practices and ideas as collapsing 'will' and 'judgement'. In the end, Urbinati, like Shapiro, gives us insufficient reason to think that minimalist democracy alone can foil the populist or plebiscitary domination she fears.

Weak judgement and behavioural Schumpeterians

Today's behavioural Schumpeterians stand at the near end of a very long line of scholars who have argued that the vast majority of citizens are not, in Philip Converse's terms, 'ideologues' or even 'near-ideologues' (1964): indeed, they simply lack any real, rooted preferences or attitudes about politics and policy at all. For our purposes, the clearest way to locate the weaknesses and difficulties of this approach is by highlighting continuities with the work of Schumpeter himself. For the behavioural Schumpterians' difficulties can be understood as the result of their adopting the thesis of weak citizen judgement as a stand-alone position – abstracted from both a satisfying account situating citizen judgement within a historically attuned political sociology of groups, identity and ideology – and at the same time shorn of Schumpeter's elite proclivities.

Central to the work of Christopher Achen and Larry Bartels is a stark contrast between two implausibly dichotomous possibilities: either individual voters start with firm, abstract principles from which they rationally and autonomously derive policy and electoral decisions, or we must accept that they 'don't really know what they want' (2016, 30), and do not think on their own at all (267–296), but instead are just passive receptacles of group ideas, just repeating to researchers 'what their party tells them they should be thinking' (312). This way of conceptualising the possibilities not only invites us to adopt, to borrow a phrase from Clifford Geertz, a 'flattened view of other people's mentalities' (1973, 210), it also steers us away from recognising what are arguably some of the most serious threats to democratic politics. For Achen and Bartels, as for their predecessors, the crucial danger for democracy revealed by survey research can be summed up this way: there can be no democratic accountability if people lack stable preferences against which the actions of elected officials can be judged (2016, 4). But their approach obscures a different, crucial and rather more straightforward source of risk for any democratic polity, one that Europeans and North Americans can no longer see as someone else's problem: the growing prevalence of undemocratic and even anti-democratic movements and ideologies.[5]

Like Schumpeter, Achen and Bartels do not merely present certain findings of research in political behaviour on their own, so to speak – but rather they present them in stark contrast to elements of a stylised ideal model of citizen judgement, one they attribute to the 'folk theory' of democracy (Achen and Bartels 2016, 1, 21, 49, 213). And they cite Schumpeter as their authority on the nature and prevalence of the 'folk theory' (3, 10, 22, 50). The elements of 'folk theory's' stylised ideal model of judgement frame their whole analysis.

The first of these elements is what I termed, in reference to Schumpeter, the assumption of 'deduction from abstract principles'. Like many students of political behaviour, Achen and Bartels rely heavily on the somewhat ambiguous catch-all term 'preferences' rather than referencing 'abstract principles'. It is political 'preferences' of a certain kind that most citizens lack, they say. But it is pretty clear that the sort of thought elements Achen and Bartels have in mind would be (for those few who employed them) fairly abstract principles or commitments, and ones that would constitute the premises of political judgement. Citizens with the sort of preferences they are referring to would be what Converse termed 'ideologues', voters who employed 'relatively abstract and far-reaching conceptual dimension[s]' to explain their judgements (1964, 14). Commenting and drawing on Converse, Achen and Bartels write that what is missing from most citizens' judgement is 'ideological concepts at the core of elite political discourse', especially labels like liberal or conservative (2016, 32). These concepts or principles, for those few who employed them in their political thinking, would stand above or behind the judgements citizens make – would serve as 'yardsticks,' as Converse put it (1964, 14). They would be, as Achen and Bartels put it, 'the starting point and the foundation' of political judgement (2016, 213). Moreover, such ideas would foster judgements of a categorically different kind than judgements about identity and social position (Converse 1964, 15; Achen and Bartels 2016, 4, 213–231).

Much of the behaviour scholarship devoted to assessing whether citizens deduce electoral decisions and other political judgements from such abstract principles does not directly assess fluency with ideological terms, like liberal or conservative, let alone feminist, white supremacist, environmentalist, or socialist – or freedom, justice and oppression. Instead, it focuses on what Converse termed 'constraint', defined as 'the success we would have in predicting, given initial knowledge that an individual holds a specified attitude, that he holds certain further ideas and attitudes' (1964, 3). Such predictive success would surely depend on correctly specifying the full range of possible ideologies available to citizens, as well as a sense of their meaning to them – though Converse did not make this clear. (I return to this issue shortly.)

It is easier to see how Achen and Bartels rely on the assumption of 'stability'. Schumpeter himself emphasised that citizens' beliefs were generally indefinite, weakly held and subject to manipulation – not at all stable. Converse famously tested the stability of voters' preferences by drawing on surveys in which some were asked the same questions at intervals over several years, and then measuring the correlation or consistency among their answers. As critics have pointed out, if the hypothesis to be tested is, first, that citizens derive their issue judgements from higher-level abstractions and, second, that those abstractions are stable, Converse's empirical test, focused on the stability of specific issue responses, may not be ideal. But it has set the standard for later investigators. And Achen and Bartels rest heavily on Converse's finding that 'successive responses to the same question turned out to be remarkably *in*consistent' (2016, 33).

The final element of the model of citizen judgement Schumpeter attributed to the 'classical doctrine' was autonomy, as we have seen, and his contemporary heirs place a similar emphasis on this assumption, which they attribute to the 'folk theory'. Schumpeter focused much of his attention not on exploring the meaning of autonomy, per se, but more on the ability of political parties and demagogues to manipulate citizens and so to violate autonomy. So here again, the key is not any assumption that behavioural Schumpeterians themselves adopt, but rather one they attribute to their antagonists: a stringent, causal understanding of individual autonomy, autonomy not merely as a capacity for uncoerced action or choice, but as action or choice that is actually determined solely internally, solely according to self-chosen 'preferences', without influence by others. Achen and Bartels insist that the 'folk theory' posits preferences as 'the starting point and the foundation' of political judgement (2016, 213), thus attributing to the theory's reputed proponents a very strong assumption about autonomy. For them, the 'folk theory' assumes that nothing comes before and nothing lies beneath individual preferences. Tellingly, they attribute this ideal of autonomous judgement to Enlightenment 'monadic individualism' or to an 'individualist' mentality they associate with 'rationalistic liberalism' (18, 213, 217). And while they derogate the belief that people can or do form political judgements in this purely autonomous way, they are more fixated on debunking this ideal than on building up a more plausible alternative.

In part, this is a reflection of the stark way they posit their alternatives in terms of simple causal determination. Either preferences or foundational judgements about issues cause individuals' candidate choices, or their fundamental identifications with candidates cause their issue positions. (Missing is the fairly innocuous idea that the same individual might at one time derive candidate choices from her beliefs or preferences and at another be influenced by the beliefs espoused by people she finds trustworthy, including candidates and parties.) Given these choices, Achen and Bartels argue that partisanship, overwhelmingly, causes ideology rather than vice versa (2016, 234). All this points ahead to their treatment of a 'group theory' of politics, whereby group identification or membership determines political judgement, a theory they see as a stark alternative to the 'folk theory' and its emphasis on autonomous individual judgement.

Overall, Achen and Bartels offer no detailed account of their own of how ordinary people reason about politics – of what political judgement looks like from the standpoint of lay political agents themselves. Their emphasis is negative, offering three main kinds of arguments about why ordinary people do not live up to the standards of 'folk theory'. One is that although citizens could do better, they are busy, and political judgement is not very important to them (2016, 9–10, 14, 37–38). Another more ominous strand of explanation is that citizens often act quite instinctively, unreflectively and irrationally. Retrospective voting occurs, according to this account, but it is 'blind' (118–145). As Achen and Bartels put it, '[u]nder sufficient pressure, voters sometimes lash out blindly' (145). I shall take up their third explanation – the influence of group politics – shortly.

There are a few preliminary reasons to be doubtful about the basis on which behavioural Schumpeterians in the Converse-Achen-Bartels mould reach the conclusion that most citizens have no stable preferences from which to derive voting and other decisions. First, one's judgement of whether a person is ideological can only be as reliable as one's a-priori understanding of the full range of existing ideologies in society. This is true in a broader and a narrower sense. In the broader sense, according to Achen and Bartels's way of thinking, each distinct ideology should in principle be characterised by a relatively unique pattern of responses to questions about issues – with libertarians or white nationalists differing from other conservatives. For each ideology, different beliefs – and here I mean not just policy preferences or abstract values but also views about how society, politics and the economy work – are likely to be central to their forms of judgement. If a person does not exhibit one of the expected ideological patterns, it could mean he is not ideological at all – or it could mean he subscribes to some ideology not anticipated by researchers.

In the narrower, more methodological sense, one's judgement of a person's ideological cogency or constraint can only be as good as the issue questions one asks to assess her preferences. Stephen Ansolabehere, Rodden and Snyder (2008) have sought to demonstrate that much of Converse's influential finding that most Americans have no stable ideological preferences is attributable to measurement error: survey questions that are, taken individually, unstable and unreliable guides to citizen preferences. They find that simply averaging many different survey items related to the same 'issue area' results in measures that show rather 'structured and stable' ideological preferences (215).

And there is another difficulty. Converse, at least, seems to have regarded patterns of association between stated issue preferences ('constraint') and the spontaneous use of certain ideological concepts in open-ended survey questions as nearly equivalent measures of how ideological voters are. As we have just seen, 'constraint' points to one set of issues about identifying the ideological commitment of voters. But whether or not, in a given instance, people employ particular ideologically significant concepts in explaining their choices points to a different set of issues. For the skilled use of ideological concepts surely depends in part on agents' 'discursive capabilities': their ability at any given moment to recall concepts, facts and considerations, and put them together in an explanatory, narrative form (Giddens 1986, 57). The fact that at a given moment a person cannot or does not draw on a given concept does not mean it plays no role in his thinking, or that he is unaware of what it refers to. In fact, a person's failure to use one of the concepts Converse and his followers recognised as ideological – terms like liberal, conservative or radical – could at times signify political competence, in the sense of knowledgeable responsiveness to political discourse, as it changes over time, focusing at one time on such ideological labels and at another time on competing visions of how society is structured, or on who has power, or what groups are worthy contributors to society.

If the definition of ideological political judgement motivating Achen, Bartels and Converse is rather narrow and exclusive – so too, in an opposite way, is Achen and Bartel's understanding of how group and identity may affect political judgement. They conceive of ideological political judgement and the effect of social identity on voting as categorically different from each other – different as to substance and as to mechanism. An ideologue (of the sort Achen and Bartels say is vanishingly rare) would derive voting decisions syllogistically from abstract principles and preferences. By contrast, a voter acting on her identity is little more than a mimic, engaged in little thinking at all. Identity-based voting is not derived from relatively abstract preferences or principles and does not reflect individual autonomy, they say. At best, people motivated by identity construct 'preferences or beliefs consistent with' their group commitments (2016, 294). (Party is the most important group identity, Achen and Bartels argue, although they talk about other collective attachments.) And while constructing preferences in this way might sound like a sort of thinking, it is really only 'pseudo-thinking', involving rationalisation, imitation and the docile acceptance of instruction (294). '[P]eople tend to adopt beliefs, attitudes, and values that reinforce and rationalise their partisan loyalties' (296), they argue. What passes for thinking among even well-informed citizens is just 'mechanical reflection of what their favorite groups and party leaders have instructed them to think' (12). They surrender any possible autonomy and 'let their party tell them what to think about the issues of the day' (266).

Identity, for Achen and Bartels, is then the 'key moving force' in [p]olitical behaviour; it straightforwardly *causes* ideology, rather than ideology *causing* identity (2016, 234, 235). And identity itself, viewed this way, is not thought-ful or reflective, it is simply a given impulse about 'where 'people like me' belong' (266). It provides no 'meaningful basis for democracy' (233). In this conceptualisation of group- or identity-based judgement, then, there is no room for the possibility that group identity might itself be composed of or thoroughly entwined with shared beliefs and judements, a common narrative sense of history, or visions of how the social world works or is ordered; no room for the idea that identity, like these sorts of judgements and beliefs, might thus be subject to reflection or to cultural change; no elaborated model of the influence of groups or group membership on cognition, between the extremes of pure individual autonomy and an individual simply accepting what the group tells her or him.

It is fair to ask at this point: If most people lack meaningful preferences on most issues and simply mimic the judgements of those they take to be in *their group*, why not follow Schumpeter in embracing elite rule, in recognising that rule of the politician is all democracy ever can or should be? For Achen and Bartels, the answer is that, while their conclusions about lay political judgement *should* lead them to an elite interpretation of minimal democratic institutions, they do not share Schumpeter's normative comfort with elite pre-eminence. They are in this sense members of the family of traditional democrats. As a result, their normative commitments, their starkly dichotomous and anti-idealist mode of thinking and their conclusions about lay political capacities – taken together – put Achen, Bartels and other behavioural Schumpeterians in a peculiar position: committed to aims for which they can posit no plausible agent or means. At one point, they suggest that their realist account requires that we adjust the values we associate with democracy, to less idealistic matters, such as the establishment of legitimate rule, turnover of leadership and toleration of opposition. But when they turn to the topic of 'truer and deeper' democracy, they consider not the securing of these more modest goods, but the attainment of a higher degree of 'economic and social equality' in order to reduce political inequality (2016, 325–328), a goal that resonates with other work by Bartels (2008). Yet they immediately concede that it is not clear 'how to accomplish such a change,' in the US, for example, given their view that 'Americans lack the ideas, the will and the political organisation' (2016, 326).

With this initial analysis of Achen and Bartels in hand it becomes relatively easy to understand the essential characteristics of other work that builds on behavioural Schumpeterian assumptions. Much of Jeffrey Edward Green's work on plebiscitary or plebeian politics builds on a similar critique of political judgement, one explicitly influenced by Converse and Schumpeter. He also employs an argumentative strategy like Achen and Bartels's, focused on debunking a stylised ideal – albeit the model of the 'citizen-governor' rather than the 'folk theory' of democracy targeted by Achen and Bartels (Green 2010a, 32). Green holds that 'most citizens on most issues lack opinions, preferences, interests, and values waiting to be represented' (2010b, 269). As a result, 'nonparticipation, nondecision, hierarchy, nonpreference, [and] spectatorial passivity' are 'foundational features' of contemporary democracy (2010b, 273; 2010a, 45–47). Green, like Achen and Bartels, also holds fast to certain democratic values – especially freedom and equality (2016, 1–8). This combination of premises and forms of reasoning leads to the same problem: the quite literal lack of an agent who could rectify the flaws Green perceives in contemporary democracy. Green, however, adopts a novel strategy for dealing with this: positing the people as a solution, while at the same time denying that they can be conceived as an agent or a collection of agents. In one version of Green's vision, this means the 'people' passively discipline politicians through their spectatorial gaze, without actually acting so as to hold them accountable (2010a, 120–139, 152–157). In another, he counsels contemporary plebeians not to engage in a particular form of collective action, but to accept the permanence of second-class citizenship, harness envy to a programme of burdening the superrich, engage in vulgar discourse and find extrapolitical sources of solace (2016, 8–14).

It is not within my remit to propose a fully elaborated conception of political judgement. But to lay the groundwork for further criticism of behavioural Schumpeterians, it is important to point to some conceptual possibilities forsworn by them in their single-minded focus on refuting the mythic 'folk theory'. To this end, it may help to begin by identifying the problem of political judgement that actually confronts most citizens: not writing an essay applying the principles of few fixed ideologies to contemporary politics, but making recurrent practical choices in a complex, changing political environment, drawing on concepts from public discourses that vary from one social location to another and are always in flux. Given the varied, changing nature of this challenge, there is no reason, a priori, to think that people who explain themselves with concepts other than abstract general ideological labels can offer no plausible, coherent account of their political choices at all. Nor, given all this, should we think a shift in how someone responds to a question necessarily signifies that her responses are meaningless.

With this understanding of the challenge of political judgement in mind, what should we make of individual 'autonomy' and the role of groups? Behavioural Schumpeterians are surely right to reject an unduly individualist conception of political judgement, but rejecting what is misguided in what they term 'monadic individualism' (2016, 18) does not require us to think that most individuals just thoughtlessly adopt their group's ideas. First, no individual's thinking can ever be purely autonomous; it always requires concepts, styles and methods developed by and shared with others. And judgement also frequently involves consulting the views of those whose opinions and knowledge we trust – something even experts do. Neither of these considerations refutes the idea that individuals indeed think.[6]

And consideration of the role of groups in thinking takes us directly to the problem of ideology. One of the oddities of the nomenclature Achen and Bartels adopt from Converse is its treatment of 'ideology' as an essentially individual characteristic centred around logical inference from abstract ideas and preferences. In the long interdisciplinary history of debates about the matter, the study of ideology has almost always indicated something quite different: an inclination to see groups, classes or movements of one kind or another as bearers or sharers of belief systems, concepts and styles of thought. We speak of socialist ideology, or bourgeois ideology, or the ideology of ethnic nationalists – not the ideologies of particular, isolated individuals. More broadly, debates about ideology in social theory generally involve disagreements concerning how, exactly, social structure, social position and interests, and social change condition thinking. In fact, Converse, Achen and Bartels's individualist conception of ideology actually puts them sharply at odds even with Schumpeter, who under the heading of 'ideology' consistently explored people's social and political ideas as products of 'historical conditions' and the attempts of 'groups or classes to explain to themselves their own existence' (Schumpeter 1946, 270, 2008, 11). As I have pointed out, Achen and Bartels treat group-influenced political judgement as an alternative to 'ideological' thinking, thus categorising as non-ideological one's view of who one's group may be, the nature or character of that group, and what the position, needs and interests of the group are. But a vision of how society is structured, of what its component groups and parts are, how those groups relate to each other, their relative power and what one's place in all this may be – this is a consummately ideological matter. Ideologies, that is, do not consist just of abstract ideals and labels alone, but also such a vision of society and one's place in it.

A final element of an alternative conception would be the recognition that political judgement is prone to many psychological phenomena that cause it to diverge from the path of the syllogistic reasoning envisioned by the supposed believers in 'folk theory'. In particular, considerable bodies of research now attest to the importance of motivated reasoning, and of various emotions in forming political judgements. As to the first phenomenon: people tend to find plausible-sounding arguments to reach conclusions that they already want to reach, searching their memories for supporting considerations and rejecting factual correction (Kunda 1990; Nyhan and Reifler 2010). But rather than support the case for the pervasiveness of non-attitudes, the recognition of such motivated reasoning may underscore the power of diverse ideological pre-commitments to shape perceptions and conclusions. And we should be interested in how motivated reasoning may interact with social power and position to favour certain kinds of arguments and interests. From the standpoint of democratic values and concerns, it is particularly important, for example, that those with more powerful social and political positions are likely motivated to resist arguments and considerations that call the fairness of the existing social structure into question (Bagg 2015). There may often be, as well, parties with a vested economic interest in providing some citizens with considerations that will support their pre-existing misconceptions, thus staving off regulation and oversight that challenge their privileges and interests (Hochschild and Einstein 2015). In the broad, traditional sense of the term, these are classically *ideological* phenomena, ones concerning the way that social position and structure affect the way people think about politics and social life.

Like the effect of motivated reasoning, the effects of emotions on political judgement seem not to be uniform across all possible ideologies. The most significant examples of emotions' effects are linked to particular problems and social relations. Perceived terrorist threats and the array of emotions they can trigger (including but not limited to fear) tend to cause citizens to trust in 'strong' leaders, become more favourable to foreign intervention and to become less tolerant of outgroups (Merolla and Zechmeister 2009). Thus, the perception of such threats has close links to aspects of authoritarian and nationalist ideologies. Related research shows that sensitivity to images that often provoke disgust – such as maggots and putrid meat – is associated with conservative attitudes towards issues such as gay marriage, and more generally with authoritarian and socially dominant attitudes (Inbar, Pizarro and Bloom 2009; Inbar and Pisarro 2016).[7]

Like their institutional counterparts, contemporary behavioural Schumpeterians, as we have seen, perceive a danger for democracy: voters lack the sort of real, rooted preferences that could be the basis of democratic accountability. But in rehearsing their evidence for 'nonattitudes', in dismissing the view of political judgement they ascribe to the 'folk theory', Achen and Bartels simply do not make a strong case that lay political actors are non-ideological. They are surely right, that is, that group identity or affinity powerfully shape citizens' choices, but this does not rule out the need to study and understand ideology. Fundamentally, the problem is the sharply dichotomous way behavioural Schumpeterians conceive of political judgement, as either ideological in their sense (characterised by stability, individual autonomy and deduction from abstract preferences) or characterised by empty group mimicry. But insofar as ideologies include beliefs about the structure of society and one's place in it, they can powerfully shape one's sense of group membership and group needs. Moreover, while emphasising a supposed generic weakness of citizens' political judgement, Achen and Bartels have little to say about emotion and motivated reasoning, psychological tendencies that can interact in important ways with judgements and perceptions about the relationship between social groups in society.

Conclusion: white nationalism, far right movements and democracy

All the considerations just reviewed point towards a set of related questions specifically ignored by behavioural Schumpeterians: What kinds of group-centred ideologies are most significant to the life and health of contemporary democracy? What sort of ideologies might be threatening to democratic practices and values? Here, the critical analysis of behavioural Schumpeterianism converges with that of institutional Schumpeterianism. For while Shapiro's entirely appropriate democratic concern about domination leads him to worry about indivisible goods related to race and ethnicity, this does not lead him – though it should, or could – to consider the social relations that structure conflict over such goods, and by extension, the way that many citizens conceive of those social relations and formulate their indivisible needs and demands concerning them.

In both contemporary Europe and the US, there is growing evidence of the resurgence of movements of traditionally dominant ethnic and racial groups that believe their position is threatened by out-groups such as immigrants, and so embrace programmes to degrade the value of others' democratic citizenship, often by extraordinary political means that undermine democratic commitments to democratic rights and procedures. In Europe, such far-right parties have participated in coalition governments in about a dozen countries (Golder 2016, 478). In the US, both survey research and simple observation show that the Tea Party movement that began in 2011 was significantly animated by fear that the position of white men was being threatened on all sides by newly assertive groups, such as African Americans and immigrants (Parker and Barreto 2013; Williamson, Skocpol and Coggins 2011). Similar evidence shows that Donald Trump was propelled into office significantly by the same social forces and beliefs (Nteta and Schaffner 2016; Sides and Tesler 2016; Tesler and Sides 2016). These movements may not be explicitly hostile to democracy, per se, but they embrace positions that are counter to democratic practices and values. As Matt Golder notes, what far right parties [in Europe] have in common is a desire to create an authoritarian system that is strictly ordered according to the 'natural' differences that exist in society, as well as a law-and-order system that severely punishes deviant behaviour.

(2016, 479)

Meanwhile, Trump supporters rallied enthusiastically to their candidate's calls to jail political opponents, commit violence against dissenters and expand the security state in order to carry out mass deportations, while also tolerating his admiration for authoritarians like Vladimir Putin.

It is far beyond the scope of this chapter to provide a full account of the far-right or white-nationalist wave. My purpose, rather, connects this troubling phenomenon to the weaknesses of institutionalist and behaviourist Schumpeterian approaches to democracy. It seems strange to have to point out the seriousness of this threat to democracy, but both branches of contemporary Schumpeterianism tend to obscure it. Contemporary institutional Schumpeterianism, while rightly understanding opposition to domination as an abiding aim of democracy, identifies democracy too narrowly with certain minimalist democratic institutions and threats to democracy too narrowly with certain uses of the instruments of state. In its current form, then, it can have little directly to say about social relations and structures that foster domination – including social relations of ethnicity and race that people often rally to challenge or defend. Meanwhile, contemporary behavioural Schumpeterians, while giving plausible weight to the role that group and identity play in politics, think wrongly that this underwrites an approach that dismisses ideologies as important factors in political judgement – and so dismisses the possibility that the growing prominence of certain ideologies could constitute a democratic danger.

My analysis culminates with a brief consideration of the resurgence of white-nationalist and far-right movements and ideologies because of the limitations of behavioural and institutional Schumpeterianism to conceptualise the problem as a critical danger to democratic practices and institutions. I do not mean to suggest, however, that this resurgence is the only significant challenge contemporary democracy faces. And this is something that can be seen when starting with the critical analysis of these two branches of Schumpeterianism. The contemporary institutional branch, in focusing so narrowly on the state as a potential site of domination, deflects attention from dominating social and economic relations. The behavioural branch, in dismissing ideology as a factor in democratic politics, illicitly neglects the whole traditional subject matter of ideology critique: how substantive ways of thinking arise in relation to particular social relations and structures, and as ways of making sense and responding to those social relations and structures. One way to think of white nationalism and the far right, then, is as movements that 'make sense' of a variety of related social, economic and political relations – relations often characterised by profound differences in power and privilege –

in a very particular and dangerous way. Both in academia and in public discourse, there is debate about whether disadvantages faced resulting from unequal economic relations cause Trump supporters and European populists to scapegoat immigrants, or whether, on the contrary, racial resentment causes the same people to perceive economic unfairness and dislocation in a particular way. That starkly binary causal choice is probably too simplistic, especially if we consider how processes of ideological change play out in historical time. But the question does correctly identify the broader terrain of concern for democratic theory: all the social, economic and political relations that may foster domination and undermine political freedom and equality.

Contemporary democratic theory can still learn a great deal from Schumpeter – with provisos derived from the analysis here. First, ignoring or bracketing Schumpeter's own elite and inegalitarian sympathies cannot undo their thorough conditioning of his democratic theory. Some of the most pronounced strains in both behavioural and institutional Schumpeterianism arise from forgetting this, and attempting to bind elements of Schumpeter's thought to democratic commitments and aims he did not share. A better approach would be to explore the practical challenges of theorising democracy by reflecting, comprehensively and critically, upon Schumpeter as an example of a social theorist enmeshed in given historical context – analysing the difficulties and the choices he confronted, as an admirer of elite rule and of the European old regime who had to come to terms with the transformative rise of democratic practices and beliefs. Second, democratic theorists can profit more from adopting the polymathic approach to social theory he employed throughout his career, encompassing everything from mathematical economics to interpretive history, than from adopting specific assumptions and definitions plucked from *Capitalism, Socialism and Democracy*. There is much to appreciate in an approach to democratic theory that emphasises the continual struggle against domination, but relying so heavily on Schumpeter's definition of democracy as an electoral 'institutional arrangement' has distracted institutional Schumpeterians from reflecting broadly on the many forms of domination at work in the contemporary world, and envisioning what democratic opposition to these forms of domination might entail. Such an approach would be, methodologically, a Schumpeterian endeavour – a historically informed exploration of social relations of power – though of course not an endeavour linked to his particular anti-democratic political commitments. Similarly, a realistic account about modes of political judgement that endanger democratic life would be a most welcome addition to contemporary political thought. But adopting Schumpeter's searing conclusions about ordinary people's judgement, treating observed weaknesses as permanent fixtures of human cognition, categorically distinct from the historically varied problem of ideology, from the varieties of shared beliefs that shape judgement – these choices are in themselves conceptually suspect. And they divert attention from critically analysing the substantively anti-democratic and undemocratic ideologies we find around us. A democratic theory that incorporated critical analysis of anti-democratic and undemocratic ideologies could build on Schumpeter's own understanding of ideology critique: a study of how groups understand the social world and explain to themselves their place in it, and the implications this has for politics. In short, a contemporary democratic theory that learned from Schumpeter – in these ways, *critically* – would be well positioned to investigate twenty-first-century movements and beliefs and twenty-first-century forms of domination that continually challenge the ability of people to govern themselves on terms of equality.

Notes

1 Schumpeter's later democratic theory should be viewed not only in this context, but also in light of his political commitments and the trajectory of his view of democracy over several decades (Medearis 2001, 2009, 1–33, 68–94).
2 The focus of Schumpeterian democracy (or his version of it), Shapiro says, is 'political institutions narrowly defined' (2003, 58).
3 For an earlier statement of the same distinction, see Shapiro's *State of Democratic Theory* (2003, 158). I am doubtful of this distinction between civil and political – especially the idea that there is some apolitical or non-contentious 'superordinate good' for every type of civil institution (Shapiro 2016, 32). But that is a debate for another place or time.
4 But see his different, earlier formulation in *The State of Democratic Theory* (2003, 4).
5 Much of Achen and Bartels's book is devoted to assessing retrospective voting theory (90–212). The authors claim that coastal New Jersey voters in the 1916 election punished Woodrow Wilson, the incumbent, for a series of shark attacks he could not possibly have caused or prevented (2016, 118–128). Achen and Bartel's argument is not so much that voters do not base their votes on events during incumbents' terms in office, as it is that they do this poorly and irrationally. But this portion of the book is less significant to me than their dismissal of ideological judgement and their proffered alternative: identity or group-based voting.
6 In their chapter on a 'group theory of politics', Achen and Bartels make only a fleeting reference to Karl Mannheim, but his 'sociology of knowledge' provides just the antidote they are seeking to undue individualism (1985). Mannheim writes that 'it is far from correct to assume' that what Achen and Bartels call the 'monadic individual' – in his words, 'an individual of more or less fixed absolute capacities' – generally 'confronts the world and in striving for the truth constructs a world-view out of the data of his experience' (26). But for Mannheim, this does not mean most individual human beings are just political ciphers or mimics. For Mannheim, it is a reminder only that '[K]nowledge is from the very beginning a co-operative process' (26).
7 We can put aside, for the moment, the precise causal connections between these emotions and ideologies, which are likely to be multiple and complex rather than simple and unidirectional.

References

Achen, C.H. and Bartels, L. M. (2016). *Democracy for Realists: Why Elections do not Produce Responsive Government*. Princeton, NJ: Princeton University Press.

Ansolabehere, S., Rodden, J. and Snyder, J.M. Jr. (2008). The strength of issues: Using multiple measures to gauge preference stability, ideological constraint, and issue voting. *American Political Science Review*, 102(2): 215–232.

Bagg, S. (2015). Can deliberation neutralise power? *European Journal of Political Theory*, online before print.

Bartels, L.M. (2008). *Unequal Democracy: The Political Economy of the New Gilded Age*. New York: Russell Sage Foundation.

Converse, P.E. (1964). The nature of belief systems in mass publics. *Critical Review*, 18(1–3): 1–75.

Geertz, C. (1973). Ideology as a cultural system. In: *The Interpretation of Cultures: Selected Essays* (pp. 193–233). New York: Basic Books.

Giddens, A. (1986) [1979]. *Central Problems in Social Theory: Action, Structure and Contradiction in Social Analysis*. Berkeley, CA: University of California Press.

Golder, M. (2016). Far right parties in Europe. *Annual Review of Political Science*, 19: 477–497.

Green, J.E. (2010a). *The Eyes of the People: Democracy in an Age of Spectatorship*. Oxford: Oxford University Press.

Green, J.E. (2010b). Three theses on Schumpeter: Response to Mackie.' *Political Theory*, 38(2): 268–275.

Green, J.E. (2016). *The Shadow of Unfairness: A Plebeian Theory of Liberal Democracy*. Oxford: Oxford University Press.

Hochschild, J. and Einstein, K.L. (2015). 'It isn't what we don't know that gives us trouble, it's what we know that ain't so.' Misinformation and democratic politics.' *British Journal of Political Science*, 45(3): 467–475.

Inbar, Y. and Pisarro, D.A. (2016). Pathogens and politics: Current research and new questions. *Social and Personality Psychology Compass*, 10(6): 365–374.

Inbar, Y., Pisarro, D.A. and Bloom, P. (2009). Conservatives are more easily disgusted than liberals. *Cognition and Emotion*, 23(4): 714–725.

Kunda, Z. (1990). The case for motivated reasoning. *Psychological Bulletin*, 108(3): 480–498.

Mannheim, K. (1985) [1936]. *Ideology and Utopia: An Introduction to the Sociology of Knowledge*. New York: Harcourt Brace Jovanovich.

Medearis, J. (2001). *Joseph Schumpeter's Two Theories of Democracy*. Cambridge, MA: Harvard University Press.

Medearis, J. (2009). *Joseph A. Schumpeter*. New York: Continuum.

Medearis, J. (2015). *Why Democracy is Oppositional*. Cambridge, MA: Harvard University Press.

Merolla, J.L. and Zechmeister, E.Z. (2009). *Democracy at Risk: How Terrorist Threats Affect the Public*. Chicago, IL: University of Chicago Press.

Nteta, T.M. and Schaffner, B. (2016). New poll shows trump supporters more likely to fear a majority-minority U.S. *Washington Post* 5 March. Available at www. washingtonpost.com/news/monkey-cage/wp/2016/03/05/new-poll-shows-trump-supporters-more-likely-to-fear-a-majority-minority-u-s/?utm_term=.63daec67820d.

Nyhan, B. and Reifler, J. (2010). When corrections fail: The persistence of political misperception. *Political Behavior*, 32(2): 303–330.

Parker, C.S. and Barreto, M.A. (2013). *Change They Can't Believe In: The Tea Party and Reactionary Politics in America*. Princeton, NJ: Princeton University Press.

Przeworski, A. (1991). *Democracy and the Market: Political and Economic Reforms in Eastern Europe and Latin America*. Cambridge: Cambridge University Press.

Przeworski, A. (1999). Minimalist conception of democracy: A defense. In: I. Shapiro and C. Hacker-Cordón (Eds.), *Democracy's Value* (pp. 23–55). Cambridge: Cambridge University Press.

Schumpeter, J.A. (1946). Review of *The Road to Serfdom* by F.A. Hayek. *The Journal of Political Economy*, 54(3): 269–270.

Schumpeter, J.A. (1989) [1949]. Science and Ideology. In: R.V. Clemence (Ed.), *Essays on Entrepreneurs, Innovations, Business Cycles, and the Evolution of Capitalism* (pp. 272–286). New Brunswick, NJ: Transaction, 1989

Schumpeter, J.A. (2008) [1942]. *Capitalism, Socialism and Democracy*. New York: HarperPerennial.

Shapiro, I. (1999). *Democratic Justice*. New Haven, CT: Yale University Press.

Shapiro, I. (2003). *The State of Democratic Theory*. Princeton, NJ: Princeton University Press.

Shapiro, I. (2016). *Politics Against Domination*. Cambridge, MA: Harvard University Press.

Sides, J. and Tesler, M. (2016). How political science helps explain the rise of Trump: Most voters aren't ideologues. *Washington Post*, 2 March. Available at www. washingtonpost.com/news/monkey-cage/wp/2016/03/02/how-political-science-helps-explain-the-rise-of-trump-most-voters-arent-ideologues/?utm_term=. f57e9c6defe1.

Tesler, M. and Sides, J. (2016). How political science helps explain the rise of Trump: The role of white identity and grievances. *Washington Post*, 3 March. Available at www.washingtonpost.com/news/monkey-cage/wp/2016/03/03/how-political-science-helps-explain-the-rise-of-trump-the-role-of-white-identity-and-grievances/?utm_term=.e2bc53cc0497.

Urbinati, N. (2006). *Representative Democracy*. Chicago, IL: University of Chicago Press.

Urbinati, N. (2014). *Democracy Disfigured: Opinion, Truth and the People*. Cambridge, MA: Harvard University Press.

Williamson, V., Skocpol, T. and Coggins, J. (2011). The Tea Party and the remaking of Republican conservatism. *Perspectives on Politics*, 9(1): 25–43.

10 Bringing the state into Schumpeter's model

Entrepreneurial states, socialisation of investment, creative-destruction management and China

Leonardo Burlamaqui

Introduction

> During the twentieth century, the line of evidence from Schumpeterian ideas to policies to outcomes is perhaps clearest in the high-performing East Asian economies of the late twentieth century, especially Japan, Korea, Taiwan, and Singapore.
>
> (McCraw 2007, 182)

McCraw's observation is an appropriate starting point for an inexcusably absent discussion with respect to Schumpeter's development theory: the absence of a proper role for the state within it.[1] As already mentioned and briefly discussed in Chapter 2, this constitutes another puzzle in Schumpeter's evolution, given the fact that early on, in 1918, in 'The crisis of the tax state', he explicitly acknowledged the key role of the state and of fiscal measures, and of policy in general, in shaping development processes.[2]

> Fiscal measures have created and destroyed industries, industrial regions, even where this was not their intent, and have in this manner contributed directly to the construction (and distortion) of the edifice of the modern economy.
>
> (1918, 101)

However, as Swedberg has pointed out, that essay was mostly concerned with whether the Austrian state as well as its economy would be able to withstand the financial pressures of World War I, or whether they would break down (1991, 47). The answer given by Schumpeter was that they should not break down, but only if reconstruction was left to the market economy and private entrepreneurs, and, ultimately, that an appropriate level of taxation was engineered, a tax policy that could preserve the state finances without putting too much pressure on private enterprise (1918, 126–127). Therefore, markets and private enterprise are seen as the engines of growth, which stands in conformity with his theory of economic development (TED). Notwithstanding the sentence above, '[f]iscal measures have created and destroyed industries, industrial regions ...' stands, along with the supremely insightful observation that ... '[t]here is a great difference between ... *entrepreneurial and rentiers states*'[3] (1918, 111, my emphasis), but they are not developed further and end up, from a theoretical point of view, orphans in the text.

The take-away here is that the 'tax state' essay is fundamentally a historical excursus within which an institutional and policy message is attempted: the modern state is dependent on a healthy private economy from which it extracts revenue. If no wealth is generated, there will be nothing to tax (1918, 112–114). A special emphasis is placed on not burdening entrepreneurial profit, the prize for successful innovation, with a heavy tax load. Ultimately, Schumpeter's characterisation of the tax state is essentially Austrian, with a Von Misean flavour, a perspective that would resurface with full force under the public choice approach championed by Buchanan, Tullock, Wagner and others (Buchanan and Wagner 1977, Buchanan, Tollison and Tullock 1980).

In point of fact, there is no incoherence so far. The way Schumpeter conceived his *The Theory of Economic Development* (1961), excludes the state by design. As I showed in Chapter 2, the economic system is analysed as self-regulating, and the roots of innovation and structural transformation are to be found in private entrepreneurial activity and credit creation by private banks. They are necessary and sufficient conditions for development. The state – the *tax* state – is bound to become a burden on that process if taxation is not carried out in a way that preserves entrepreneurial activity and innovation.

However, it's likely that Schumpeter's ideas started to change, or evolve, right after the publication of the 'tax state' essay. It is well known that in 1919 he was invited by Rudolf Hilferding and Emil Lederer, his former socialist colleagues in Boehm-Bawerk's seminar, to take part in the German Socialisation Commission (cf. Allen 1991, Vol. 1, Ch. 9). Although not a socialist, Schumpeter promptly accepted the invitation, quipping when asked about it that 'if somebody wants to commit suicide, it is a good thing if a doctor is present' (Allen 1991, Vol. 1, 163). Although the quip would underwrite his previous Austrian view on state-market boundaries, it did not reflect Schumpeter's work in the commission. He endorsed the commission's rationale of finding ways to increase the productivity of the German coal industry by bringing it under social or public control and worked hard to set it up. Specifically, he favoured 'a *public coal corporation* that would take *strong leadership* from the existing Coal Board' (Allen 1991, Vol. 1, 163–164, my emphasis). Such public enterprise would be run on the basis of productivity improvements and efficiency, and independently of (central) government interference and direction.

The commission's work was not exactly a success, but here I find three elements that are central for the discussion ahead: first, Schumpeter was hinting at a possibility he would further develop: the entrepreneurial action could take many forms. Not only 'new men' but 'new organisational forms' could get the job done, given the appropriate institutional settings, or circumstances.[4] Second, the state could develop, or acquire entrepreneurial skills and perform entrepreneurial functions. It could become an innovator. Schumpeter would come back to this point and I will show it. Third, this new organisational arrangement would concoct a sort of socialisation of investment, which, if managed properly in regard to productivity, efficiency and political independence, could rival (or even outpace) private entrepreneurship.

All three themes would be developed further, and more coherently, only in *Capitalism, Socialism and Democracy* (*CSD*), especially in the its third part, on socialism. I will try to show how they shape up there, and argue for their contemporary relevance. The truth of the matter is that Schumpeter's reflections and insights, demonstrated vividly by the Asian developmental states, as suggested by McCraw, and on 'steroids' by China, never made it into his 'models': neither the cycles models (*TED* and *BC*) nor the 'creative destruction' paradigm. However, there is no theoretical reason preventing us from working in that direction. The state functioning both as an entrepreneur for all seasons and as a lender of first resort is perfectly compatible with the 'creative-destruction' paradigm. In fact, it is a much-needed complement that shall improve it.

Capitalism, Socialism and Democracy constitutes, as just mentioned, the closest of a coherent set of propositions by Schumpeter on state action in economic affairs. They cover roughly three elements: the entrepreneurial state, socialisation of investment and 'creative-destruction management'. Nevertheless, there is a, slippery, trail in his previous works where these themes are already referenced.

Schumpeter and the state: entrepreneurial leadership, socialisation of investment and creative-destruction management

> In his 'Tax-State' paper, Schumpeter recognises the legitimate role of government, a theme that was developed at length in Capitalism, Socialism and Democracy.
>
> (Musgrave 1992)

In his substantive reworking of *The Theory of Economic Development* (which was in order for it to be published in English, which happened in 1934), the closing pages exhibit a new view, already taking place in his thinking about state action. In referring to the process of 'abnormal liquidation' brought about by the depressions and the possible measures towards mitigation of their predatory effects, he argues:

> But [instead of a policy of indiscriminate credit restriction] a *credit policy* is also conceivable – on the part of the individual banks as such, *but still*

more on the part of the Central Banks, with their influence upon the private banking world – which would differentiate between the phenomena of the normal process of the depression, which have an economic function, and the phenomena of the abnormal process, which destroy without function. *It is true, such a policy would lead far into a special variety of economic planning* which would infinitely increase the influence of political factors upon the fate of individual and groups.... Theoretically, it is of interest to establish that such a policy is not impossible and is not to be classed with chimeras or with measures which are by nature unsuited to attain their ends.

(Schumpeter 1961, 254, my emphasis)

In fact, what is being raised by the author is the functionality – and theoretical support – of a selective credit policy, orchestrated by the Central Bank and intended to differentiate the 'old' from the 'new' so as to prevent innovations from undergoing the destructive process inherent in depressions. The outcome would be a selective intervention, by the state, in order to preserve successful innovations from financial bankruptcy. It is obviously an exaggeration to label these actions as suggestive of a full-blown, state-directed industrial policy, but it is also evident that Schumpeter's arguments display a considerable change in his appraisal of state capacities and their potential to help manage creative destruction. The excursions get more explicit in *Business Cycles*.

Although absent from the theoretical sections of the book,[5] there are a host of passages in the 'historical outlines' chapters, which, very explicitly, address the state's entrepreneurial action in forging industry, and shaping economic rationalisation:

Was it not – again, in *Germany – the state rather than the entrepreneur which initiated modern industry? The answer is ... in the affirmative,* and with the dosing appropriate to each case, similar answers would have to be returned for other countries. The German principality in many cases ... directly filled the entrepreneurial function, particularly in mining. Beyond that it conditioned enterprise by reshaping the institutional framework (legal reforms and so on) and improving the environment (canal and road building and the like), and by fostering it in various ways, some of which in fact come within what we usually understand by mercantilist policy.

(1939, Vol. 2, 235, my emphasis)

However, Schumpeter's most comprehensive endorsement for the entrepreneurial state, in the book, comes from his analysis of the 'State-directed economy of Germany' between 1933 and 1938. At that time, the German economy was operating at almost full capacity and its investments were filled with innovations (Schumpeter 1939, Ch. 15; Landes 1969, Ch. 6; Tooze

2006). That chapter of *Business Cycles* allows for a critical evaluation of my argument,[6] inasmuch as it places us before Schumpeter's interpretation of a fully developed version of state-led capitalism in whose core was a state-induced industrial strategy.

> The outstanding feature is the rapid progress, practically without relapse, toward full employment of resources in general and labour in particular, in fact more than that: unmistakable symptoms of overemployment in our sense.... In many industries, shortage of labour.
>
> (Schumpeter, 1939, Vol. 2, 971)

In his attempt to diagnose the nature and effects of the 'government leadership and control' (ibid., p. 972), Schumpeter focuses on the state's leadership towards building a self-sufficient economy and on the measures for speeding expansion by analysing them through the lenses of their impact upon the introduction of innovations. In his words:

> A large part of the new investments in industry was for the development of resources that were to replace imported materials.... But that was not all. New things were done involving *the distinct entrepreneurial act that constitutes creative adaptation*.

To which he adds a note specifically referring to the role of the state:

> It gave leads. It exerted pressure. It helped in various ways in financing and promoting.... This active leadership was, of course, something very different from mere *control* or *regulation*, and also from mere *conditioning*.
>
> (Ibid., 973, my emphasis)

Schumpeter's argument concerning this matter is subtle but extremely relevant for the discussion. The crucial point in his interpretation does not concern state-directed investment or expansionary fiscal policy alone, but their operation under the framework of his theory: as fundamental structural transformation parameters, as carriers of industrial rationalisation, productivity increases and innovation. Therefore, policies should be selective and directed to maintain and speed the innovative process.

In contradistinction, antitrust – or trust busting – policies aiming to chain them according to a neoclassical 'perfectly competitive' normative standard could result, in a depression, and from an evolutionary perspective, in deepening market structure instabilities and even in discouraging future innovations. State intervention could thus also have a perverse effect, jeopardising the system's performance: it would, in addition, produce conflicts between public bureaucracy and private managers, bringing about a situation of reciprocal distrust which, according to Schumpeter, would neither be useful nor efficient. This argument is the basis of his rejection of Roosevelt's New Deal, or more precisely what he dubbed an anti-business bias of the New Deal policies.

However, in a piece on 'Economic theory and entrepreneurial history', written in 1949, one year before his passing, Schumpeter reinforces his changed perception of entrepreneurship, as a *function*, not necessarily attached to a person, and enthusiastically endorses state action towards innovation by the US Department of Agriculture:

> Finally, as has been often pointed out, the entrepreneurial function need not be embodied in a physical person and in particular in a single physical person. Every social environment has its own ways of filling the entre-preneurial function. For instance, the practice of farmers in this country has been revolutionised again and again by the introduction of methods worked out in the Department of Agriculture and by the Department of Agriculture's success in teaching these methods. *In this case then it was the Department of Agriculture that acted as an entrepreneur.*
>
> (1949, 260)

No doubt his views had changed at that point. Back to the German state-directed economy, and into the financial policies' sphere, Schumpeter explicit approval of targeted credit, curbing speculative behaviour and, if needed, 'business and social disciplining' policies, were justified on the same grounds, stimulating investments, productivity increases and innovations. In this regard, we read:

> It is reasonable to attribute [such success] to the manner in which it was done in this case, and to concomitant policy.... Creation of purchasing power was an incident but it was not pursued as an end. Speculation was not encouraged, infraction of social discipline was discouraged. No attempt was made to raise costs.... Saving and accumulation were encouraged ... and in many instances, enforced.
>
> (1939, Vol. 2, 975)

To which he adds in a footnote:

> ... Compulsion to invest in some lines frequently implied prohibition to invest in other lines, but these prohibitions were no longer dictated by the recovery purpose and carry a different meaning.
>
> (Ibid.)

The crucial point is Schumpeter's positive evaluation on this redesign of the boundaries between public and private spheres. It should be stressed that his opinion is not grounded on the political regime in course, but rather on the position of the state vis-à-vis long-term economic rationality. In Schumpeter's words:

The strength of the Fascist State as against group interests [rested in] its
fundamental attitude to economic life (which) facilitated a behaviour in
accordance with the rules of long economic rationality.

(1939, Vol. 2, 976)

Based upon this diagnosis, Schumpeter makes a consideration that calls our
attention to the relationship between structural change and macroeconomic
stability:

Theoretically it is possible so to plan the sequence of innovations as to
iron out cycles: but after strenuous periods of advance there will be recessions even in the corporate State: most of the symptoms of *depressions*,
however, need not occur at all....

(1939, Vol. 2, 977)

That's clearly a receipt for socialisation of investment and 'creative-destruction
management' which would, as he points out, in a similar way Keynes did,
smooth the range of economic fluctuations – or the business cycle – and
eliminate the wasteful, and theoretically unnecessary, 'abnormal liquidation'
brought about by depressions. In addition, it is worth recalling those were the
same policies that in Joan Robinson's phrasing, caused the German economy
'to eliminate unemployment when Keynes was still concerned about explaining its causes' (Robinson 1972).

Summing up: state-guided selective intervention, entrepreneurial leadership, encouragement of investment cartels, efficiency and productivity
improvements, and industrial rationalisation were the elements stressed by
Schumpeter in his rather positive account of the German economic policy
and industrial strategy in the thirties.[7] The extraction of analytical considerations from this maze of massive historical evaluation is not the easiest task, but
once one gets through them, it appears that Schumpeter was developing an
approach – a hidden one – to state involvement in economic activity. To use
his own taxonomy, it is more than a 'vision', but less than a theory. Nonetheless, it provides us with enough material to propose that it is possible to
extract from Schumpeter an analytical framework where development can be
forged, facilitated and accelerated by state action. If this will in fact happen is
a matter of state structures, capacities and type of political coalitions in place.
In case it does happen, the linchpin is an entrepreneurial state.[8]

The elaboration on these arguments would only be done, however, in his
1942 book. In *Capitalism, Socialism and Democracy*, Schumpeter is already fully
operating, as we have seen in Chapter 2, on the concepts of competition via
innovations, creative destruction and corporate capitalism where big companies and oligopolistic market structures shape the typical economic structure. In this context, there is a whole set of industrial policy measures that
acquire their substantive rationality only within this theoretical framework.
State-guided cartel policies, as instruments of stabilisation and/or speeding

technical progress, are fully understandable only under this theory of competition as a creative-destruction process filled with technological and financial uncertainties, the threat of cut-throat price competition and the possibility of bankruptcies and involuntary unemployment.

> Restraints of trade of the cartel type, as well as those consisting only of tacit understandings about price competition may *be effective under conditions of depression. As far as they are, they may in the end produce not only steadier but also greater expansion of total output* than could be secured by an entirely uncontrolled rush that cannot fail to be studded by catastrophes.
>
> (1942, 91, my emphasis)

Its counterpart would be a cartel-monitoring set of measures designed in order to guarantee their 'efficiency commitment' and encourage entrepreneurial strategies concerning technological creativity and organisational rationalisation.

> It is certainly as conceivable that an all-pervading cartel system might sabotage all progress as it is that it might realise, with smaller social and private costs, all that perfect competition is supposed to realise. *That is why our argument does not amount to a case against state regulation. It does show that there is no general case for 'trust-busting' or the prosecution of everything that qualifies as a restraint of trade.* Rational as distinguished from vindictive regulation by public authorities turns out to be a an extremely delicate problem, which not every government agency … can be trusted to solve.
>
> (1942, 91 my emphasis)

However, as already mentioned, Schumpeter's most effective support of an active entrepreneurial state along with an institutional framework where investment is largely socialised is not contained in the second part of *CSD*, but rather in the third part, where he discusses and compares the potential efficiency of corporate capitalism to an eventual 'socialist project' of economic administration. His key thesis is that just as corporate capitalism represents an acceleration of potential growth and economic rationality vis-à-vis Adam Smith's early stage capitalism, a 'socialist economy' might as well surpass corporate capitalism by means of these same criteria. Here two issues must be clarified: (a) what Schumpeter understood as a socialist economy, and (b) what was his reasoning to support its potential superiority.

The analysis departs from a, well-known, rhetorical question: Can socialism work? His answer is 'of course it can' (1942, 167). Yet, Schumpeter's definition of socialism does not focus on state seizure of the means of production nor on the eradication of private property, but rather on their socialisation, which involves essentially redesigning the frontiers and modes of interaction between the private and public spheres.[9] In his own words:

By socialist society we shall designate an institutional pattern in which the control over means of production and over production itself is vested with a central authority – or, as we may say, in which, as a matter of principle, the economic affairs of society belong to the public and not to the private sphere.

(1942, 168)

The core concept in the definition is control by a central authority. The author also does not mention absence of private property that could, and should exist. About the day-to-day operations of that system, 'regulated managerial freedom' should be the norm:

There may also be a supervising and checking authority – a kind of *cour des comptes* that could conceivably even have the right to veto particular decisions. As regards the second point, some freedom of action must be left, and almost any amount of freedom might be left, to the 'men on the spot,' say, the managers of the individual industries or plants. For the moment, I will make the bold assumption that the rational amount of freedom is experimentally found and actually granted so that efficiency suffers neither from the unbridled ambitions of subordinates nor from the piling up on the desk of the minister of reports and unanswered questions.

(1942, 168)

Third, the innovative process could be coordinated, taking into account timing and locational considerations. In the process of creative destruction, creation would be performed in a coordinated manner and destruction by means of exit policies:

... *the planning of progress*, in particular the systematic co-ordination and the orderly distribution in time of new ventures in all lines would be incomparably more effective in the prevention of bursts ... and of depressive reactions ... than any automatic or manipulative variations of the interest rate or the supply of credit can be.... And the process of discarding the obsolete, that in capitalism – specially in competitive capitalism – means paralysis and losses that are in part functionless could be reduced to what discarding the obsolete actually conveys to the layman's mind within *a comprehensive plan providing in advance for the shifting to other uses of the non-obsolete complements of the obsolete plants or pieces of equipment*.

(Ibid., 200, my emphasis)

Fourth, the relation between technological change and employment could be also rationalised by coordination policies so that it would be possible to 're-direct the men to other employments which, if planning lives up to its possibilities at all might in each case be waiting for them' (ibid., p. 201).

Finally, the resistance to changes could be 'strongly discouraged', and consequently the promotion of innovations would be operated in a quicker and more rational way.

Summing up: what Schumpeter considered as possibilities of a 'socialist economy', measures whose implementation would render it more rational and efficient than corporate capitalism itself, are, in my view, crucial elements of a structural transformation agenda tied to a different type of capitalism: although rejected on an a priori basis by mainstream economic theory, and therefore largely absent[10] from Anglo-American thinking about market-capitalism,[11] they are the 'bread and butter' of the German-Scandinavian pattern of 'alliance capitalism'. Their central elements are grounded exactly on the ideological acceptance of state involvement in the economic sphere besides a non–individualist economic culture (although compatible with a high degree of individual freedom, as Germany and the Scandinavian countries unmistakably show), and on an economic and institutional structure marked by a substantively higher degree of socialisation. It should be stressed that this is my interpretation of Schumpeter's ideas, although the author appears to be pointing in the same direction when he states that:

> ... the whole of our argument might be put in a nutshell by saying that *socialization* means a stride beyond big business on the way that has chalked out by it or, what amounts to the same thing, that socialist management may conceivable prove as superior to big-business capitalism has proved to be to the kind of competitive capitalism of which the English industry a hundred years ago was the prototype.
>
> (Schumpeter 1942, 196)

The crucial point I want to underline here is the author's definition of 'socialism' as 'an institutional pattern ... where the economic issues of society belong to the public sphere'. There should not be any doubt what this definition really addresses: the centrality of the economic role of the state in forging and guiding structural transformation. The Asian developmental state, which piloted the most astonishing development 'explosion' of the twentieth century's second half presents strong evidence of the power of Schumpeter's conception. Yet, it is China, the most successful case of development as leapfrogging, that impersonates the core traces of the Schumpeterian entrepreneurial state. The Chinese state executes simultaneously, as I will try to show below, the functions of ephor in finance, entrepreneur-in-chief in science, innovation and crucial decisions in investment, and creative-destruction manager, which means it works within Schumpeter's conception of socialisation of investment. In the next section I will show how China's *managed* structural transformation provides a solid empirical foundation for Schumpeter's analytical insights on the entrepreneurial state.

Schumpeter (rekindled) goes to China: the Chinese entrepreneurial state and structural transformation

> Firms around the world face ever more intense competition from their Chinese rivals. China is not the first country to industrialise, but none has ever made the leap so rapidly and on such a monumental scale. Little more than a decade ago Chinese boom towns churned out zips, socks and cigarette lighters. Today the country is at the global frontier of new technology in everything from mobile payments to driverless cars.
>
> (*The Economist*, 24 September 2017)

In 1976, China barely managed to cover the costs of sending its highest-ranking dignitary to speak at the UN (Walter and Howie 2012, 12). By 2014, the country had become the second larger national economy, the largest exporter, the largest manufacturer, the possessor of the world's largest current account surplus,[12] the holder of the biggest amount of foreign reserves as well as the largest sovereign wealth fund (World Bank 2012, 25; Bergsten, Freeman, Lardy and Mitchell 2010, 9–10). The country also exhibits the fastest rate of growth of any nations over the past two decades, an extremely fast rate of technological upgrading (Zhou, Lazonick and Sun: 2016; Keidel and Burlamaqui 2015; Keidel 2007 and 2011; Gallagher and Porzecanski 2010, Ch. 4; Pettis 2013) and one of the most successful set of policies for poverty alleviation, which allows it to take millions above the poverty line every year. In a phrase: China has become an economic superpower.

In fact, in 2014, according to the International Monetary Fund (IMF), China *surpassed* the US economy in size, measured in purchasing power parity terms. The Chinese economy is now worth $17.6tn, slightly higher than the $17.4tn the IMF estimates for the US (Giles 2014). This is highly symbolic data: for the first time in more than 140 years, the US has lost the title of the world's largest economy – it has been overtaken by China. The bottom line is clear, China did not 'catch-up' with the West. It leap-frogged.[13] In addition, let me recall that the country is a nuclear power and has veto power at the UN Security Council.[14]

To answer the question of how all this happened is well beyond the purpose of this chapter, but that's the 'factual background' that I think is appropriate to use when discussing the kind of institutional configuration that brought China to these highly successful achievements. The reason is, that looking at China as a 'big success case' (although obviously not lacking problems) should invite searching for lessons instead of recommending emulation (especially of Anglo-American practices and institutions).

However, the main purpose in what follows is analytical, not descriptive, and the central claim is that China's speed and ability to leapfrog its peer nations in the last three decades stems, largely, from the fact that it possesses a fully developed entrepreneurial state (ES).[15] From a theoretical point of view,

China's achievements reaffirm all the elements contained in Schumpeter's vision of successful state involvement in economic activity: the centrality of selective credit for innovation and development, the key role of the state in steering innovation and exercising leadership towards development, the strategic role of investment-development banks to provide the necessary funding, and the functionality of financial restraint to avoid the build-up of 'financial casinos'.

China's development trajectory has them all. Briefly discussed below, they point towards a two-fold conclusion: first, it suggests that the concept of entrepreneurial state, whose roots are in Schumpeter, as we saw, should synthesise three core elements: (a) A 'Hilferding-Schumpeter' type of banking system; (b) state-directed involvement in forging structural transformation agendas and implementing them, which means performing the Schumpeterian entrepreneurial function; and (c) a robust degree of socialisation of investment, which would allow it to implement 'creative destruction management policies' and exercise financial regulation (or 'restraint speculation'). The second conclusion is that the Chinese State encapsulates all three dimensions and therefore should be taken as the prototype of a Schumpeterian entrepreneurial state. These are admittedly bold propositions, which should invite further debate and discussion.

Conceptualising the entrepreneurial state in China

The state was (is) a prominent, key, actor in East-Asian industrial transformation. China followed the path, and went further. Concerning ES's first element: from a financial perspective, China is Schumpeter on steroids (see Burlamaqui 2015 for a first attempt at this conceptualisation). To be more precise, what Minsky characterised, echoing Hilferding, as a (reinvigorated) form of 'finance capitalism'[16]; a financial system dominated by development banks with close ties with commerce and, especially, industry, and geared towards finance for development (Hilferding 1981; Minsky 1978, 1996; and Wray 2010, for a discussion of finance capitalism, as well as its demise in the West).[17]

If accessed through its finance-investment behaviour, China's banking system – the 'Big 4' banks plus China's Development Bank and their SIV's ramifications[18] – is the newest incarnation of the Hilferding-Schumpeter model of finance capitalism. Furthermore, they are, today, the biggest banks in the world. And they are public-policy and development banks. The particularly 'Minskyian' traces in the model are the pervasiveness of speculative finance, the build-up of situations of 'financial fragility', but also the presence of a 'Big Bank' and of robust financial governance.[19] An important point to stress here is that animal spirits in the Chinese version of the Hilferding-Schumpeter model come largely from the public policy and investment banks, that is, from the state. It is public-issued credit, not private wealth, that funds the bulk of structural transformation. In that institutional configuration, development springs largely from 'socialised investment'.

The second element backing up the ES concept refers to forging science and innovation. Again, the Chinese state is the prototype for executing these functions. China's five-year plans, as well as its strategic longer-term proposals, such as China 2030 and – more recently – the One Belt One Road (OBOR) initiative, configure full-blown cases of exercising Schumpeter's entrepreneurial function. In fact, the developmental states – especially in their Asian incarnations – are different forms of a 'Schumpeterian- or innovation-oriented State'.[20]

The third element for structuring the concept of ES is the presence of a robust degree of socialisation of investment. I showed this is key in Schumpeter's endorsement of public entrepreneurship, but Keynes provides, in that realm, a broader understanding of its meaning. As stated in *The General Theory*'s last chapter:

> The State will have to exercise a guiding influence on the propensity to consume partly through its scheme of taxation, partly by fixing the rate of interest, and partly, perhaps, in other ways. Furthermore, it seems unlikely that the influence of banking policy on the rate of interest will be sufficient by itself to determine an optimum rate of investment. I conceive, therefore, that a somewhat comprehensive socialisation of investment will prove the only means of securing an approximation to full employment; though this need not exclude all manner of compromises and of devices by which public authority will co-operate with private initiative.
>
> (1936, 377–378)

Keynes's central message for conceptualising the entrepreneurial state, I suggest, is that it should extend itself much beyond the strictly 'Schumpeterian dimensions' (finance, entrepreneurship, innovation and creative-destruction management). Income distribution, employment, regulation and supervision and public–private partnerships were already at the core of Keynes vision. However, the relevant, and scarcely noticed, fact I would like to call the reader's attention to is the close resemblance between Keynes's idea of socialisation of investment and Schumpeter's, previously discussed, conceptualisation of 'socialism'. Schumpeter's broad – and unconventional – characterisation of socialism provides us with a concrete illustration of his arguments of why 'socialism' *can* work and *can* beat 'capitalism' on the grounds of conflict management and economic efficiency. If we take China as the materialisation of the Schumpeter-Keynes concepts of entrepreneurial state plus socialisation of investment, the result is, I submit, a very strong case for their policies and institutional reform prescriptions. And China should be presented as their poster country.

McGregor (2010) gives a good example, which sums up the whole picture:

> Most foreigners dealing with large Chinese state companies in the early days of economic reform – he writes – felt much like the Japanese executives from the giant Mitsubishi conglomerate negotiating to build a power plant for Baoshan Steel.... The Japanese were aggrieved when the Chinese side got the better of them during the talks and they were forced into concessions. *'Yes, you win the negotiations,'* the Mitsubishi *executives exclaimed. 'But it was your national team fighting our company team!'* Chen Jinhua, a titan of state industry who recounted this story in his biography, said the Japanese were right. 'We had invited many capable experts from China's electrical power system to join our negotiating team, but Mitsubishi, as a single company, had been unable to do so,' Chen wrote. 'This example showed the superiority of our wide socialist co-operation.'
>
> (McGregor 2010, Locations 1155–1161, my emphasis)

An institution that combines the functions of macro-strategist (managing interest and exchange rates, capital flows along with prices and financial stability); venture-capitalist-in-chief (forging and funding industrial, innovation and technology policies) and creative-destruction management (stimulating the creative part of the process in order to speed productivity enhancement and innovation diffusion and acting as a buffer to its destructive dimension) clearly 'qualifies' as entrepreneurial.[21] Summing up, from a Schumpeterian (rekindled) perspective, the Chinese entrepreneurial state encompasses the functions of ephor, entrepreneur-in-chief and policy coordinator.

The entrepreneurial state in finance

China's development trajectory fully supports Schumpeter's emphasis on reliance on credit and the banking system as sine-qua-non-conditions for successful development processes. However, the first fact to register when looking at the Chinese financial sector is that the state and publicly owned banks are by far the biggest players. The framework of China's current financial system was set in the early 1990s. The process of establishing a legal framework for these reforms gathered momentum with the passage by the National People's Congress (NPC) of a central bank law, a commercial bank law and a company law. China in the mid-1990s created the so-called policy banks, for agriculture, foreign trade and domestic infrastructure, as a way of relieving commercial banks of the burden of making government policy-directed loans – which continued on a large scale nevertheless (Keidel 2007, 1). As for financial regulation, the Chinese system is lean and quite straightforward. The financial sector is regulated by one bank – the People's Bank of China (PBOC, the central bank[22]) and three commissions: the regulatory commissions for banking, securities and insurance.

The banking sector falls under the supervision of the People's Bank of China and the China Banking Regulatory Commission (Cousin 2011, 21). The China Banking Regulatory Commission (CBRC) was established in March 2003 with the aim of increasing the independence of the central bank and, especially, making the regulatory function of financial institutions more robust. The CBRC is the supervisor of financial institutions under the leadership of the State Council. It turned to be a key player in the guidance of the financial system through reform and recapitalisation after the Asian Crisis and, even more, in preventing China's financial system from diving into the kind of 'casino capitalism' that had been growing in the US and all over Europe since the eighties.[23] Lardy affirms this very clearly:

> Most obviously, since China's financial regulatory agencies had steadfastly refused to permit the creation of complex derivative products in the domestic market and severely limited financial institutions' exposure to foreign sources of these products, Chinese financial institutions had little exposure to toxic financial assets.
>
> (2011, Kindle Locations 452–454)

In fact, when in the summer of 2008, a small group of foreign 'financial experts' headed to China to give financial advice, Wang Qishan, the vice-premier in charge of China's financial sector, quickly made it clear that China had little to learn from the visitors about its financial system. His message was, concisely: 'You have your way. We have our way. And our way is right!' (McGregor 2010, Locations 51–52). In the same vein, Chen Yuan, the celebrated chair of China's Development Bank was thinking along these same lines when he declared, in July 2009: '[We] should not bring that American stuff and use it in China. Rather, we should develop around our own needs and build our own banking system' (Yuan quoted by Walter and Howie 2012, 27).

They had a point. If we look at Chinese Banks's capitalisation and non-performing loans at the height of the 'global financial crisis' (compared to JP Morgan, the go-to bank for the Obama administration), the data speak for themselves.

Figures 10.1 and 10.2 provide a snapshot of what 'socialisation of finance' (Schumpeter-style) can produce by combining robust financial regulation with countercyclical measures and a strategic stimulus package (Keynes and Minsky).[24] However, the most *entrepreneurial* player in China's finance is China's Development Bank (CDB). Sanderson and Forsythe put it concisely: 'In one decade, CDB has become the financial enabler of both China's global expansion and domestic boom' (2013, Introduction).

With that strong statement, the authors begin their analysis of what they claim to be 'the core of China's state capitalism' … '[a] system of

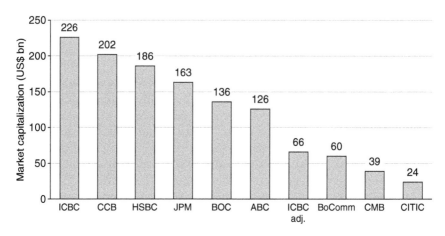

Figure 10.1 Chinese Bank's capitalization compared with J P Morgan (JPM) in 2010.
Source: Walter and Howie, Kindle Location 1069.

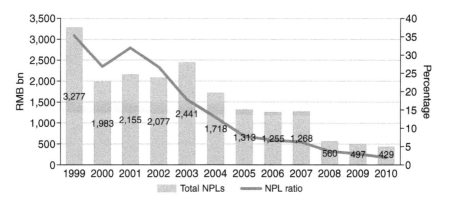

Figure 10.2 Non-performing loans of top Chinese banks: 1999–2010.
Source: Walter and Howie, Kindle Location 1114.

government-controlled banks and companies that many development countries see as an alternative to a freer market-focused system' (ibid.). Founded in
1994, with 'global operations springing from Asia to Africa and Latin-
America', with total assets of 1.7 trillion dollars and a non-performing loan
ratio of 0.4 per cent, CDB is in fact the 'pilot agency' of China's aggressive
financial diversification in the last ten to 15 years. In 2011 CDB had a loan
portfolio of around US$884 billion and 'a business presence in 116 economies
around the globe (Chairman's message for the 2011 CDB Annual Report
www.cdb.com.cn/english/Column.asp).

CDB's hallmark financial innovation was the system of local government
finance, which transformed China's landscape in just over a decade. To

understand this innovation, I have to refer to the reversal of one of the core principles of the Communist Revolution: the redistribution of land from rich property owners to landless peasants. Between 1996 and 1997, as the Asian crisis started, countercyclical spending on infrastructure in China doubled, and by 2002, it had risen by nearly three times. This massive urbanisation was a sensible response to collapsing 'global demand', an event that would be repeated in 2008–2009. However, it came with a serious downside, requiring a reappropriation of land by the state as a condition to create 'development zones' where bullet trains, sports complexes, shopping malls, apartment blocks and all kinds of urban facilities were produced/erected at a very fast pace.

The land reappropriation was the equivalent of a vast enclosure movement where millions of peasants were obliged to leave their land in order to give way to urban expansion.[25] This growth spurt of urban construction required finance and funding on a large scale, but there was still a problem to solve. In 1994, China's premier Zu Ronjin cut local government off from direct borrowing due to spiralling inflation. In the words of Chen Yuan:[26] 'While our national government enjoys virtually unlimited credit, the initiators of urbanisation projects, local governments, have little' (www.cdb.com.cn/english/NewsInfo.asp, and Sanderson and Forsythe 2012). Here, CDB enters the scene. The bank is funded by treasury bonds, which are typically bought by China's commercial banks, and had no difficulty in giving seed money to local governments to start the projects. However, more credit would have to follow in order to provide for the full funding of the projects. Collateral was the problem to solve.

Here, Yuan's, or, better, the state's, entrepreneurial vision coupled with CDB's innovation solved it. Yuan knew that urbanisation would vastly increase land prices and land was, now, in the hands of local governments, which meant that local governments were sitting on a potential 'gold mine'. The innovation was the local-government financing vehicle (LGFV), a public SIV, a company set up by local governments to allow them to spend beyond the limits of their budgets (Sanderson and Forsythe 2012). They would get additional money from CDB but through LGFVs, giving land as collateral, collateral whose value was bound to increase because of investments made possible by the bank's strategy. Higher land prices would mean more local government income; hence, more room for loans – and spending.

This was a self-fulfilling strategy, a type of financial operation already devised by Soros (1987) who pointed out that the willingness of a bank to finance an investment project has a direct impact on its viability and thus, on its returns, and therefore, on its price (Kregel 2001). It was also a Schumpeterian strategy where credit allowed investment to occur, raised the value of collateral and, as the investment matured, generated the cash-flows to repay the loan. The 'Wuhu Model', as it was labelled,[27] worked. As Sanderson and Forsythe recount: '[this system] managed to transform a sleepy city into a bustling metropolis that today is home to one of China's most prominent car makers, Chery Automobile, which happens to be owned by one of the first LGFVs'.

Furthermore, the model's success in Wuhu was replicated across the country, with CDB lending money to LGFVs in Shanghai (home to former president Jiang Zemin), Tianjin (home to Premier Wen Jiabao) and Suzhou. The system spread across the country, and came into its own in 2008 when it helped shield China from the worst effects of the global financial crisis. Now, every province in China has set up such companies to finance infrastructure investments (Sanderson and Forsythe 2013, 9–12).

At this point, the reader should be wondering the obvious: Wasn't that precisely the type of financial behaviour that produced the sub-prime crisis in the US – a leveraged lending binge backed by the assumption that real-estate prices would never collapse? If so, why so much enthusiasm for it? My answer to that question is no, and for several reasons, all related to the existence and course of action of the Chinese entrepreneurial state. First, all the players involved were public entities. The loans came from public banks, to local governments, and had guarantees from both the People's Bank of China and the Ministry of Finance (MOF). Second, under those circumstances what we have is a state-sponsored, public-bank-funded expansion, which could last for a very long time. And it did. The non-performing-loan rates consistently declined for the top Chinese banks between 1999 and 2010 (see Figure 10.2 above).

Third, in the worst-case scenario, the banks could become filled with 'bad loans'. Even then, they would never face credit freeze or a 'let the market do its job' in the way that it happened in the – difficult to under-stand – Lehman Brothers decision.[28] The banks would be recapitalised again, and the collateral would still be there, waiting for the urban migra-tion already gaining momentum. However, that scenario never material-ised. Fourth, and critical, there was no 'destructive lending' in the process: no 'NINJA' loans, no synthetic layers of leverage over leverage (naked selling or derivatives such as CDOs and CDSs) pilling over the loans to enhance trader's gains, and no betting against a 'client' such as Goldman Sachs – ABACUS, Paulson style.

Finally, and most importantly, the Party treats its banks as basic utilities that provide unlimited capital to the cherished state-owned enterprises (McGregor 2010, 27). Zhou Xiaochuan, a PBOC director framed the purpose of the banking system in a straightforward way when discussing the need for the previous banking reforms-cum-recapitalisation: '… China's financial system would be a drag on its economic growth, making it imposs-ible for the system *to service the economy and support development*' (2009, quoted by Cousin 2011, my emphasis).

I close this section with a reference to the current discussion over China's escalating debt coupled with the speedy increase of 'shadow banking' organisa-tions. Both issues are of concern – no doubt about that. From a Minskyan per-spective, they are also destabilising factors in China's financial evolution, as Wray, Kregel, Pettis, Sheng and others have warned. The easy escape from that discussion would be the suggestion that it's too early to tell – which is true.

However, let me make two points here and leave them for further reflection. First, in contrast with other financial systems in place, China, beside having a smooth relationship between its treasury and central bank, is home to five of the largest banks in the world, and they are all public. In case of any financial distress, these institutions can, as I pointed out above, absorb a vast amount of bad debts and expand their balance sheets considerably and continually – in the same fashion the FED did – with the advantage of having no legislative constraints to doing so. In sum, China has Minsky's Big Bank and Big Government, on steroids, along with its hands-on financial regulation. As Schumpeter put it, in another context, it's like a car that can speed up more confidently *because* it has good brakes.

Second, in their recently released books, Barry Naughton and Andrew Sheng, two seasoned researchers of China's economic and financial affairs, back what I have just affirmed with robust empirical investigation. According to Naughton and Tsai: 'Despite progress toward marketization and opening of finance, and the ongoing reality of shadow banking, on balance, state control over finance remains considerable. This is evident both in the banking system and in equity markets' (2015, Kindle Location 796). As for Sheng:

> With the economy still growing at 6–7 percent per annum, low fiscal deficit, a high savings rate and very large foreign reserves, the book concludes that a systemic financial meltdown is unlikely as China has adequate resources and policy flexibility to address what is essentially a domestic debt problem with no direct global implications'
>
> (Sheng and Soon 2016, Kindle Locations 311–312)

Past and current performance doesn't guarantee future outcomes but, so far, the evidence does not look bad.

The entrepreneurial state in industrial and technology policy

China's twelfth five-year plan for 2011 to 2015 was launched in March 2011. The plan highlights the importance of the 'magic seven' industries: (1) energy saving and environmental protection, (2) next-generation information technology, (3) biotechnology, (4) high-end manufacturing, (5) new energy, (6) new materials and (7) clean-energy vehicles. The plan's objective is to 'shape' those industries in order to raise their share from 3% to 15% of the economy by 2020.[29] No wonder that, way before the plan's announcement, China's banks were already pouring money in, in order to fund the long-term projects whose purpose is to turn that scenario into reality.

In fact, Chinese companies have started to win first places in global markets. Huawei has overtaken Sweden's Ericsson to become the world's largest telecoms-equipment maker. The company is becoming an increasingly powerful global player, capable of going head-to-head with the best in intensely competitive markets. It follows Haier, which is already the leading white-goods maker; now Lenovo is challenging Hewlett-Packard as the world's biggest PC maker. Much more will follow (cf. *The Economist*, 2012). *The Economist*'s piece also raises a key issue from the perspective of 'Western competitors': 'Western governments are also suspicious of the subsidies, low-interest loans and generous export credits lavished on favored champions'. The article has the right perception. The arsenal behind China's industrial and technology policies is formidable and to downplay it would be a huge mistake.

Take environment: in 2010, China invested some $51.1 billion into clean energy, the largest investment by any country in the world. However, in 2006, four years before that record, two Chinese companies were already on the list of the top ten solar-cell producers. In 2010, six made the list, according to a BNEF report.[30] Among them is Yingli, founded in 1998, and one of the biggest beneficiaries of CDB loans in the solar industry, borrowing at least $1.7 billion in dollar-denominated loans from CDB from 2008 through early 2012.[31] In 2009, Yingli opened offices in New York and San Francisco; by the year's end, it held 27% of the California market. China simply took over. *'In 2011, the country supplied some 72 percent of global crystalline-silicon module production, the most popular type of solar module that converts light to energy'* (Sanderson and Forsythe 2012, 150, my emphasis). A clear and stunning case of leapfrogging.

In fact, 2010 saw an explosion of loans to renewable energy, mostly from CDB. The bank lent $14.7 billion to clean energy and other energy-saving projects. The European Investment Bank lent 8 billion for clean energy projects in 2010; BNDES lent $3.16 billion and the US Federal Financing Bank $2.12 billion. In all, since 2010, CDB – alone – has made available at least $47.3 billion in credit lines to support Chinese solar and wind companies .

Let's return to telecom and, in particular, to Huawei. A private firm founded in 1987 with just 21,000 Yuan, a bit more than $5,000 at the time, Huawei at first struggled to win customers even in China. In 2012, as mentioned, it surpassed Ericsson to become the world's largest telecoms-equipment maker. Now, it is a $32-billion business empire with 140,000 employees, customers in 140 countries and 65% of its revenue coming from outside China. In Europe, it is involved in over half of the superfast 4G telecoms networks that have been announced, and it has become a strong competitor in mobile phones, In Africa, Huawei's cheap but effective equipment helped make the continent's mobile-telecoms revolution possible (The Economist 2012).

On 27 December 2004, in Beijing, Huawei and CDB signed a $10 billion agreement for overseas markets, the first of many CDB credit lines to its customers across the developing world that would allow it to gain significant market share. It was also the beginning of CDB's support of Chinese firms to 'go global'. In April 2005, Huawei and CDB signed a risk-sharing 'win–win' agreement to share information on clients and projects after the loan had been dispensed. In December 2005, Vodafone Group, then the world's largest

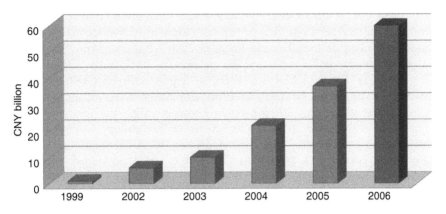

Figure 10.3 Huawei's overseas sales after CDB loan (CNY billion).[33]
Source: Sanderson and Forsythe.

mobile phone company, named Huawei its first Chinese-approved supplier of network equipment. Huawei's road to global domination had begun[32] (Sanderson and Forsythe 2012, 160) (Figure 10.3). I am not aiming to provide a comprehensive case-study here, but the one-liner is public funding and, ultimately, China's entrepreneurial state acted, via CDB, as the key player in forging and backing up the whole process.

The entrepreneurial state and socialisation of investment: OBOR as China's global strategy

China has amassed more than US$3 trillion in foreign reserves. This places its entrepreneurial state in a very special position in the global financial landscape. Furthermore, in implementing China's global strategy, China's Sovereign Wealth Fund (CIC) plus the 'Big 4' policy banks, and China's Development Bank (CDB) are the crucial players. By carrying out the goals of the state, China's banks, and especially CDB among them, are helping further China's goal of securing energy supplies and positioning its 'national champions' in a global strategy. Since much of the proceeds of the international loans are used to buy Chinese goods and services, from Huawei phones to CITIC-built railroads, China wins twice, and the policy and development banks help foster another Chinese goal, pushing its top companies to 'go out' (Sanderson and Forsythe 2012, 131).

Africa was its first stop. Aided by Chinese demand for its exports and raw materials, Africa has experienced its best decade and a half of economic growth since independence from colonialism.[33] CDB is at the core of that 'reversal of fortunes' by helping to change failed development policies by stimulating manufacturing and building the infrastructure that most African countries require to climb the developmental ladder (Sanderson and Forsythe 2012, 86). CIC (China's sovereign wealth fund) is another big player in those endeavours. Its operations include the establishment of five special economic zones, promised by President Hu Jintao in 2006 – Nigeria, Mauritius, Egypt, Algeria, Ethiopia and Zambia and the creation, in 2007, of the China-Africa Development Fund (CADF) as a private equity arm of CDB to 'boost investment in Africa by Chinese firms and offshore, to Africa, some of China's manufacturing. Adittionaly, in February 2012, the fund signed an agreement with Xinjiang Goldwind Science & Technology, a wind-turbine manufacturer, to develop the African market. In 2010, CDB had already given the company a $6 billion credit line for international expansion (Sanderson and Forsythe 2012, 98–99). It also formed a venture with carmaker Chery Auto, to set up factories in Africa.

In Latin America, Chinese lending is continuously gaining momentum. It has taken off from almost nothing prior to 2008 to the point where, in 2010, its loan commitments were more than those of the World Bank, Inter-American Development Bank and the US Export-Import Bank combined (Gallagher, Irwin and Koleski 2012, 5). CDB seems confident about the soundness of its oil-for-loans programme; so confident that in 2010 it lent Ecuador $1 billion in a four-year loan at 6% interest, two years after the Country had defaulted on $3.2 billion-worth of bonds. Chinese lending to Venezuela and Ecuador is filling in for the private players in the sovereign debt markets which vanished.

> Chinese financing is often the 'lender of last resort.' It is not a cheap one, but due to the concern the international financial community has over Venezuela and Ecuador, and the large risk premiums they would charge, Chinese lending is an attractive option.
>
> (Tissot quoted by Gallagher *et al.* 2012, 8)

The loan-for-oil model seems to be broader. It is being used around the globe, 'from Russia, to Ghana, to Brazil, as a means for China to secure energy supplies and for its state-owned infrastructure companies to win contracts'. In sum, Chinese banks maintain some oversight over their loans by attaching either purchase requirements or oil sale agreements. Most Chinese loans require the borrowers to use a portion for Chinese technology or construction (Gallagher *et al.* 2012, 17).

As of 2015 China has become the second major investor in the global economy. Chinese global investments have risen at a compound rate of 16% from 2011 to 2014. The volume of foreign direct investment from China reached US$183.2 billion, surpassing the foreign direct investment into China which amounted to US$126.0 billion in 2016. In 2015 Chinese firms executed 579 mergers and acquisitions abroad covering 62 countries and regions with a transaction value of US$54.44 billion out of which US$37.28 billion were financed by sources within China. In 2016 Chinese companies spent US$227 billion on acquiring foreign companies; outbound mergers and acquisitions have grown 33% per year for the past five years (Financial Times 2017)

Yet, the apex of that state-guided strategy, at the time of writing this chapter,[34] is the 'one belt, one road' (OBOR) initiative. Launched in 2013, OBOR has two parts. There is a land-based 'belt' from China to Europe, evoking old Silk Road trade paths, then a 'road' referring to ancient maritime routes. OBOR will span 65 countries and China has so far invested over $900bn in projects ranging from highways in Pakistan to railway lines in Thailand. In May 2017, more than 100 world leaders gathered in Beijing for un update on the strategy. The host, president Xi, labeled OBOR the 'project of the century' and reaffirmed the estimated $5 trillion in infrastructure spending spanning Asia, the Middle East, Europe, and Africa. The *Financial Times* (*FT*) had 'President Xi Jinping positions China at centre of new economic order' as a headline, adding 'President Xi of China delivered a sweeping vision of a new economic global order on Sunday, positioning his country as an alternative to an inward-looking United States under President Trump' (*Financial Times*, 3 August 2017).

At the same gathering, China's prime minister pledged more than $100 billion from Chinese development banks for the next round of infrastructure renewal. The next gathering, in Beijing, will take place in 2019. Public entrepreneurship and public funding on that scale is unheard of. However, as I have tried to show in the previous section, that is precisely what Schumpeter had in mind when he wondered if 'socialism' could work. China incarnates, in fact, Schumpeter on steroids. Or, I must add, the Chinese state should be seen also as the materialisation of Hubert Henderson's wishes, expressed in 1943, one year after *Capitalism, Socialism and Democracy* was published. In a little-noticed exchange with Keynes, his co-author, Henderson, wrote:

> What I really suggest is that the state should assume the role of Entrepreneur-in-Chief, directing the flow of productive resources to the employments in which can best serve human needs.
>
> (1943, 233)

The required amendments here are: … best serve China's interests and needs on a global scale.

Conclusion: beyond Schumpeter–state structures, public leadership and structural transformation

> A context of deliberately created stability achieved by risk-spreading mechanisms … can facilitate industrial deepening, export expansion, and political compromises to share adjustment costs.… Unassisted entrepreneurs may not have either the foresight or the access to capital to follow long-term prospects. Their decisions may lock in the country into a specialisation in industries with inferior prospects.
>
> (Wade 1990)

Given the arguments discussed so far, and despite the current (sometimes enraged) neo–liberal statements that continue to view state action and bureaucracies as always ineffective, or at best irrelevant (cf. Buchanan, Tollison and Tullock 1980,) the reason seems to remain with Max Weber, whose statement that '[c]apitalism and bureaucracy found each other and belong intimately together' is as true today as when it was written, at the beginning of last century (1968, 1395, n. 14).

China's compressed 'case-study' provides us, I trust, with sufficient empirical evidence to validate the claims about the effectiveness of a properly developed entrepreneurial state as a vehicle for carrying out structural transformation in a more superior fashion than 'markets alone'.[35] I also submit that a close examination of Schumpeter's writings on that subject offer a solid starting point for a theory of the entrepreneurial state. This updating and extension of Schumpeter's agenda, when accomplished, would fill two critical lacunae: (a) it would add a crucial building block to Schumpeter's 'creative-destruction paradigm', which still misses out a comprehensive role for the state as an effective player; and (b) it would provide the field of 'development studies' with a proper, theoretical, space for the economic role of the state as a key actor in forging successful development processes in evolutionary environments, which is something surprisingly lacking so far, in spite of the extremely competent studies delivered under the 'developmental state' rubric.

In the conceptual framework conceived by Schumpeter in *CSD*, where, technology, finance and competition are always pushing towards unexpected outcomes and unpredictable possibilities, let me submit that entrepreneurial states and government policies crafted to forge and assist structural transformation are a permanent necessity dictated by the market's behaviour rather than by its failures. Consequently, their making must be based upon a correct understanding of the characteristics that, under this framework, define the actually existing capitalist economy: finance as its 'headquarters', competition as creative destruction, endogenous technological progress, entrepreneurial strategies conceived to differentiate each firm from its competitors and monopolise market opportunities, irreversible decisions – 'crucial decisions', in Shackle's catch phrase (1955) – and multiple types of uncertainties.

Additionally, the perception of economic progress under capitalist conditions as turmoil, where new and old assets, firms and sectors coexist and compete, allows for the introduction of the concepts of sunrise and sunset industries, as well as potential and effective conflicts between them. On the other hand, the perception of the economic environment as a Darwinian-Lamarkian arena where survival does not necessarily belong to those with better technologies or productivity potential, but rather to those with best adaptation skills, legitimises sector-based and selective financial, technological and industrial policies,[36] as well as the need for collective entrepreneurial action in order to forge and produce the system's future competitiveness, a task that each separate sector has no means to anticipate or even map. Under this framework, policies designed to manage the creative-destruction process, and whose aims are investment coordination, innovation diffusion and conflict management become not only economically rational, and business-friendly, but badly needed. The overall desired policy result is to decrease the system's inescapable elements of financial and technological instability and uncertainty.

Drawing on Schumpeter's reflections on entrepreneurial leadership by the state paired with his economic sociology, taking on board Keynes and Minsky's discussion of the need for a 'substantive degree of socialisation of investment' in order to preserve technological dynamism[37] and applying them to China, I submit that both macroeconomic stability and structural transformation are (a) best achieved when designed and assisted, (b) best assisted by public policies designed taking a long term-term strategic orientation, and (c) best achieved when these policies are implemented by state structures that are entrepreneurial[38] but connected with corporate interests (without being captured by them), which means 'embedded'. The question of social organisations and civil society participation, or social embeddedness, raised by Evans (1995) is a crucial, and difficult, subject. However, it is outside the scope of the present discussion. It will have to wait for a follow-up.

In conclusion, I suggest that despite the slippery and unsystematic way Schumpeter handled his reflections and observations on the role of state leadership and action under his evolutionary framework, he provided us with sufficient material for extending and updating the boundaries of his own research agenda. Furthermore, the empirical evidence displayed by the East-Asian developmental transformations, and especially by the Chinese entrepreneurial state, offers the data-set for working it out. Bringing the state into Schumpeter's creative-destruction paradigm doesn't harm or violate it. It is a needed improvement.

Acknowledgements

I want to thank Dick Nelson, Linda Weiss, Fred Block, John Mathews and Rainer Kattel for their useful comments, with the usual proviso that the neck I am sticking out here is my own.

Notes

1 This lacuna is also highlighted and briefly discussed by Callegari in his contribution to this volume.
2 See Burlamaqui 2000 for a previous attempt to recover Schumpeter's important, but unsystematic, comments on state action and leadership as well as their convergence with the East-Asian developmental states' structural transformation strategies, and some policy and institutional building lessons. This chapter is an effort to build on that discussion and to give it more analytical robustness, focusing exclusively on China for empirical corroboration. Ebner 2009 provides another contribution to, essentially, the same end. Covering substantially the same ground I did in the referred-to paper – but without knowledge of it – underlining the importance of the concept of entrepreneurial state in Schumpeter – which I did

not in 2000 – and pointing to very similar conclusions in respect to the nature of the East-Asian development states' industrial strategy (however, not referring China), his brilliant paper clearly constitutes a travelling companion to the present chapter. I will come back to Ebner's reasoning.

3 Although scarcely explored from a theoretical point of view, the *idea* of an 'entrepreneurial state' has a respectable pedigree in development thinking that goes back, at least, to Hamilton, List, Carey, the German Historical School, Hilferding, Lenin and Gerschenkron. It also percolates Keynes' thinking on the role of state, his exchanges with Hubert Henderson resurfacing in the flood of books and papers on the Asian developmental state as well as in recent works by Fred Block and his collaborators and Linda Weiss (see Reinert 2007 for the early literature and a wonderful historical exploration on the subject, Keynes 1936; Henderson 1943; Gerschenkron 1962; Crabtree and Thirlwall 1993; Woo-Cummings 1991 Block and Keller 2011; Weiss: 2014). Mazzucato 2013 did a laudable job not only recasting the term but, more important, carrying the discussion to a much wider audience. Previous books that feature 'entrepreneurial state' in their titles include Holland 1972; Eisinger 1989; and Tiberghien 2007.

4 Which was obviously not the case in Weimar Germany.

5 Considering that few people read the first four chapters of the first volume, we wonder whether a great number of Schumpeter-minded researchers have *indeed* read the second volume.

6 And Ebner's as well.

7 I'm well aware that this positive, even enthusiastic, diagnosis by Schumpeter of the Nazi state is, from a political perspective – and in retrospect – difficult to swallow. However, let's recall he was writing from a strictly economic point of view, and well before the Third Reich imposed war and destruction both East and West, and exposed the madness of its holocaust actions. Furthermore, let's also recall Keynes' preface to the 1936 German edition to *The General Theory*, which raised a host of debates after Schefold's note in CJE (1980): '[…] For I confess that much of the following book is illustrated and expounded mainly with reference to the conditions existing in the Anglo-Saxon countries. Nevertheless, the theory of output as a whole, which is what the following book purports to provide, is much more easily adapted to the conditions of a totalitarian state [the German text carries the official expression: Totaler Staat], than is the theory of the production and distribution of a given output produced under conditions of free competition and a large measure of laissez-faire. This is one of the reasons which justify calling my theory a *General* [emphasis in the original] theory. Since it is based on less narrow assumptions than the orthodox theory, it is also more easily adapted to a large area of different circumstances. Although I have thus worked it out having the conditions in the Anglo-Saxon countries in view – where a great deal of laissez-faire still prevails – it yet remains applicable to situations in which national leadership [staatliche Führung] is more pronounced. To balance the search for understanding with the commitment to persuade and the demands of what today goes under the rubric of "political correctness" is certainly not an easy task.'

8 Here, a mandatory comment on Gerschenkron's thesis is due. Gerschenkron, the doyen of economic history in Harvard during the 1950s and 1960s, was a product of the same cultural constellation Schumpeter had experienced in Europe and, like Schumpeter himself, he influenced a whole generation of Harvard economists through his required graduate course in economic history. Although often associated with catch-up narratives, his thesis on the 'advantages of backwardness' (Gerschenkron 1962, Ch. 1) puts him far away from stages theories à la Rostow, and brings him very close to the hypothesis advanced by Kattel and myself, of 'development as a leapfrogging process, not convergence, not catch-up' (Burlamaqui

and Kattel 2016). In his 2003 review of the classic book, Fishlow provides a well-balanced perspective pointing toward that conclusion:

> Gerschenkron's analysis is conspicuously anti-Marxian. It rejected the English Industrial Revolution as the normal pattern of industrial development and deprived the original accumulation of capital of its central force in determining subsequent expansion. It is likewise anti-Rostovian. There were no equivalent stages of economic growth in all participants. Elements of modernity and backwardness could survive side by side, and did, in a systematic fashion. Apparently, disadvantageous initial conditions of access to capital could be overcome through new institutional arrangements. Success was indicated by proportionally more rapid growth in later developers, signaled by a decisive spurt in industrial expansion.
>
> (2003, 1)

I cannot delve into a comprehensive discussion of his thesis here, but will say it offers a complement to Schumpeter's entrepreneurial state. However, in my view, Schumpeter brings more analytical material than Gerschenkron to this endeavour of making the state a central subject of economic theory, and especially to the theory of economic development, where its absence is appalling. Nonetheless, Gerschenkron's thesis, historically and institutionally rather than theoretically crafted, would certainly be a key supplement in this task of putting the state into the core of development theory (see Shin and Chang 2003 for a clever use of Gerschenkron's thesis for analysing South Korea's development spurt).

9　This discussion builds on Burlamaqui 2000.

10　Or formulated in a rather ad hoc way.

11　And I underline mainstream *thinking* because there is a shelf of economic history books that describe and analyse state involvement both in the US and the UK. For the US, see Bensel 1990 and 2000. For the UK, see Brewer 1990. Furthermore, recent work – already cited in note 2 – by Block and associates, Mazzucato and Weiss reiterate the historian's case: behind the endurance and economic preeminence of the US (and of the UK in the past) there was/is an active entrepreneurial, state.

12　Direct investment overseas by Chinese companies has increased from just $5.5bn in 2004 to $56.5bn in 2009. About 70% of the money invested in 2010 went to other parts of Asia. Latin America came in second place with 15% ('The China Cycle' *Financial Times* 2010.)

13　For a discussion, from an evolutionary perspective, of the pertinence of using that concept instead of 'catch-up', see Burlamaqui and Kattel 2016, and Gerschenkron 1962 for historical illustrations of leapfrogging without using the concept.

14　And this wholesale structural transformation went beyond dry economic statistics: when deplaning in Beijing for the 2008 Olympic games, McGregor recounts, the *New York Times* architecture correspondent, Nicolai Ouroussoff, compared arriving at the city's new airport 'to the epiphany that Adolf Loos, the Viennese architect, experienced in New York more than a century ago. He had crossed the threshold into the future' (2010, Locations 529–531).

15　China scholars have been using the entrepreneurial state rubric to help explain the countries' stunning structural transformation for a while. Mathews in his chapter for the boo provides a few examples. Therefore, my claim in terms of adding to the discussion is, obviously, not in linking the term to the country, but rather in presenting it as a concept, as part of a theoretical construct that should improve the comprehension of the Chinese developmental trajectory through an evolutionary, Schumpeter-based approach.

16　As opposed to a 'money manager capitalism' where the value-extraction component of finance went much beyond its value-creation dimension.

17 Minsky treated these as 'phases of capitalism' instead of *varieties*. According to him, that phase of finance capitalism collapsed in the Great Depression. What emerged afterwards was a new stage of capitalism: managerial welfare-state capitalism (Wray 2010). I don't agree with that taxonomy. It is very much US-rooted. A state-led variety of 'finance capitalism' resurfaced in Asia and was a key feature of the 'Asian miracles'. China is the latest example of that pattern.

18 From the nineteenth century to World War II, Germany had in its own Big 4s, the '4 Ds': Deutsche, Dresdner, Darmstader and Disconto (Hilferding 1981; Landes 1969, Ch. 5). They were private universal banks that operated mostly as development-oriented financial institutions.

19 Which were not in Hilferding's model.

20 See Lundvall 1992 and Nelson 1993 for attempts to fill that gap, but the emphasis is mostly on 'collective entrepreneurship' – Lundvall – and 'the institutions and mechanisms supporting technical innovation … in various countries – Nelson. The state is there, but not front and centre.

21 See Ruttan 2006; Block and Keller 2011; Mazzucato 2013; and Weiss 2014 for analyses of the US case. On the developmental state for East-Asia's cases see Johnson 1982; Amsden 1989; Wade 1990; Vogel 2011; Kim and Vogel 2011.

22 Founded in 1948.

23 When the savings-and-loan fiasco erupted in the US.

24 For a comprehensive analysis of China's response to the financial crisis, see Lardy 2011.

25 They received compensation, but well below their market value and especially to their 'expected future value' once urbanisation was in place. Of course, if we stay within this somewhat *Marxist* way of looking at the picture, the same stroke also helped produce a sizable labour force, Marx's 'industrial reserve army', available to sell its labour force in the new factories for a very modest price by any international standard.

26 Echoing one of modern money theory's key statements.

27 Because it started in the city of Wuhu.

28 Note that after Lehman, there were many mergers and acquisitions as well as restructurings and an ocean of cash and guarantees injected by the FED and the Treasury in the US 'too big to fail' banks, insurance and corporations. After Lehman, no other big institution closed in the US, supposedly the 'land of the market' (see Blinder 2013 for an excellent discussion of these issues). From that perspective China's pre-emptive policy action of recapitalising the banks when they needed it and then making sure that finance and funding would be there when needed was not surprising at all: as mentioned before, Big Government *plus* Big Bank *plus* industrial policy. A Keynes–Minsky–Schumpeter approach to 'policy in hard times'.

29 For a thorough analysis of the plan, see 'China 2030 – Building a modern, harmonious, and creative high-income society' (The World Bank and Development Research Center of the State Council, the People's Republic of China 2012).

30 BNEF: Bloomberg New Energy Finance.

31 When fiscal deficits were ballooning and the credit for long-term projects from private finance were frozen in most of the 'North'.

32 At that point, a high official of Alcatel-Lucent remembers telling his boss, the Chairman … 'We won't die at the hands of Huawei; if we die, it will be at the hands of China Development Bank.'

33 For a broader analysis and discussion of China's strategy for Africa, see Carmody and Owusu in Leão, Pinto and Acioly 2011.

34 Summer 2017.

35 Something (structural transformation by markets alone) that, by the way, never happened in history. That makes the comparison irrelevant, and I'm only referring to it because it's so embedded in the encyclopaedia of economic fairy tales.

36 In order to either encourage or discourage investments according, for instance, to sunrise and sunset industry criteria.
37 Ever ahead of his time, Minsky submits the following observation in closing his 1990 paper on 'Schumpeter: finance and evolution': 'Capitalism *may require intervention to remain technologically dynamic* in an era of managed money capitalism' (37, my emphasis). It seems Chinese policymakers caught the message.
38 Which means, states possessing capacities that enable them to forge long-term, strategic agendas for structural transformation as well as the means to help implement them.

References

Allen, L. (1991). *Opening Doors. The Life and Work of J.A. Schumpeter* (2 vols). New York: Transaction Books.

Amsden, A.H. (1992). *Asia's Next Giant: South Korea and Late Industrialization.* Oxford: Oxford University Press.

Bensel, R.F. (1990). *Yankee Leviathan: The Origins of Central State Authority in America, 1859–1877.* Cambridge: Cambridge University Press.

Bensel, R.F. (2000). *The Political Economy of American Industrialisation, 1877–1900.* Cambridge University Press.

Bergsten, C.F., Freeman, C., Lardy, N.R. and Mitchell, D.J. (2010). China's Rise. Challenges and Opportunities. Washington, DC: The Peterson Institute.

Blinder A. (2013). *When the Music Stopped: The Financial Crisis, the Response, and the Work Ahead.* Penguin Press: Kindle edition.

Block, F. and Keller, M. (Eds.) (2011). *The State of Innovation, The U.S Government's Role in Technology Development.* Boulder, CO: Paradigm Press.

Brewer, J. (1990). *The Sinews of Power: War, Money, and the English state, 1688–1783.* Cambridge, MA: Harvard University Press.

Buchanan, J.M. and Wagner, R.E. (1977). *Democracy in Deficit.* New York: Academic Press.

Buchanan, J.M., Tollison, M. and Tullock, G. (1980). *Toward a Theory of the Rent-Seeking Society.* College Station, TX: Texas A & M University Press.

Burlamaqui, L. (2000). Evolutionary economics and the role of state. In: L. Burlamaqui, A.C. Castro and H.-J. Chang (Eds.), *Institutions and The Role of the State.* Cheltenham, UK: Edward Elgar.

Burlamaqui, L. (2015). Finance, development and the entrepreneurial state: Schumpeter, Keynes, Minsky and China. In: L. Burlamaqui, A.C. Castro and M. Vianna (Eds.), *The Present and Future of Development Financial Institutions: Theory and History.* Rio de Janeiro: MINDS.

Burlamaqui, L. and Kattel, R. (2016). Development as leapfrogging, not convergence, not catch-up: Towards schumpeterian theories of finance and development. *Review of Political Economy*, 28(2), 270–288.

Cousin, V. (2011). *Banking in China.* New York: Palgrave.

Ebner, A. (2009). Entrepreneurial state: The schumpeterian theory of industrial policy and the East Asian 'Miracle'. In: U. Cantner, J.-L. Gaffard and L. Nesta (Eds.), *Schumpeterian Perspectives on Innovation, Competition and Growth* (pp. 369–390). New York: Springer.

Eisinger, P. (1989). *The Rise of the Entrepreneurial State: State and Local Economic Development Policy in the United States.* La Follette Public Policy Series.

Evans, P. (1995). *Embedded Autonomy: States and Industrial Transformation*. Princeton, NJ: Princeton University Press.

Financial Times (2010). The China cycle. 13 September.

Financial Times (2017). President Xi Jinping positions China at centre of new economic order. 3 August.Fishlow, A. (2003). Review of Alexander Gerschenkron, *Economic Backwardness in Historical Perspective: A Book of Essays*. Economic History Association (EH.net).

Gallagher, K. and Porzecanski, R. (2010). *The Dragon in the Room: China and the Future of Latin American Industrialisation*. Palo Alto, CA: Stanford University Press.

Gallagher, K., Irwin, A. and Koleski, K. (2012). The new banks in town: Chinese finance in Latin America. *Inter-American Dialogue* (February 2012).

Gerschenkron, A. (1962). *Economic Backwardness in Historical Perspective*. Cambridge, MA: Harvard University Press.

Giles, C. (2014). MoneySupply: The new world economy in four charts. *Financial Times*, 7 October.

Henderson, H. (1943). Note on the problem of maintaining full employment. Reprinted in: H. Henderson, *The Inter-War Years and Other Essays*. Oxford: Oxford University Press, 1955.

Hilferding, R. (1981) [1910]. *Finance Capital*. London: Routledge.

Holland, S. (Ed.) (1972). The State as Entrepreneur: New Dimensions for Public Enterprise: The IRI State Shareholding Formula. London: Weidenfeld and Nicolson.

Johnson, C. (1982). *MITI and the Japanese Miracle*. Stanford, CA: Stanford University Press.

Keidel, A. (2007). China's financial sector: Contributions to growth and downside risks. Paper delivered at the Conference 'China's changing financial system: Can it catch up with or even drive economic growth?', Indiana State University.

Keidel, A. (2011). China economic developments, prospects and lessons for the international financial system. Unpublished paper.

Keidel, A. and Burlamaqui, L. (2015). China Development Bank's Strategy and its implications for Brazil. In: L. Burlamaqui, A. Castro and M. Vianna (Eds.), *The Present and Future of Development Financial Institutions: Theory and History*. Rio de Janeiro: MINDS.

Keynes, J.M. (1936). *The General Theory of Employment, Interest and Money*. New York: Harcourt Brace.

Kim, B. and Vogel, E. (2011). *The Park Chung Hee Era: The Transformation of South Korea*. Cambridge, MA: Harvard University Press.

Kregel, J. (2001). Derivatives and global capital flows. Applications to Asia. In: H.J. Chang, G. Palma and D.H. Whittaker (Eds.), *Financial Liberalisation and the Asian Crisis*. Basingstoke, UK: Palgrave.

Landes, D. (1969). *The Unbound Prometheus*. Cambridge: Cambridge University Press.

Lardy, N. (2011). *Sustaining China's Economic Growth After the Global Financial Crisis*. Peterson Institute: Kindle Edition.

Leão, Pinto and Acioly (Eds.) (2011). *A China na Nova Configuração Global*. Brasilia: IPEA.

Lundvall, B-Å. (1992). User-producer relationships, national systems of innovation and internationalisation. In: *National Systems of Innovation: Toward a Theory of Innovation and Interactive Learning* (pp. 45–67). UK: Pinter Publishers.

Mazzucato, M. (2013). *The Entrepreneurial State*. London: Anthem Press.

McCraw, T.K. (2007). *Prophet of Innovation*. Cambridge, MA: Harvard University Press.

McGregor, R. (2010). *The Party: The Secret World of China's Communist Rulers.* HarperCollins: Kindle Edition.

Minsky, H. (1978). The financial instability hypothesis: An interpretation of Keynes and an alternative to Standard Theory. In: H. Minsky, *Can 'It' Happen Again: Essays on Instability and Finance.* New York: Routledge, 1982.

Minsky, H. (1996). Uncertainty and the institutional structure of capitalist economies. *Jerome Levy Institute, Working Paper* no. 155.

Musgrave, R.A. (1992). Schumpeter's crisis of the tax state: An essay in fiscal sociology. *Journal of Evolutionary Economics*, 2(2), 89–113.

Naughton, B. and Tsai, K. (Eds.) (2015). *State Capitalism, Institutional Adaptation and the Chinese Miracle.* Cambridge: Cambridge University Press, Kindle edition.

Nelson, R.R. (1993). *National Systems of Innovation: A Comparative Study.* Oxford: Oxford Univesity Press.

Pettis, M. (2013). *The Great Rebalancing: Trade, Conflict, and the Perilous Road Ahead for the World Economy.* Princeton, NJ: Princeton University Press.

Reinert, E. (2007). *How Rich Nations Got Rich ... And Why Poor Countries Stay Poor.* London: Constable Press.

Robinson, J. (1972). The second crisis of economic theory. *The American Economic Review*, 62(1/2), 1–10.

Ruttan, V. (2006). *Is War Necessary for Economic Growth?* Oxford: Oxford University Press.

Sanderson, H., and Forsythe, M. (2012). *China's Superbank: Debt, Oil and Influence: How China Development Bank is Rewriting the Rules of Finance.* New York: John Wiley & Sons.

Schefold, B. (1980). The General Theory for a totalitarian state? A note on Keynes's preface to the German edition of 1936. *Cambridge Journal of Economics*, 1980.

Schumpeter, J.A. (1918). The crisis of the tax state. In: R. Swedberg, *Schumpeter: A Biography.* Princeton, NJ: Princeton University Press,1991.

Schumpeter, J.A. (1939). *Business Cycles* (2 vols.) New York: Mac-Graw Hill.

Schumpeter, J.A. (1942). *Capitalism, Socialism and Democracy.* New York: Routledge.

Schumpeter, J A. (1949). Economic theory and entrepreneurial history. In: R.V. Clemence (Ed.), *Essays on Entrepreneurs, Innovations, Business Cycles and the Evolution of Capitalism.* New Brunswick, NJ: Transaction, 1989.

Schumpeter, J.A. (1961) [1911]. *The Theory of Economic Development.* Oxford: Oxford University Press.

Shackle, G.L.S. (1955). *Uncertainty in Economics and other Reflections.* Cambridge: CUP Archive.

Sheng, A. and Soon, N.C. (Eds.) (2016). *Shadow Banking in China: An Opportunity for Financial Reform.* New York: Wiley, Kindle edition.

Shin, J.S. and Chang, H.J. (2003). *Restructurin 'Korea Inc.': Financial Crisis, Corporate Reform, and Institutional Transition.* New York: Routledge.

Soros, G. (1987). *The Alchemy of Finance.* New York: Simon and Schuster.

Swedberg, R. (1991). *Schumpeter: A Biography.* Princeton, NJ: Princeton University Press.

The Economist (2012). Huawei: The Company that Spooked the World. August.

The Economist (2017). How China is battling ever more intensely in world markets. September.

The World Bank and Development Research Center of the State Council, the People's Republic of China (2012). China 2030 – Building a modern, harmonious, and creative high-income society.

Thirlwall, A.P. and Crabtree, D. (Eds.) (1993). *Keynes and the Role of the State: The Tenth Keynes Seminar Held at the University of Kent at Canterbury, 1991.* New York: St Martin's Press.

Tiberghien, Y. (2007). *Entrepreneurial states: Reforming corporate governance in France, Japan, and Korea.* Ithaca, NY: Cornell University Press.

Tooze, A. (2006). *The Wages of Destruction.* London: Penguin Books.

Vogel, E. (2011). *Deng Xiaoping and the Transformation of China.* Cambridge, MA: Harvard University Press.

Wade, R. (1990). *Governing the Market.* Princeton, NJ: Princeton University Press.

Walter, C. and Howie, J.T. (2012). *Red Capitalism.* New York: Wiley.

Weber, M. (1968). *Economy and Society* (2 vols). Berkeley, CA: University of California Press.

Weiss, L. (2014). *America Inc.?* Ithaca, NY: Cornell University Press.

Woo, J-E. (1991). *Race to the Swift: State and Finance in Korean Industrialization.* New York: Columbia University Press.

Wray, R. (2010). What should banks do? A Minskyian analysis. Public Policy Brief 115, September.

Zhou, Y., Lazonick, W. and Sun, Y, (Eds.) (2016). *China as an Innovation Nation.* Oxford: Oxford University Press.

Index

Page numbers in **bold** denote tables, those in *italics* denote figures.

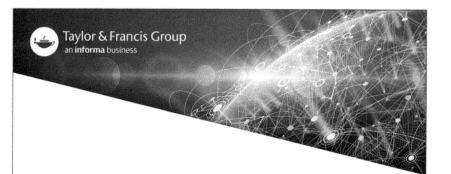

For Product Safety Concerns and Information please contact our EU
representative GPSR@taylorandfrancis.com
Taylor & Francis Verlag GmbH, Kaufingerstraße 24, 80331 München, Germany

www.ingramcontent.com/pod-product-compliance
Ingram Content Group UK Ltd.
Pitfield, Milton Keynes, MK11 3LW, UK
UKHW021018180425
457613UK00020B/972